Chocolate Cake

BROADWAY BOOKS   NEW YORK

Chocolate

FROM THE SIMPLE TO THE SUBLIME

Cake

Michele Urvater

Broadway Books titles may be purchased for business or promotional use or for special sales. For information, please write to: Special Markets Department, Random House, Inc., 1540 Broadway, New York, NY 10036.

BROADWAY BOOKS and its logo, a letter B bisected on the diagonal, are trademarks of Broadway Books, a division of Random House, Inc.

Visit our website at www.broadwaybooks.com

Library of Congress Cataloging-in-Publication Data
Urvater, Michele.
    Chocolate cake / Michele Urvater.— 1st ed.
        p.   cm.
    1. Cake.   2. Cookery (Chocolate)   I. Title.
TX771. U78   2000
641.8'653—dc21   00-022006

FIRST EDITION

Designed by Ralph L. Fowler

Illustrated by Jackie Aher

ISBN 0-7679-0607-1

10   9   8   7   6   5   4   3   2   1

For Maria G. Cook,

MY BELOVED AND ADMIRED MOTHER-IN-LAW

WHO TAUGHT ME MUCH ABOUT BAKING

AND ABOUT FAMILY DEVOTION.

CONTENTS

ACKNOWLEDGMENTS   IX

INTRODUCTION   1

PART ONE

Ingredients, Equipment, and Techniques
7

INGREDIENTS   9
BAKING EQUIPMENT   35
BAKING INFORMATION AND TECHNIQUES   50

PART TWO

The Recipes
59

PLAIN AND EASY BATTER CAKES   61
CHEESECAKES   94
BUTTER AND SHORTENED CAKES   100
LAYER CAKES   136

FOAM CAKES   178

BISCUIT CAKES   207

FLOURLESS CAKES   232

SPECIAL, INDIVIDUAL, AND REFRIGERATED CAKES   262

PART THREE

The Icing on the Cake

293

FROSTINGS, BUTTERCREAMS,
ICINGS, FILLINGS, AND GLAZES   295

PART FOUR

Decorative Techniques

333

DECORATING WHOLE CAKES   335

HOW TO GLAZE, ICE, FILL, FROST, AND ASSEMBLE CAKES   339

DESIGNING THE DECORATIVE TOUCHES   343

PRESENTATION AND THE PLATED DESSERT   351

SAUCES   357

GARNISHES   371

QUICK AND EASY CHOCOLATE DECORATIONS   379

Appendixes

A: MICHELE'S FAVORITE RECIPES   383

B: GLOSSARY OF TERMS AND PHRASES   385

C: SOURCE LIST   389

D: SELECTED BIBLIOGRAPHY   393

INDEX   395

ACKNOWLEDGMENTS

*N*O BOOK IS THE RESULT of a single person's effort, and this book is certainly no exception.

For my new-found pastry knowledge and expertise, I want to thank all my teachers at the French Culinary Institute, especially Dieter Schorner, who is no longer there but whose enthusiasm for the field of pastry is inspirational; Vicki Wells, whose plated desserts are the most beautiful; Steven Iglinsky, who is the most patient of teachers; and Jurgen David, who brought an old-world European sensibility to his work and always brought a smile to my face.

I want to thank pastry chefs Eric Hubert from Jean Georges Restaurant; Jacques Torres formerly at Le Cirque 2000; and Wayne Brachman for letting me spend time observing in their kitchens.

As always, I owe a huge thanks to my amazing agent Susan Ginsburg, who brings so much enthusiasm and positive energy to her work and who always makes me feel more talented than I am.

At Doubleday, I want to thank Judy Kern for great editing and Jennifer Josephy for seeing the project through.

On the personal side, thanks to the Bank Street teachers and kids, who tasted so many chocolate cakes and who proved once and for all that everything in life is indeed a matter of taste. Thanks to my daughter Alessia's friends from Dalton, who were an eager set of guinea pigs but who, I believe, enjoyed every minute of their tasting task.

Thanks to Janice Rubino and David Leite for testing recipes. And speaking of recipes, thanks to the following for letting me use and adapt their recipes for this book: Maria Cook, Linda Dann, Jurgen David, Karen Fohrhaltz, Eric Hubert, Martin Johner, Francis Lorenzini, Ann Rothschild, and Dieter Schorner. A big thanks as well to my favorite baking company, King Arthur Flour Company, for their Chocolate Pudding Cake recipe, and to Pillsbury Company for letting me include the latest version of their famous Tunnel of Fudge Cake recipe.

And even though I know my husband, Michael, and my daughter, Alessia, did not exactly suffer through this book and found every crumb of chocolate cake delicious, I still must thank them for the loyal support they show for every project I embark on and every career move I make.

How I Came to Write a Baking Book

AFTER TWENTY-THREE YEARS away from the business, I found myself, at fifty-two years old, at work again in a restaurant and this time around as a pastry chef. What in the world possessed me, at my age, to return to restaurant work? My love of baking and an unexpected twist in my career path.

Some twenty-five years ago, I began my long, exciting journey into the food world by abandoning my first career as a librarian to attend baking and culinary classes in the hospitality division of what was then New York City Community College in Brooklyn, New York (New York City Technical College today). The classes led to my association with two other women students, which in turn led to our sharing a single chef's job in a small restaurant on the Upper West Side of Manhattan in New York City. Eventually I gave up restaurant work because it was night work and my husband is a teacher and we never saw each other. Instead, I found work as a day chef for the private dining room of a corporation and at the same time worked on my first cookbook and ran a series of successful cooking classes from my home.

After my daughter was born, I gave up my cooking school but continued to write and work as a chef in a corporate environment. The difficulties I had in balancing cooking for my family and managing a career led to my *Monday-to-Friday* series of cookbooks (Workman Publishing, New York, 1991–98), which in turn led to a two-year television career at the Food Network. When the TV work dried up, I found myself at loose ends, had some difficulty in finding work, and was undecided about what my next career move would be.

During that uncertain time, I taught a culinary arts course in the hotel and management division at New York City Technical College, the same school I had attended in the 1970s. While teaching there I found myself continually enticed into the baking classes by the exquisite aromas wafting from the kitchen. I thought that if I could find a way to deepen my basic baking skills, perhaps I could teach baking as well as culinary arts. In seeking out specialized pastry training, I discovered what was then the almost-brand-new pastry arts program at the French Culinary Institute in New York City. I fell in love with the program after one visit to the school and enrolled immediately. Some 600 hours and ten months later, I found myself a bona fide diploma-toting pastry chef, and what had begun as a way of brushing up on basic skills ended in a whole new career possibility.

To those who did not know me, taking such a lengthy and expensive professional pastry course and then working as a pastry chef seemed like an odd move, but to those who knew me well, it made sense. I confess that during all the twenty-five years of my career devoted to matters culinary, I have, in fact, been a closet baker. Everything about baking gives me pleasure: the heady aroma of warm yeast bread fresh out of the oven, the crisp bite of a shortbread cookie, the silky feel of buttercreams, and the artistic process of decorating a cake. When I was six years old, my most treasured toy was a miniature baking set, complete with 1-inch round baking tins, tiny boxes of cake mixes, and colorful jimmies. To this day, I recall how ecstatic I was when those perfect lilliputian cakes emerged from the oven. I recall too that my first amateur attempts in the kitchen were baking experiments. On my first try, I boldly attempted a classic French strawberry tart layered with pastry cream. The results were dismal—the crust was underbaked and tough, and the pastry cream a tad scorched. I was only eighteen years old and undaunted, so I forged ahead and continued to experiment with pastries, breads, cookies, and cakes. With each try, I got a little better and a little more expert.

It may seem odd today that when I started out in the food world, in the 1970s, I chose the culinary arts over the pastry arts as the focal point of my career. That was because in those days, in most restaurants where I wanted to work, desserts and cakes, along with salads and appetizers, were prepared in the cold station and that was the only station where women were allowed. At that time, fresh out of the revolutionary 1960s and a budding feminist to boot, I decided I was going to break new ground, become a restaurant chef (against the advice of countless male French chefs), and follow in the footsteps of Leslie Revsin, the first woman ever to work in the kitchens of the Waldorf Astoria Hotel in New York City.

Now, much older and somewhat wiser, I no longer feel I must prove anything to myself or to my colleagues, so I am free to follow my heart and passion. While my professional career as a restaurant pastry chef fizzled out after a year because of the sheer physical demands of the job, my enthusiasm for baking and pastry endures. I am happiest baking for friends and family and have channeled my newfound baking knowledge and pastry experience into this book. Never has work been so much fun and never has writing a book given me as much joy as has writing *Chocolate Cake*.

Why Chocolate Cake?

UPON HEARING of my intent to write a book titled *Chocolate Cake,* a friend—not a baker—cracked sarcastically, "I see . . . a book with ten recipes!" Little did she know the number and range of cakes I could make fit into those two words. Why *Chocolate Cake?* The idea came to me one night when I was about to complete my course of study to become a pastry chef. I had spent close to a year doing what I love best: baking delightful pastries like cream-filled fruit tarts, brioche topknots, napoleons, angel food cakes, chocolate chip cookies, decorative breads. I tangled with pulled sugar and tempered chocolate and struggled with icing a cake so that it looked *almost* perfect. I created decorative plated desserts and spent endless hours at home fashioning dozens of tiny marzipan roses destined to adorn a wedding cake, which was the centerpiece of my practical final exam.

During the final phase of my training, I decided it would do me some good to intern for a few hours in the pastry kitchens of our finer New York City restaurants. I spent some time in the extraordinarily well-appointed pastry kitchen at Jean Georges Restaurant, working two or three days a week for a couple of weeks with Eric Hubert, a truly original pastry chef. One Saturday night the restaurant was closed for a special birthday party. When I arrived, prepared as always to help peel rhubarb or pitch in to assist with plating desserts, I walked into a frenzied kitchen where Eric and his assistant were creating a 2- by 4-foot honeycomb chocolate rectangle designed to cover the wooden table on which the birthday cake would be carried into the dining room. Into each of the tiny honeycomb openings Eric had piped a different pastel-colored filling so that the chocolate rectangle looked like a mosaic-tiled table. This table,

along with an assortment of pulled sugar accoutrements, were created just to display the pièce de résistance, the birthday cake, *the chocolate cake!*

When I asked Eric's assistant about the cake itself, anticipating a confection of unimagined tastes and textures, he replied nonchalantly, "Oh, you know, a chocolate mousse cake." When the cake was unveiled, it turned out indeed to be a conventional chocolate mousse cake, baked in single layers of different sizes, unworthy, in my opinion, of the extraordinary chocolate stand designed to display it.

Not only did I think this cake did not deserve its stand, but to me, chocolate mousse cake hardly qualifies as chocolate cake at all. Then I asked myself, What type of chocolate cake would I have wanted it to be? That got me thinking about chocolate cake in all its forms, and the more I thought about it, the more I realized those words evoke different cakes depending on the culture in which you were raised.

I thought about how, to Americans, a chocolate cake is a triple-decker devil's food cake frosted with peaks of fudge icing, whereas to my mother-in-law, of Austro-Hungarian background, a chocolate cake is a flat, flourless nut torte shimmering under a thin chocolate glaze. To the French housewife, a chocolate cake can be a *quatre quarts,* a chocolate pound cake, but to a French pastry chef, a chocolate cake is probably the syrup-soaked genoise filled with pale chocolate buttercream that is ubiquitous in pastry shops throughout France.

The more I thought about the number of chocolate cakes in the existing pastry repertoire, from the simple to the complex, from the round to the square, from the traditional to the wildly inventive, from the individual cupcake to the grand multitiered wedding cake, the more I was convinced it would be great fun to write *Chocolate Cake* and bring together a collection of classic and original recipes devoted entirely to America's favorite cake.

When Is It Cake and When Is It Chocolate?

THE TITLE OF this book might mislead the reader into thinking *Chocolate Cake* would be the slimmest of volumes, but only if the words *chocolate* and *cake* are taken at their most literal of meanings. I have interpreted the words so broadly that any and every cakelike confection imaginable is acceptable provided it looks or tastes like cake and includes dark, milk, or white chocolate, either in the cake layers themselves or in the frosting.

How did I decide which cakes to include, given my rather catholic interpretation of the words *chocolate* and *cake*? Well, the sources of inspiration were abundant. First I decided that the classic chocolate cakes from the American and European pastry repertoires had to be represented, from the range of cakes prepared at home, like devil's food cake, to those made only in professional pastry shops in France, like the classic bûche de noël or the astonishing Sacher torte, Dobos Torte, and Black Forest cakes that come to us from Germany, Hungary, and Austria.

For even more inspiration, I decided to include restaurant-style cakes both classic and new, like the forgotten Coach House cake, a James Beard favorite of the 1960s, and today's almost ubiquitous ganache-oozing, warm individual cakes as served in trendy Manhattan restaurants. And finally, so that this book would appeal to as wide an audience as possible, I made sure to include a range of cakes that could be accomplished by bakers of different levels of expertise and that could be prepared for different occasions.

This is how you end up with a book like this, which includes the very humble Wacky Chocolate Cake, of the mix-and-dump school of baking even a child could prepare, to my interpretation of the Marjolaine cake, an exquisite masterpiece of the 1950s created by the legendary Fernand Point for his three-star restaurant, La Pyramide, considered at the time to be the best restaurant in France.

About the Recipes

THE PROVENANCE OF my recipes has always intrigued my friends. As with all themed recipe collections, some recipes in this book are timeless classics, while others are adaptations of forgotten old favorites or interpretations of trendy new recipes, and a very few are pure inventions.

I combed hundreds of cookbooks to make sure I would have a selection of the best of the timeless chocolate-cake classics. I pored over dozens of handwritten recipes passed on to me by my mother, who had collected them from her mother and aunts and assorted friends. I went through my files to retrieve personal favorites collected over the last thirty years and in the process rediscovered forgotten treasures.

I cajoled friends and colleagues into sharing their recipes with me. I spent hours typing into English my mother-in-law's translations from the German of her family's treasured recipes for wonderful flourless nut-torte recipes, which her mother had culled from a 1917 cookbook.

When I say I have invented my share of these cakes, I must explain what I mean. In baking, there are parameters to how inventive one can be, because the structure of the cake itself and the techniques required to make the icings and fillings are dictated more often than not by chemistry and by how ingredients interact with each other.

Where the pastry chef can become endlessly inventive, however, is in how she puts together different cake elements. She can alter the feel of a cake by building it with layers of different textures, so that two moist flour layers are counterpointed by a crunchy layer of nut meringue in the middle. She can introduce subtlety of taste and nuance by including more than one type of filling or by accompanying a slice of cake with an exotically flavored sauce.

So how does a creation come about?—sometimes by design and sometimes by accident. What I like to do is read through recipe books by pastry chefs I admire, then perhaps take a flavor combination seen in one type of cake and pull that taste into a different type of cake. Or I work from an existing recipe, like the White and Black Chocolate Cheesecake, which I tested first just by marbling some cheesecake batter with the same batter flavored with melted bittersweet chocolate. The first try was good but yielded a cake too sweet for my taste. To intensify the chocolate flavor, I changed the bittersweet chocolate to unsweetened, increased the amount of chocolate by 30%, and introduced grated orange zest to make the taste more exciting. Other creations come about haphazardly, like Michele's German Chocolate Cake. It started out by my testing a classic recipe for German Chocolate Cake. Recipe after recipe for the filling, including the one on the package for German's Sweet Chocolate, instructs one to cook together evaporated milk, sugar, butter, and egg yolks directly over heat. I kept on thinking "egg yolks cooked over direct heat curdle, but maybe this experience will be different." I went ahead and tried this method with unmitigated disastrous results: the filling curdled and scorched. On the next attempt I cooked the ingredients in a double boiler, and the filling thickened, but it took 20 minutes. Then I tried the filling another way, by heating cream instead of evaporated milk, using brown sugar instead of white sugar, tempering the yolks with some of this mixture, and returning the mixture to cook slowly until thickened. This method thickened the filling in 5 minutes without curdling but it was too runny. I added bittersweet chocolate to thicken it and voilà—the birth of a new filling for German Chocolate Cake, which in turn led to my renaming the cake Michele's German Chocolate Cake.

A Word About Taste

*F*OR AS LONG as I remember, I have been more interested in the taste of food than in its presentation, and in discovering intriguing flavor and texture combinations. Years before the popularization of "fusion" cooking—in *Cooking the* *Nouvelle Cuisine in America* (Workman Publishing, New York, 1979), my first cookbook, coauthored with David Liederman—I worked on combining French technique with non-French flavors. That early exploration led to such unusual (for those days) combinations as homemade mayonnaise made with Asian sesame oil rather than olive oil, reduced demi-glace bases finished with gumbo filé or flavored with star anise, and filet mignon seasoned with fresh ginger. Today, my interest in using classic techniques to explore new flavors continues with pastry and baking.

My interest in flavor manifests itself in this book in a couple of ways: by introducing into the cake itself spices or other tastes not usually found in conjunction with chocolate, or more typically by pairing an intriguingly flavored sauce with a slice of chocolate cake. The inspiration for these combinations of flavors comes from two sources: from reading about the history of chocolate and how the Mayans and Aztecs flavored their chocolate drinks with achiote, allspice, black pepper, flowers, honey, and chiles; and

from tasting the chocolate candies manufactured in France by Michel Richart. Michel Richart, a Parisian chocolate maker, has a boutique on Fifth Avenue in Manhattan, where I first tasted his unusual chocolates and discovered an astonishing array of exotically flavored fillings such as the unlikely basil, star anise, curry, cumin, and ginger. While I didn't like all the combinations, some were truly inspirational, and I have carried some of these tastes into my cakes.

Always mindful of the fact that most people feel comfortable with the familiar rather than the new, however, I have for the most part limited my fascination with pairings of chocolate and intriguing flavors to plated dessert combinations. This way, a new flavor can be tried out in a suggested accompanying sauce so that those who are not so adventurous can omit the sauce and stick to the chocolate cake on its own.

The Stars

YOU WILL NOTICE that the titles of some recipes are preceded by two little asterisks, which mean they are my favorite cakes. These asterisks are not to be confused with the stars that follow the phrase "level of difficulty." One "level of difficulty" star means the cake is easy enough for a novice to make; two stars mean it takes a certain amount of knowledge and patience to make the cake; and finally, three stars mean the cake takes time and patience, as well as some skill.

PART ONE

Ingredients, Equipment, and Techniques

INGREDIENTS

*H*OW DELICIOUS YOUR cakes taste and how well they come out depends on the quality of the ingredients and how you handle them. I think about ingredients in two categories: those like eggs, butter, sugar, and flour that are essential to the structure and flavor of the cake, and those like spices, nuts, and vanilla extract that are "add-ins" for flavor and texture.

EGGS

All the recipes in this book were tested with U.S. Grade AA or Grade A large eggs, which weigh about 1.67 ounces each out of the shell or 2 ounces in the shell.

Eggs are a most amazing and perfect food, essential to the art of baking. They are part of the liquid content of the cake, and their protein coagulates so that they bind the ingredients together as they give structure to the cake. They help cakes rise as well as contribute to color, nutrition, and, of course, flavor.

Egg yolks are natural emulsifiers so they help to produce smooth batters, which in turn help in the leavening and texture of the finished cake. They are rich in fat, which tenderizes the cake because the fat weakens ("shortens") the gluten strands in the flour. The fat in the yolks is also what thickens custards, sauces, and fillings.

Egg whites, too, have a unique function in cake-making: They are rich in albumen so they can be stretched enough to hold in air bubbles when beaten, which is why they are essential to the structure of angel food and chiffon cakes.

There is no difference between brown and white eggs in terms of nutrition and other properties; in fact, the only difference between them is the pigment in the shells, which varies according to the breed of chicken. In some parts of the country, brown eggs are more expensive because they are less popular, so you should buy what is freshest and cheapest.

Buying and Storing Eggs

Eggs have recently been implicated in salmonella poisoning, so the American Egg Board recommends you take special care in their handling. Check the expiration date on the carton and make sure the eggs are clean and without cracks. Refrigerate the eggs immediately when you get them home and store them in the carton toward the back wall of the refrigerator, not in the door where they deteriorate more quickly because of the temperature swings that come from opening and closing the refrigerator door.

Whole eggs out of the shell can be stored in a covered jar in the refrigerator for up to 3 days. To freeze whole eggs, first stir them gently to blend without incorporating air, and freeze them in a container, leaving ½ inch of headroom at the top, for up to 9 months.

Store egg yolks in the refrigerator, by keeping them covered with water in a glass jar so they don't dry out, but use them within 2 days. You cannot freeze whole egg yolks because, upon thawing, they turn into an unusable sticky gel. To freeze them correctly, first pierce each yolk gently with a toothpick, then combine each ¼ cup of yolks with 1 teaspoon of sugar if you are going to use them in sweet dishes or with ⅛ teaspoon of salt if you are going to use them in savory ones. Transfer them to a container with a tight-fitting lid, leaving ½ inch of headroom for expansion, and freeze for up to 9 months.

Store leftover egg whites in the refrigerator in a covered glass jar for up to a week, or freeze them for up to a year. Be sure to thaw them in the refrigerator, however, before using, and don't refreeze them.

Dried Egg Whites

These are dehydrated egg whites that have been pasteurized so they are safe to eat and great to use in situations where you don't cook the egg whites. I use them only for crystallizing flowers.

Handling Eggs in Baking

THE RIGHT TEMPERATURE Before baking, other ingredients should be between 68° and 70°F, but eggs should be even a bit warmer. Warm eggs behave more efficiently: Egg whites whip up to a greater volume and egg yolks emulsify more readily. Remove the eggs from the refrigerator about 20 minutes before you are ready to assemble the batter, but if you forget, then set the whole eggs, in their shells, in a bowl of warm water and they will be ready to use within minutes.

ADDING WHOLE EGGS TO A BATTER When one of my recipes instructs you to "add the eggs one at a time," please don't crack them open right into the batter. To make sure you don't get any shell or blood spots in the batter, crack the egg into a small bowl, then add the egg to the batter. If there are large blood spots in an egg, discard it.

TO SEPARATE EGGS Even though eggs should be at room temperature when you add them to a cake batter, they are easier to separate when cold because the yolk is less likely to run into the white. When I need separated eggs, I separate them while cold, then leave the egg whites and egg yolks to come to room temperature. As they are coming to room temperature, set a piece of plastic wrap directly on the surface of the egg yolks so they don't develop a surface skin and crust over.

To crack open an egg, tap it gently in the center with the back of a knife. Separate the two shell halves along the crack and let the egg white drip into a bowl while you pass the yolk back and forth between the two shell halves. A messier way but less likely to break the yolks is to tap open the egg and let it drop into your slightly cupped hand. Let the egg white drip through your slightly opened fingers while the yolk remains in your hand. A final way is to use an egg separator, which is a little contraption that catches the yolk in the center while the egg white slips through side openings.

Even though I have never seen a professional chef work this way, I recommend that the home baker separate eggs over three bowls to ensure there is no trace of fat or egg yolk in the egg whites, because fat inhibits aeration and foaming. Begin by cracking open the egg over one bowl, then transfer the egg yolk to the second bowl and the egg white to the third. Repeat this procedure with the second egg over the first bowl and continue until all the eggs are separated. The reason it is wise to work this way is that if you have almost finished separating a batch of eggs and accidentally get some yolk from the last egg into the whites, the entire batch of whites will be lost. However, if you work over three bowls and get some yolk into a single egg white, then you can either discard the egg or save it for some other use.

BEATING AND "BURNING" EGG YOLKS When you beat egg yolks with sugar, begin by beating the yolks on their own to break them up, then add the sugar as you continue to beat. If the recipe advises you to beat the yolks with the sugar until "ribbons" form, that means beating them on medium-high speed until they turn a pale lemon yellow and, when

you lift up the beaters, the batter falls back onto itself in flat "ribbon" shapes.

Before adding egg yolks to a batter, don't premix them with other ingredients such as vanilla extract or lemon zest because they will curdle or "burn," as the French like to say. And finally, add sugar to egg yolks at the last possible moment because if you combine egg yolks and sugar in advance and let them stand on the counter for a while, again the yolks will "burn" or turn grainy.

Whipping Egg Whites: The Different Stages

Learning how to whip egg whites properly and make a meringue (whipped egg whites with sugar) is crucial to the art of making cakes. If you underbeat the egg whites, your cakes won't have the texture you want, nor rise enough. Conversely, if you overbeat the egg whites, your cakes might collapse in the oven.

In this book I refer to several stages of beating egg whites, and each is described in the recipe by a crucial word or phrase that is explained more fully below.

BEFORE YOU BEGIN
- Beat the egg whites in a nonreactive metal bowl made of stainless steel or copper, but not of aluminum, which reacts with eggs, nor of plastic, which doesn't provide enough friction to whip up the eggs. Glass and porcelain work fine but are breakable.
- Make sure the bowl in which you are going to beat the whites is absolutely spotless, dry, and grease-free because fat inhibits the proper aeration of the egg whites.
- Make sure the egg whites are at room temperature so they can incorporate as much air as possible when you whip them. (A trick to maximize the amount of air you incorporate is to first warm the egg whites in a bowl set over simmering water, then start to whip them.)

- Use an electric mixer, either stationary or hand-held, for whipping up more than one egg white. Whipping egg whites by hand requires a very strong arm and the patience of Job. When I have only one egg white to whip, I do it by hand, using a large balloon whisk, because it's faster and easier than using an electric mixer.

THE STAGES

Stage # 1: Beat until frothy. Using an electric mixer fitted with the whip attachments, beat on low speed until the whites have large bubbles in them, are still somewhat yellowish clear in color, and look "frothy."

Stage # 2: Beat until soft peaks form. When the egg whites are frothy, add the salt and cream of tartar as indicated in the recipe, increase the speed to medium, and beat until soft peaks form. Salt breaks up the albumen in the whites so they whip up more easily, and the cream of tartar acts as a stabilizer to prevent the beaten egg whites from deflating too quickly. At the soft peak stage, the egg whites are much whiter than before, the bubbles are smaller, more like the foam in a head of beer, and when you lift up the beaters, the egg whites form peaks, the tips of which droop.

Stage # 3: Beat until stiff and glossy peaks form. To get to this stage you increase the speed to medium-high and beat until the egg whites are stiff and, when you lift up the beaters, form stiff peaks, the tips of which point almost straight up, with the teensiest of droops. The whites will be snow white in color and the bubbles will be microscopic. The other key word in this description is *glossy* because the egg whites must have a sheen to them which indicates they are still moist. If they look dry and dull, like large curds of cottage cheese, they have been overbeaten. When overbeaten, they can't hold moisture and water begins to seep out of the eggs into the bowl, their structure can't stretch any further when the hot air in the oven expands the air cells, and the batter will collapse.

TO WHIP MERINGUES Whip egg whites with salt, cream of tartar, and sometimes a pinch of sugar until the soft peak stage.

For soft meringues, add the remaining sugar at this stage slowly, 1 tablespoon at a time, and to one side of the bowl, so the sugar does not deflate the egg whites.

For stiff meringues, add half the sugar slowly, when the eggs are at the stiff peak stage, then add the other half rather quickly at the end and don't beat much after all the sugar is in. This last method is for the type of meringue you dry out slowly in the oven so that it emerges crisp and crunchy.

TROUBLESHOOTING: SAVING OVERBEATEN EGG WHITES If you think you have overbeaten egg whites, just add 1 more egg white for every 4 to 6 whites and whip by hand for a few seconds just to moisten the whipped whites.

FATS

Fats, another essential element in cake-baking, contribute to the tenderness, texture, flavor, and keeping qualities of the cake. The word *fats* is a rather inelegant term used to describe butter, solid vegetable shortening, vegetable oils, margarine, and lard.

Fats contribute to the volume and leavening of a cake by helping in its aeration. Solid fats like butter, margarine, and vegetable shortening can be beaten with sugar ("creamed"). As you cream the fat and sugar, the facets of the sugar cut into the fat, creating tiny pockets that trap air. Fats are also emulsifiers, so they help to keep the liquids suspended in the batter, and because fats draw and keep in moisture, they increase the shelf life of the cake.

Even though I don't like its taste, if you must, for

religious or dietary reasons, you can substitute margarine for butter in these cakes. Lard is not used in cake-making.

Butter

All the recipes in this book were tested with unsalted U.S. Grade AA or Grade A butter.

UNSALTED BUTTER Butter is a substance comprised of about 80% fat with the remaining percentage consisting of water, milk solids, and minerals. I prefer butter to vegetable shortening for almost all of my cakes because it tastes better and it melts at a temperature slightly lower than body temperature, which means cakes made with butter always leave you with a good feeling on the tongue.

I always use unsalted (also sometimes known as "sweet") butter in my recipes because salted butter contains too much water and its saltiness can sometimes mask a less than fresh taste.

The national brand of butter I prefer is Land O'Lakes, which invariably tastes fresh, rich, and sweet.

TO STORE BUTTER Buy unsalted butter packaged in foil rather than in waxed paper because foil is less porous and the butter will stay fresher longer. Check the expiration date and buy the freshest butter possible. Once the package is open, be sure to rewrap the butter well, because butter is highly perishable and seems to be a magnet for the other flavors and aromas in your refrigerator. It is wise to store butter away from strong-smelling foods, in the special compartment of your refrigerator designed for that purpose. If you don't use butter within 10 days of purchasing, store it in the freezer, where it will keep superbly for 6 months.

Hydrogenated Vegetable Shortening

Hydrogenated vegetable shortening, also known as solid vegetable shortening, is nothing more than a solid fat fabricated from purified vegetable oils that are heated and then pressurized with hydrogen so that they are transformed from a liquid into a solid state. Vegetable shortening is pliable, flavorless, and white at room temperature, but is clear when heated.

This shortening is 100% fat so that when you cream it with sugar, it envelops and protects the fragile air bubbles better than butter does, which means cakes made with solid shortening can be somewhat lighter. That said, I still prefer butter in almost all cases because solid shortening melts at a higher temperature than your body temperature and leaves you with a slight "coated" feel on your tongue. I use solid vegetable shortening, however, when I want a very light crumb or when I want a neutral-flavored cake that allows the taste of the frosting to come to the fore.

I use Crisco brand vegetable shortening, and because I use it infrequently, I store it in the refrigerator. If you use it frequently, store it at room temperature, in a cool dry place.

Vegetable Oil

In general, cakes made with vegetable oil have a tender crumb and are particularly moist but don't have the rich flavor of cakes made with butter. I use vegetable oil in American classics like Wacky Chocolate Cake and in chiffon cakes, which call for oil as a key ingredient. Use a neutral-flavored oil such as safflower, canola, or a nonspecific vegetable oil. Avoid olive oil, which is overpowering and will ruin your cakes.

Cream Cheese

Cream cheese, a high-in-fat, fresh (unaged) cheese, is essential in cheesecakes but is also a great addition to icings. I love the flavor and texture of cream cheese blended with butter in confectioners' sugar frostings, because it brings with it a certain tanginess that is delicious with chocolate.

Flour is perhaps the single most important ingredient in cake-baking because it creates the strength and structure of the cake and because the type of flour used determines in part how tender or tough the cake will be.

Flour is the very finely ground, sifted meal of any type of grain, but for the purposes of this book we are talking about wheat flour exclusively. The use of wheat flour is essential in cake-baking because of the presence of starch and because wheat, unlike other grains, contains two important proteins: gliadin and glutenin. These proteins, when combined with water or another liquid, create a new substance called gluten. Gluten is elastic and strong enough to hold the carbon dioxide created by chemical leaveners or yeast. This in turn allows the cake batter to set in the oven without collapsing so your cakes end up light.

Wheat flours differ from one another depending on the strains of wheat the flour comes from, the environment and climate in which the wheat is grown, and where and how the wheat is milled. All the home baker needs to know is that there are two broad categories of wheat flours: the "strong" flours, high in protein, milled from "hard" wheat, which are great for yeast doughs; and the "weak" flours, low in protein, milled from "soft" wheat, which are perfect for pastries and cakes.

The other crucial component of flour is its starch, which absorbs liquid, swells up (this process is known in baking jargon as "gelatinization"), and thus sets the structure of the cake.

Bleached, Unbleached, Bromated, and Enriched Flour

Freshly milled flour is somewhat weak in strength and yellowish in color because of the natural pigments found in wheat. All flours are then aged to lighten the color and strengthen the proteins. Some flours are aged and lightened (bleached) naturally over time but are described as "unbleached" because no chemicals have been added. But natural aging or bleaching is costly, so millers hasten the process artificially by aging or bleaching flours with chemicals.

Cake flours are bleached with chlorine gas, which is good for cake-baking. This chlorine gas is slightly acidic, and this acidity allows for better liquid absorption, which in turn yields a finer, smoother, and more even-textured cake.

Potassium bromates are chemicals that bleach flours and enhance their baking characteristics, but unbleached flours may contain bromates as well, in which case the package must indicate that the flour is bromated.

Enriched flour means vitamins and minerals have been added to the flour to make up for the nutrients lost in the milling and refining process.

The Strength of Flours

The lower the protein content of the wheat flour, the higher the starch and the better for cakes. So how do you know which flour is low or high in protein, weak or strong? Some package labels indicate the protein content, but if that information is unavailable, write to the manufacturer to find out what it is. Years ago the package label indicated the grams of protein per 1 cup or 4 ounces of flour rounded up to the nearest whole number. So if a particular flour was 8.7 grams of protein per 1 cup of flour, the package would indicate it was 9 grams per 1 cup of flour.

These days the labeling guidelines have changed and the numbers are misleading because the protein grams are listed per ¼ cup of flour, and that number is then rounded up to the nearest whole number. So if you have a flour with 9 grams of protein per 1 cup of flour, that equals 2.25 grams per ¼ cup, which, rounded up to the nearest whole number, becomes 3 grams of protein. However, flour with 12 protein grams per 1 cup of flour is also 3 grams of protein per ¼ cup of flour, and the gluten power difference is enormous between 9 grams and 12 grams of protein per 1 cup of flour.

To help you figure this out, I have listed below the average protein content of the better-known brand-name flours. For lesser-known brands, inquire directly from the manufacturer. King Arthur's *Baker's Catalogue* indicates clearly, to the decimal point, the protein content of each of their flours.

CAKE FLOUR (ABOUT 8 GRAMS PER 1 CUP FLOUR) These flours (national brands like Swan's Down or King Arthur Guinevere) are low-protein flours, milled from soft wheat, high in starch, weak in gluten, and bleached. Some cake flours are self-rising, which means they include salt and chemical leavening mixed into the flour. Be very careful to check the box and don't substitute self-rising for regular cake flour in any of these recipes.

PASTRY FLOUR (ABOUT 9 GRAMS PER 1 CUP FLOUR) Pastry flour is made from a soft wheat and is considered a low-gluten flour but is slightly stronger than cake flour. I like it especially for pie and tart doughs because it gives them a slightly stronger structure than cake flour does yet is not as tough as all-purpose. I have been told by French pastry chefs that it is almost identical to French flour, which is why we used it for all our pastry- and cake-baking at the French Culinary Institute. The only pastry flour I have worked with is available from King Arthur's *Baker's Catalogue* and is identified as King Arthur Round Table pastry flour. It is unbleached and has about 9.2 grams protein per cup of flour. If you have it on hand, you can substitute it in these recipes for cake flour.

ALL-PURPOSE FLOUR (FROM 11 TO 12 GRAMS PER 1 CUP FLOUR) In this book all recipes that call for all-purpose flour were tested with a national-brand bleached and enriched all-purpose flour.

All-purpose flour is a blend of strong and weak flours and comes bleached or unbleached. It was developed for the home cook so that it can be used for all cooking and baking needs, for sauces as well as yeast doughs and cakes. However, not every all-purpose flour is the same and they too vary in protein content.

- Unbleached all-purpose flour is high in protein
    Hecker's or King Arthur:
       12+ grams protein per 1 cup flour
- Bleached all-purpose flours
    Gold Medal, Pillsbury:
       11 to 12 grams protein per 1 cup flour
- Southern bleached all-purpose flours (so weak they qualify as cake flour)
    White Lily, Martha White:
       9 grams per 1 cup flour

BREAD FLOUR (ABOUT 13 GRAMS PER 1 CUP FLOUR) This is a high-protein, high-in-gluten flour milled from "hard" wheats, which absorbs more liquid, is low in starch, and is best for breads and yeast doughs. Bread flours come either bleached or unbleached.

Handling Flour

STORING FLOUR White wheat flour will keep well for up to 1 year in a dry cool cupboard away from light and moisture. If you don't know how long you have had flour on your shelf, smell it before you use it; it will give off a rancid smell if it is spoiled and should be thrown out.

MEASURING FLOUR For baking, it is better to weigh ingredients, especially flour, than it is to measure them by volume. That said, I realize the majority of American cooks are more comfortable with the volume measurement, so here is how I measure flour the "cup" way.

Set a dry measuring cup (or fraction of a cup if the recipe so requires) on your counter, *spoon* the flour into the cup, mounding in more than is required. To level the measurement, sweep off the excess flour by passing the back of a knife or a straight metal spatula across the cup. *Don't* dip your cup in the flour and then sweep off the excess because you will get more weight than is required in the recipe. Also, be sure you know the difference between dry and liquid measuring cups (pages 41–42), making sure to use the dry measuring cups.

To measure tablespoonfuls or teaspoonfuls of flour, dip the measuring spoon into the container of flour and sweep off the excess with the back of your knife, just as you do with a cupful measure.

SIFTING FLOUR You need to sift flour to aerate it so that it properly absorbs moisture and is lump-free. Cake flour is finer than all-purpose and must always be sifted because it tamps down. You will also need to sift flour with other dry ingredients such as baking soda or cocoa powder in order to thoroughly and evenly distribute these throughout the flour. After you have accurately measured the flour, transfer it to a sifter or to a double-meshed strainer. To sift through a strainer, hold the strainer with one hand as you tap the side with the other hand. Sift it over a large sheet of parchment or waxed paper or over a mixing bowl. If the recipe instructs you to sift twice, return the sifted ingredients to the strainer or sifter and repeat the procedure.

STARCHES

Cornstarch

This is a gluten-free pure starch made from the endosperm of the corn kernel. Cakes made with corn-

starch are velvety smooth and tender. Cornstarch is also used to thicken pastry creams and other dessert fillings and sauces.

If you are trying to weaken the gluten structure of an all-purpose flour to simulate a cake flour, substitute 2 tablespoons of cornstarch for 2 tablespoons of flour for each 1 cup of flour called for in the recipe.

Potato Starch

This gluten-free pure starch is extracted from cooked dried and ground potatoes. Like cornstarch, it is used in cake batters as a substitute for flour and produces a moist velvety texture. It is used a lot in Passover cakes when the use of flour is forbidden.

LEAVENERS

Leaveners such as baking powder, baking soda, and yeast are added to cake batters to give them volume and hold up their structure.

Chemical Leaveners

Chemical leaveners refer to baking soda and baking powder, which, in reaction to moisture, acids, or heat, release gases into the dough that help cakes rise and become stable structures.

BAKING SODA This is the common name for sodium bicarbonate, which, in the presence of moisture and some type of acid, releases carbon dioxide gas into the batter. I use baking soda in many of these cakes because almost all of them have the requisite acid, in the form of chocolate or cocoa, to make the baking soda work. Other acidic ingredients include buttermilk, sour cream, yogurt, fruit juices, fruit purées, honey, and molasses.

Because baking soda reacts immediately once introduced into the batter, you must quickly get the cake in the oven or much of the leavening power will dissipate.

The leavening power of baking soda, in the presence of acid, is about four times as strong as that of baking powder. You might think it a good idea then to add more baking soda than is called for in order to give your cakes greater lift, but please resist that temptation. You need very little baking soda to enhance the air bubbles already present in the batter— no more than ¼ teaspoon per cup of flour. If you add too much baking soda to a batter, your cake may have a nasty soapy aftertaste.

Note that baking soda and cocoa cause the batter to develop a reddish hue.

BAKING POWDER Baking powder is a compound that includes sodium bicarbonate (baking soda), an acid that activates the baking soda, and a starch (usually cornstarch) to prevent lumping and to stabilize the leavening power. While single-acting baking powder exists (although it is no longer available commercially), the baking powder used in this book is double-acting. Single-acting baking powder starts to work immediately in the presence of moisture, so as soon as you mix it into the batter, you must get the cake into the oven fast or the leavening power is lost.

Double-acting baking powder works twice. The first reaction begins immediately when you mix the baking powder with liquid and a small percentage of the gases are released into the batter. A second and more powerful reaction occurs when the cake batter goes into the oven and most of the gases are released by the heat. The advantage of double-acting baking powder is that you can mix the batter and let it stand for some time before baking without loss of leavening power.

As with baking soda, don't use more baking powder than is called for or your cakes could have an unpleasant bitter aftertaste, could rise too rapidly in the oven and then sink, or could end up with a crumbly texture.

Store baking soda and baking powder in tightly closed containers away from heat and moisture, because if they are left exposed to air, they absorb moisture and their leavening power is diminished. Baking powder especially loses power fast, and once the can is opened, it should be replaced every 3 months.

Yeast

This is a one-celled, live, microscopic fungus. When combined with flour and liquid, the yeast eats the starch in the flour, then converts it to sugar and, in the process, gives off carbon dioxide and alcohol. It is the release of these gases that produces the leavening action. There is only one yeast cake in this book, which was tested with dry active yeast (dormant, yet still alive). You can find dry active yeast on the refrigerated dairy shelves of your supermarket. Check the expiration date on the package to make sure the yeast is fresh and that you are not buying "rapid-rise" yeast, which is a yeast that makes the dough ferment twice as fast.

LIQUIDS

Liquids are an essential part of any cake batter for several reasons. They activate the gluten in the flour, which gives structure to the cake; they turn to steam in the oven, which then pushes up the cells of the batter, thus giving the cake its lift and delicate texture. The moisture also activates the baking powder and baking soda, which would remain inert if left dry.

It is important that the ratio of liquids to flour and other solids be correct so that the final structure and texture of the cake be right. Too much liquid overactivates the gluten, thus making the cake tough, whereas too little makes the cake leaden.

Fresh Milk Products

CREAM The percentage of butterfat in cream determines how you are going to use it.

Heavy cream (sometimes identified as "whipping cream" or "heavy whipping cream") has a 36% to 40% butterfat content. Heavy cream is reserved for cake fillings and icings like whipped cream or ganache, as well as for sauces.

Try to buy heavy cream that is not ultrapasteurized. Ultrapasteurized means the cream was boiled for a longer time than regular pasteurized cream and at a higher temperature so as to destroy bacteria and prolong the cream's shelf life. This process makes it harder to whip the cream, so manufacturers introduce stabilizers to make up for the decreased whipping ability.

Ultrapasteurized cream has a slightly "cooked" taste.

Light whipping cream has a 30% to 35% butterfat content and can be whipped somewhat but will never achieve the volume of whipped heavy cream.

Light cream has an 18% to 20% butterfat content and is sometimes known as "table" or "coffee" cream.

Half-and-half has only a 10% to 12% butterfat content. I use light cream and half-and-half in certain cake batters, icings, and in dessert sauces.

MILK Milk is a crucial element in baking. It is 91% water, so it functions in baked goods mostly in the development of gluten. The milk solids and butterfat contribute to flavor, color, and keeping qualities of baked goods. Unless otherwise stated, all milk used in this book is whole, pasteurized, and homogenized, with a 3.5% butterfat content. Please don't substitute low-fat for whole milk because it will throw off the balance of the cake.

Pasteurized means the milk has been heated up to a fairly high temperature for a specific period of time in order to thoroughly kill bacteria.

Homogenized means that the butterfat in the milk is evenly distributed throughout the liquid and won't separate and come to the top as a layer of cream.

Evaporated Milk is whole milk that has been heated until about 60% of the water is evaporated. It is a canned product used in frostings.

Sweetened Condensed Milk is a mixture of whole milk and sugar that has been heated until about 60% of the water is evaporated. It is a sweet and thick, sticky canned product that can be used in frostings.

Fermented Milk Products

The advantage of adding fermented milk products to cake batters, fillings, and sauces is that they are acidic and tangy. The tanginess changes the flavor, and the acidity helps cut or shorten the gluten strands, which makes the cakes more tender. Do not substitute fresh milk for fermented milk products as it will throw off the balance of baking soda and baking powder.

BUTTERMILK Originally, buttermilk was a naturally occuring, slightly sour residual liquid left after churning milk into butter. Buttermilk is thus low in fat because all the original butterfat has been congealed and solidified into butter.

Today buttermilk is a "cultured" product, which means skim milk has been cultured with a lactic-acid bacteria that makes it taste slightly sour. For recipes in this book, I use 1% butterfat buttermilk sold in the refrigerator case in the supermarket.

If you come across the phrase "sour milk" in an old cookbook, use buttermilk instead.

SOUR CREAM This is an 18% "light" cream that has been soured by adding a lactic-acid bacteria. Sour cream makes the cake crumbs especially tender.

YOGURT This is either a whole, low-fat, or skim milk that has been cultured by adding a special type of bacteria. The yogurt used in this book is plain and unflavored. Each recipe specifies whether to use whole or low-fat yogurt.

Other Liquids

UNSWEETENED COCONUT MILK In my coconut cakes, as all or as part of the requisite liquid, I use unsweetened coconut milk to accentuate the flavor of the coconut. This is an unsweetened canned product that comes from grinding the meat of the coconut with milk or water and then extracting the juice from that pulp. It is readily available in gourmet stores and even in the larger, better-stocked supermarkets, where it is often stashed alongside other food products used in Hispanic cuisine. Do not substitute sweetened coconut milk for the unsweetened milk; the sweetened milk is used in mixed drinks and candies, and it is way too sweet and will throw off the balance of your cake.

ORANGE JUICE CONCENTRATE Sometimes, to really develop a deep orange flavor, I add undiluted, thawed, frozen orange juice concentrate; the flavor is intense and the density adds to the texture as well.

SUGARS

Sugar is a substance that is extracted from sugarcane or from sugar beets. The extracted juice is combined with water, and that solution is then put through an elaborate and extensive refining process that transforms the sugar from a colored liquid into the white crystals we know as "refined, white granulated sugar." Liquid sweeteners such as honey and molasses cannot be substituted for granulated sugar in these recipes.

The role of sugar in baking is multifaceted. Besides its obvious contribution to the sweetness and flavor of the cake, sugar weakens the gluten structure in flour and thus helps to tenderize the cake. Sugar helps in the creaming and foaming process of cake batters; it attracts and absorbs moisture so that cakes keep fresher longer; and when subjected to heat, sugar caramelizes, so it also provides color to baked goods (an almost irrelevant factor in this book, where most of the cakes are deeply colored with chocolate). Sugar is also food for yeast, so it helps in the fermentation and ultimately results in a better rise and lighter texture in yeast doughs.

Granulated Sugar

Granulated sugar is the all-purpose sugar we use in the home. While professional bakers have at their disposal various grades of granulated sugar, in my recipes, granulated sugar is the stuff you get from the supermarket.

The size of the crystals in granulated sugar vary from package to package, even when manufactured and distributed by the same company. Granulated sugar that is too coarse will not dissolve during baking, so your cakes could develop surface spots of undissolved sugar. Sugar that is too coarsely ground doesn't hold as much air during the creaming or foaming process, so your cakes won't rise as well nor be as light. I did not want to discourage people by making my recipes too complicated, so when I say "granulated sugar," it is okay to use it straight from the bag. However, if you want an especially fine and even crumb in your butter cakes and foam cakes, or if the sugar you are about to use looks too rough and coarse, grind it further by giving it a few spins in the food processor. Another solution is to substitute, measure for measure, superfine sugar (discussed on the next page) for granulated sugar.

Superfine, Instant, or Bar Sugar

This is a sugar that has been ground into very fine crystals. Because the crystals are so fine, they dissolve almost instantly in cold liquid, which is why it is the sugar of choice for making mixed drinks in bars. Superfine sugar is also the best for all sorts of cakes, buttercakes, meringue cakes, angel food, and chiffon cakes. While the tiny facets in superfine sugar make it perfect to use in butter or shortening cakes, you can substitute granulated sugar, which works well enough and is more likely to be on hand in the pantry of most home kitchens. For a super-delicate crumb texture, however, do as I recommend and use superfine rather than granulated sugar.

Strain or sift superfine sugar before using because it cakes upon standing.

Confectioners' or Powdered Sugar

This is a refined sugar ground to a powder and mixed with about 3% starch to prevent it from caking. The pastry chef has available to her several grades of confectioners' sugar, but my recipes call for 10X confectioners' sugar, which is the finest grind and the one the average consumer can buy at the supermarket.

Confectioners' sugar dissolves instantly, so it is great in uncooked icings and whipped cream. Do not, however, substitute it for granulated or superfine sugar in making cakes.

You must always strain or sift confectioners' sugar before using because it cakes upon standing.

Brown Sugar

Originally, brown sugar was sugar that had not been completely refined. The residual impurities left in the sugar, including caramel or molasses, gave the sugar its characteristic brown color and light caramel flavor. Today, however, for the sake of consistency, brown sugar is a manufactured, refined white sugar combined with some molasses to give it the old-fashioned color and flavor.

Brown sugar is available in a couple of grades, and the darker it is, the stronger it tastes. I often use light brown sugar in my recipes because of its more subtle taste.

"Granulated" or "instant" brown sugar is a crystallized form of brown sugar that does not harden and lump like ordinary brown sugar. You can substitute it, measure for measure, for light brown sugar.

Brown sugar is moistened with molasses, which, when exposed to air, evaporates, thus leaving the sugar clumped into tiny hard rocks on which you could break your teeth. To keep the sugar from hardening this way, once the package is open, I leave the sugar in its original plastic wrapping, which I staple shut. Then I stick the closed package in a zippered plastic bag, which I then stick in an airtight container. Believe me, the brown sugar will remain moist this way for months!

If, however, your brown sugar does harden, stick a slice of apple in the package, staple it shut, and wait a few days for it to soften. If you need to use the hardened sugar immediately, sprinkle it with water, wrap it airtight in foil and stick the package in a 200°F oven for 15 to 20 minutes, or until it softens. Cool the sugar before using it.

Vanilla Sugar

This is granulated or superfine sugar that has been flavored with vanilla. You can buy small packages of vanilla sugar from specialty gourmet stores, or you can create your own. To make vanilla sugar, stick a vanilla pod, emptied of its seeds, in a closed jar of superfine or granulated sugar. Over time, the sugar will pick up the flavor of the vanilla.

How to Measure Sugar

As I've said, I prefer to weigh my ingredients, especially flour and sugar, but I must admit that the difference in accuracy between measuring sugar by volume or weight is negligible because sugar does not tamp down the way flour does.

To measure granulated sugars by volume, dip the measuring cup or spoon in the canister of sugar, scoop it out, and set it on the counter. Sweep off the excess sugar back into the canister by passing the back of a knife or a straight metal spatula across the measuring cup or spoon.

To measure brown sugar, measure the sugar into the cup, press down with your hands to pack it into the measuring cup, and stop when the cup is filled to the brim.

To measure confectioners' sugar, spoon the sugar into the measuring cup, mound it up past the brim, and sweep off the excess by passing the back of a knife or a straight metal spatula across the cup.

How to Sift Sugar

Granulated sugar is so carefully packaged these days that it rarely clumps unless some moisture has seeped into the package, so you don't need to sift it.

However, superfine sugar tends to clump, so it should be sifted before using (that is, passed through a single-mesh strainer), and confectioners' sugar must always be sifted before using. If for some reason you are working with a lot of confectioners' sugar, as when making large batches of frosting, wear a mask while you work to avoid inhaling the microscopic particles that float into the air and that are bad for your lungs.

Brown sugar offers the most problems in terms of lumps. Dump the sugar into a bowl and check for lumps. Press soft lumps through your fingers to dissolve them and discard rock-hard ones. Measure after the lumps have been removed.

LIQUID SWEETENERS

Corn Syrup

Corn syrup is made from cornstarch converted into a liquid sweetener along with water and a vegetable gum. Corn syrup comes in a light form, which is flavorless and colorless and which I prefer over the dark corn syrup to which caramel has been added for flavor and color.

In this book, I use corn syrup mostly for making sugar syrups and for cooked frostings because it prevents some of the crystallization of the sugar.

Honey

This is a natural liquid sugar obtained from the nectar of flowers that varies widely in color and flavor depending on the source of the nectar. It has the same sweetening power as sugar but cannot be substituted for sugar in these recipes because it doesn't work in the same way.

I use honey in some of my cakes because of its unique flavor and because it adds moistness, which extends the keeping quality of a cake.

Molasses

Molasses is a by-product of the process of refining sugar; it is what remains after most of the sugar has been extracted from the sugar solution. Sulfured molasses contains sulfur dioxide, which is added to clarify it, but it also gives it a particular strong sulfur flavor that can be quite unpleasant. Unsulfured molasses is not a natural by-product of the refining process; instead it is a specially produced sugar syrup that is slightly less bitter than sulfured molasses and is what I use in my recipes.

How to Measure Liquid Sweeteners

Liquid sweeteners, like honey and molasses, should be measured in liquid cups or in volume spoons for smaller measurements. To make it easier to remove these sticky liquid sweeteners from the measuring implements, grease the measuring implement first with vegetable oil, then measure. The liquid sweetener will pour out effortlessly.

EXTRACTS, ESSENCES, AND FLAVORINGS

Extracts are essential oils extracted from the fruit or bean of a plant, which are then dissolved in an alcohol solution. I use pure extracts because they taste better than anything synthetic and are less volatile so they hold up better to heat. It is worthwhile spending some extra money on the real stuff, because the use of imitation extracts will lower the overall quality of taste.

Store extracts in a cool dry place, away from light, because they are volatile and dissipate in the presence of light.

Citrus Oils and Natural Flavorings

I have recently discovered a source of natural flavorings and citrus oils, which heretofore were available only to professional pastry chefs through wholesale baking distributors. Boyajian is the manufacturer of these oils and natural flavorings. They are available through the King Arthur's *Baker's Catalogue* and the Williams-Sonoma catalogue (see source list, pages 309 and 391). I love these flavorings and oils. They are so concentrated that you need only a tiny bit to perfume an entire cake or sauce, so you never have to add an excess that could throw off the balance in your recipe.

Coffee Extract

Coffee extract plays a big role in the professional pastry kitchen but is not available to the home baker. However, it is easy to create your own "coffee extract"

by dissolving instant espresso coffee powder in very hot or boiling-hot water. The proportion of coffee to water varies from recipe to recipe.

Ginger, crystallized

Crystallized ginger, also known as candied ginger, is cooked ginger that is cut into bits and coated with granulated sugar. I add it to cakes when I want an extra-sharp bite of ginger.

Herbs

Herbs don't play a major part in the flavoring of cakes; the only fresh herb used in this book on occasion is mint—used either as a garnish or to flavor custard sauces.

To store fresh mint, set the stems in a jar or glass filled with an inch or so of water. Cover the leaves loosely with a plastic bag and store the jar in the refrigerator—the mint will keep vibrant and fresh for up to 1 week.

Orange Flower Water

This flavoring, a highly aromatic distillation of orange blossoms, is used extensively in Middle Eastern and Indian kitchens. I like to use it in custard sauces and in cakes to reinforce other orange flavorings.

Rose Water

This flavoring, a distillation of rose petals, is also used in Middle Eastern and Indian cuisine. I love its aroma, in minute amounts, in sauces because it is a great flowery counterpoint to the assertiveness of bittersweet chocolate.

Salt

Salt is used in cake batters to bring out the taste of the other ingredients. The salt used in these recipes is ordinary table salt, not the coarse kosher variety.

Spices

Spices refer to a variety of seasonings extracted from plant parts, such as bark, flower buds, and roots. In these cakes I have used primarily ground spices. An excellent mail-order source for the freshest and most fragrant spices is Penzeys Spices (see page 390 for address).

The aroma and power of spices is volatile and easily dissipated, so store them in a cool dry place away from light. If you can't remember how long you've had a spice on your shelf, smell it before using it. If the spice gives off little aroma, it has lost its strength and won't add any flavor to your baked goods.

Spirits

Brandies and liqueurs should be of good quality because cheaper brands are harsh and will ruin fillings or cakes.

Vanilla Extract and Beans

The vanilla bean is the fruit of a particular variety of orchid. Extracting the vanilla essence from the pod is so involved and labor intensive that it pushes up the price of vanilla. Do not substitute imitation vanilla for the pure extract because its overwhelmingly artificial flavor will ruin your desserts.

Vanilla beans are grown in different parts of the world, but the three that are available to the consumer are Tahitian (most expensive), Bourbon-Madagascar (most common and reasonable), and Mexican (unusual). Experiment with different varieties until you find the one that suits your taste. Purchase vanilla beans from a reputable source and check to see that they look plump, flexible, and glossy. Once you open the package, check the smell to make sure the vanilla beans are highly aromatic. If they are not, return them to the store and get your money back! I buy vanilla beans and extracts from King Arthur's *Baker's Catalogue* or from Penzeys Spices.

You can use both the outside pod and the inside seedy pulp of the vanilla bean. With a small paring knife, split a vanilla bean in half lengthwise to expose the flavorful pulp and tiny seeds. With the tip of the knife, scrape out the pulp and seeds and reserve the pod. Use the pod as is, or if you have used it to flavor a sauce, rinse the pod with water and let it dry at room temperature, then stick it in a container of granulated or superfine sugar to create vanilla sugar. Use vanilla sugar to lightly dust cakes or cookies.

Zest

Zest refers to the brightly colored part of the peel of citrus fruits such as orange, lemon, or lime. In the colorful part of the peel resides the fruits' essential and flavorful oils. I like to use freshly grated zest in recipes where the juice of the fruit is called for as well. First I grate the zest, then squeeze out the juice. If very little zest is called for in a recipe, I am more inclined to use a "pure" citrus extract or oil. Before you remove the zest, wash the fruit to remove any bacteria or chemical spray.

HOW TO GRATE ZEST Using a box or handheld grater, remove only the part of the peel that has color. Avoid grating the bitter white pith, located right below the colored part of the peel.

HOW TO MINCE ZEST Remove the colored part of the peel with a sharp paring knife or little tool known as a "zester." Mince the peel as finely as possible with a chef's knife. This method is best for cakes in which you don't mind fine bits of peel.

FRUITS AND FRUIT PRODUCTS

Dried Fruits

When selecting dried fruit, look for bright-looking, plump, and moist fruit. I like the quality of prunes, raisins, and currants from the supermarket. I prefer buying apricots, cranberries, cherries, figs, and dates from a gourmet or health food store, where I can sample the merchandise first to make sure it is moist and fresh.

To restore hardened dried fruit, steep it in hot water until soft enough to bite into.

Once the package or bag of fruits has been opened, repackage the fruit in an airtight glass jar or transfer it to a plastic bag, squeeze out the air, and tape it shut. Store dried fruit in a cool dry cupboard away from light, where it will keep for a month, or store it in the refrigerator, where it will keep for up to 1 year.

APRICOTS I prefer Californian or Australian dried apricots to the Turkish variety because they taste sweeter and have more fruit flavor.

CURRANTS Dried currants are not a dried version of fresh currants, which are berries, but a dried variety of the tiny grape known as the Zante grape. I often choose currants over raisins because I like their smaller bite in baked goods.

DATES Avoid the supermarket variety, which can be brittle and sugary. An easy way to cut dried dates is to use scissors instead of a knife.

FIGS Sample one first to make sure the figs are moist and fresh, and don't forget to remove the stem before cutting.

RAISINS Raisins are merely dried grapes. In these recipes, you can substitute golden raisins, which are a little sweeter, for the dark ones.

Canned and Jarred Fruits

In general I prefer fresh fruit over dried and dried over canned, but in some instances the canned or jarred variety is perfectly acceptable. Sour cherries in the jar or bing cherries in the can, for example, are great in cake fillings.

I am also fond of canned sliced mango or canned mango pulp to use as the basis of dessert sauces. I buy Alphonso brand, imported from India and available in stores that carry foreign foods.

Frozen Fruit and Fruit Purées

The professional pastry chef has at her disposal a wide and wonderful world of frozen fruit and fruit purées, available in the most exotic flavors, from passion fruit to blood orange. These are usually imported from France and available only from a wholesaler. However, the home baker need not despair because we are not without resources of our own. The supermarket freezer is a hidden treasure trove. There is fresh frozen fruit which is great in baked goods. Be sure to look for the IQF, or Individually Quick Frozen, variety, which is the best. I purée the frozen fruit with a sugar syrup, and presto, a quick dessert sauce is ready in minutes. Frozen raspberries packed in syrup make the best raspberry sauce imaginable.

There is also a line of tropical frozen fruit, either puréed or in chunks, available in Hispanic markets. Passion fruit and mango are the flavors I use in dessert sauces. And, finally, available from King Arthur's *Baker's Catalogue*, are raspberry and mango coulis, which are ready-to-eat sauces.

NUTS AND SEEDS

I confess to having an insatiable penchant for the taste of nuts, so much so, in fact, that I have to refrain from adding them to every cake I make. I learned quickly when working in a restaurant, however, that nut-filled pastries are not great sellers, either because people are allergic to nuts or because they don't care for the taste (incomprehensible to me).

Perhaps some of this aversion to nuts results from

the fact that the precious oils that give nuts their distinctive flavor rapidly go rancid, and this rancidity comes through even in baked goods. The most important piece of advice I can give you is to buy nuts from a reputable source where you can actually taste before buying. If you buy prepackaged nuts and find them spoiled, be sure to return them and get your money back; whatever you do, don't use them in your baked goods.

Store vacuum-packed nuts in a cool dry place, where they will keep for a few weeks, but store opened packages of nuts in the freezer, where they will keep for a year. You don't have to thaw them before using.

Measuring Nuts

My recipes instruct you to measure the nuts first, then chop or grind them; don't reverse the procedure or you might throw the recipe out of balance.

Chopping Nuts

I find it easier to chop nuts by hand, on a cutting board with a chef's knife, than to do so in a food processor because I can exert more control over the size of the particles. However, grinding nuts should be done in a food processor, provided you take the proper precautions (described below) so they don't turn oily.

"Coarsely chopped" nuts are chopped by hand into pieces about ½ inch in size.

"Finely chopped" nuts are chopped by hand or in a food processor into ¼-inch or smaller pieces.

"Ground" nuts are ground in the food processor until they are almost as powdery as flour. Years ago, nuts were put through a hand-operated nut grinder, which reduced them to very fine, dry particles. Today, the action of the food processor can quickly turn nuts into an oily paste, which you don't want. To prevent this, grind the nuts by pulsing the machine on and off until the nuts are chopped into the size you wish. Another safeguard is to grind the nuts with 1 or 2 tablespoons of sugar taken from the amount you need in the recipe.

Toasting Nuts

Toasting nuts before you add them to batters makes them taste immeasurably better. To toast nuts, preheat the oven to 375°F, spread the nuts in a single layer on a baking sheet, and bake for about 20 minutes, depending on how golden, toasted, and aromatic you want them to be. Let your nose be your guide: The nuts are done when you can begin to smell their toasty aroma.

Almonds

Almonds are sold in various forms. They are the nut of choice in baked goods because they add texture without too distinctive a taste, which could overshadow other flavors in the cake.

"Whole" almonds refers to the entire almond with its brown skin left on.

"Blanched" almonds refers to almonds with the brown skins removed. You can buy blanched almonds in bulk or packaged in 4-ounce cans. (To blanch almonds at home, plunge them in boiling water for a minute, drain, cool under cold running water, and slip off the skins.)

"Slivered" almonds are blanched and cut lengthwise into long thin "slivers."

"Sliced" almonds are not blanched but have been cut across the width of the nut into wafer-thin slices. (When a recipe specifies sliced instead of slivered, stick to the instructions.)

"Almond flour," a professional product available through wholesalers, is made from blanched almonds pulverized to a powdery flour; it is used instead of, or as part of, the flour in a recipe. I prefer the uneven coarse texture I get from grinding almonds in a food processor to the very fine texture of commercial almond flour.

"Almond paste," a prepared product available in cans (Solo is the most common brand available), is composed of 50% ground almonds and 50% sugar, with some glycerin added. (In certain European countries, where almond paste is prized, it is made of 75% almonds and only 25% sugar.)

Do not confuse almond paste with marzipan, which is a candy made from almond paste plus additional sugar; don't substitute one for the other.

Chestnuts

A chestnut is a very sweet, mealy nut often used in Europe, and sometimes in Asia, in both savory and sweet dishes. There are many forms of chestnuts: fresh, dried, roasted, canned, and candied. Fresh chestnuts are available in the United States from September through January. Buy very firm ones without bruises or soft spots.

To peel fresh chestnuts, make an incision on the side of each chestnut and boil them for 10 minutes. Drain and cool them under cold running water. Peel the outer and inner skins (this is a lot of work, but the taste makes the effort worthwhile).

Canned chestnuts come either whole, in pieces, or as a purée, and either sweetened or unsweetened. You can also get them roasted whole and packaged in jars. Each recipe in this book specifies which type you need. You can find them through mail-order catalogue sources or, most easily, in some canned form in a gourmet store.

Marrons glacés is a popular French confection made from whole chestnuts cooked in a sugar syrup. See page 373 for how to make Sugared Chestnuts, which come close to the original.

Chestnut flour is made from dried chestnuts pulverized into flour. It is a pure starch, so it produces a velvety smooth crumb in cakes and adds a distinctive and very sweet taste. You can buy chestnut flour imported from France or Italy from specialty gourmet stores and from certain mail-order catalogues.

Coconuts

Coconuts are not botanically true nuts, but we use their white nutmeat in the way we do other nuts. Fresh coconut has a brown, hard, hairy husk surrounding an inner thin, brown skin, which in turn envelops the white nutmeat. Inside the white nutmeat is an opaque, almost flavorless liquid known as coconut water, not to be confused with coconut milk.

FRESH COCONUT I use fresh coconut in some of my cakes, so here is what you need to look for when buying a fresh coconut. It should feel heavy and you should shake it to hear if it is full of liquid. Don't buy it if you can't hear the liquid because it will be dried out. Make sure the shell is not cracked and there is no mold around the "eyes" (the three blackish indentations on one end).

To open the coconut, pierce two of the three eyes with a screwdriver and turn it upside down to drain the juice (reserve the juice in the refrigerator and drink it as is).

Preheat the oven to 400°F and bake the coconut for 20 minutes. Remove the coconut and wrap it in towels; use a hammer to smash it in a few places. The coconut shell will fall away in several large pieces. Then, with the help of a screwdriver, pry the meat with its peel away from the outer husk. Use a vegetable peeler to peel away the thin brown skin.

PACKAGED COCONUT You can buy packaged shredded and sweetened coconut at the supermarket, or desiccated and unsweetened coconut from a health food store, or frozen fresh coconut from a Hispanic grocery store.

COCONUT MILK AND COCONUT CREAM Coconut milk and coconut cream refer to the liquid obtained by steeping grated fresh coconut meat in boiling water and pressing out the liquid from the pulp. Years ago I made my own coconut milk, but today it is readily available, unsweetened in cans, from grocery stores or large supermarkets that cater to an Asian or Hispanic clientele.

If you can't find canned coconut milk, this is how you do it from scratch: Bring equal parts of water and grated fresh coconut or unsweetened desiccated coconut to a simmer; let stand for 10 minutes and strain out the liquid through a cheesecloth-lined sieve; refrigerate. To make coconut cream, proceed as you would with coconut milk but use 3 parts coconut to 1 part milk, and let the mixture stand for a few hours to get the richest extraction possible.

Hazelnuts

I think that, of all the nuts, hazelnuts have the greatest affinity to chocolate. Hazelnuts are less popular in this country than in Europe, so the turnover is slower. The nuts go rancid quickly, so be sure to taste one before buying them.

You need to remove the skins before using hazelnuts in baked goods. To do so, toast them in a hot oven until the skins blister and the nuts smell toasted. Then rub the nuts, while they are still hot, between dry clean towels; most of the skin will flake off.

PRALINE PASTE This is another one of those miraculous and indispensable products used in the professional pastry kitchen that is impossible to make at home. It is a paste of toasted hazelnuts and caramelized sugar ground and pressed so fine that the natural oils in the nuts are released and turn the mixture into paste. Up until recently one could get this product only through bakery supply houses, but now consumers can purchase praline paste from King Arthur's *Baker's Catalogue*. It is sold under the brand name American Almond (the best domestic brand) and comes in 8-ounce cans. When you open the can, you'll notice the oil will have separated to the top as it does in peanut butter. To rehomogenize the mix, put the contents of the can in a food processor and purée until smooth. Transfer the paste to a tightly closed container and keep it in the refrigerator or freezer indefinitely.

Macadamia Nuts

The macadamia nuts I use in my recipes are the unsalted ones available in certain gourmet stores. If only the salted variety is available to you, remove the excess salt by quickly rinsing the nuts under cold running water and drying them for a few minutes in a 200°F oven.

Pecans

I buy pecans from a health food store where I know they are always fresh, but the vacuum-packed variety available from the supermarket is quite acceptable.

Pistachios

The pistachios called for in these recipes are shelled, unsalted, and lightly roasted. You can buy them from a baking supply or gourmet store.

Poppy Seeds

A couple of recipes call for poppy seeds and one calls for ground poppy seeds. While you can buy a specialty poppy-seed grinder or grind them yourself in a spice grinder, for my recipe, it is easier to use the canned filling. The canned filling is basically a mixture of ground poppy seeds combined with some corn syrup.

Walnuts

These come vacuum packed but still can turn rancid. Taste a nut, and if it is spoiled, return the package to the store.

Sift through the nuts before adding them to your baked goods and remove any stray bits of hard shell. You could break your tooth if one of these slipped unnoticed into your cake.

MISCELLANEOUS INGREDIENTS

Cream of Tartar

Cream of tartar, also known as potassium acid tartrate, is a white power made from the ground crystalline deposits found on the inside walls of wine barrels. It has many functions in dessert-making. It helps stabilize beaten egg whites so they remain moist and pliable, and a small amount prevents the crystallization of sugar in cooked frostings and icings.

Gelatin

Gelatin is a ground-up protein derived from pig skin or beef and veal bones, cartilage, and hooves. Gelatin is a tasteless, colorless, and odorless substance used to stabilize and thicken mousses, whipped creams, and Bavarian creams; without it, they would separate and liquefy over time.

Gelatin comes packaged either in clear sheets, or "leaves," favored by chefs or powdered in the ¼-ounce envelopes available in supermarkets. I use the powdered variety in this book because it is easier for the consumer to find, but I happen to prefer the leaves because they are easier to work with and dissolve more easily. You can find them through bakery supply catalogues or specialty stores.

Regardless whichever form you buy, always rehydrate the gelatin in a *cold* liquid for 3 to 5 minutes (10 minutes for the sheets) so that it softens, swells, and dissolves easily. Then heat it up or add it to a hot liquid so it liquefies and begins to gel. After the gelatin is dissolved into the base, cool the bowl with the base in a larger bowl of ice until the mixture begins to set

slightly. After the mixture begins to set, you can fold in the whipped cream or beaten egg whites. With the bowl still on ice, stir the mixture occasionally with a rubber spatula so that it cools and sets evenly. Once the mixture is fully gelled, don't continue to fold or stir, or it will begin to break down.

For more information on ingredients used specifically in decorating cakes, see: Decorating Whole Cakes: Equipment and Ingredients, pages 335–337.

CHOCOLATE

From Cacao Seed to Cocoa Bean

Over and over again, people ask: "Which chocolate do you like best?" Ah, if chocolate were that simple! I can't give a quick and easy answer because chocolate is endlessly complex. The best chocolate for cake-making is not necessarily as good for eating out of hand, nor the right type for making a frosting. To select the right chocolate, it helps to know what goes into making quality chocolate.

Chocolate has been in existence for thousands of years, although not in the form we know it today. At the outset, chocolate was a bitter drink made from pounding cacao seeds (beans) until the cacao butter oozed out, turning the beans to a paste; the paste was combined with spices, and sometimes honey, flowers, chiles, or almonds, then mixed with water, and whipped until frothy. We know that the ancient Indians—like the Toltecs, Mayans, and Aztecs—loved this drink, and legend has it that the Aztec Emperor Montezuma consumed fifty cups of it a day, ostensibly because it was an aphrodisiac!

So how does this ambrosial substance come about? Not easily. It all starts with the seed of *Theobroma* (meaning "food of the gods") *cacao*. In order to bear fruit, this plant must be grown in a geographical area either 20° north or 20° south of the equator—thus in an area with high humidity, low altitude, and a consistently warm temperature of around 68°F. A cacao tree produces large ovoid pods, each weighing 1 to 1½ pounds. Within each of these pods lie an average of fifty precious cacao seeds from which chocolate is derived. Surrounding these seeds is a tangy, refreshing white or pinkish pulp that, at this point, is far better tasting than the hard and bitter seeds. It is believed that the white pulp, not the seeds, originally attracted humans to this food.

One of the determining factors in the ultimate taste and quality of chocolate is the type of cacao bean used in its production. There are two main species of cacao trees: the criollo and the forastero, with crossbreeds such as the trinitario in between. The criollo bean produces the smoothest, richest, and best chocolate in the world. Unfortunately, the criollo tree, which grows primarily in Central and South America, accounts for only about 2% of the world's cacao beans because it is so susceptible to blight and disease. On the other end of the spectrum is the forastero tree grown in Africa and Brazil. The forastero is hardy, which is why it accounts for 90% of the world's cacao beans; perhaps the qualities that make the forastero resistant to disease also result in beans that produce a more astringent bitter chocolate. The trinitario cacao is a crossbreed that came about in the eighteenth century when the criollo trees planted on the island of Trinidad were killed off by pests. Forastero trees were imported and planted and were crossbred with criollo seeds to produce the new tree, trinitario. The trinitario tree has some of the sturdy characteristics of the forastero tree, and its cacao beans have some but not all of the more delicate qualities of the criollo.

One of the most interesting developments in the history of chocolate is a new breed of cacao, grown in Hawaii and introduced by Jim Walsh, whom I had the great pleasure of meeting. He is a former advertising executive who made a life change and now devotes his time and energy to growing cacao. Today, he must be one of the world's great authorities on growing cacao and manufacturing chocolate. Walsh manufactures "vintage chocolate," which, like vintage wine, tastes different from year to year, depending on the crop, weather, and production. Unfortunately for the home cook, this chocolate, named Hawaiian Vintage Chocolate, is available only to professional cooks.

The next step in determining the quality of the cacao bean is how well they are handled at the plantation. In the wild, after the pods ripen, they fall to the ground and split open, and the pulp and seeds begin to rot—to ferment, actually—in the intense heat and humidity of the equator. This rotting or fermentation is actually a good thing, in fact crucial, because it begins to transform the bitter bean into something edible and eventually delicious.

Today, of course, fermentation is a deliberate and controlled process, because bad fermentation adversely affects the aroma and flavor of the beans. On the plantations, the pods are carefully opened and their seeds and pulp left to ferment—either in boxes or on banana leaves—for five to seven days, during which time the beans are carefully turned so their moisture is sweated out. During fermentation the white pulp turns liquid and drains away, the seeds germinate briefly, which is crucial because ungerminated ones never develop the requisite "chocolate" flavor. Eventually the germ within the seed is killed off, the cacao bean changes color from a yellowish tan to a deep brown, and most important, the seed begins to lose some of its astringency and bitterness.

The final step on the plantation is the drying of the beans. After fermentation, the beans are still high in moisture, which must be evaporated or they become moldy and would be unfit for transportation and storage. The beans are dried in the hot tropical sun, continuously turned by hand, for about a week, during which time their moisture is reduced to about 7% and the flavor continues to develop. It is also during this time that the specific taste of each variety of bean begins to show its unique identity. The fermented dried beans are put into sacks and shipped to the factories where they will be transformed into chocolate as we know it today.

From Cocoa Bean to Chocolate

After fermentation and drying, the cacao beans are referred to as cocoa beans. After they are shipped to the plant, they are thoroughly cleaned and roasted. Just as coffee beans develop their final aroma and taste through controlled, careful roasting, so do cocoa beans. This is a critical point because too much roasting makes the beans bitter, whereas too little leaves the taste underdeveloped. And just as with coffee beans, different markets have different preferences, with Spain liking cocoa beans deeply roasted, and the United States liking them mild.

Once the beans are roasted, they are cracked to separate the hard shell from the precious kernel wherein resides the valuable cocoa butter. The roasted cracked kernels are now referred to as "nibs." The nibs, composed of about 50% cocoa butter, are pressed through rollers to remove a lot of the cocoa butter; what remains is a paste known as chocolate liquor. This liquor (not to be confused with "liqueur," an alcoholic drink) is the very essence of chocolate. It is a thick paste containing both the unctuous cocoa butter and the cocoa solids that carry all the precious flavor. This chocolate liquor becomes the basis for the further processing of chocolate, because when combined, in varying degrees and proportions, with more cocoa butter, sugar, milk solids, flavorings, and emulsifiers, it becomes that luxurious substance we love to eat.

The penultimate phase of refining the chocolate is conching, a special heating and mixing process that purges the chocolate of volatile acids and excess moisture, perfects its pouring quality, develops the chocolate aroma, and reduces the particle size in order to yield a velvety smooth texture. Finally, the chocolate is tempered, which means it is heated, cooled, and heated slightly again to the perfect temperature so that when hard and at room temperature, the finished chocolate (whether dark, milk, or white) snaps when you break it and has a beautifully glossy sheen.

Varieties of Chocolate

The chocolate available to the consumer comes in a mind-boggling array of qualities, and you will have to taste and decide which you prefer. Manufacturers develop their own well-guarded secret formulas, blending varieties of cacao beans, varying roasting times, and mixing chocolate liquor, cocoa butter, and sugar in myriad proportions. The market has become so sophisticated, in fact, that specialty chocolates have been developed for the professional pastry chef and confectioner, and even these more exotic chocolates sometimes find their way into the ordinary consumer's kitchen.

UNSWEETENED CHOCOLATE Unsweetened chocolate, also known as "baking" chocolate, is pure chocolate liquor that must, by federal law, contain no less than 50% cocoa butter. It has no sugar at all and is used for baking, in the United States more than in Europe. Any one of the national brands is acceptable; at various times I have used Baker's, Nestle's, and Hershey's unsweetened chocolate. I tend to buy the cheapest one.

BITTERSWEET, SEMISWEET, AND SWEET CHOCO-LATE The distinctions between what are basically "dark" chocolates is a bit confusing because there is no law that governs what has to be contained in each variety. What one manufacturer identifies as semi-sweet might, in fact, be less sweet than what another manufacturer labels bittersweet. So, once again, it will be up to you to investigate and discover which is more suitable to your needs and taste.

Bittersweet chocolate usually contains at least 35% chocolate liquor combined with additional cocoa butter, sugar, vanilla, and an emulsifier like lecithin to produce an intense chocolate taste. Bittersweet chocolate is what I prefer over all other chocolates for eating and baking because of its intense flavor. My absolute favorite is the Swiss brand Lindt, which is readily available.

Extra bittersweet chocolate, or 70% (Lindt) or 71% (Valrhona) chocolate, is much higher in cocoa liquor than ordinary bittersweet. While I find this type of chocolate almost too bitter for eating, I do like it in some fillings and frostings. If I call for it in this book, but you can't find it, substitute regular bittersweet.

Semisweet chocolate, depending on the manufacturer, can be more or less sweet than bittersweet, but in general it is sweeter. This is the chocolate taste Americans seem to like best. In this book, I specify in which recipes you can use semisweet and bittersweet chocolates interchangeably.

Sweet chocolate is the sweetest of all the "dark" chocolates. The one available in the supermarket is sold as German's Sweet Chocolate and is used primarily in the famous German Chocolate Cake. This sweet chocolate was developed in the Midwest by a Mr. Sam German, which is how the cake and chocolate got its name, but is now manufactured by Baker's. I can't recommend specific brand names for semisweet or sweet chocolates because I prefer bittersweet and use it almost exclusively in my cakes and fillings.

MILK CHOCOLATE Milk chocolate is composed of about 10% chocolate liquor, about 12% dry milk solids, sugar, vanilla, and lecithin. It is much sweeter than semisweet, with a far more elusive chocolate taste. It melts at a lower temperature than dark chocolates and has to be handled carefully so that it doesn't scorch. I use milk chocolate in a few fillings, glazes, and mousses, as well as in a few cake batters where I want the faintest of chocolate flavors.

I especially like the Swiss brand Lindt, which has caramelized overtones, but Valrhona might appeal to more people because it is milkier.

WHITE CHOCOLATE White chocolate is not a true chocolate at all because it is without the chocolate liquor that gives chocolate its identifiable taste. Instead, it is a blend of cocoa butter (it must contain 30% to 55% cocoa butter) and sugar, milk solids, vanilla, and an emulsifier. If the white chocolate doesn't include cocoa butter, it is not the real thing and is known as "summer" coating or "confectionary" white chocolate. Like milk chocolate, white chocolate is very heat sensitive, melts at a lower temperature than regular chocolate, and must be handled carefully so it doesn't scorch and seize up when heated. I use it selectively in a few cake batters where I want its velvety smooth texture. By using white chocolate in cake batters, I get to cheat a bit and work with flavors, such as tea or lemon, that don't marry successfully with dark chocolate.

White chocolate varies widely in quality, and you will have to determine which you like best. I like the Swiss brands Lindt and Tobler.

CHOCOLATE MORSELS OR BITS These are small pieces of molded semisweet, milk, or white chocolate that hold their shape during baking because they contain less cocoa butter than ordinary eating chocolate.

Supermarket brands are what I use when I call for these in some of my recipes.

IMITATION, "COVERING," "CONFECTIONARY," OR "COATING" CHOCOLATE Imitation chocolate is made by combining an artificial chocolate flavor with a vegetable fat like coconut or palm oil. It does not contain cocoa butter or chocolate liquor, so *don't* substitute it for real chocolate because the results will be disappointing. It is used in large professional bakeries and kitchens as a quick and cheap way to coat pastries such as eclairs. Whenever you see a pastry with an icing that looks dark and appetizing but is tasteless, you are almost guaranteed it was made with a "coating" chocolate. Imitation white chocolate is also sometimes known as "summer" chocolate or "baking" white chocolate. If you read the label and don't see the words cocoa butter, you know you are in artificial land.

CHOCOLATE BUTTONS OR *PISTOLES* The industry now sells chocolate—dark, milk, and white—in round button shapes so that the professional pastry chef doesn't have to chop chocolate every time she needs to melt it. In French, these are known as *pistoles*, a word that refers to coins. Sometimes I have seen these repackaged, in smaller quantities, for the retail domestic market. If you see these, buy them and store them in the freezer; they melt evenly and quickly and are nice as a decorative element on cakes.

Storing Chocolate

Store chocolate in a cool dry place, preferably not in the refrigerator, where it picks up moisture that could give you trouble when you melt it. If you store chocolate in too warm a place, the cocoa butter might seep out, causing ugly gray streaks on the surface.

Properly stored, unsweetened, bittersweet, and semisweet chocolates will keep for years, whereas white or milk chocolate will keep only for up to a year because the milk solids make it more perishable.

Cocoa Powder

Cocoa powder is the dry residue that remains after the cocoa butter is pressed out of the chocolate liquor. It is ground and sifted, and is known as "unsweetened cocoa powder." This powder has residual cocoa butter in it, from 8% to 24%, which is what manufacturers refer to when they identify some cocoas as "high-fat" cocoa.

NONALKALIZED VERSUS DUTCH-PROCESSED COCOA POWDER When the cocoa butter has been extracted from the chocolate liquor, the residual cocoa powder is somewhat astringent and not easy to blend with cold water. In 1828, a Dutch chemist by the name of Mr. Coenraad Johannes Van Houten, in search of a way to make cocoa powder mix more readily with water, treated it with alkaline salts, thus creating a neutralized, nonacidic cocoa known today as "Dutch-process" or "Dutch-processed" cocoa. As a by-product of this process, the cocoa tastes milder and is deeper in color, which leads people mistakenly to believe it has a more intense chocolate flavor than natural cocoa. The two varieties of cocoa powder taste pretty much the same.

However, in baking cakes, if a specific type of cocoa powder is called for, don't substitute one for the other. Nonalkalized cocoa powder, which is acidic, works with baking soda, whereas the neutral Dutch-processed cocoa works with baking powder. In these recipes I specify whether you should use Dutch-processed or nonalkalized cocoa powder; and if either one is acceptable, as in cake frostings, my recipe will say "unsweetened cocoa powder."

The brands of Dutch-processed cocoa powder I like are Van Leer, available through King Arthur's *Baker's Catalogue*, Ghirardelli, or Droste, available in supermarkets. I use Hershey's natural nonalkalized cocoa powder.

"INSTANT COCOA" is a mix in which dry milk solids and sugar have been added to the cocoa powder. It should never be substituted for unsweetened cocoa.

Handling Chocolate

CHOPPING CHOCOLATE To melt chocolate properly, first chop it into pieces that are roughly ½ to ¾ inch in size. If the pieces are chopped into different sizes, the chocolate won't melt evenly and you risk having to heat it too long for all of it to melt.

At home, I chop thin pieces of chocolate with a chef's knife and thicker chunks with an ice pick. I also chop chocolate, nuts, fruits, and other items on cutting boards reserved exclusively for baking so that these ingredients do not pick up the residual taste of garlic, onions, or other aromatic savory items.

MELTING CHOCOLATE Chocolate can be a bit tricky to melt because it is an emulsion of cocoa butter and cocoa solids. If the chocolate is heated too much, the cocoa butter separates from the cocoa solids, streaking the chocolate gray. Chocolate must be heated without a drop of moisture and never to more than 115°F for dark chocolate or 110°F for milk and white chocolates. If you overheat chocolate, it scorches and becomes grainy, as it will if a drop of moisture falls into the melting mass. To avoid overheating it, always melt chocolate slowly over indirect heat. Another foolproof way is to partially melt the chocolate by whichever method you choose, remove it from the heat source, and let the remaining chunks of chocolate melt by the heat of the surrounding warm chocolate. For small amounts of chocolate, use the double-boiler or microwave method. For large amounts of chocolate, use the double-boiler or oven method.

Double-Boiler Method of Melting Chocolate: For the double-boiler method, chop the chocolate fine, place it in a clean stainless-steel bowl or the top of a double boiler, and set the bowl over a saucepan of very hot or gently simmering (not boiling) water. You do not want the bottom of the bowl to come directly in contact with the water below nor the water to be boiling and spewing up large masses of steam, which could fall into the chocolate and turn it lumpy. Also, *do not cover* the bowl or double boiler because steam could collect under the lid and fall back into the chocolate, causing the mass to harden and become grainy. As the chocolate begins to melt, stir it with a heat-resistant spoon or rubber spatula, working the chocolate from the sides of the bowl into the center mass. When the chocolate pieces are almost entirely melted, remove the bowl from the heat, stir, and let the remaining chocolate melt by the heat of the larger mass.

Microwave Method of Melting Chocolate: For the microwave method, finely chop the chocolate and place it in a clean microwavable plastic or glass bowl. Set the bowl in the microwave oven and heat it, uncovered, at 100% power for 15-second intervals, or at 50% power for 1-minute intervals, stirring between intervals. When you melt chocolate in the microwave, it retains its shape, which can fool you into thinking it is not melting. Be sure then to stir it between heating intervals or you won't be able to gauge if it has melted, and you might overheat it.

You can remove the chocolate from the oven when it has almost melted, then stir and let any tiny undissolved lumps melt by the heat of the surrounding mass. Read the back of the box to find out how to microwave those 8-ounce packages of chocolate from the supermarket that contain smaller, individually wrapped 1-ounce chunks. They suggest melting the chocolate in its paper wrapping in the microwave oven. I have tried this method and it works well.

Oven Method of Melting Chocolate: For the oven method, place the chocolate in a moisture-free, ovenproof pan, and set it, uncovered, in an oven that has a pilot light. Leave the oven door ajar and wait until the chocolate has melted, 5 to 7 minutes.

Melting Chocolate with Liquid: Even though I said earlier that you cannot melt chocolate with a drop of liquid because it will seize up, you *can* melt chocolate in liquid if you have the proper ratio of liquid to chocolate. To be on the safe side, melt chocolate in 1 tablespoon of liquid for 1 ounce of chocolate, even though for certain chocolates, such as milk and white, which contain fewer cocoa solids than dark, you need only 1 tablespoon of liquid for 2 ounces of chocolate.

A much-used preparation in cake-making is "ganache," a superb cream and chocolate mixture used as either a filling or a glaze. To make a ganache, bring heavy cream to just under the boil and pour it over chopped chocolate set in a bowl. It is crucial that before you blend them together, you let the mixture stand for 30 seconds to make sure the heat of the cream has been absorbed by each piece of chocolate. If you don't wait, you might end up with microscopic bits of undissolved chocolate that would make your icing bumpy.

Troubleshooting

- If, despite all your good intentions and precautions, the chocolate seizes up while you melt it, try to salvage the mess by whisking in, for each ounce of chocolate, 1 teaspoon solid vegetable shortening (not butter, which contains water).
- If you feel you have overheated the chocolate and it is about to scorch, immediately transfer the mass to a large clean bowl or dump it on a marble counter, and scrape it back and forth a few times to cool it down quickly, then scrape it back into a clean bowl.

BAKING EQUIPMENT

*B*AKING CAKES IS easy, provided you have good recipes, are organized, and have the proper equipment. I am not going to recommend a comprehensive list of the equipment you should buy because beginner bakers, (see my one-* recipes), need a lot less than more experienced bakers (two- and three-* recipes). What I want to do here is to describe the major appliances and basic small equipment, as well as why I use this type of equipment and how the proper tools can help you to achieve a happy baking experience.

MAJOR APPLIANCES

Ovens

CONVENTIONAL OVENS Conventional ovens, electric or gas-fueled, are best for baking cakes because they radiate heat evenly. To be successful in all your baking endeavors, make friends with your oven and accept its shortcomings. No oven is perfect, not even professional ones. "Making friends with your oven" means learning where the hot spots are and whether or not it is a "fast" or "slow" oven, which means finding out if it is hotter or cooler than what the thermostat indicates.

I have had my gas range for thirty years and always knew it was slightly on the "slow" side, but I didn't worry much about it as it has given me great results over time, in spite of its being consistently and evenly "slow." When I embarked on this project, however, I was determined to know the exact temperature of my oven, so I invested in an expensive oven thermometer which indicated my oven was 50° cooler than it was supposed to be. This didn't seem right to me, so I invested in two more oven thermometers, with the result being that each one gave me yet a different reading. So, with all my oven thermometers appearing inaccurate, I went back to setting my oven thermostat slightly above the temperature a recipe calls for, just as I had been doing for over a quarter of a century with good results. However, if your oven appears to be completely off—that is, really hot or cold—use a good mercury-type oven thermometer to find out what temperature the oven registers, and if it appears to be off by more than 50°, call in a professional to check it out and recalibrate the thermostat.

CONVECTION OVENS A convection oven is an electric oven with an interior fan that blows heat around and causes food to cook faster than a conventional oven. In the early 1980s, convection ovens were all the rage, maybe because they were used in restaurants and whatever professionals used was believed to be superior. Well, I invested in a countertop model with disappointing results: The continual hot air blowing around was good for roasted meats and certain baked goods but not so great for delicate cakes, which emerged too crusty on top and a little dried out. When I was baking for restaurants, however, I had no choice but to make use of the convection oven, so I compensated for the action of the fan by baking my cakes at much lower temperatures than in a conventional oven and for much less time as well.

MICROWAVE OVENS Whereas I never use my microwave oven for straight baking, I find it indis-

pensable for melting chocolate, for defrosting, and for reheating slices of cake I like to serve warm.

Mixers

It is true that a mere one hundred years ago, cakes were beaten by arm power, not electric power, and there are a few "plain and easy" batter cakes in this book that can be assembled by hand. Most of these recipes, however, are easier to do and faster to put together with an electric mixer.

STATIONARY MIXERS While a handheld electric mixer is better than no electric mixer at all, I recommend you buy a quality "stand" or "stationary" mixer, which will be an investment you will never regret. The stationary mixer is invaluable because the bowl doesn't move and the beaters are powered by the machine, which leaves both your hands free to do other work, like gradually pouring liquid into the batter or a hot sugar syrup into eggs as they are whipping up. While you can always improvise with a handheld electric mixer, the more complicated recipes, especially the cooked sugar buttercreams, icings, and fillings become much more difficult to accomplish without a stationary mixer. Once you have decided on this investment, the question becomes which stationary mixer to buy.

KitchenAid. This is the mixer I own and have used for the last twenty-five years. It is a smaller version of the professional mixers you see in bakeries and restaurants. Whether in 10-quart or 10-gallon capacities, all these mixers operate basically the same way—that is, one bowl anchored down to the arms of the machine and a large wire whip, paddle, or dough hook turning in the center and doing all the work. The great advantage of the KitchenAid is that it is operated by a powerful motor that can handle heavy, dense batters without burning out. Its large balloon whip aerates better and produces greater volume. Its other unique feature is the "paddle" attachment, a flat beater that is perfect for creaming butter with sugar because it whips some air into the mixture without overbeating and dense mixtures don't get stuck in the wire beaters. And, of course, thinking beyond cake-making, this machine also comes with a dough hook, which is very useful for kneading certain types of yeast doughs.

I like the KitchenAid Model K-5S or 5-quart capacity because it is the most powerful with the largest capacity bowl. Some people prefer the slightly smaller Model K45SS or 4.5-quart capacity because it is as good, a tad cheaper, has the same nifty paddle and dough hook, and the head of the machine swivels back, which makes it easier to reach down into the bowl to scrape down batters or add ingredients.

The only disadvantage to this mixer is that the paddle and whip attachments don't reach all the way down to the bottom of the bowl, so you must frequently scrape down the beaters and sides of the bowl with a rubber spatula. To make sure the wire whip attachment aerates your mixtures properly, you can lift up the bowl slightly from the arms that anchor it to the machine so the paddle or whip reaches the bottom and can work the whole mass of the batter. (This trick works for the Model K-5S only; for the Model K45SS, where the bowl sort of screws into the base, don't turn the bowl all the way down so it remains slightly elevated and the beaters or paddle then reach to the bottom.) I do this trick in brief bursts and for short periods of time only because this action, in the long run, distorts the shape of the wire whip and scratches the bowl.

Stationary Mixers with Revolving Beaters. The KitchenAid is an expensive machine, so some folks might opt for a more common stationary mixer which comes with a bowl that rotates and two inner whips that beat the batter. The advantage of this machine is that it is smaller and takes up less room on the counter, and some models come with two bowls—one for larger amounts, the other for smaller. The disadvantage is that this type of mixer does not have the paddle attachment, which I find extremely useful.

HANDHELD ELECTRIC MIXERS If you don't have the space for, or inclination to buy, a stationary mixer, a handheld one will do for many tasks although it is less efficient when beating dense batters like pound cakes and cheesecakes. I like handheld electric mixers for specific tasks like whipping cream or small amounts of egg whites and, best of all, because it is portable, for whipping something at the stove, over hot water, like the Seven-Minute Icing.

Because it is less powerful than a stationary mixer, to get the right result, you will have to spend more time at the task than what is recommended in my recipes.

Food Processors

I can't imagine life without a food processor. Not only do I use it constantly for cooking, but for baking it is an invaluable tool as well. I use it for chopping nuts or for turning them into paste, for pulverizing cookie crumbs, and for mixing and blending ingredients.

SMALL FOOD PROCESSORS The only disadvantage to my food processor is that its large bowl makes it inefficient for processing small quantities. This is why I love my "mini-food chopper," which is a small version of a food processor that I rely on for chopping small amounts of ingredients like the handful of pistachios I might need for decorating a cake.

Baking Pans

Don't feel compelled to rush out and buy every single one of the items listed below. Instead, buy what you need to make a specific recipe and over time you will build up an impressive collection of pans as well as other baking tools. When you do need to buy a new cake pan, invest in a high-quality item, which might be more expensive but will last a lifetime. I still use the 9 × 1.5-inch round cake pans I bought over thirty years ago.

I have tried to design my recipes so that, for the most part, you will need only standard-size pans. The recipes at the beginning of the book call for the most widely available cake pans, but as you work your way through to the back of the book and the recipes progress from easy to complex, you might find the need for a few more exotically sized pans.

For best cake-baking results, you need pans made of a durable material that conducts heat uniformly, and that have straight sides, which also help the cake bake evenly. The best materials for cake pans are medium-gauge aluminum or tinned steel, which are ideal because they conduct heat evenly and don't warp. Black steel pans are not good for baking cakes because they absorb too much heat and the outside of the cake will get too crusty (and, of course, for nonchocolate cakes, also too dark in color).

For square or loaf pans, glass is acceptable because it conducts heat well, but the cakes will bake faster, so you will have to reduce the recommended oven temperature by 25° and bake the cakes for a shorter period of time as well.

In general I don't like baking pans with nonstick coatings because the pans are cheap and thin and the coating wears off or gets scratched. The only exception to this rule is for a flat-bottomed tube pan, which I like in a nonstick material because it's easier to remove the cakes from these pans than from the regular aluminum ones.

Springform pans are made of tinned steel or nonstick coated aluminum and consist of a round metal base that is enclosed by a 3-inch-high ring which latches shut around the base. These are great pans for heavy, sticky cakes like cheesecakes, which you can't possibly unmold from the pan in a standard fashion. The only problem is that because these are fairly lightweight pans, over time they warp and the seal between base and sides becomes imperfect so that the batter can weep out. The best insurance against this is to wrap the outside of the pan with aluminum foil and bake with the pan set on a sheet or jelly roll pan to catch the drips.

Tube, Bundt, and kugelhopf pans are useful for dense cakes with lots of volume. The inner tube transfers the heat to the middle of the cake so the interior bakes at the same time as the outside. If you baked a large volume of dense, heavy cake batter in a standard round cake pan, the outside would be overbaked before the interior was cooked through. Sometimes the differences between tube, angel food, Bundt, and kugelhopf pans can be confusing, because different manufacturers use the names interchangeably. What I mean by a kugelhopf or a Bundt pan is a tube pan with a ridged or fluted bottom. A tube pan has a flat bottom. An angel food pan looks like a tube pan but has a removable base with three little "legs," which elevate the pan from the counter, allowing air to circulate around the cake as it cools upside down.

Jelly roll or half-sheet pans should be made of a heavy material so they don't warp. What I mean by a jelly roll pan is a flat, rectangular shallow pan that is about 10 × 15 × 1 inch in size. A half-sheet pan is slightly bigger, 12 × 16 × 1 inch and is called "half-sheet" because it is exactly half the length of a full-sheet pan, which is 16 × 24 × 1 inch in size and is the standard baking sheet in the commercial restaurant and baking industry. You can purchase half-sheet pans in stores that cater to a more serious gourmet crowd. I like this size because nonstick baking mats and parchment papers are cut to fit half-sheet pans rather than jelly roll pans. However, you can substitute for this size an 11 × 17 × 3/4-inch-size jelly roll pan, which is a more standard size used in home kitchens.

Below is a list of the standard cake pans used in this book as well as a recommendation of how many of each you should have.

ROUND CAKE PANS
Three 8 × 1.5-inch layer pans
    (American layer cakes)
Two 8 × 2-inch layer pans
    (French sponge cakes)
One 9 × 1.5-inch false bottom pan
Three 9 × 1.5-inch layer pans
    (American layer cakes)
Two 9 × 2-inch layer pans
    (French sponge cakes)
One 8 × 2.5-inch springform pan
One 9 × 2.5-inch springform pan
One 9 × 3-inch springform pan
One 10 × 2.5-inch springform pan
One 10 × 3-inch springform pan
One 8.5- or 9-inch (10-cup) kugelhopf or
    Bundt pan
One 10-inch (12-cup) kugelhopf
    or Bundt pan
One 10 × 4-inch (2 quarts + 2 cups)
    flat-bottomed tube pan
One 10 × 4-inch (2 quarts + 2 cups)
    angel food pan with detachable bottom

SQUARE PANS
Two 8 × 8 × 2-inch
Two 9 × 9 × 2-inch

RECTANGULAR AND LOAF PANS
One 9 × 13 × 2-inch baking pan
Two 9 × 5 × 3-inch loaf pans
Two 8 × 4.5 × 2-inch loaf pans

SHEET PANS
One 10 × 15 × 1-inch jelly roll pan
One 12 × 16 × 1-inch half-sheet pan
    or
One 11 × 17 × 3/4-inch sheet pan

OTHER
Two 12-cup muffin pans
One 6-cup large muffin pan

BAKING PAN SUBSTITUTIONS AND PAN VOLUME CHART It is important that you stick to the pan size recommended in each recipe for your cakes to be successful. Baking in too small a pan results in batter overflowing onto your oven floor, and baking in too large a pan results in burned or dried-out cake layers.

Although I am not inclined to encourage you to substitute one size pan for another because of the adjustments you would have to make in baking times, there are some standard pan substitutions that always work and that don't require major timing adjustments.

The same amount of batter, more or less, can be baked in

Two 9 × 1.5 or 2-inch round cake pans
Two 8 × 8 × 2-inch square pans
One 9 × 13 × 2-inch baking pan
One 10 × 15 × 1-inch jelly roll pan
Two 12-cup muffin pans

In case you have an odd-size pan you want to use and must figure out its capacity, you can fill it with cups of water, or use the handy geometry formulas you learned in high school, which you probably have forgotten.

To figure out the volume of a square or rectangular pan, the formula is

Length × width × height.
E.g.: 9 × 13 × 2 = 234 square inches
8 × 8 × 2 = 128 square inches

To figure out the volume of a round cake pan, the formula is

½ diameter × ½ diameter × pi (3.14) × height
E.g.: 9 × 2-inch round cake pan
4.5 × 4.5 × 3.14 (pi) × 2 = 127 square inches

If you compare the numbers, you can see how to get the pan size equivalences I describe above; even though their volume capacity is not identical, it is close enough so that you can substitute one for the other.

Two 9 × 2-inch round pans =
    254 square inches
Two 8 × 8 × 2-inch square pans =
    256 square inches
One 9 × 13 × 2-inch pan = 234 square inches

Kitchen Scales

In a professional setting, the first thing you learn about baking is how to measure ingredients accurately, not by volume as the home baker is in the habit of doing, but by weight, using a scale. Get into the habit of measuring ingredients by weight rather than by volume, because weight measurements are constant while measurement by volume varies. I proved this to myself over and over when, for many of the recipes in this book, I measured flour both by weight and by volume, and the weight of the volume cup varied each time I measured. Granted, the weight was off by one-quarter or at most one-half ounce, which does not spell disaster with small amounts of flour for one cake, but it would spell disaster if, when

baking in large volume for a restaurant, the difference added up, literally, to pounds of flour.

There are several types of scales on the market, the big divide these days being between the balance and spring type of scales and the electronic digital ones. Balance scales are fabulous and are used in commercial bakeries. I own a gorgeous iron and brass one given to me by my mother-in-law that measures only in grams. On the down side, balance scales are expensive and take up a lot of counter space.

Whatever type of scale you buy, make sure it registers both in grams and ounces because you never know which recipes you will be working from at some future time. I inherited my mother-in-law's European gram-based pastry recipes, and it's much easier for me to weigh the ingredients in grams, rather than having to convert them to ounces.

Choose a scale with at least a 2-pound capacity and with a platform top rather than a basket so you can vary the container used to hold the ingredients according to the volume you are weighing. If you are weighing small quantities, weigh the ingredients on a piece of aluminum foil or plastic wrap. Weigh larger quantities in lightweight containers like recycled aluminum foil or plastic take-out containers. Once you set the container on the platform, reset the dial to zero so that you take into account the weight of the measuring container, and be sure to read the scale markings at eye level.

I happen to like the Pelouse spring scale, which measures up to 2 pounds. It's a good choice for the amateur baker who uses it on occasion, even though if handled carelessly, it does not hold up.

If you invest in a digital scale, buy an expensive one because inexpensive ones break easily. I had the pleasure of working as a pastry intern at Le Cirque 2000, a four-star New York City restaurant, where I was introduced to the Rolls Royce of digital scales: the Edlund DS-10. It is an extraordinary tool, sensitive enough to register in 0.1-ounce increments up to 10 pounds (or 2 grams to 5 kilograms). It is fabulous but too expensive a toy for me or the average home cook.

Knives

Even the baker should have a good set of knives. A few basic types will do, the serrated one being the most essential.

SMALL PARING KNIFE You'll need a small paring knife, from 3 to 4 inches long for peeling citrus, trimming fruit, etc. It should be made of high-carbon stainless steel or carbon steel.

CHEF'S KNIFE You'll need a heavy-duty chef's knife for chopping chocolate, nuts, and fruit. Don't stint on quality here; go to a reputable store and have someone help you find a carbon steel or high-carbon stainless-steel knife of the right length and weight to fit your hand. I have been collecting kitchen knives for the last thirty years and have always spent money on quality. The proof that it is worthwhile is that I still have and use the very first chef's knife I bought thirty years ago. The wooden handle is worn, and the blade is getting smaller from all the sharpening, but it is as useful as it has always been. Always keep the edge sharp, and dry the knife right after washing.

OLD CHEF'S KNIFE (NOT ESSENTIAL BUT USE-FUL) Every now and then, especially for the more advanced touches in cake-baking, you will need to heat the blade of a chef's knife over an open flame so you can cut through caramel. This is, for example, how you mark portions and cut through the top caramel layer of a Dobos Torte. However, heating the blade this way isn't good for the knife, so I recommend you do this only with a knife you don't use much or were about to discard.

SERRATED KNIFE To slice a cake horizontally, to level off the top and trim off edges, nothing works quite like a serrated knife. If you are serious about baking, invest in a very high-quality serrated knife with a blunt rounded top 12 to 14 inches long. (It needs to be longer than the diameter of the largest cake you bake.) Make sure the teeth are closely set so they cut through delicate cakes cleanly. The knife also doubles as a decorating tool: You can pass it lightly over an icing to form wavy lines.

CAKE KNIFE This is shaped like a cake server but has an edge with fine teeth to cut through cakes cleanly. Its wedge shape makes the knife double as a cake server because it slips easily under the sliced wedge of cake.

DECORATING KNIFE This is not essential (I don't own one) but is interesting to know about because it looks like a baker's serrated knife, only shorter. This knife, made of stainless steel, has a ridged blade that forms wavy lines when you slice through hard root vegetables or potatoes. However, the knife can also double as a decorating knife if you use it to shape wavy lines in soft frostings.

Measuring Tools

As much as I wish Americans would measure ingredients by weight rather than by volume, we are stuck with our present system so we might as well do it right and have the proper measuring tools.

DRY MEASURING CUPS Dry ingredients like flour and sugar are measured with dry measuring cups. Dry measuring cups come in graduated sizes, most commonly in nesting sets, which include capacity measures of ¼ cup, ⅓ cup, ½ cup, and 1 cup. Some sets come with an ⅛-cup capacity, which I find very useful, and even more useful is the 2-cup measuring cup you can purchase separately (available from King Arthur's *Baker's Catalogue*). If you bake a lot and often, it makes sense to have two complete sets;

they never wear out, and it will make your life a lot easier. Even though you can purchase plastic dry measuring cups, I recommend durable stainless-steel ones with sturdy handles that don't bend.

To measure correctly, spoon the dry ingredient you are measuring into the cup up to and past the rim, then sweep off the excess by passing a straight edge, like the back of a knife, over the cup.

LIQUID MEASURING CUPS Liquid measuring cups are obviously for liquid ingredients and can't be used interchangeably with dry measuring cups. These also come in different sizes, and I have several, ranging from the 1-cup capacity to the ½-gallon size. The best ones, like Pyrex brand, are made of a heat-resistant glass, which, unlike plastic, won't stain or absorb odors. The cups have lines on the side to indicate various quantities. You should have at least one each of the following: 1-cup, 2-cup, and 1-quart capacity. As you collect equipment, you will find it invaluable to have two each of the 1- and 2-cup capacity cups.

To measure liquid correctly, pour the liquid in the cup to just under the line that indicates the required volume. Be sure to set the cup on a flat surface and read the line at eye level or your measurement will be inaccurate.

MEASURING SPOONS Measuring spoons also come in plastic and metal, and I recommend the sturdy ones made of stainless steel. Start out with one set that includes four measurements: ¼ teaspoon, ½ teaspoon, 1 teaspoon, and 1 tablespoon. Some newer sets include a ⅛ teaspoon and a 1.5 teaspoon as well. I have six sets of measuring spoons, but two or three sets are sufficient for the home baker.

MEASURING CHART Over the years, I have done a lot of teaching, both to amateur bakers and in professional schools, and I am continually amazed at how misinformed people are about standard measurements. Here then, to refresh your memory, is a handy chart of essential measurements:

1 pint = 2 cups
2 pints = 1 quart
1 quart = 4 cups
1 cup = 16 tablespoons
½ cup = 8 tablespoons
⅓ cup = 5⅓ tablespoons
¼ cup = 4 tablespoons
⅛ cup = 2 tablespoons
1 tablespoon = 3 teaspoons
½ tablespoon = 1.5 teaspoons

Mixing Bowls

Purchase a variety of mixing bowls, in stainless steel and heatproof glass, because these inert materials are "nonreactive" and thus don't discolor, flavor, or react to any of the chemical elements in foods.

For mixing ingredients together it makes sense to have, in a variety of sizes, stainless-steel mixing bowls with flat bottoms so they don't tip over as you are beating. Also purchase a few stainless-steel mixing bowls with rounded bottoms in a variety of sizes, because you can use them as molds for refrigerated cakes and as the top part of a makeshift double boiler.

For mixing ingredients and heating them in a microwave oven, heatproof glass (Pyrex) mixing bowls in varying sizes are indispensable. In addition to the 1- to 2-quart-capacity mixing bowls, I have on hand a half dozen or so ½-cup and 1-cup custard cups for mixing small quantities of ingredients and for holding premeasured ingredients. They, too, are heatproof Pyrex, so they go in the oven and can double as baking molds.

Saucepans

For pastry creams and custard sauces, you will need nonreactive, durable, heavy-duty saucepans that distribute and conduct heat evenly and rapidly.

They should have straight or sloping sides and be made of a stainless steel–lined aluminum with either an aluminum or a copper-cored bottom.

DOUBLE BOILER A double boiler is a two-part pan designed to cook ingredients over indirect heat. It is composed of a saucepan or another type of insert that sits inside a slightly larger saucepan in which you simmer water. Double boilers are made of different types of materials (the insert must be made of a nonreactive material), from stainless steel to heatproof glass, enameled aluminum (which chips), and the deluxe model: a copper base and a heavy porcelain insert. I own a double boiler that I use rarely because it is too small for my needs.

I find it more efficient to create my own double boiler by using a stainless-steel mixing bowl with a rounded bottom of an appropriate size, which varies according to what I am heating, and setting it inside a smaller saucepan. You never want the simmering water below to touch the bottom of the bowl above because whatever you are cooking in the upper vessel might get too hot.

UNLINED COPPER SAUCEPAN A heavy, unlined copper pot with a pouring spout is the pastry chef's dream tool, although an unessential one. It is perfect for cooking sugar syrups for buttercreams and meringues, or for making caramel because it brings the sugar to the right stage very quickly. You must not cook anything but sugar in this pot because bare copper reacts adversely to other foods. An ideal pot for the serious home baker has a 1.5-quart capacity and a wooden handle (rather than a copper one), which doesn't retain heat.

Thermometers

There are several types of thermometers, each designed for a different purpose and each useful to the home baker.

CANDY THERMOMETER A candy thermometer is a mercury-filled glass tube fastened to a stainless-steel casing and is designed to measure the temperature of the sugar syrups that are used in the making of mousses, buttercreams, and other cake fillings. There are excellent candy thermometers designed for the home baker, and Taylor is a reliable brand name. The noncommercial candy thermometer often has temperature markings, like 230°F, on one side of the glass tube, as well as words like "soft ball," designed to describe the texture of the sugar syrup at the different temperatures. Good thermometers should have both Celsius and Fahrenheit markings to give the cook maximum flexibility in terms of the recipes she uses. These candy thermometers for the home cook have a clip on the back to help fasten them to the pot, but I have found that feature not useful because when clipped to the side of the pot, the bulb tip of the thermometer, which is the sensor, often isn't immersed in the sugar syrup and the temperature can't be registered accurately. I recently discovered, and now use, a professional Taylor-brand candy thermometer, which is heavy so it is stable in a pot. It is tall enough so I can comfortably hold on to the wooden handle, which is high enough above the scalding steam that wafts up from the sugar syrup cooking below. Its sensor sits low enough so that it can be properly immersed in a shallow amount of sugar syrup to accurately measure the temperature. (You can purchase this type of thermometer through the J. B. Prince catalogue; see page 390.)

Reading a candy thermometer can be tricky because the markings are often obscured by the steam that rises from the sugar syrup and because the home baker works with such small quantities that often the tip isn't immersed deep enough in the syrup to register on the thermometer. If you are working with small quantities, tip the saucepan to one side until you get a quantity deep enough for the thermometer's mercury tip to be immersed in the sugar syrup to get a reading. Also, to help you see through the steam, read the thermometer at eye level but stand slightly to one side of the thermometer.

INSTANT-READ THERMOMETER These are thermometers used to "instantly" gauge the temperature of a food or mixture. The stainless-steel stem of the thermometer is dipped into the food and, after you read the temperature, is then removed. This is commonly used to gauge the temperature of roasted meats, but I use it for determining the temperature of pastry creams and custard sauces.

OVEN THERMOMETER Before you embark on any serious baking project, you must first determine how accurately your oven is calibrated, and you will need to purchase a good mercury thermometer to gauge this. Oven thermometers come mounted either on a stainless-steel stand or with a hook to hang them from the oven rack. Replace them every now and then to make sure they are accurate.

CARING FOR YOUR THERMOMETER All the thermometers we have discussed consist of mercury enclosed in glass, and you must handle them with care so the glass doesn't break, allowing the toxic mercury to escape. When you remove a candy thermometer from a scalding-hot sugar syrup, set it on a cutting board to cool down; don't immerse it in cold water, or you risk shattering the glass. Also, it is best to store these thermometers from a hook rather than in a drawer, where they can knock against other sharp implements and break.

MISCELLANEOUS SMALL EQUIPMENT

Baking Parchment

Baking parchment is a greaseless, silicone-treated paper that is perfect for lining cake pans and bak-

ing sheets. The paper prevents sticky batters like meringues from adhering to the pan. Baking parchment is sold in rolls like waxed paper or foil, or in precut sheets to fit full- or half-sheet pans, as well as round cake pans of various sizes. There is even a doughnut-shape precut paper specifically designed to fit a tube pan.

New on the market are reusable, fawn-colored nonstick baking sheets. They are coated on both sides with teflon, can be cut to fit any pan, and can be wiped down and reused up to two hundred times per sheet. They are marvelous and available through baking supply stores like J. B. Prince or from mail-order sources like King Arthur's *Baker's Catalogue*. (See Source List, page 390.)

Bench Knife

A bench knife is a stainless-steel rectangular blunt blade fastened to a wooden or textured plastic handle. I use this in countless ways—to clean off my counter, to lift heavy batters into mixing bowls, to cut through, push, pull, score, and knead thick yeasted doughs, as well as to give a straight edge to the icing on the sides of a cake.

A device similar to this, made of flexible thick plastic, is known as a "dough scraper" or a "bowl scraper." It is great for cleaning dough from a mixing bowl, and for folding ingredients together and leveling batter in a pan, but a rigid metal blade is more effective as a cutter.

Cake Breaker

This looks like a comb with 3-inch-long teeth set wide apart. It is used to slice through angel food or chiffon cakes because it doesn't squash the cake.

Cake Dome

This old-fashioned item, seen these days mostly in diners, is the best way of keeping nonrefrigerated cakes fresh and moist. It is a dome made of glass or acrylic that you lift over the cake and the surface on which it sits. It is tall and wide enough so it doesn't mess up the icing and decorative work on your cake as can airtight foil or plastic wrappings. I have a 12-inch-wide and 6-inch-high plastic one purchased from King Arthur's *Baker's Catalogue* that covers the tallest cake imaginable, and a daintier, smaller glass one purchased from Lechters Housewares store. I also have some pretty glass ones that I purchased from the *Martha By Mail* mail-order catalogue. (See Source List, page 390.)

Cake Lifter

A cake lifter is shaped like a bench knife, is about 10 inches square, and comes in a lightweight metal or plastic material. Its large surface is perfect for lifting up cake layers or entire frosted cakes to help move them from counter to cake board or from wire rack to turntable.

Cake Testers and Wooden Skewers

A cake tester is designed to determine if your cake is cooked through to the center. It is nothing more than a tinned-steel needle topped by a plastic-coated ring handle so you don't burn your hand. It is skinny enough so it doesn't tear the cake when you insert it into the center yet has enough of a surface to which unbaked cake batter can cling. There are lots of other little household tools that you can use instead of a cake tester—a clean broom straw, a wooden or bamboo skewer (the kind you would use for shish kebabs), or even a wooden toothpick if the cake layers are not too tall.

Cardboard Boxes

Nothing is better for transporting cakes and even storing them than cardboard boxes designed specifically for that purpose. What is fabulous about them

is that they come in all sizes, are tall enough so your icing does not get squished, and they allow for enough air circulation so the icing doesn't form beads of moisture. For some odd-shaped cakes such as long rectangular ones, you might have to fashion a box out of two smaller boxes taped together and shaped to the right size. You can get these from New York Cake and Baking Distributor or Broadway Panhandler, or order them by mail from the Sweet Celebrations catalogue. (See Source List, page 390.)

Cardboard Rounds and Rectangles

Rounds and rectangles of corrugated cardboard are invaluable for supporting cakes so you don't risk breaking them when you transport or store them for any period of time. I also use them to turn layers upside down or right side up from cake pan to wire rack. They are sold in several sizes that correspond to the dimensions of standard cake pans. I use the plain corrugated type, which is brown on one side and white on the other, but some come covered with gold or silver foil or glassine and are more appropriate for the presentation of fancy decorated cakes.

The more common 8- or 9-inch round sizes are available in small quantities in some gourmet or bakeware stores. More unusual sizes and shapes can be purchased from New York Cake and Baking Distributor or ordered by mail from the Sweet Celebrations catalogue. (See Source List, page 390.)

Charlotte Mold

This is a tall tin mold traditionally used in the making of charlotte russe. I use it for some of my refrigerated chocolate cakes, but it is not essential.

Cutting Boards

For cooking and for baking I have an assortment of cutting boards, some made of hardwood and others of polyethylene. Because it is hard to completely eliminate the aroma of garlic and onions that seep into wooden boards, I set aside a few of my plastic boards to use exclusively for baking tasks like chopping chocolate, nuts, or fruit. It was believed for a long time that the polyethylene boards were more sanitary than the hardwood ones, but this has proved not to be true.

Doilies

Doilies—made of paper, glassine, or foil—add a lovely inexpensive professional touch to your cake presentations. You can stick them onto cardboard rounds with double-sided tape. The glassine ones are greaseproof and prevent the cardboard from absorbing moisture from the cake and disintegrating.

Graters

You'll need at least one all-purpose grater to grate citrus zest, nutmeg, or ginger. A decent all-purpose one is a box or four-sided stainless-steel grater, or the rubber-handled OXO stainless-steel grater. My favorite one, though, is the long, slender Japanese grater (available only from the *Martha Stewart Living* mail-order catalogue), shaped like a ruler. I like the OXO grater because citrus peel never gets caught on the widely spaced rasplike perforations, but I love the Japanese one because it is razor sharp and you get the best and most finely grated citrus peel.

A stainless-steel nutmeg grater or lemon grater, or a ceramic ginger grater, which releases the ginger juices as it catches the ginger fibers are useful but not essential.

Ice Chipper

An ice chipper, designed for ice carving, is a tool made of a band of very sharp spikes attached to a wooden handle. It has become the pastry chef's implement of choice with which to break up large blocks of chocolate. Chocolate is sold, on a wholesale

level, in 10-pound blocks at least 2 inches thick. These thick blocks, broken down into small quantities for resale to the consumer, are hard to chip with a chef's knife but yield under the sharp teeth of the ice chipper. If, however, you work with small amounts of chocolate or thin chocolate bars, don't buy an ice chipper because good ones are expensive. You can buy inexpensive ice chippers from household bakery-supply catalogues, but they don't work well because the points of the spikes aren't sharp enough. The only one I found to work beautifully is sold through the J. B. Prince mail-order catalogue or at retail stores.

Icing, Decorating, or Pastry Combs

These are comblike implements used to mark soft icings, leaving decorative zigzag impressions. They are sold as square or ruler-shaped plastic pieces with triangular or rounded grooves set along one edge. You can also purchase metal or plastic triangles with triangular teeth of different sizes, set along each of the edges.

Kitchen Shears

Multipurpose kitchen shears are useful for innumerable pastry tasks; I like the Joyce Chen kitchen shears best. They are small but strong enough to cut through cardboard, and sharp enough to notch out a tiny opening in a parchment-paper cone.

Lemon Zester

If you don't own a Japanese grater, this is a handy tool used to grate the zest off lemon and other citrus fruit. It is basically a metal strip held by a handle. The metal strip has five tiny sharp-edged holes that remove tiny strips of skin when dragged along the surface of the fruit. What is so handy about this particular tool is that the rasplike holes catch only the colorful skin of the fruit, which contains the flavorful oils, but leave the bitter white pith behind.

Nonstick Baking Mats

In pastry school I was introduced to a miraculous silicone baking mat known as a Silpat. Since then I have learned that Silpat is just one of the brand names for this silicone mat, which also goes by the name Exopat. It is a flexible nonstick baking mat made of a type of silicone that is impervious to heat. When you lay this on a regular baking sheet or jelly roll pan, you transform the surface of the pan into a nonstick surface. This amazing quality makes these mats indispensable in the pastry kitchen, and I do not know of any serious pastry cook who doesn't use them. I use them to line sheet pans when I am making sticky meringuelike cake batters, and after baking, the cake just lifts up like a dream. In pastry school, I also used these mats for pulled sugar work.

Up until just a few years ago, these miracle mats were available only to the professional baker or pastry chef and only in full-sheet pan sizes. Now they are available to home bakers in half-sheet pan sizes. You can buy them at Bridge Kitchenware, Broadway Panhandler, J. B. Prince, Williams-Sonoma, or through King Arthur's *Baker's Catalogue*. They can be cut down to size, if necessary, with kitchen shears. Never cut a cake directly on the mat or you risk ruining it for future use, because batters will run through the mat onto the pan surface below and stick.

Pastry Bags

Pastry bags are made of nylon, plastic-coated fabric, or of disposable plastic. You should have several of these in different sizes. The ones I like best are the plastic-lined canvas ones because they insulate the filling from the heat of your hands. The nylon ones are good because they are flexible and easy to wash, and nothing stains them. But they are so thin, the heat of your hand transfers quickly to the filling inside the bag.

Buy a couple of the 16- to 18-inch-long bags, which are large enough to handle a generous volume of foamy batter or meringue, and buy a few of the smaller, 12- to 14-inch bags, which are appropriate for piping out buttercreams and whipped cream fillings. Disposable plastic bags are good for small quantities, when you don't want to bother washing out a durable bag, and I like them especially when I use a pastry bag with a coupler.

For fine lettering and other small decorative piping work, it is preferable to make a disposable paper cone out of parchment (see Thin Icings and Paper Cone Designs, page 348).

Pastry Brushes

Bakers, like artists, need a range of brushes, preferably made of natural bristles, with which to brush flour off pie doughs, to moisten cake layers with flavored syrups, to wash down the insides of a saucepan when cooking sugar for frostings, to apply melted butter to coat cake pans, or to apply glazes to cakes. Mark with tape the brushes you use exclusively for brushing off flour from doughs so you don't mix them up with ones you use for stickier work like applying sugar syrups or glazes to cakes.

Pastry Tubes or Tips and Couplers

Pastry tubes, also known as tips, are metal cones whose ends are cut into various shapes that determine the configuration of the icing as it comes out of the pastry bag. Plain round tips give you straight lines while star tips give you rosettes or shell-like shapes. You can buy pastry tips in sets of anywhere from six to fifty-two. A few pastry tips is all you really need. Buy a few plain round ones with ¼-inch and ½-inch openings, a five-point "closed" star shape to make stars, and a six-point "open" star shape to pipe out shell shapes.

If you are interested in learning how to make buttercream roses, buy a rose petal tip and a leaf tip.

Basket-weave shapes can be piped out only with tips designed for that purpose. With these few essential tips, you will be able to accomplish just about all the basic decorative work. More rarefied pastry tips are designed for shaping specific flowers and are of interest only to the most serious of cake decorators.

I find it easier to plop the pastry tip down into the pastry bag and get to work, but if you are likely to do more complicated cake-decorating you will need a coupler, a two-part plastic gadget consisting of a plastic tube threaded onto a disk. You slip the plastic tube down the bag, fit the metal pastry tip over the tube, and screw the plastic disk over the tip to anchor it to the tube. The advantage of the coupler is that you can switch tip sizes to create different icing shapes without first having to empty the pastry bag to fit in a new pastry tip. The ½-inch-wide coupler fits 12-inch-long pastry bags, whereas the ¾-inch-wide one fits the 14- to 18-inch bags.

Sifters, Strainers

You will need an implement of some sort to aerate flour before folding it into batters or to sift confectioners' sugar or cocoa powder to eliminate lumps. There are many sifters on the market, and you should choose one that has a large enough capacity and a fine- or medium-meshed single or double screen, and you should use the sifter only for flour. Don't wash sifters because some flour when it comes in contact with water creates a paste that tends to harden and stick in the mechanism. Instead, shake out as much of the flour as you can, then wipe down the sifter with a damp sponge or paper towel, and dry it immediately.

In lieu of a sifter, and especially for sifting confectioners' sugar or cocoa powder, use a fine-mesh strainer through which you push the ingredients with a spoon. I use a small, very fine–mesh strainer to sift confectioners' sugar or cocoa over the tops of finished cakes or onto plates for plated dessert presentations.

Spatulas

There are three types of spatulas I refer to in this book: flat or offset metal spatulas, and rubber spatulas.

FLAT METAL SPATULAS Flat spatulas are round-tipped blunt blades used to spread batters in pans, smooth frostings on cakes, and transfer pastries to cardboard rounds. For icing cakes you need a blade that is longer than the diameter of the cake itself, and I find that one 10-inch and one 12-inch flat spatula are sufficient for most of my icing needs. For delicate icing work I have a 4-inch spatulalike blade that I bought in an art supply store and is really an artist's palette knife.

I also have a couple of 16-inch flat metal spatulas that I use primarily to help me lift up and transfer whole cakes from one surface to another. I place the spatulas in a "crossed sword" or "X" pattern underneath the cake to lift it. This gives the cake enough support so it doesn't wobble or tip over.

OFFSET METAL SPATULAS An offset spatula is like a flat metal spatula, but part of the blade is slightly bent at an angle, which allows you to spread icings in hard-to-reach places, like deep inside a tall tube cake pan. I like working with both 10-inch and 12-inch offset spatulas as well as smaller 4- or 6-inch ones for applying small amounts of icing to small areas.

RUBBER SPATULAS Rubber spatulas have flat, squarish synthetic rubber "heads" that come in different sizes and are attached to wooden or plastic handles. You need one with a 3 × 4-inch "head" to fold large volumes of delicate foams and whipped egg-white mixtures into dense batters, along with a couple of medium-size 2 × 3-inch ones for mixing and for scraping out the inside of bowls and saucepans.

New on the market and incredibly useful are heavy-duty, heat-resistant rubber spatulas, which I use for stirring and mixing hot custard sauces into which I don't want to incorporate air bubbles as I would were I to stir with a whisk. These heatproof spatulas are also fine for scraping scalding-hot sugar syrups out of saucepans.

Spoons

New on the market and far better for stirring than wooden spoons are fiberglass spoons that can withstand temperatures as high as those of caramel syrups. Unlike wooden spoons, they don't splinter with age, nor do they discolor or absorb odors. I have a long-handled one that I use for sugar work and a shorter-handled one that I use for savory cooking tasks. You can purchase them from J. B. Prince.

Squeeze Bottles

Squeeze bottles are soft plastic bottles with nozzles. They are used in the professional pastry kitchen to squeeze out sauces used to garnish the plate on which you center a slice of cake. You can buy regular 8-inch plastic squeeze bottles or fine-tipped 6.5-inch ones in pastry supply stores like J. B. Prince. What also works well is the type of plastic bottle with a nozzle used to color hair, which you can buy in a drugstore.

Swivel-action Vegetable Peeler

I use a swivel-action vegetable peeler for shaving strips of chocolate off blocks. I like ones with a wide slot size because paring and cutting is faster, and I use either an OXO brand vegetable peeler or the French type, which has a narrow rectangular swivel-action head.

Whisks or Wire Whips

A whisk, also sometimes referred to as a "whip" or "wire whip," is a balloon-shaped tool made out of a network of pliable wires. It is used to incorporate air into cream or egg whites and is preferable to a rubber spatula or a spoon for homogeneously blending a liquid ingredient with a dense one. The larger, rounder whips are known as balloon whips, whereas the more slender ones are known as French whips. The best whisks are heavy, with thick wires that won't bend out of shape over time. Make sure the wires are bundled and welded together inside the metal handle.

Wire Racks

When I refer to a "wire rack," I mean a tool designed to help cool baked goods. It is a metal, rectangular or circular rack made up of metal rods. The rack has little feet that elevate it up from a flat surface, thus allowing air to circulate underneath whatever baked goods you are cooling. The rectangular ones are about the size of a jelly roll pan, and the wire rods are set more widely apart than they are in the circular wire racks designed specifically for cooling round cakes. Sufficient for all my needs are two 12-inch circular cake racks and two rectangular 11 × 16-inch wire racks.

There is also something called an "icing grate," which is a fine metal mesh grid set in a rectangular frame with feet to elevate it above a flat surface. It is designed to drain away the icing you pour over cakes during final glazing, but it can double as a cake cooling rack.

For additional information on tools and equipment used exclusively for intricate cake-decorating or decorative chocolate work, see Part Four: Decorative Techniques.

*I*T IS IMPORTANT that you learn to master a few basic techniques so your batters are well put together and your cakes come out fine.

FOLDING

"Folding" is a term that describes how to blend an aerated mixture like whipped cream with a heavier one like melted chocolate. The principle is to combine two preparations of different densities without deflating the aerated mixture. This technique is not difficult but can present problems if you don't understand how to do it.

You begin by placing the aerated mixture in a large bowl. Add a portion of the heavier ingredient on top of the aerated ingredient and start to fold. If you are folding in flour, be sure to sift it evenly over the surface of the whipped ingredient or it will sink to the bottom like a stone in water.

If you are folding in a very heavy ingredient, like melted butter, lighten it first by folding about a quarter of the whipped ingredient into it, then folding this lightened mixture back into the aerated mixture. The recipe will indicate if this step is necessary.

For almost all folding, except for foam cakes where folding with your hand is more effective, use a rubber spatula with a head that is wide and long; the wider the head of the spatula, the faster and more effective the folding. Be careful not to lapse into a mixing or stirring motion, which will deflate the precious air bubbles.

To fold the ingredients together, stabilize the bowl with one hand and hold the rubber spatula with the other hand. Use the edge of the spatula, not the flat side, to cut down through the center of the batter. Pull the ingredients from the bottom up along the side of the bowl to the top. Flip the spatula to deposit the mixture from the bottom of the bowl over the top of the mixture. As you are folding with one hand, turn the bowl with the other hand. Repeat until the mixtures are homogenized.

To fold using your hands: In professional kitchens, when you are dealing with masses of batter, it is far more efficient and effective to fold ingredients together using your hand and arm rather than a rubber spatula. At home I use this method for angel food, chiffon, and sponge cakes because I invariably get at least one clump of flour in my cake when I use the spatula, but never when I use my hand. The other advantage to using your hand as a spatula is that you can feel a clump of flour and press it through your fingers to dissolve it as you fold. Your fingers also help you locate the heavier ingredients, which tend to sink to the bottom of the bowl and get left behind.

If you are turned-off by the idea of using your hand, remember that you should always wash your hands before you touch food anyway, and bacteria deposited in the batter will be destroyed by the heat of the oven. Do not, however, use this technique for uncooked preparations.

MEASURING INGREDIENTS

For best results, measure your ingredients as accurately as possible. As I have said before, the most consistent measurement is by weight rather than by volume, but short of that, measure the ingredients by volume.

In these recipes, I indicate the volume measurement first, followed by the weight equivalence in parentheses. In almost all instances, ingredients are measured or weighed first, then sifted or further prepared as the recipe indicates.

Measurements are sometimes given in whatever form makes the most sense. If, for example, there is not enough volume of a particular ingredient, like ¼ teaspoon of salt, the weight of the ingredient is omitted, and if the weight of the ingredient doesn't make a difference in the outcome of the recipe, it too is omitted.

CHART OF VOLUME AND WEIGHT EQUIVALENCES

Listed below are the volume and weight equivalences I use throughout the book. I round the weight to the nearest measurable fraction of an ounce. For example, if 1 cup of cake flour weighs 4.5 ounces, then 1¾ cups weighs 7.875 ounces. To make it easier for the baker, I round this measurement up to 8 ounces—a tenth of an ounce won't make a difference in a single cake. Furthermore, scales used in the home don't even register such small weight differentials.

Cocoa powder
1 cup = 3.2 oz.
5 tablespoons = 1 oz.

Cornstarch
1 cup = 4 oz.
¼ cup = 1 oz.

Flour, all-purpose and bread
1 cup = 4.75 oz.

Flour, cake and pastry
1 cup = 4.5 oz.

Nuts
1 cup = 3.5 oz.

Sugar, granulated, superfine, and brown
1 cup = 7.5 oz.

Sugar, confectioners'
3.5 cups = 1 lb.
1 cup = 4.5 oz.

PREPARING THE OVEN

The oven must be preheated for 20 minutes before you begin to bake. If you set your batter in a cold oven, the results will be dismal.

Before you preheat the oven, make sure the racks are set in the right position and as close to the center of the oven as possible. If you are baking a tall tube cake, set the rack in the lower third of the oven so the mass of the cake, as it rises, is centered.

I happen to have a wide enough oven so I can bake three cake rounds on one rack, but if you need more than one rack, position one in the upper third of the oven and the other in the lower third. Remember to rotate the cakes from the top to the bottom halfway through the baking time to be sure each pan gets an equal amount of heat. When you change the cake pans from one level to the other, do so gently so that your cakes don't collapse. When baking on two levels, stagger the pans so one is never directly above the other in order to make sure the cakes get even distribution and circulation of heat.

Set the baking pans in the oven at least 2 inches away from the sides and back of the oven, leaving space between them, so the hot air circulates evenly around the pans.

Don't overload your oven by baking too much at once. If you do, your cakes will take much longer to bake.

If you need to check on your cake, remove it from the oven and set it on top of the stove. *Close the oven door to keep the hot air in.* You would be surprised to learn how rapidly your oven loses heat when you leave the door open and how much this affects the outcome of the baking.

If you have a "fast" oven, cover your cakes with a double thickness of aluminum foil in the last 10 minutes or so of baking, so they don't get too dark or crusty.

PREPARING THE PANS

How to prepare the pans depends on the type of cake you are baking. For layer and pound cakes, high in fat, you must grease and flour the pans as well as line them with paper so the cake can be easily unmolded.

Lean, egg-foam cakes like sponge cakes should be baked in pans with the bottoms lined with paper but the sides left ungreased, so the batter can adhere to a rough surface as it climbs up the sides.

Angel food and chiffon cakes are usually baked in pans that are left ungreased.

Batter cakes that are cut and served straight from the pan can be baked in pans that have been greased but not lined.

Greasing the Pan

To grease a pan means to rub the inside surfaces lightly with a hard fat such as solid vegetable shortening or softened butter.

There are several ways to coat the pans. At home I grab about a tablespoon or so of softened butter and rub it on the pan with my fingers or with a paper towel. When I am working in a restaurant, I use a pastry brush to grease the pan. I have a container of butter that sits close to the ovens so it is soft but not melted, and I keep a pastry brush in the container at all times. This way, whenever I need it, I have butter at the right consistency. What I like about using a pastry brush is that it coats the pan sufficiently without overgreasing it.

Whichever method you choose for greasing your pans, make sure you get into the corners of rectangular and square pans, where batter tends to stick.

It is important that you lightly grease the pans rather than saturate the surfaces. Too much grease might end up coating the outside of your baked cake. The only time you can be more generous with the grease is when you are preparing a Bundt pan, because these pans have numerous little crevices where the batter tends to stick.

Other materials used to grease the pan are nonstick vegetable sprays pumped out of an aerosol can, but I find that too much often gets pumped out and I have to wipe out the excess. There is also a product many amateur bakers swear by, known as Baker's Joy. It is a combination of oil and flour that comes in a spray can and is available in specialty bakery supply houses.

Vegetable oil isn't good for greasing pans because it gets absorbed by the cake and imparts a "fried food" flavor to the finished product.

Dusting the Pan with Flour

When the recipe says to grease and "dust" a pan with flour, it means that after you have lightly greased it, you need to coat the pan with a fine dusting of flour.

Use all-purpose flour for dusting pans, rather than cake flour, which tends to clump. Scatter a small handful of flour in the pan, then turn and rotate the pan continuously so that all the interior surfaces are coated. Then (a very important step), turn the pan upside down and rap it firmly, several times, over the kitchen sink or a garbage pail to get rid of the excess flour. If you don't get rid of the excess flour, the out-

side surface of the finished cake might be lightly coated with lumps of baked-on flour and grease.

Lining the Pans with Paper

As a precautionary measure, even after greasing and flouring the pan, you should line the bottom with parchment or waxed paper. You can always run a knife around the cake if it sticks to the sides of the pan, but there is not much you can do when it sticks to the bottom. You will never have this problem if you line the bottom of the pan with paper.

I prefer baking parchment to waxed paper for lining the pans because it is durable and more effective. You can, in a pinch, use waxed paper, but you must grease and flour the paper as well.

If you are serious about baking cakes, invest in precut parchment rounds. They come in a multitude of sizes, and there are even ones cut to fit tube pans. They are inexpensive and will save you loads of time. However, don't assume the precut parchment circles will fit your pan. To check, set the paper circle in the pan and, if the paper is too big, cut it down to fit your pan exactly. If you don't, part of the paper will run up the sides of the cake and tear the cake as you pull off the paper circle.

If you don't have precut circles, or if you have to cut the paper to fit a rectangular, square, or other pan, set the pan on the paper and trace the outline of the pan on the paper with a pencil. Cut the paper *inside* the pencil tracings to cut out the pencil markings, which could rub off on your cake.

Filling the Pans

Don't fill your pans to the brim or the batter will run over. In general, pans should be filled from ½ to ¾ full, depending on the type of cake batter and how much the cake will rise. Batters made with aerated eggs or whipped egg whites need more headroom than heavy, dense cakes, which barely rise.

If you are baking a cake in two or three pans, make sure each pan has the same amount of batter so that the layers will be of even height. If you were working in a bakery, you would weigh the batter and distribute it among the pans by weight. At home it is easier to use a volume measuring cup to distribute the batter among the pans.

Fluid batters tend to spread out in the cake pan, but dense, thick ones need to be spread in the pan with a rubber or offset spatula to make sure the top is level and even.

Take special care when filling jelly roll pans. If you don't spread the batter evenly and well into the corners, the cake won't be level and the corners will be brittle. The cake will tend to break when you try to roll it up.

For many cakes in this book, after filling the pans, I say to give the pans a couple of sharp raps on the counter. This is to make sure any large air pockets burst so your cakes won't emerge from the oven with crater-sized holes.

Checklist—Pan Preparation

- High-fat cakes: grease and flour pans and line bottoms with paper.
- Sponge cakes: grease and line bottoms with paper but leave sides ungreased.
- Angel food and chiffon cakes: leave pans ungreased or line bottoms with tube-pan liners.
- For jelly roll or half-sheet pans, line bottoms with greased parchment or a nonstick baking mat.

TESTING A CAKE FOR DONENESS

The best way to determine if a cake is done is to insert a cake tester in the center, where the batter takes longest to set. Unless otherwise indicated, if the tester comes out dry, without batter clinging to it, the cake is done.

Another test of doneness is the look and feel of a cake. If the cake begins to shrink from the sides of the pan, it is baked through, and if you press the top gently and feel resistance, that too is an indication of doneness. If you are baking two or three cake layers at once, test each one.

For some special cakes, which need to be a tad underbaked, like brownies or cheesecakes, the recipe will indicate that it is okay for some moist crumb to cling to the tester. That is because the cake firms up upon standing and if you were to bake it longer, it would be dry.

If you test the cake and the center is still wet and jiggles, return the cake to the oven and keep checking it for doneness at 5-minute intervals.

The Timing of a Recipe

Whenever I asked my teachers in pastry school how long it would take to bake something, they would reply: "Until it is done!" And for good reason, because the timing of a recipe varies widely depending on the type of oven, the weather outside, how many cakes are in the oven, as well as the temperature of the ingredients when the batter goes into the oven.

I know that it seems improbable that there could be such discrepancies between ovens, but I remember that when I used to teach cake-making at the New York Culinary Center, it seemed to me that all my cakes were done in half the time it took them to bake in my oven at home. Also, every time I gave out a recipe to be tested by someone else, they would claim the cake needed more or less time to bake than what the recipe said.

My recipes, which were each tested at least twice, do give a time frame to determine when the cake is done, but please don't follow this timing to the letter because your oven might be slower or faster than mine. Always begin to check the cake before it is due to be finished. If a recipe gives you a range of times—for example, "bake for 40 to 50 minutes"—start to check at 35 minutes. For a cake baked within 25 to 30 minutes, check it after 20 minutes of baking, but for a sheet cake baked within 15 minutes, check it no sooner than at the 13-minute mark.

COOLING AND UNMOLDING CAKES

The first step in cooling cakes is to transfer them, still in their pans, to a cake cooling or wire rack. Set the cakes on a cooling rack so that air can circulate underneath the pans and cool the cakes more rapidly.

I find it easier to unmold most types of cakes after they have cooled to room temperature in the pan, because they are less fragile. If the cake adheres to the sides of the pan, loosen it by running a table knife or a flat metal spatula around the cake. Place a plate or cake cooling rack over the cake and invert the pan. If the cake sticks to the bottom, turn the cake right side up and bring the pan to the stove. Set the pan, for a few seconds, on an electric burner on a low setting or lift the pan up above the gas heat, also set on low. Keep rotating the pan over the heat until the bottom feels warm. This helps melt any hardened shortening or butter in the pan, which is what is making the cake stick. Invert the cake again and it should pop out.

Cakes that should be cooled out of the pans should first cool for 20 minutes in the pan. Cakes are too hot when fresh out of the oven and would break were you to attempt to unmold them right away. After 20 minutes, loosen the cakes from the sides of the pan and unmold them. Cool them to room temperature on a wire rack but still on the paper liner so the cake does not stick to the wire rack. If you do not have a paper liner, lightly grease the wire rack.

Angel food and chiffon cakes are cooled upside down so that gravity does not squash the cake and pull it down. It is best to bake these types of cakes in special pans with little "feet" on the rim that lift the pan from the counter as the cake cools upside down. If you have baked the cake in an ordinary tube pan, cool it upside down in the pan set over a funnel or a soda bottle.

Rolled cakes are cooled in the pan on a nonstick baking mat or are immediately turned out of the pan onto a sugar- or cocoa-dusted towel or paper. The sugar or cocoa lifts the cake slightly from the paper so that it does not stick.

STORING CAKES

At Room Temperature

Unfrosted pound, sponge, angel food, chiffon, nut cakes, and brownies keep well at room temperature in a cool dry place, wrapped airtight in plastic or under a glass cake dome.

Cakes iced with nonperishable frostings like a confectioners' sugar glaze or a hard chocolate icing can also be stored at room temperature. A cake frosted with a boiled icing should be kept at room temperature but eaten within one day or the icing will collapse and collect beads of moisture. Iced cakes, kept at room temperature, should be covered loosely with foil or, better yet, to allow the proper amount of air to circulate around the cake, kept in a cake box, under a glass cake dome, or under an inverted bowl.

In the Refrigerator

Cakes that include perishable ingredients like cream cheese or nuts, or those frosted with perishable fillings, need to be refrigerated. However, because refrigeration dries out cakes, it is best to frost and assemble the cakes and refrigerate them on the day of serving.

How you store the cakes in the refrigerator depends on how they are finished. Cakes frosted with whipped cream or iced with fancy decorative touches that can be damaged under a tight wrapping should be stored under an inverted bowl, a cake dome, or in a cardboard cake box. If this is not possible, keep the cake uncovered in the refrigerator for up to one day. Once you cut into these cakes, the cut sides will dry out unless protected with a piece of parchment or waxed paper, set flush against the cut side. After a day of keeping them uncovered in the refrigerator, however, you must cover them so they don't pick up refrigerator odors. Wrap them loosely with foil so the frosting does not bead up and become slick under a tight wrapping.

Some cakes are frosted with the types of glaze that need to set up before you can wrap them. Refrigerate these cakes, uncovered, long enough for the icing to set. Once the icing is hard, wrap the cakes in plastic wrap. For most all of these cakes, I give guidelines on how long to store them. It is not that the cakes will be bad if stored longer, they just will not be at their best.

In the Freezer

Some cakes are best frozen unfilled, whereas others freeze beautifully even when frosted.

Un-iced high-fat cakes—like pound cakes, nut tortes, and most American layer cakes—freeze best. Un-iced lean cakes—like sponge and angel food cakes—can also be frozen but for a shorter period of time.

To wrap unfrosted cakes so they don't get freezer burn, place the cooled cake on a cardboard round, or another rigid surface, and wrap it in two or three layers of freezer paper or plastic wrap. I don't like wrapping cakes with foil because foil tears, reacts to certain acidic ingredients, and can deposit micro-

scopic pieces of foil on the top of the cake. Pop the wrapped cake in a plastic bag and freeze.

You can freeze high-fat cakes for up to three months and lean cakes for six to eight weeks only.

To defrost the cakes, take them out of the freezer, set them, still wrapped, on a counter; thaw at room temperature for two to three hours. Or thaw them, still wrapped, overnight in the refrigerator.

Cakes filled and frosted with buttercreams, mousses, Bavarian creams, or confectioners' sugar frostings can be assembled and frozen for up to two months. Do not freeze cakes filled with whipped cream, custard, or meringue frostings.

To freeze decorated cakes so you do not damage the decorations, partially freeze them first, uncovered. Once the cake is partially frozen and the decorations are firm, wrap the cake with several layers of plastic or freezer wrap and slip it into a plastic bag. Press as much air as possible out of the bag so the cake does not take up too much room in the freezer.

Frosted and filled cakes are best thawed slowly in the refrigerator. Remove the wrappings, set the cake on a plate, cover it loosely with foil so the cake does not absorb refrigerator odors, and thaw it overnight in the refrigerator.

HANDLING CAKES FOR TRANSPORT

Baking a cake to give as a gift, to add to a potluck supper, or to bring to a Thanksgiving celebration is a lovely idea, but getting the cake, intact, to its destination can be a difficult task.

Choosing the Right Cake for Transport

The first step in transporting a cake successfully is to select the right cake for the occasion and weather. If you must travel far and in hot weather, select a pound, angel food, chiffon, or nut cake frosted with a nonperishable icing. Whipped cream or butter-cream-filled cakes are best to transport during the cold winter months or for short distances only.

Packing the Cake for Transport

Before packing the cake, make sure it is on a rigid, stable surface, like a corrugated cardboard round.

The best way to transport a cake is in a cardboard cake box like those you see in bakeries, because the sides, top, and bottom of the box are rigid and the box is high enough so it won't squash the top of the cake or ruin the decorations. The box should be only slightly larger than the cake, or the cake will slide around the box and might sustain some damage. Cake boxes come in standard sizes. You can buy them in a bakery supply house or from a mail-order catalogue. However, if you need only the occasional cardboard box, try to buy one from a neighborhood pastry shop or bakery.

Once the cake is in the box, tape the box shut with the flaps on the outside so they don't damage the sides of the cake.

Decorations for Transport

When transporting a decorated cake, pack additional decorative elements so you can refinish the cake or do patch-up work after you get to your destination.

Include some crystallized or fresh flowers because they always look great in the middle of a cake and you can strew them on a platter to hide damaged bottom edges.

For patch-up work, bring extra frosting along with a small pastry bag and an offset spatula.

HIGH-ALTITUDE BAKING

I have never baked at a high altitude, so the information outlined here is simply a summary of my understanding of what happens when you do bake at high altitudes.

At elevations of more than 3,000 feet, the air is thinner and the humidity and air pressure are lower, which affects the physics of baking. At lower air pressure, water boils at a lower temperature. This means that water boils at 212°F at sea level, but by the time you reach an altitude of 7,500 feet, it boils at 198°F. Food takes longer to cook at high altitudes, moisture is lost, and this can mean dry cakes.

To compensate for these problems, here are the adjustments you can make: Set the oven 15° to 25° higher than normally recommended, so that food cooks more quickly. Depending on the elevation, reduce the sugar from 1 to 3 tablespoons per cup to compensate for the loss of moisture that results from an overconcentration of sugar. Because of the decreased humidity in the air, flour absorbs more moisture, so more liquid is required in a recipe. And because the air is thinner, cakes tend to rise too much and then collapse in the oven, so underbeat the eggs slightly, and decrease the quantity of chemical leaveners.

The best way to deal with these recipe adjustments is to bake from recipes specifically designed for higher altitudes or, better yet, developed for the region of the country in which you live. You can also send away for a U.S. Government Printing Office pamphlet on high-altitude cooking or consult your local library for more information.

BEFORE YOU BEGIN THE RECIPES

I know there is a tendency to skip over written matter and plunge right into the recipes, but I strongly recommend that you read about a few essential bits of information before you begin so that your baking experience will be a successful one.

- Read through the entire recipe before you begin.
- Make sure you have the correct equipment and of the right size.
- Make sure you have the ingredients you need, and don't make substitutions.
- Make sure the ingredients are at the right temperature and are accurately measured.
- If you don't understand a phrase, a term, or a technique, research it elsewhere in the book, where it will be more fully explained.
- Read the front matter for each chapter because important technical information is included.
- Don't forget to preheat the oven.
- Follow the order of the recipe.
- If a recipes indicates 1 cup (3.5 ounces) pecans, chopped, that means you measure or weigh the pecans first, then chop them. Conversely, if the recipe indicates ¾ cup chopped (3 ounces) pecans, that means you chop the pecans before you measure or weigh them.

PART TWO

The Recipes

PLAIN AND EASY BATTER CAKES

I'VE BEGUN MY book with chocolate cakes even the neophyte baker can master. These are the easiest of chocolate cakes to put together in terms of technique, and the batters are assembled without special or expensive equipment. The cakes are served plain, lightly dusted with confectioners' sugar, with whipped cream, or with a simple sauce on the side. For special occasions, there are some frosted layer cakes in this chapter as well, but they, too, are put together with icings and fillings that are a snap to prepare.

I deliberately chose many types of cakes to include in this chapter so that bakers too unsure to experiment with more difficult techniques can choose from a good selection of cakes to bake for different occasions. These range from the simplest of brownies to festive three-layer cakes and warm pudding cakes, along with a few unique cakes such as those made with fruits or vegetables. Given how uncomplicated they are, these cakes are remarkably delicious and some are surprisingly sophisticated.

Batter cakes are also called "one-bowl" or "mix-and-dump" cakes. Basically these are cakes that are high in fat (butter, oil, or shortening), and the fat is mixed into the batter along with all the other ingredients rather than being creamed first with sugar as it is in the cakes in the next chapter. The result is that the fat melts into the cake rather than wrapping around air cells, so cakes made by this method aren't as light or springy as the ones in the next chapter, but they are as moist and delicious.

Before you begin, make sure all the ingredients are at room temperature so that the batter can be effectively homogenized. Sift or whisk together the dry ingredients such as flour, leavener, salt, spices, or cocoa powder to combine them and make sure that the leavener is properly dispersed throughout and the flour gets aerated.

First beat the eggs and sugar until light, then add other liquids such as milk, cream, or melted chocolate. Blend the dry ingredients with the wet ones, mix the batter until smooth, dump it into the prepared cake pan, and bake—voilà, that's the method. Even the baking time for these cakes is forgiving; a couple of minutes over or under the recommended baking time won't ruin anything.

BEFORE YOU BEGIN, READ ABOUT:

- Preheating the oven and positioning of racks (page 52)
- How to measure ingredients (page 51)
- Preparing pans (page 52)
- How to melt chocolate (page 33)
- How to sift (page 16)
- How to whip egg whites (page 11)
- Testing for doneness (page 54)
- Cooling cakes (page 55)
- How to slice, fill, and frost cakes (page 339)

Wacky Chocolate Cake

The unusual name of this cake, also known as "Crazy," "Mixed-Up," "Mix-in-the-Pan," or "Three-Hole" cake, was inspired from the fact that the ingredients are sifted, mixed, and baked in the same pan. The result is a surprisingly light chocolate cake, quick to make, which kids love to help prepare because it is so easy. I like it plain (for breakfast!) or with whipped cream and fresh berries on the side.

Makes one 8-inch square cake

Serves 8 to 12

Level of difficulty ★

1½ cups (7 ounces) bleached all-purpose flour

¼ cup (0.75 ounce) unsweetened, nonalkalized cocoa powder

½ teaspoon baking soda

½ teaspoon salt

1 cup (7.5 ounces) granulated sugar

1 teaspoon vanilla extract

1 tablespoon white or cider vinegar

6 tablespoons vegetable oil

1 cup water

---

1. Position a rack in the center of the oven and preheat to 375°F. Lightly grease an 8-inch square pan.
2. Sift the flour, cocoa, baking soda, and salt directly into the baking pan, then add the sugar. With your finger, poke 2 small holes and 1 large one in the dry ingredients. Into one of the small holes pour the vanilla, into the other one the vinegar, and into the larger one the oil.
3. Pour the water over all the ingredients and stir the ingredients together with a table fork, reaching into the corners, until you can't see any more flour and the batter looks fairly well homogenized.
4. Bake for 35 to 40 minutes, or until the top is springy and a tester inserted in the center comes out dry. Cool the cake in the pan on a wire rack, then cut and serve it from the pan.

STORAGE: Keep at room temperature, wrapped airtight, for up to 3 days; refrigerate after that.

NOTES: In my files I found a mayonnaise chocolate cake recipe my aunt gave to me, which I used to bake frequently when I was in college because it was so simple to make. Now that I take a closer look at it, I wonder if she didn't mix up a mayonnaise cake recipe with this "Wacky" one. Anyway, her cake is delicious and easy to make: In a mixing bowl, combine 2 cups unsifted bleached all-purpose flour with ¼ cup unsweetened cocoa, 1 teaspoon baking soda, ¼ teaspoon salt, and 1 cup granulated sugar. Add 1 cup mayonnaise (instead of the oil and vinegar) to the dry ingredients, and blend in 1 teaspoon vanilla extract and 1 cup water. Transfer the batter to a greased 9-inch square pan and bake for 30 to 35 minutes.

Not-So-Wacky Chocolate Cake

This cake came about as the result of a few changes I made in the preceding Wacky Choco-late Cake. I use butter instead of oil, milk instead of water, then I bake the batter in three layers, fill, and frost it. This is a great place to start if you are an inexperienced baker yet want to create, from scratch, a layer cake for a special occasion. I prefer raspberry or red currant jelly between the layers, but for a more traditional approach, make a full batch of the frosting and use it to fill the cake as well as to frost the top and sides. You'll definitely want to drink a tall glass of ice-cold milk with this delicious, comforting chocolate cake.

Makes one 9-inch,
3-layer cake

Serves 12 to 14

Level of difficulty ★

CAKE

3⅓ cups (1 pound) bleached all-purpose flour

⅔ cup (2 ounces) unsweetened, nonalkalized cocoa powder

¾ teaspoon baking soda

½ teaspoon salt

2 cups (15 ounces) granulated sugar

1½ sticks (6 ounces) unsalted butter, melted and cooled

2 teaspoons vanilla extract

2 tablespoons white or cider vinegar

2 cups milk

FILLING AND FROSTING

½ cup raspberry jam or red currant jelly

½ recipe Classic American Chocolate Frosting (page 298)

TO MAKE THE CAKE

1. Position a rack in the center of the oven, or if you have to use two racks, position them as close to the center as possible. Preheat the oven to 350°F. Lightly grease three 9 × 1.5-inch round layer-cake pans, then line the bottoms with parchment or greased waxed paper circles.
2. Sift the flour, cocoa, baking soda, and salt into a large mixing bowl, then blend in the sugar with a whisk. Add the melted butter and vanilla to the dry ingredients. Pour the vinegar into the milk and add this to the batter. Blend the batter with a rubber spatula until it looks homogenized.
3. Divide the batter evenly among the prepared pans and bake for 35 minutes, or until the tops are springy and a tester inserted in the center comes out dry. (If you are baking the cakes on two racks, halfway through the baking, switch the pans on the top rack with those on the bottom so they bake more evenly.)
4. Cool the cakes in their pans on a wire rack for 20 minutes. Then turn the cakes out of the pans onto the racks and cool them to room temperature before filling and frosting. Remove the paper circles before frosting.

TO FILL AND FROST

1. Stack the layers with jelly evenly spread between 2 of them.
2. Spoon a generous amount of frosting in the middle of the top of the cake. Working from the center outward, spread the frosting over the top of the cake and then around the sides to cover the cake completely.

STORAGE: Refrigerate the cake, unwrapped, until the frosting sets. Then wrap the cake loosely in plastic wrap and keep it in the refrigerator for up to 3 days.

PLATED DESSERT SUGGESTION (per portion)

1 slice of cake   *Raspberry Squeeze Sauce (page 368)*

Set the slice of cake on the plate to the left or right of center. Opposite the cake, squeeze raspberry dots in a crescent shape, beginning with tiny circles and gradually increasing their size until they are ½ inch in diameter.

Pecan Chocolate Mayonnaise Cake

Years ago, the Best Foods company printed a chocolate mayonnaise cake recipe on the side of the Hellmann's mayonnaise jar—not such an amazing invention, given that mayonnaise is nothing more than an emulsification of oil and eggs with a bit of flavoring and seasoning. This cake was inspired by the original, and once refrigerated, has the dense texture of a brownie.

Makes one 9-inch square cake

Serves 12 to 15

Level of difficulty ★

---

1 cup (4.75 ounces) bleached all-purpose flour

⅓ cup packed (1 ounce) unsweetened, nonalkalized cocoa powder

¼ teaspoon baking soda

¼ teaspoon salt

2 large eggs

Scant 14 tablespoons (7 ounces) granulated sugar

⅓ cup (3 ounces) good-quality mayonnaise

1 teaspoon vanilla extract

1 cup plus 2 tablespoons milk

2 cups (7 ounces) chopped pecans

½ cup (2 ounces) dried cranberries, chopped

---

1. Position a rack in the center of the oven and preheat to 350°F. Lightly grease a 9-inch square pan.
2. Sift the flour, cocoa, baking soda, and salt into a large mixing bowl and blend the ingredients with a whisk.
3. In a separate bowl, with an electric mixer on medium speed, beat the eggs with the sugar for 2 to 3 minutes, or until the mixture has an ivory hue and a texture like whipped cream. Add the mayonnaise and beat on low speed for 1 minute.
4. Stir the vanilla into the milk. With a rubber spatula, fold the sifted ingredients into the eggs in three additions, alternating with the milk, in two additions. Fold ½ the nuts into the batter.
5. Spread the batter evenly in the prepared cake pan. Sprinkle the remaining nuts and the cranberries on top, and bake for 45 minutes, or until the top begins to crack and a tester inserted in the center comes out somewhat moist. Cool the cake in the pan on a wire rack, then cut and serve it from the pan.

STORAGE: Keep at room temperature, wrapped airtight, for up to 3 days; refrigerate after that.

PLATED DESSERT SUGGESTION (per portion)

Confectioners' sugar
2-inch square piece of cake
¼ cup Grand Marnier Sauce (page 365)
½ navel orange, cut into "supremes" (see Note)
6 dried cranberries
1 fresh mint leaf

Through a fine sieve, sift ½ teaspoon confectioners' sugar over each slice of cake, then center the piece of cake on a 10-inch plate.

Carefully spoon or pour (from a measuring cup) the sauce around the cake. Place 5 orange supremes on top of the sauce, arranged like the spokes of a wheel around the cake. Place 5 of the cranberries in between the orange segments, then pose an orange segment, cranberry, and mint leaf on top of the cake square.

NOTE: To cut an orange into supremes: With a sharp knife, peel off all the skin and white pith from an orange. Cut between the membranes to loosen skinless sections of orange, which are known as supremes.

Chocolate Pudding Cake

Pudding cakes, which I think taste more like soufflés than puddings or cakes, are the result, I bet, of an error, but a good error it was, because the dessert is delicious. A pudding cake is nothing more than a cake batter in which the proportion of ingredients is out of balance so that, during baking, the cake separates into a top layer with a cakelike texture and a bottom layer that is more like a custard. The most classic of these types of pudding cakes is a lemon one, but I think this chocolate version is quite lovely. It is most delicious when eaten warm, fresh from the oven.

Makes one 8-inch square cake

Serves 4 to 6

Level of difficulty ★

---

2 tablespoons bleached all-purpose flour

¼ cup (0.75 ounce) unsweetened, nonalkalized cocoa powder

¾ cup (5.5 ounces) granulated sugar

3 large eggs, separated

1 cup milk

1 teaspoon vanilla extract

⅛ teaspoon salt

Confectioners' sugar, for dusting

2 cups fresh raspberries

---

1. Position a rack in the center of the oven and preheat to 350°F. Lightly grease an 8-inch square pan. Fold a cloth towel in the bottom of a 13 × 9 × 2-inch baking pan, or one large enough to accommodate the 8-inch square pan.
2. In a mixing bowl, blend the flour, cocoa, and sugar with a whisk.
3. With an electric mixer on low speed, beat the egg yolks, milk, and vanilla for a few seconds, or until foamy. Pour this over the dry ingredients and blend with a rubber spatula.
4. In a separate bowl, with an electric mixer on medium speed, whip the egg whites with the salt until stiff and glossy. Fold the beaten egg whites into the batter and spread the batter evenly in the greased pan. Set the pan on the towel in the larger baking pan and pour boiling or very hot tap water into the larger pan over the towel.
5. Bake for 35 to 40 minutes, or until the cake looks puffy and the top looks set (you can't gauge this with a tester because the center remains damp).
6. Remove the cake pan from the larger pan and serve while hot, with each portion dusted with confectioners' sugar and fresh raspberries on the side.

STORAGE: Keep in the refrigerator, wrapped airtight, for up to 3 days, but warm portions in a microwave oven before serving.

King Arthur Chocolate Pudding Cake

I can't say enough wonderful things about King Arthur Flour Company. I adore this company and would be lost without their catalogue for easy access to many of the ingredients I use in this book. They kindly gave me permission to use their recipe for Chocolate Pudding Cake, which appears in The King Arthur Flour 200th Anniversary Cookbook. Any adjustments made in the recipe are editorial, so that the recipe style conforms to that of the other recipes in this book. This recipe is more like a cake than the previous pudding cake, and because it is not very sweet, I like it served with a custard sauce. The addition of nuts make the top layer crunchy, which is an especially nice contrast to the gooey layer underneath. Like all pudding cakes, this one, I think, is best served warm, straight out of the oven.

Makes one 8-inch square cake

Serves 8

Level of difficulty ★

---

1 cup (4.75 ounces) King Arthur all-purpose flour

2 teaspoons baking powder

¼ teaspoon salt

1½ cups (11.25 ounces) granulated sugar

6 tablespoons (1.25 ounces) unsweetened, Dutch-processed cocoa powder

1 teaspoon vanilla extract

½ stick (2 ounces) unsalted butter, melted and cooled

2 cups water

¾ cup (3 ounces) chopped pecans or walnuts

Vanilla Custard Sauce, or any one of the flavored custard sauces, optional (page 358)

---

1. Position a rack in the center of the oven and preheat to 350°F. Lightly grease an 8-inch square pan.
2. Blend the flour, baking powder, salt, sugar, and cocoa in a mixing bowl. Add, but don't blend yet, the vanilla and butter. Pour the water over everything, blend thoroughly, and fold in the nuts.
3. Spread the batter evenly in the prepared cake pan and bake for 45 minutes (you can't gauge this with a tester because the center remains damp). Cut the cake into portions and transfer them to small bowls. If you wish, spoon the sauce around the cake.

STORAGE: Keep leftover cake in the refrigerator, wrapped airtight, for up to 3 days, but warm it up for a few seconds in a microwave oven before serving.

The Classic Brownie

What makes this brownie a classic is that a crackling sugary surface tops a moist, chewy interior. In pastry parlance, a brownie is considered a bar cookie rather than a cake because the batter is assembled like a cookie dough. But a brownie tastes more like a cake than a cookie, and a chocolate cake book without a brownie recipe would be incomplete. Here, then, is what I consider to be the classic brownie, along with its sweet variations.

Makes one 9-inch square cake

Serves 9 to 12

Level of difficulty ★

4 ounces unsweetened chocolate, finely chopped
1 stick (4 ounces) unsalted butter, cut into 1-inch chunks
1 cup (4.75 ounces) bleached all-purpose flour
⅛ teaspoon baking soda
⅛ teaspoon salt
4 large eggs
1½ cups (11.25 ounces) granulated sugar
1 teaspoon vanilla extract
1 cup (3.5 ounces) walnuts or pecans, coarsely chopped, optional

1. Lightly grease a 9-inch square pan. Melt the chocolate and butter in a microwave oven or in the top of a double boiler set over simmering water. Stir occasionally, and when just melted, transfer the chocolate and butter to a clean bowl and set it aside to cool to room temperature.
2. Position a rack in the center of the oven and preheat to 350°F. In a mixing bowl, blend the flour, baking soda, and salt with a whisk.
3. Beat the eggs, sugar, and vanilla with an electric mixer on medium speed for about 2 minutes, or until the mixture has an ivory hue and looks fluffy.
4. With a rubber spatula, fold the flour mixture into the eggs, then fold in the cooled melted chocolate and the nuts, if using. Spread the batter evenly in the prepared pan.
5. Bake for 40 to 45 minutes (if you want the brownies to be incredibly moist, bake for only 35 minutes), or until the top looks cracked. You can't gauge this with a tester because the inside remains moist.
6. Cool the brownies in the pan on a wire rack. Cut and serve the brownies from the pan.

STORAGE: Keep at room temperature, wrapped airtight, for up to 3 days; refrigerate or freeze after that. Serve at room temperature.

COCONUT BROWNIES

Reduce the sugar by ¼ cup. Omit the walnuts or pecans. Instead, add ½ cup chopped macadamia nuts and 1 cup sweetened coconut flakes to the batter.

ESPRESSO BROWNIES

Dissolve 1 tablespoon instant espresso coffee powder in 2 teaspoons boiling or very hot tap water, and add this to the batter instead of the vanilla extract.

JAMMY BROWNIES

Omit the nuts. After you have transferred the batter to the pan, dot the top with teaspoonfuls of ½ cup apricot jam, red currant jelly, or seedless raspberry jam. Draw a knife or wooden skewer through the batter to swirl in the jam. Sprinkle ½ cup sliced blanched almonds over the top and bake.

Best Brownies

This is my "best" brownie because of the balance of flavor and texture, along with moistness and the depth of chocolate flavor.

Makes one 9 × 13-inch sheet cake

Serves 15 to 18

Level of difficulty ★

4 ounces bittersweet chocolate, finely chopped

2 ounces unsweetened chocolate, finely chopped

1 cup (4.75 ounces) bleached all-purpose flour

¼ cup (0.75 ounce) unsweetened, Dutch-processed cocoa powder

¼ teaspoon baking soda

¼ teaspoon baking powder

¼ teaspoon salt

1½ sticks (6 ounces) unsalted butter, softened

1½ cups (11.25 ounces) granulated sugar

4 large eggs

1 teaspoon vanilla extract

2 cups (7 ounces) walnuts or pecans, coarsely chopped

1. Lightly grease a 9 × 13 × 2-inch pan. Melt the two types of chocolate in a microwave oven, or in the top of a double boiler set over simmering water. When almost melted, remove the chocolate from the heat and stir until completely melted. Transfer the chocolate to a clean bowl and set it aside to cool to room temperature.

2. Position a rack in the center of the oven and preheat to 350°F. Sift the flour with the cocoa, baking soda, baking powder, and salt into a mixing bowl.

3. Beat the butter and sugar with an electric mixer set on medium speed for about 1 minute, or until it has an ivory hue. Add the eggs and vanilla, and beat for another minute, or until blended.

4. With a rubber spatula, fold the flour and cocoa mixture into the eggs, then add the melted chocolate and stir until combined. Stir in the nuts.

5. Spread the batter evenly in the prepared pan and bake for 30 to 35 minutes, or until a tester inserted in the center comes out somewhat moist.

6. Cool the brownies in the pan on a wire rack, then cut and serve from the pan.

STORAGE: Keep at room temperature, wrapped airtight, for up to 3 days; refrigerate or freeze after that. Serve at room temperature.

The Brownie Torte

I've named this cake "Brownie Torte" because its texture and flavor are dense, moist, and rich, like that of a brownie. In German the word torte *can mean "fancy cake," but in our family, it describes any single-layer cake that is as flat as this one!*

Makes one 9-inch, single-layer cake

Serves 8

Level of difficulty ★

¾ stick (3 ounces) unsalted butter, cut into 1-inch chunks

3 ounces unsweetened chocolate, finely chopped

1½ cups (11.25 ounces) superfine sugar

3 large eggs

1 teaspoon vanilla extract

⅛ teaspoon salt

¾ cup (3.5 ounces) bleached all-purpose flour

1 cup (3.5 ounces) chopped pecans or walnuts

Maria's Best Chocolate Glaze, mocha variation (page 331)

---

1. Lightly grease a 9 × 1.5-inch round cake pan, then line the bottom with a parchment or greased waxed paper circle.

2. In the top of a double boiler set over simmering water, melt the butter, chocolate, and sugar, stirring occasionally. When melted, remove from the heat, transfer to a clean bowl, and set aside to cool to room temperature.

3. Position a rack in the center of the oven and preheat to 350°F. In a mixing bowl, blend the eggs, vanilla, and salt with a whisk, add the cooled chocolate mixture, and mix well. Fold in the flour and nuts with a rubber spatula, then spread the batter evenly in the prepared pan.

4. Bake for 35 to 40 minutes, or until a tester inserted in the center comes out almost dry. Remove the cake from the oven and cool it on a wire rack for an hour before unmolding.

5. Unmold the cake and cool it to room temperature, right side up, with the paper still in place, on a wire rack. Remove the paper circle just before icing.

6. With a small offset spatula or table knife, spread some of the glaze around the sides of the cake. Pour the remaining glaze on top of the cake and spread it from the middle out to and over the edges. Spread any glaze that drips over the edges around the sides of the cake. Refrigerate the cake, unwrapped, until the glaze sets.

STORAGE: Keep in the refrigerator, loosely wrapped, for up to 3 days, but remove the cake 30 minutes before serving.

Boozy Mud Cake

This cake has a rich, gooey interior that may look like mud but tastes divine. My experience with mud cakes is limited to eating them in not-too-swanky restaurants, and they always taste like underbaked brownies. My research into chocolate cakes known as "Mississippi Mud" turned up several versions, none of which seemed to have much in common with the others. I found something like this cake in a New England community cookbook, and it was called "Mississippi Mud," whereas an almost identical cake turned up in a Mississippi Junior League cookbook but was called "Bourbon Cake"—go figure! Whatever the origin, this is a delicious taste sensation, and while I prefer it plain, my husband loves it with vanilla or butter pecan ice cream.

Makes one 9 × 13-inch sheet cake

Serves 12 to 15

Level of difficulty ★

1½ cups freshly made double-strength coffee or 2 tablespoons instant espresso coffee powder dissolved in 1½ cups boiling water

6 ounces unsweetened chocolate, finely chopped

2 sticks (8 ounces) unsalted butter, cut into 1-inch chunks

2 cups (15 ounces) granulated sugar

6 tablespoons bourbon whiskey

2 cups (9 ounces) cake or pastry flour

½ teaspoon baking soda

⅛ teaspoon salt

2 large eggs

1. Position a rack in the center of the oven and preheat to 375°F. Lightly grease a 9 × 13 × 2-inch pan.
2. In a medium saucepan, bring the coffee and chocolate to a boil over medium heat, stirring occasionally. Remove from the heat, add the butter, and stir with a whisk until the butter is dissolved and the mixture is smooth. Transfer the mixture to a bowl, add 1 cup of the sugar along with the bourbon, and whisk until combined. Set aside to cool.
3. Sift the flour, baking soda, and salt into a large mixing bowl.
4. With an electric mixer on medium speed, beat the eggs with the remaining 1 cup sugar for about 1 minute, or until it has an ivory hue and is light. Add the chocolate mixture and beat on low speed for a few seconds, just to combine. Slowly add the chocolate mixture to the flour, stirring with a whisk until homogenized.
5. Transfer the batter to the prepared cake pan and smooth the top with a spatula. Bake for exactly 30 minutes; the interior should remain moist and "muddy."
6. Cool the cake in the pan on a wire rack for 1 hour. Cut and serve directly from the pan.

STORAGE: Keep at room temperature, wrapped airtight, for up to 2 days; refrigerate after that. Bring the cake back to room temperature before serving.

Cherry Milk-Chocolate Cake

This cake is a lovely combination of milk chocolate cake, milk chocolate ganache, and kirsch-marinated cherries. The kirsch and sour cherries add a felicitous and contrasting note to the sweetness of the chocolate.

Makes one 9-inch,
2-layer cake

Serves 12 to 14

Level of difficulty ★★

CAKE

4 ounces milk chocolate, finely chopped

½ stick (2 ounces) unsalted butter, cut into 1-inch chunks

1½ cups (7 ounces) cake flour

1 teaspoon baking powder

¼ teaspoon salt

1 cup (7.5 ounces) granulated sugar

¾ cup heavy cream

½ cup sour cream

3 large eggs

FILLING AND FROSTING

1 jar (about 24 ounces) sour cherries packed in syrup, drained

6 tablespoons kirsch

Chocolate Shavings made with a 4-ounce piece of milk chocolate (page 380)

Whipped Ganache, made with milk chocolate, chilled (page 321)

TO MAKE THE CAKE

1. Position a rack in the center of the oven and preheat to 350°F. Lightly grease two 9 × 1.5-inch round cake pans, dust them with flour, and tap out the excess. Line the bottoms with parchment or greased and floured waxed paper circles.

2. In a mixing bowl or the top of a double boiler set over simmering water, melt the chocolate and butter, stirring occasionally. When melted, remove from the heat and set aside to cool to room temperature.

3. Sift the flour, baking powder, and salt into a large mixing bowl. Add the sugar and blend with a whisk.

4. In a separate bowl, with a whisk, combine the cream, sour cream, and eggs, then add the cooled chocolate and butter. With a rubber spatula, fold the dry ingredients into the wet ones and transfer the batter to the prepared cake pans. Rap the pans sharply on the counter a few times to break up any large air bubbles.

5. Bake for 35 to 40 minutes, or until the cakes begin to shrink from the sides of the pan and a tester inserted in the center comes out dry.

6. Cool the cakes to room temperature in their pans on a wire rack. Peel off the paper circles just before frosting.

TO FILL AND FROST

1. Dry the sour cherries on paper towels, transfer them to a bowl, and marinate them in 2 tablespoons of the kirsch for at least 4 hours or, preferably, overnight. Make the chocolate shavings and chill them in a bowl for at least 4 hours or, preferably, overnight.

2. Set one cake layer on a cardboard round, cut slightly larger than the diameter of the cake. Sprinkle the cake with 2 tablespoons of the remaining kirsch. Spread 1 cup of whipped ganache on the cake layer and imbed the ganache with the cherries, making sure they are evenly distributed. Sprinkle the second cake layer with the remaining 2 tablespoons kirsch and set it, upside down, over the first layer, making sure the two layers are lined up evenly. Spread the ganache around the sides of the cake, then spread all but 1 cup of the remaining ganache on top.

3. Fill a 16-inch pastry bag fitted with a ½-inch star tip with the reserved 1 cup ganache and refrigerate the bag while you finish the cake. With your cupped hand, press the chilled chocolate shavings around the sides of the cake, working fast so the chocolate shavings don't melt. Remove the pastry bag from the refrigerator and pipe 16 large rosettes around the top outside edge of the cake. Spoon a few chocolate shavings in the center of each rosette, and refrigerate the cake, uncovered, until the frosting has set.

STORAGE: Keep in the refrigerator, covered with a cake dome or an inverted large mixing bowl, for up to 3 days.

ADVANCE PREPARATION TIPS

- Bake the cake, make the whipped ganache, marinate the cherries, and prepare the chocolate shavings 1 day ahead of assembling the cake.
- You will find it is easier to assemble the cake when all the components have been thoroughly chilled.

Christmas Chocolate Fruit Cake

This is great for a Christmas buffet because it is incredibly simple and quick to prepare, can be made weeks in advance, and a small slice goes a long way. I have hated fruit cakes for as long as I can remember because they're filled with candied fruit, which I detest. This lovely version, however, is chock-full of rum-soaked raisins, dried cranberries, apricots, pecans, walnuts, and pistachios. You can make it as a traditional fruit cake—that is, wrap it in cheesecloth and soak it with booze for months before eating—or serve it as I prefer, one plain slice set in a pool of cool vanilla custard sauce and drizzled with warm chocolate sauce.

Makes one 10-inch
tube cake

Serves 20 to 24

Level of difficulty ★

---

2 cups (9 ounces) golden raisins

1 cup (4 ounces) dried California apricots, quartered

1 cup (4 ounces) dried cranberries

1 cup dark rum, bourbon, or brandy

3 cups (14.25 ounces) unbleached all-purpose or bread flour

¾ cup (2.5 ounces) unsweetened, Dutch-processed cocoa powder

½ teaspoon baking soda

1 teaspoon baking powder

¼ teaspoon salt

2 teaspoons ground cinnamon

¼ teaspoon ground cloves

1 teaspoon ground cardamom

¾ cup (9 ounces) honey

1¼ sticks (5 ounces) unsalted butter, melted and cooled

3 large eggs

2 cups (15 ounces) granulated sugar

1½ cups (5.25 ounces) walnuts, chopped

1½ cups (5.25 ounces) pecans, chopped

½ cup (2 ounces) roasted unsalted pistachios

---

1. Position a rack in the lower third of the oven and preheat to 350°F. Lightly grease a 10 × 3-inch tube pan with butter, then dust it with flour, and tap out the excess. You can also line the bottom with a special parchment designed for tube pans.
2. Soak the raisins, apricots, and cranberries in the rum.
3. Sift the flour, cocoa, baking soda, baking powder, salt, cinnamon, cloves, and cardamom into a large mixing bowl.
4. In a separate mixing bowl, with a rubber spatula, blend the honey, melted butter, eggs, and sugar. Add the dry ingredients to the honey mixture and blend until smooth. Fold in the nuts, raisins, apricots, and cranberries (along with any liquor not absorbed by the fruit).
5. Spoon the batter into the prepared tube pan and rap the pan sharply on the counter a few times to level the batter. Bake for 1½ hours, or until a cake tester inserted in the center of the cake comes out dry.
6. Cool the cake in the pan on a wire rack for 1 hour. Tip the cake out of the pan and cool to room temperature, right side up, on a wire rack.

STORAGE: Keep at room temperature, wrapped airtight, for up to a week; freeze after that.

TO FINISH THE CAKE AS A TRADITIONAL FRUIT CAKE

Once cool, wrap the cake in cotton cheesecloth and keep on soaking the cheesecloth with rum or bourbon for several weeks, or until you've had enough of the aroma. Wrap in plastic and freeze for Christmas.

PLATED DESSERT SUGGESTION (per portion)

*¼ cup chilled medium-thick
   Vanilla Custard Sauce (page 358)
1 thin slice of cake*

*2 tablespoons warm Deadly
Delicious Chocolate Sauce
(page 362)*

Spoon the vanilla sauce in the center of a dessert plate and center the cake on the sauce. Imagine a line running diagonally across the cake and spoon the chocolate sauce over the cake just on one side of that imaginary line. (One triangular side is glazed with chocolate sauce and the other is unglazed.)

Ginger Honey Cake with Chocolate

This fabulously moist cake is rich in spices and reminds me of the honey cakes I ate as a child growing up in Antwerp, Belgium. At the time, I didn't understand the beauty of these spicy cakes, but now I appreciate their bold flavor and great texture. In the cake there is but a hint of chocolate, which I sometimes like to echo with a chocolate icing.

Makes one 9 ×
13-inch sheet cake

Serves 15 to 16

Level of difficulty ★

2 sticks (8 ounces) unsalted
butter, melted and cooled

3 ounces unsweetened
chocolate, melted and cooled

2½ cups (12 ounces) bleached
all-purpose flour

1 teaspoon baking soda

1½ teaspoons ground ginger

½ teaspoon ground cinnamon

½ teaspoon salt

4 large eggs

1 cup packed (7.5 ounces)
dark brown sugar

1 cup (12 ounces) dark and richly
flavored honey such as lavender,
wildflower, or buckwheat

1 teaspoon vanilla extract

1 cup milk

Sour Cream Chocolate Icing
(page 326), optional

1. Position a rack in the center of the oven and preheat to 325°F. Lightly grease a 9 × 13 × 2-inch pan.

2. Combine the butter and chocolate with a whisk and set aside. Sift the flour, baking soda, ginger, cinnamon, and salt and set it aside.

3. With an electric mixer on low speed, beat the eggs with the dark brown sugar for about 1 minute, or until combined. Add the chocolate and butter mixture and beat until mixed, then add the honey and vanilla, and mix until smooth.

4. With a rubber spatula, fold in the sifted ingredients, then beat the batter on low speed for 1 to 2 minutes, or until blended. With the machine running, drizzle in the milk and when all of it is in, beat for 1 minute.

5. Pour the batter into the prepared pan and bake for 50 minutes to 1 hour, or until a tester inserted in the center comes out dry and the cake begins to pull away from the sides of the pan.

6. Cool the cake to room temperature in the pan on a wire rack. Spread the icing over the top, if using, and cut and serve from the pan.

STORAGE: Store in the refrigerator, lightly covered with aluminum foil, for up to 5 days, but bring the cake back to room temperature before serving.

PLATED DESSERT SUGGESTION (per portion)

1 slice of cake
Ginger Custard Sauce (page 360)

2 teaspoons finely chopped
candied ginger

Center a slice of cake on a 10-inch plate and spoon the sauce around it. Scatter the chopped ginger over the sauce.

**Gisèle's Raspberry Chocolate Cake

I love this cake. I received the recipe for it from my late aunt Gisèle, but I suspect it came from the back of a package of chocolate morsels. This is one of the first cakes I used to make when I was young because it is as foolproof as it is delicious. Today, I continue to make it because it is the perfect little cake for occasions when I entertain just a couple of friends. Fresh raspberries and whipped cream make deliciously appropriate garnishes.

Makes one 8-inch,
2-layer cake

Serves 6 to 8

Level of difficulty ★

CAKE

1 stick (4 ounces) unsalted butter, cut into chunks

2 ounces semisweet or bittersweet chocolate, finely chopped

¾ cup (3.5 ounces) bleached all-purpose flour

½ teaspoon baking powder

⅛ teaspoon baking soda

⅛ teaspoon salt

⅔ cup (5 ounces) sugar, preferably superfine

½ cup milk

½ teaspoon vanilla extract

2 large eggs

FILLING AND GLAZE

4 ounces semisweet or bittersweet chocolate, finely chopped

1 tablespoon unsalted butter

2 tablespoons milk

3 tablespoons seedless raspberry or apricot jam

TO MAKE THE CAKE

1. Position a rack in the center of the oven and preheat to 350°F. Lightly grease two 8 × 1.5-inch round cake pans, line the bottoms with parchment or greased waxed paper circles.
2. Melt the butter with the chocolate in a small saucepan over low heat, stirring occasionally. Remove the pan from the heat and transfer the mixture to a clean mixing bowl.
3. In a separate mixing bowl, blend the flour, baking powder, baking soda, and salt with a whisk.
4. Stir the sugar, milk, vanilla, and eggs into the chocolate, then add the flour mixture. Blend the ingredients with an electric mixer on low speed, then increase the speed to high and beat for 2 minutes.
5. Divide the batter evenly between the prepared cake pans, and smooth the tops with a rubber spatula or a small offset spatula. Rap the pans sharply on the counter a couple of times to break up any large air bubbles. Bake for 30 minutes, or until a cake tester inserted in the center comes out dry and the cake begins to shrink from the sides of the pan.
6. Remove the cakes from the oven and cool them to room temperature in their pans on a wire rack. Unmold the cakes and remove the paper circles just before filling and glazing.

TO FILL AND GLAZE

1. In the top of a double boiler set over simmering water, melt the chocolate with the butter and milk, stirring occasionally. Transfer the chocolate glaze to a clean bowl to cool to lukewarm.
2. Set one cake layer on a cardboard round cut slightly smaller than the cake, and spread the top with ½ the jam. Set the second cake layer, upside down, over the jam and spread it with the remaining jam.
3. Spread the sides of the cake with a thin layer of the chocolate glaze, then pour the remaining glaze over the top of the cake. With a small offset spatula or a table knife, spread the glaze across and over the edges of the cake; spread any chocolate that falls off the edges around the sides of the cake. Refrigerate the cake, unwrapped, to firm up the chocolate glaze.

STORAGE: Keep in the refrigerator, wrapped airtight in plastic, for up to 3 days, but remove the cake 30 minutes before serving.

Fissure Spiced Chocolate Cake

I've given this cake its unusual name because, when done, the top looks fissured like desert earth. The cracked top gets hidden later when the cake is turned upside down after cooling. This cake has the deepest chocolate flavor imaginable and feels like velvet on the tongue. The subtle use of spices gives the cake its mysterious aromatic quality, making it far more complex than if you were to flavor it simply with vanilla. It is so rich, it is best served plain, with a dollop of whipped cream.

Makes one 9-inch, single-layer cake

Serves 10 to 12

Level of difficulty ★

1 stick plus 2 tablespoons (5 ounces) unsalted butter, cut into chunks

12 ounces bittersweet chocolate, finely chopped

1 cup (4.5 ounces) cake or pastry flour

⅛ teaspoon ground allspice

¼ teaspoon ground black pepper

¼ teaspoon ground cinnamon

⅛ teaspoon ground ginger

¾ teaspoon baking powder

⅛ teaspoon salt

4 large eggs

¾ cup (5.5 ounces) granulated sugar

Superfine or vanilla sugar, for dusting (page 20)

Whipped Cream or Spiced Whipped Cream (page 318)

1. Lightly grease a 9 × 3-inch springform pan and line the bottom with a parchment or greased waxed paper circle.
2. In a mixing bowl or the top of a double boiler set over very hot or simmering water, melt the butter with the chocolate, stirring occasionally. When melted, transfer the butter and chocolate to a clean bowl and set it aside to cool to room temperature.
3. Position a rack in the lower third of the oven and preheat to 375°F. In a large mixing bowl, sift the flour with the allspice, black pepper, cinnamon, ginger, baking powder, and salt.
4. Whip the eggs until foamy with an electric beater on high speed. Gradually add the sugar with the machine running and beat for 2 to 3 minutes, or until the mixture has an ivory hue and is light.
5. With a rubber spatula, fold the melted chocolate and butter into the eggs. Sift the dry ingredients over the batter and fold until homogenized.
6. Transfer the batter to the prepared cake pan, smooth the top with a rubber or small offset spatula, and place the cake pan on a baking sheet to catch any drips. Bake for 45 minutes, or until the top looks cracked and dry (a cake tester, when inserted in the center will come out moist, which is how it should be).
7. Remove the cake from the oven and cool it to room temperature in the pan on a wire rack. Unlock the springform and turn the cake upside down onto a plate or cake board and peel off the paper. Lightly dust the top with superfine or vanilla sugar, and serve at room temperature with whipped cream on the side.

STORAGE: This cake tastes best served on the day it is baked. If there are leftovers, wrap them airtight in plastic wrap and keep at room temperature for 1 day. Refrigerate the cake after that, but be sure to bring it back to room temperature before serving.

NOTE: If the spices don't appeal to you, flavor the cake with 1 teaspoon vanilla extract added after you beat the eggs with the sugar.

One-Bowl Chocolate Cake with Tutti-Frutti Filling

You'll understand the name of this cake once you read how it's made. Combine all of the ingredients in one bowl, beat them together, and bake. The cake is so light that it needs a filling as airy as whipped cream with fresh fruit to match it perfectly.

Makes one 9-inch, 4-layer cake

Serves 12 to 14

Level of difficulty ★

CAKE

2 cups (9.5 ounces) bleached all-purpose flour

½ cup (1.5 ounces) unsweetened, Dutch-processed cocoa powder

1 teaspoon baking powder

¼ teaspoon baking soda

¼ teaspoon salt

1 cup plus 14 tablespoons (14 ounces) granulated sugar

½ cup (4 ounces) solid vegetable shortening, at room temperature

½ stick (2 ounces) unsalted butter, softened

1¼ cups milk

1 teaspoon vanilla extract

3 large eggs

FILLING AND FROSTING

1 pint strawberries

1 large banana

Whipped Cream, plain or flavored (see page 318)

½ pint raspberries

Confectioners' sugar

TO MAKE THE CAKE

1. Position a rack in the center of the oven and preheat to 350°F. Lightly grease two 9 × 1.5-inch round cake pans. Line the bottoms with parchment or greased waxed paper circles.

2. Sift the flour, cocoa, baking powder, baking soda, and salt into a large mixing bowl (or into the bowl of a stationary electric mixer). Add the sugar and blend the dry ingredients with a whisk.

3. To the dry ingredients, add the shortening, butter, milk, vanilla, and eggs. Beat the ingredients with an electric mixer on low speed for a few seconds to just combine, then increase the speed to medium and beat for 1 minute. Scrape down the sides of the bowl with a rubber spatula and beat for 2 minutes longer.

4. Divide the batter evenly between the prepared cake pans and smooth the tops with a rubber or small offset spatula. Bake for 45 to 50 minutes, or until the tops are springy, the cakes begin to shrink from the sides of the pan, and a cake tester inserted in the center comes out dry.

5. Cool the cakes to room temperature in their pans on a wire rack. Unmold and peel off the paper circles just before filling and frosting.

TO FILL AND FROST

1. Trim and cut the strawberries into very thin slices. Peel and thinly slice the banana.

2. With a serrated knife, split each cake layer horizontally in two. Set one cake layer, cut side up, on a cardboard round slightly larger than the diameter of the cake. Spread about ¾ cup whipped cream on the layer and scatter a mix of strawberries, banana, and raspberries over the cream.

3. Set the second layer, cut side down, over the fruit and spread it with whipped cream and fruit. Repeat this procedure with the third cake layer, and end with the fourth layer, set cut side down.

4. Spread the remaining whipped cream around the sides of the cake, leaving the top unfrosted. Chill for a couple of hours before serving.

5. Just before serving, dust the top of the cake with confectioners' sugar passed through a very fine sieve.

STORAGE: Keep in the refrigerator, under a cake dome or an inverted large mixing bowl, and eat within 2 days.

Orange-Blossom Chocolate Cake

This honey cake has a beautifully intriguing taste, vaguely reminiscent of the Mediterranean. While it hints at chocolate, it shouts "orange" because of the quadruple dose of this fruit flavor in the zest, juice, honey, and orange flower water.

Makes one 9 × 5-inch loaf cake

Serves 12 to 14

Level of difficulty ★★

---

4 ounces bittersweet chocolate, finely chopped

2 tablespoons (1 ounce) unsalted butter

Scant ½ cup (2 ounces) whole or slivered blanched almonds

Scant ½ cup (2 ounces) roasted unsalted pistachios

2 cups (9.5 ounces) bleached all-purpose flour

½ teaspoon baking soda

¼ teaspoon baking powder

⅛ teaspoon salt

½ cup (6 ounces) orange blossom honey

½ teaspoon grated orange zest

¾ cup orange juice

1 teaspoon orange flower water

1 teaspoon anise seeds

3 large eggs

½ cup (3.75 ounces) granulated sugar

---

1. Position a rack in the center of the oven and preheat to 350°F. Lightly grease a 9 × 5 × 3-inch loaf pan. Line the bottom with parchment or greased waxed paper.
2. In a mixing bowl or the top of a double boiler set over simmering water, melt the chocolate with the butter, stirring occasionally. Set aside to cool to room temperature.
3. Finely grind the almonds and pistachios in the bowl of a food processor fitted with the steel blade, pulsing the machine on and off so the nuts don't turn oily.
4. Sift the flour, baking soda, baking powder, and salt into a mixing bowl. Add the almonds and pistachios, and combine with a whisk. In a separate mixing bowl, blend the honey, orange zest, juice, orange flower water, and anise seeds with a whisk.
5. With an electric mixer on medium speed, beat the eggs for a few seconds, or until foamy. Add the sugar and beat on high speed for 2 minutes, or until the mixture has an ivory hue and looks light. Add the honey mixture and melted chocolate to the eggs and beat until combined.
6. With a rubber spatula, fold the flour and nut mixture into the eggs. Transfer the batter to the prepared loaf pan and smooth the top with a rubber or small offset spatula.
7. Bake for 1 hour to 1 hour and 10 minutes, or until a cake tester inserted in the center comes out dry. Cool the cake in the pan on a wire rack for 30 minutes, then tip it out of the pan, remove the paper, and cool to room temperature, on its side, on a wire rack.

STORAGE: The honey makes this a good keeper, so you can store the cake at room temperature, wrapped airtight in plastic, for up to 5 days.

PLATED DESSERT SUGGESTION (per portion)

1 slice of cake
3 to 4 tablespoons sour cream
2 to 3 tablespoons Fig Compote (page 372)

Fresh mint leaf
1 teaspoon minced pistachios
Honey

Center the slice of cake on a 10-inch plate. Spoon the sour cream on the lower left or right of the cake and top with the fig compote and then a mint leaf. Sprinkle the pistachios around the cake and over the figs. Dip a fork in honey and sparingly drizzle over the cake and the plate.

Peanut Chocolate Cake

This is a dream cake for Reese's Peanut Butter Cup fans because it includes milk chocolate and peanut flavors in both the cake and the frosting. This definitely resides in what my husband calls the "kid cake" category (even though he eats it with as much joy as my teenager and her friends do). If you prefer a more intensely chocolate flavored frosting, substitute Classic American Chocolate Frosting (page 298).

Makes one 9-inch, 2-layer cake

Serves 12 to 16

Level of difficulty ★★

CAKE

¾ cup (3 ounces) unsalted roasted peanuts

¾ cup (5.5 ounces) dark brown sugar

⅔ cup double-strength coffee (or 1 heaping teaspoon instant espresso coffee powder dissolved in ⅔ cup boiling water)

6 ounces milk chocolate, finely chopped

1 stick (4 ounces) unsalted butter, cut into 1-inch chunks

1¾ cups packed (8 ounces) cake or pastry flour

¾ teaspoon baking powder

¼ teaspoon allspice

⅛ teaspoon salt

¾ cup (5.5 ounces) granulated sugar

2 large eggs

¾ cup sour cream

TO MAKE THE CAKE

1. Position a rack in the center of the oven and preheat to 375°F. Lightly grease two 9 × 1.5-inch round cake pans, dust them with flour, and tap out the excess. Line the bottoms with parchment or greased and floured waxed paper circles.

2. In the bowl of a food processor fitted with the steel blade, finely grind the peanuts with ¼ cup of the brown sugar; set aside.

3. Dissolve the remaining ½ cup brown sugar with the coffee in a small saucepan over low heat, stirring occasionally. Add the chocolate and bring back to a simmer, stirring until the chocolate is melted. Transfer the contents of the saucepan to a clean bowl, add the butter, and blend with a whisk.

4. Sift the flour, baking powder, allspice, and salt into a medium-size bowl. Add the sugar and the ground nut mixture, and combine with a whisk.

5. Whisk the eggs and sour cream in a large mixing bowl, then gradually add the cooled chocolate mixture and mix until homogenized. Add the flour and nut mixture, and blend with a rubber spatula.

6. Divide the batter between the prepared cake pans. With a rubber or small offset spatula, spread the batter evenly in the pans and smooth the tops. Rap the pans sharply on the counter a couple of times to break up any large air bubbles.

7. Bake for 30 to 35 minutes, or until a tester inserted in the center comes out dry and the tops feel springy. Cool the cakes to room temperature in their pans on a wire rack. Peel off the paper circles just before filling and frosting.

TO FILL AND FROST

1. Melt both chocolates in a microwave oven, or in the top of a double boiler set over simmering water. When melted, blend the two chocolates with a rubber spatula, remove from the heat, and transfer to a large mixing bowl or to the bowl of a stationary mixer.

2. Add the sugar, butter, peanut butter, and sour cream to the chocolate. With an electric mixer (fitted with a paddle if you are using a stationary mixer) on low speed, combine the ingredients. Whip them for 1 min-

ute, until light, and add enough milk or coffee to make the frosting "spreadable."

3. Set one layer on a cake board that is slightly larger than the cake, and spread the top thinly with frosting. Scatter 2 tablespoons of ground roasted peanuts over the frosting. Set the second cake layer over the peanuts, making sure the two layers are lined up. Spread the sides and top of the cake with a thin layer of frosting. Drag a decorating comb in an "S" pattern across the top of the frosting. Press the remaining peanuts around the sides of the cake. Refrigerate the cake, unwrapped, until the frosting sets.

STORAGE: Keep loosely wrapped in the refrigerator for up to 3 days.

FILLING AND FROSTING

4 ounces milk chocolate, finely chopped

4 ounces semisweet or bittersweet chocolate, finely chopped

1 pound confectioners' sugar, sifted

¾ stick (3 ounces) unsalted butter, softened

1 tablespoon unhomogenized peanut butter

¼ cup sour cream

2 to 3 tablespoons milk or coffee

¾ cup (3 ounces) roasted peanuts, ground in the food processor

Quintessential French Chocolate Cake

This glorious little cake, fashioned out of five simple ingredients—butter, chocolate, eggs, flour, and sugar—pops up throughout the French culinary repertoire, mostly in home-style and regional cookbooks. While the proportions of the ingredients vary from recipe to recipe, the cake always comes out dense, rich, and as flat as a pancake. It is best to serve this plain, with a dab of whipped cream on the side, or glazed with the thinnest of icings.

Makes one 9-inch, single-layer cake

Serves 6 to 8

Level of difficulty ★

1 stick (4 ounces) unsalted butter, softened

4 ounces semisweet or bittersweet chocolate, melted

5 large eggs, separated

1 cup (7.5 ounces) superfine sugar

¾ cup (3.5 ounces) bleached all-purpose flour

⅛ teaspoon salt

Confectioners' sugar, for dusting

1. Position a rack in the center of the oven and preheat to 350°F. Lightly grease a 9 × 2-inch springform or false-bottom pan and line the bottom with a parchment or greased waxed paper circle.
2. Tablespoon by tablespoon, whisk the softened butter into the melted chocolate and set aside. With an electric mixer on medium speed, beat the egg yolks with ¾ cup of the sugar until light and lemon colored. With a rubber spatula, fold in the butter and chocolate, then the flour.
3. Whip the egg whites with the salt until they form soft peaks. Slowly, 1 tablespoon at a time, beat in the remaining ¼ cup sugar, and whip until the whites form stiff and glossy peaks. Fold the beaten egg whites into the chocolate batter, and transfer the batter to the prepared pan. Bake for 45 minutes, or until a cake tester inserted in the center comes out dry. The top will be cracked.
4. Remove the cake from the oven and cool it to room temperature in the pan on a wire rack. Release the spring latch and lift the cake up and out of the form. Turn the cake upside down onto a cardboard round and remove the bottom of the pan. Peel off the paper circle. Dust the top with confectioners' sugar.

STORAGE: Keep in the refrigerator, wrapped airtight in plastic, for up to 3 days, but remove the cake 30 minutes before serving.

**Reine de Saba

This classic French cake, with unbeatable taste, is like my mother-in-law's Our Family's Favorite Chocolate Almond Cake (page 252), except that this cake calls for flour in addition to the ground almonds. When done, the middle sags a bit and the top might crack, but don't worry, because these imperfections are hidden by the glaze.

Makes one 9-inch, single-layer cake

Serves 10 to 12

Level of difficulty ★★

CAKE

6 ounces semisweet or bittersweet chocolate, finely chopped

1½ sticks (6 ounces) unsalted butter, softened

¾ cup (3.5 ounces) cake flour

¼ teaspoon baking powder

¼ teaspoon salt

¾ cup (3 ounces) finely ground blanched almonds

4 large eggs, separated

1 cup (7.5 ounces) granulated sugar

Pinch of salt

ICING

Maria's Best Chocolate Glaze (page 331)

¼ cup finely chopped pistachios or blanched almonds

TO MAKE THE CAKE

1. Lightly grease a 9 × 3-inch springform pan, dust it with flour or unsweetened cocoa powder, and tap out the excess.
2. Melt the chocolate in a microwave oven or in the top of a double boiler set over simmering water. Transfer the melted chocolate to a clean bowl, immediately whisk in the butter, and blend until smooth; set aside.
3. Position a rack in the lower third of the oven and preheat to 350°F. Sift the flour, baking powder, and salt into a medium-size mixing bowl. Add the almonds and combine with a whisk.
4. With an electric beater on medium speed, whip the egg yolks with ½ cup of the sugar for about 1 minute, or until thick like mayonnaise.
5. In a separate bowl, with an electric mixer on high speed, whip the egg whites with a pinch of salt and a pinch of the remaining sugar, until semistiff. While continuing to beat, slowly add the remaining ½ cup sugar and beat until the egg whites are stiff and glossy.
6. With a rubber spatula, fold the melted chocolate into the beaten egg yolks, then fold this mixture into the egg whites along with the flour and almond mixture.
7. When the batter is homogenized, transfer it to the prepared cake pan. Bake the cake for 45 minutes, or until a tester inserted in the center comes out dry.
8. Cool the cake to room temperature in the pan on a wire rack. Run a metal spatula or a table knife around the cake to loosen it from the form. Open the springform lock and lift the cake up and out of the ring.

TO ICE

1. Invert the cake onto a cardboard round of the same size or slightly smaller than the diameter of the cake. Remove the bottom of the pan.
2. Dip a small offset spatula or table knife in the glaze and spread a thin coating around the sides of the cake. Pour the remaining glaze over the top and spread it across the top and over the edges. Spread any glaze that drips over the edges around the sides of the cake.
3. Press the nuts around the lower ½ inch of the sides of the cake, and center a small clump of nuts in the middle of the top as well. Refrigerate the cake, unwrapped, until the glaze sets.

STORAGE: Keep in the refrigerator, wrapped airtight, for up to 3 days, but remove the cake 30 minutes before serving.

Rum Chestnut Chocolate Cake

The chestnuts bring a delicious texture and mysterious taste to what is really a simple cake. There are other versions of chestnut chocolate cake in this book, but this one is the easiest. If you can't find marrons glacés (glazed chestnuts), or don't care to make some yourself, spread apricot jam between the layers instead, and you'll still have a delicious, unusual cake.

Makes one 10-inch, 3-layer cake

Serves 12 to 14

Level of difficulty ★★

CAKE

8 ounces milk chocolate, finely chopped

1½ sticks (6 ounces) unsalted butter, cut into tablespoon-size pieces

2 cups (10-ounce can) unsweetened chestnuts, packed in water, drained

¼ cup Meyer's dark rum

6 large eggs, separated

1¼ cups (6 ounces) bleached all-purpose flour

2 tablespoons unsweetened cocoa powder

1 teaspoon baking powder

¼ teaspoon plus a pinch of salt

1½ cups (11.25 ounces) granulated sugar

FILLING AND FROSTING

2 cups store-bought marrons glacés, chopped, or Sugared Chestnuts (page 373)

1½ recipes Whipped Cream, plain or cocoa-flavored (page 318)

Alternate filling: 1 cup apricot preserves

TO MAKE THE CAKE

1. Position a rack in the center of the oven and preheat to 350°F. Lightly grease a 10 × 3-inch springform pan and line the bottom with a parchment or greased waxed paper circle.
2. In a mixing bowl or the top of a double boiler set over simmering water, melt the chocolate and butter, stirring occasionally. When melted, remove from the heat and set aside to cool to room temperature.
3. In the bowl of a food processor fitted with the steel blade, purée the chestnuts, rum, and egg yolks.
4. Sift the flour, cocoa, baking powder, and ¼ teaspoon salt into a large mixing bowl. Add 1 cup of the sugar and blend with a whisk. Stir the chestnut purée into the chocolate and butter.
5. With an electric mixer on medium speed, whip the egg whites with the pinch of salt until they form soft peaks. With the machine running, add the remaining ½ cup sugar, about 2 tablespoons at a time, and whip until the whites form glossy stiff peaks.
6. With a rubber spatula fold the egg whites into the chocolate-chestnut purée alternately with the dry ingredients. Spread the batter evenly in the prepared cake pan.
7. Set the pan on a larger baking pan to catch the drips, and bake for about 1 hour and 10 minutes, or until the cake begins to shrink from the sides of the pan and a cake tester inserted in the center comes out dry.
8. Cool the cake to room temperature in the pan on a wire rack. Unlock the springform and lift the cake up and out of the form. Remove the bottom of the pan and peel off the paper circle just before filling and frosting.

TO FILL AND FROST

1. Set the cake on a cardboard round cut slightly larger than the diameter of the cake. With a serrated knife, split the cake horizontally into 3 equal layers.
2. Spread ½ the chestnuts over one layer, then spread that with a thin layer of whipped cream. Repeat with the second cake layer, chestnuts, and

whipped cream; then finish with the third cake layer and refrigerate, uncovered, for 1 hour. (If you are not using the chestnuts, strain the apricot preserves through a sieve into a small saucepan and bring to a simmer, stirring continuously. Cool to room temperature and spread ¼ cup of strained preserves between each cake layer and sandwich them together.)

3. Spread the remaining whipped cream evenly around the sides and on top of the cake, and if you have any whipped cream left, use it to fill a pastry bag fitted with a ½-inch star tip and pipe a decorative circle of whipped-cream rosettes around the top outer edge of the cake. Refrigerate for at least 4 hours before serving.

STORAGE: Keep in the refrigerator, loosely covered, for up to 2 days.

White Chocolate Almond Cake

White chocolate lends a glorious velvety texture to any cake, although it does have an elusive flavor that almost disappears in the company of other tastes. This ethereal confection is similar to the dark chocolate Reine de Saba, but the white chocolate and almond paste make it taste and feel remarkably different. It is a rather sweet cake, so I finish it simply with a dusting of confectioners' sugar or a white chocolate glaze. I also like occasionally pairing the cake with a contrasting acidic taste, such as a spoonful of berries or a dice of fresh mango.

Makes one 9-inch, single-layer cake

Serves 10 to 12

Level of difficulty ★★

6 ounces white chocolate, finely chopped

1 stick (4 ounces) unsalted butter, cut into ½-inch dice

1 cup (3.5 ounces) blanched almonds (whole, slivered, or sliced)

¼ cup (2 ounces) almond paste

½ cup milk

1 teaspoon grated lemon zest

⅛ teaspoon plus a pinch of salt

4 large eggs, separated

¾ cup (5.5 ounces) granulated sugar

1 cup (4.75 ounces) bleached all-purpose flour

2 tablespoons confectioners' sugar, for garnish
   or
½ recipe White Chocolate Glaze (page 331)

1. Lightly grease a 9 × 3-inch springform pan, dust it with flour, and tap out the excess. In the top of a double boiler or a mixing bowl set over simmering water, melt the chocolate and butter, stirring occasionally. Transfer the mixture to a large bowl and set it aside.

2. Position a rack in the center of the oven and preheat to 350°F.

3. In a food processor fitted with the steel blade, pulverize the almonds with a pulsing motion until ground to a powder. Transfer the ground almonds to a mixing bowl. In the same food processor, blend the almond paste until smooth and then, with the machine running, drizzle in the milk to form a smooth paste. With a whisk, blend together the almond paste and milk mixture with the chocolate and butter mixture. Add the lemon zest, ⅛ teaspoon salt, the ground almonds, egg yolks, and ¼ cup of the sugar. Sift the flour over the ingredients and blend thoroughly.

4. With an electric mixer on medium speed, whip the egg whites with the pinch of salt until semistiff. With the machine running, slowly add the remaining ½ cup sugar in a steady stream and whip until the egg whites are stiff and glossy. With a rubber spatula, in two or three batches, fold the egg whites into the chocolate and almond mixture.

5. Transfer the batter to the prepared cake pan and set the pan on a baking sheet. Bake for 1 hour to 1 hour and 10 minutes, or until the cake begins to shrink from the sides of the pan and a tester inserted in the center comes out a bit moist.

6. Cool the cake to room temperature in the pan on a wire rack. Run a table knife or a metal spatula around the cake to loosen it from the sides of the pan. Unlock the springform and lift the cake up and out of the form. Invert the cake onto a cardboard round cut to the same dimension as the cake. Remove the bottom of the pan.

7. Just before serving, dust the top of the cake with confectioners' sugar, shaken through a very fine strainer. Or, if you are going to glaze the cake, ice the sides first. Pour the remaining glaze over the top of the cake and spread it across the top and over the edges. Spread any excess glaze that drips over the edges around the sides of the cake.

STORAGE: Keep in the refrigerator, wrapped airtight in plastic, for up to 3 days, but serve at room temperature.

PLATED DESSERT SUGGESTION (per portion)

¼ to ½ cup Fresh or Canned Mango Sauce (pages 365 and 366)

1 slice of cake, dusted with confectioners' sugar

Sour Cream Sauce, in a squeeze bottle (page 370)

3 blueberries or blackberries

Pour the mango sauce in the center of a 10-inch plate. Rotate the plate so you spread the mango sauce around the middle of the plate. Center the slice of cake in the sauce.

Squeeze 7 to 9 dots of sour cream sauce on top of and toward the out-side edge of the sauce. In a continuous circular motion, run the blunt end of a wooden skewer through the center of each sour cream dot, creating heart shapes. Randomly scatter the berries over the sauce, or set them in a clump to one side of the cake.

Cardamom Carrot Cocoa Cake

I did not come up with this particular combination of flavors because of the lovely allit-eration in the name, but because they blend to produce an intensely chocolate-tasting cake with a most unusual character and texture. So what do carrots add to a chocolate cake? They add some nutrition, of course (although that's not the point when you're baking a chocolate cake), but mostly they add moistness, sweetness, and a softly crunchy texture that complements the ground nuts.

Makes one 9-inch,
single-layer cake

Serves 8 to 10

Level of difficulty ★

CAKE

2¼ cups (8 ounces) blanched almonds or pecans

1½ cups (11.25 ounces) granulated sugar

½ pound carrots, trimmed and peeled

¼ teaspoon grated orange zest

½ cup (2.5 ounces) bleached all-purpose flour

½ cup (1.5 ounces) unsweetened, Dutch-processed cocoa powder

½ teaspoon ground cardamom

½ teaspoon baking soda

⅛ teaspoon salt

4 large eggs, separated

COCOA GLAZE

½ cup (2.75 ounces) confectioners' sugar, sifted

¼ cup (0.75 ounce) unsweetened, Dutch-processed cocoa powder, sifted

TO MAKE THE CAKE

1. Position a rack in the center of the oven and preheat to 350°F. Lightly grease a 9 × 3-inch springform pan and line the bottom with a parch-ment or greased waxed paper circle.
2. In a food processor fitted with the steel blade, use a pulsing motion to pulverize the nuts with 1 cup of the sugar until they are finely ground but not oily. Transfer the mixture to a bowl.
3. Fit the food processor with the grating attachment and grate the carrots. Add the carrots and orange zest to the nuts and sugar, and combine with a rubber spatula.
4. Sift the flour, cocoa, cardamom, baking soda, and salt into a mixing bowl.
5. Whip the egg whites with an electric mixer on medium speed until they form soft peaks. With the machine running, add the remaining ½ cup sugar, 2 tablespoons at a time, and whip until the whites are stiff and glossy.
6. Set the egg yolks in a small mixing bowl and break them up with a rubber spatula, then fold them into the whites. Sift the dry ingredients over the beaten egg whites and fold them in. When the dry ingredients are almost entirely folded into the batter, fold in the carrots and nut mixture; the batter will be quite sticky.
7. Spread the batter evenly in the prepared pan and bake for 1 hour. Lower the heat to 325° and bake for 25 to 30 minutes more, or until the cake looks set. Turn off the oven, prop the oven door open with a wooden spoon, and leave the cake in the oven for 30 minutes longer. (Because this is such a moist cake, it needs to dry out rather than bake through at a higher heat, when the edges and outside would be overdone.)
8. Cool the cake in the pan on a wire rack for 15 minutes. Unlock the springform, lift the cake up and out of the form, and cool to room tem-perature on the wire rack. Remove the bottom of the pan and peel off the paper circle just before glazing.

TO GLAZE

1. Sift the confectioners' sugar again with the cocoa powder into a mixing bowl. Add 2 tablespoons of water and combine with a fork; add more water, if needed, to achieve a slightly pourable glaze.

2. Pour the glaze over the top and around the edges of the cake so the glaze drips down the sides. With a table knife, or small offset spatula, spread the glaze very thinly over the top, then spread the glaze that drips down the edges of the cake around the sides.

STORAGE: Keep at room temperature, loosely wrapped, for up to 2 days; refrigerate after that.

Chocolate Beet Cake

Here's a novelty cake: one made with beets! I discovered cakes made with vegetables when, from 1994 to 1995, I was host of the Food Network's show entitled "Feeding Your Family on $99 a week." It was a daily program that culminated every Friday evening with a live call-in show. On Fridays, I would often have a guest on the air and take questions from the viewers. One night my guest was an editor from a parenting magazine, and the discussion centered on how to get kids to eat their vegetables. The editor brought with her several cakes made with vegetables, among them a chocolate one made with beets, and while I am grateful to her for this inspiration, I am still not convinced that it's the best way to get your kids to eat their vegetables! When you make the cake, the batter smells a little odd, but once it's baked, the cake tastes intensely of chocolate and is most delectable. It also provides good dinnertime conversation, as no one will ever guess it was made with a vegetable, let alone one so many people dislike.

Makes one 9-inch, 2-layer cake

Serves 12 to 14

Level of difficulty ★

2 cups coarsely chopped, freshly cooked or canned beets

1 cup vegetable oil

2 cups (9.5 ounces) bleached all-purpose flour

¾ teaspoon baking powder

½ teaspoon baking soda

¼ teaspoon salt

3 large eggs

1½ cups (11.25 ounces) granulated sugar

4 ounces unsweetened chocolate, melted and cooled

1 recipe Vanilla Frosting, orange variation (page 301)

1. Position a rack in the center of the oven and preheat to 375°F. Lightly grease a 9 × 2-inch round cake pan and line the bottom with a parchment or greased waxed paper circle.

2. In a food processor fitted with the steel blade, purée the beets with ¼ cup of the oil. Sift the flour, baking powder, baking soda, and salt into a mixing bowl.

3. With an electric mixer on medium speed, beat the eggs with the sugar for 2 minutes, or until the mixture looks light and airy. Lower the speed and slowly drizzle in the remaining ¾ cup oil. With a rubber spatula, fold the beets and chocolate into the eggs, then fold in the dry ingredients. Spread the batter evenly in the prepared pan.

4. Bake for 50 minutes to 1 hour, or until a tester inserted in the center comes out almost dry. Cool the cake in the pan on a wire rack for 30 minutes, then turn it out of the pan and cool to room temperature right side up, on the paper, on a wire rack. Peel off the paper circle when cool.

5. With a serrated knife, split the cake in half horizontally and set the bottom half on a cake round cut slightly larger than the cake. Spread the cake with a thin layer of frosting (some crumbs will stick to the frosting, but don't worry). Set the top half over the frosting, making sure the two layers are lined up.

6. Spread more frosting over the top and around the sides.

STORAGE: Keep in the refrigerator, loosely covered, for up to 5 days.

Chocolate Zucchini Quick Bread

Quick breads taste and feel a lot more like cake than they do bread and derive their name, perhaps, from the fact that they are baked in a bread pan. Whatever the origin of the name, this "quick bread" has a terrifically moist crumb, thanks to the zucchini, and a perfectly lovely taste. Because it is not cloyingly sweet, it is great as a weekend breakfast treat.

Makes one 9 × 5-inch loaf cake

Serves 10 to 12

Level of difficulty ★

½ pound zucchini

Salt

1½ cups (7 ounces) bleached all-purpose flour

⅓ cup (1 ounce) unsweetened, nonalkalized cocoa powder

½ teaspoon baking powder

¼ teaspoon baking soda

¼ teaspoon ground allspice

2 large eggs

½ cup (3.75 ounces) granulated sugar

½ cup packed (3.75 ounces) light brown sugar

¾ stick (3 ounces) unsalted butter, melted and cooled

1 cup (3.5 ounces) walnuts or pecans, coarsely chopped

1. In a food processor, grate the zucchini, toss it with salt, and transfer it to a sieve set over a bowl for 30 minutes. With your hands, squeeze out the excess moisture and set aside.
2. Position a rack in the center of the oven and preheat to 350°F. Lightly grease a 9 × 5 × 3-inch loaf pan and line the bottom with parchment or greased waxed paper.
3. Sift the flour with the cocoa, baking powder, baking soda, allspice, and ¼ teaspoon salt.
4. With an electric mixer on medium speed, beat the eggs with the white and brown sugars for about 2 minutes, or until smooth and thick looking. Gradually add the butter and beat until blended.
5. With a rubber spatula, fold the dry ingredients into the wet ones along with the zucchini and nuts. Transfer the batter to the prepared pan and rap the pan sharply on the counter a couple of times to break up any large air bubbles.
6. Bake for 45 to 55 minutes, or until a tester inserted in the center comes out dry. Cool the cake to room temperature in the pan on a wire rack. Invert the cake and peel off the paper.

STORAGE: Keep at room temperature, wrapped airtight in plastic, for up to 3 days in a cool place.

Date and Walnut Chocolate Cake

This is an amazingly moist cake with such an intense chocolate flavor that all you need as embellishment is a spoonful of whipped cream on the side. The lemon flavor, added in small doses, is surprisingly pleasing with the chocolate.

Makes one 10-inch, single-layer cake

Serves 12 to 14

Level of difficulty ★

1½ cups pitted dates

¾ cup (3.5 ounces) bleached all-purpose flour

½ teaspoon baking powder

¼ teaspoon baking soda

⅛ teaspoon salt

6 large eggs

1½ cups (11.25 ounces) granulated sugar

4 ounces unsweetened chocolate, melted and cooled

1½ cups (5.25 ounces) walnuts, finely ground

1 teaspoon lemon extract

1 teaspoon grated lemon zest

1. Position a rack in the lower third of the oven and preheat to 375°F. Lightly grease a 10 × 3-inch springform pan and line the bottom with a parchment or greased waxed paper circle.
2. With scissors, cut the dates into pieces about ⅜ inch thick.
3. Sift the flour with the baking powder, baking soda, and salt into a mixing bowl.
4. With an electric mixer on medium speed, beat the eggs with the sugar for about 1 minute, or until the mixture looks like mayonnaise. With a rubber spatula, fold the chocolate into the eggs along with the walnuts, lemon extract, lemon zest, sifted flour mixture, and dates. Spread the batter evenly in the prepared cake pan.
5. Bake for 30 minutes, then lower the temperature to 350°F and bake for 20 to 30 minutes longer, or until the cake begins to shrink from the sides of the pan and a cake tester inserted in the center comes out almost dry.
6. Remove the cake to a wire rack to cool in the pan for 20 minutes. Unlock the springform, lift the cake up and out of the pan, and cool to room temperature on a wire rack. Invert the cake to remove the bottom of the pan and peel off the paper when the cake is cooled, but serve it right side up.

STORAGE: Keep at room temperature, wrapped airtight in plastic, for up to 5 days; this keeps on improving with age.

Prune and Ginger Chocolate Cake

Everyone laughs at the mere mention of prunes, but in reality they have a great affinity for chocolate. In this recipe, puréed prunes soaked in Armagnac give the cake a velvety moistness not unlike that of butter, but without the fat. The ground almonds add texture and the tiny bits of crystallized ginger provide a lovely counterpoint to the sweetness of the prunes.

Makes one 9-inch, single-layer cake

Serves 10

Level of difficulty ★

---

1 cup packed (8 ounces) pitted prunes

¼ cup Armagnac, cognac, or brandy

1 cup (4.75 ounces) bleached all-purpose flour

½ teaspoon baking powder

½ teaspoon baking soda

¼ teaspoon salt

½ teaspoon ground ginger

3 large eggs

¾ cup (5.5 ounces) granulated sugar

6 ounces bittersweet chocolate, melted and cooled

¾ cup (3 ounces) blanched almonds, finely ground

¼ cup (1.5 ounces) crystallized ginger

Superfine or vanilla sugar, for dusting

---

1. Marinate the prunes in the Armagnac for 2 hours, then purée them in their liquid with ½ cup water in a food processor fitted with the steel blade.
2. Position a rack in the center of the oven and preheat to 350°F. Lightly grease a 9 × 2-inch round cake pan and line the bottom with a parchment or greased waxed paper circle.
3. Sift the flour, baking powder, baking soda, salt, and ground ginger into a mixing bowl.
4. With an electric beater on medium speed, beat the eggs and sugar until the mixture looks like mayonnaise. With a rubber spatula, fold the prune purée into the eggs, then fold in the chocolate, almonds, ginger, and sifted dry ingredients. Spread the batter evenly in the prepared cake pan.
5. Bake for 50 minutes to 1 hour, or until the cake begins to shrink from the sides of the pan and a tester inserted in the center comes out dry.
6. Cool the cake to room temperature in the pan on a wire rack. Run a table knife or metal spatula around the cake to loosen it from the pan. When cool, invert the cake onto a plate or cardboard round and peel off the paper circle. Just before serving, dust the top with sugar.

STORAGE: Keep at room temperature, wrapped airtight, for up to 3 days; refrigerate after that.

PLATED DESSERT SUGGESTION (per portion)

Deadly Delicious Chocolate Sauce (page 362)
1 slice of cake

Crystallized ginger
Whipped Cream, plain or ginger-flavored (page 318)

Spoon some warm chocolate sauce in the middle of a dessert plate and center the slice of cake on the sauce. Scatter a few bits of crystallized ginger over the sauce and spoon some whipped cream on top of the slice of cake.

CHEESECAKES

HOW TO BAKE a cheesecake so its surface doesn't crack invites endless discussion among enthusiastic bakers, with every convert to a particular technique convinced hers is the only method worth considering. One camp of bakers swears by the water bath, but I begged off that method one day when, for some reason, a little bit of water seeped into my cake crust.

Then there is the other camp, to which I belong, that believes in baking the cake, as is, in a slow and steady manner. I have found this to be a straightforward, reliable, and effective method provided you don't lose patience, because the key to success is to bake the cake for a long time at a low temperature. It has also been said never to bake a cheesecake in a convection oven because the air circulated by the fan dries it out. I had no choice but to bake my cheesecakes in a convection oven when I worked in a restaurant, and they came out fine—smooth as silk and delicious. They worked out well because I baked them at such low heat for an unusually long time. Anyway, if in the end your cake does exhibit the smallest of fissures on its surface, don't worry; remember, you're not in the professional pastry-selling business, and your cakes will taste divine no matter what slight imperfections they exhibit.

Springform pans are best for baking cheesecakes because you can easily remove the finished cake from the pan. Over time, however, springform pans tend to warp, and the perfect seal between sides and bottom is broken, so the batter leaks. To ensure this doesn't happen, wrap the outside of the form with a layer of aluminum foil, then set the wrapped pan on a baking sheet so that if, by chance, there is a tear in the foil and some batter does leak, at least it won't ruin your oven floor.

Be sure all ingredients are at room temperature before you start; this will make it easier to produce a homogeneous batter.

While you want to soften and cream the cheese so you achieve a smooth batter and ultimately a silky cake, you don't want to incorporate too much air or your cake might end up with big, ugly air bubbles on its surface, or it might rise too much, then sink in the middle and crack as it cools. If at all possible, use the paddle attachment of a stationary mixer to blend the cheese with the sugar, but if you must use standard beaters, be sure to cream the cheese and sugar on the lowest speed possible.

Be sure to scrape the sides of the bowl down every now and then with a rubber spatula or a plastic scraper as you cream the cheese and sugar so that the finished cake is free of cream cheese lumps.

Another way of ensuring a smooth and silky cake is to be patient with the creaming process. Make sure the cream cheese and sugar are completely blended and smooth before you begin to add the eggs. Take care to add the eggs one at a time and to incorporate one thoroughly before adding the next one. If you don't do this, and the eggs or other liquid ingredients are added too quickly, your batter will be lumpy and it will be hard to redistribute and integrate the chunks of cheese. (If this does happen, though, try as best you can to blend the bits of cheese by vigorously whisking them into the batter with a wire whip.)

Don't bake the cakes longer than recommended, even though they might appear wobbly in the center; they will firm up while standing and cooling.

It is easiest to slice the cake if you leave it on the bottom of the springform pan. If you have to transfer the baked cake to a cardboard round, be sure to chill it first overnight so that it is firm and easy to handle. To help release the cake from the pan with the crust intact, run the point of a paring knife around the entire cake between the crust and the pan. Then insert a 12-inch flat metal icing spatula between the crust and the bottom of the pan, and work it under the entire cake. Lift the cake with the spatula, steady it with your other hand, and transfer it to the cardboard round.

Many of you know this trick, but it bears repeating: For the neatest of slices, cut a cheesecake with unwaxed dental floss rather than a knife. Wrap a long strand of floss around a couple of fingers of one hand, and hold it taut with the other hand. Press the floss down through the cake all the way through the crust. Pull the floss out of the cake from the bottom. Repeat, making cuts of the desired width as you would were you using a knife.

Cheesecakes store well in the refrigerator for up to 10 days, and they freeze beautifully. To freeze, chill the cake first, then transfer it to a cardboard round. Wrap the cake in a double thickness of plastic wrap, then in freezer paper, and freeze for up to a month.

Chocolate Cheesecake

In general, I am not especially fond of chocolate cheesecakes, but I love this one because it tastes and feels like chocolate mousse. As with all cheesecakes, a sliver goes a long way. If you have the patience of Job and absolutely insist your cheesecake be fissure-free, leave the cake in the oven after baking, with the heat turned off, for an hour before cooling it.

Makes one
9-inch cake

Serves 10 to 12

Level of difficulty ★

24 (5.5 ounces) plain chocolate wafers, broken into pieces

3 tablespoons (1.5 ounces) unsalted butter, melted

6 ounces bittersweet chocolate, finely chopped

½ stick (2 ounces) unsalted butter, cut into 1-inch chunks

1½ pounds cream cheese, at room temperature

1 cup (7.5 ounces) granulated sugar

2 tablespoons unsweetened cocoa powder

3 large eggs

1 teaspoon vanilla extract

1 cup sour cream, at room temperature

1. Position a rack in the center of the oven and preheat to 300°F. Lightly butter the bottom only of a 9 × 3-inch springform pan, and wrap the outside of the pan with foil to prevent leakage.

2. In a food processor fitted with the steel blade, pulverize the chocolate cookies into crumbs (you'll have about 1¼ cups). Transfer the crumbs to a mixing bowl, add the melted butter, and combine with a rubber spatula. With your fingers press the crumb mixture over the bottom of the springform pan, reaching all the way to the sides so it forms a bit of a seal against leakage.

3. In a mixing bowl or the top of a double boiler set over simmering water, melt the chocolate and chopped butter, stirring occasionally. Set aside to cool to room temperature.

4. Beat the cream cheese with an electric mixer (or a stationary mixer fitted with the paddle attachment) on low speed for 2 minutes, or until soft and creamy. Scrape down the beaters and sides of the bowl. Add the sugar and cocoa, and continue to beat slowly for 2 minutes longer, scraping down the sides of the bowl as necessary.

5. Add the eggs, one at a time, beating well after each addition. Add the melted chocolate, vanilla, and sour cream, and blend with a rubber spatula until the batter is smooth and homogenized.

6. Pour the batter into the prepared pan and set the pan on a baking sheet. Bake for 15 minutes, lower the heat to 275°F, and bake for 1 hour and 30 to 45 minutes longer, or until the edges just begin to pull away from the sides of the pan and the top looks puffy and no longer wet. The cake will still appear wobbly, but you want it that way so it will be creamy and moist.

7. Remove the cake to a wire rack and cool it in the pan for 1 hour. Unlock the springform and lift out the cake, but leave it on the metal base. Cool the cake to room temperature, then refrigerate for at least 4 hours before serving or even attempting to remove the cake from the bottom of the springform pan.

STORAGE: Keep in the refrigerator, wrapped airtight in plastic, for up to 5 days, but remove the cheesecake 1 hour before serving. You can also freeze this cake for a couple of months.

White Chocolate Cheesecake

While this cake is somewhat plain, it is scrumptious nonetheless.

Makes one
9-inch cake

Serves 10 to 12

Level of difficulty ★

22 (5 ounces) 2-inch-square
chocolate graham crackers

3 tablespoons (1.5 ounces)
unsalted butter, melted

1½ pounds cream cheese, at
room temperature

1 cup (7.5 ounces) granulated
sugar

10 ounces white chocolate,
melted and cooled

4 large eggs

½ cup heavy cream

1 teaspoon vanilla extract

1. Position a rack in the center of the oven and preheat to 300°F. Lightly butter a 9 × 2.5-inch springform pan and wrap the outside of the pan with foil to prevent leakage.

2. In a food processor fitted with the steel blade, pulverize the graham crackers into crumbs (you'll have about 1¼ cups). Transfer the crumbs to a mixing bowl, add the melted butter, and combine with a rubber spatula. With your fingers, press the crumb mixture over the bottom of the springform pan, reaching all the way to the sides so it forms a bit of a seal against leakage.

3. Beat the cream cheese with an electric mixer (or a stationary mixer fitted with the paddle attachment) on low speed for 2 minutes, or until soft and creamy. Scrape down the beaters and sides of the bowl. With the machine running, add the sugar, about ¼ cup at a time, and continue to beat for 2 minutes longer, scraping down the sides of the bowl as needed.

4. Add the chocolate, then the eggs, one at a time, beating well after each addition. Add the cream and vanilla, and blend with a rubber spatula until the batter is smooth and homogenized.

5. Pour the batter into the prepared pan and set the pan on a baking sheet. Bake for 15 minutes, lower the heat to 275°F, and bake for 1 hour and 10 to 20 minutes longer, or until the edges just begin to pull away from the sides of the pan and the top looks puffy. Don't worry if the center appears jiggly—this means the cake will be creamy and moist.

6. Remove the cake to a wire rack and cool it in the pan for 30 minutes. Unlock the springform and lift out the cake, but leave it on the metal base. Cool the cake to room temperature, then refrigerate for at least 4 hours or, preferably, overnight.

STORAGE: Keeps in the refrigerator, wrapped airtight in plastic, for several days. Remove the cheesecake 1 hour before serving. You can also freeze this cake for a couple of months.

White and Black Chocolate Cheesecake

This cheesecake, with its generous amount of dark and white chocolates, is incredibly rich. This is to consider for a holiday dinner party or as a centerpiece on a buffet table because it can be made days ahead of serving. A nice touch, which cuts the richness of the cake, is to serve some peeled fresh orange segments on the side.

Makes one
10-inch cake

Serves 16 to 20

Level of difficulty ★★

---

22 (5 ounces) 2-inch-square
graham crackers

¾ stick (3 ounces) unsalted
butter, melted

6 ounces bittersweet chocolate,
very finely chopped

2½ pounds cream cheese, at
room temperature

1¾ cups (13 ounces) granulated
sugar

1 teaspoon grated orange zest

3 tablespoons bleached
all-purpose flour

⅓ cup heavy cream

5 large eggs

4 ounces white chocolate,
melted and cooled

6 ounces unsweetened
chocolate, melted and cooled

---

1. Position a rack in the lower third of the oven and preheat to 350°F. Lightly butter the bottom only of a 10 × 3-inch springform pan, and wrap the outside of the pan with foil to prevent leakage.

2. In a food processor fitted with the steel blade, pulverize the graham crackers into crumbs. (You'll have about 1¼ cups.) Transfer the crumbs to a mixing bowl, add the melted butter, and mix with a rubber spatula. With your fingers, press the crumb mixture over the bottom of the springform pan, reaching all the way to the sides so it forms a bit of a seal against leakage. Bake for 10 minutes.

3. Remove the pan from the oven and immediately scatter the chopped chocolate evenly over the crust. Return the pan to the oven for a minute to melt the chocolate, remove it from the oven, and with a small offset spatula or the back of a spoon, quickly spread the chocolate over the crust. Set aside and lower the heat to 300°F.

4. With an electric mixer (or a stationary mixer fitted with the paddle attachment) on low speed, beat the cream cheese for 2 minutes, or until soft and creamy, scraping down the sides of the bowl as needed. With the machine running, add the sugar, ¼ cup at a time, beating well after each addition. Add the orange zest, flour, and cream, and continue to beat slowly until homogenized. Add the eggs, one at a time, beating for 15 seconds between additions to make sure each one is thoroughly incorporated.

5. Pour 3 cups of the batter into a separate bowl and blend in the white chocolate. Blend the unsweetened chocolate into the remaining batter.

6. Alternately and randomly spoon the dark and white batters into the prepared pan. With a knife, or the blunt end of a wooden skewer, swirl the chocolate batter into the white one, but don't over mix.

7. Set the pan on a baking sheet and bake for 1 hour. Lower the heat to 250°F and bake for 50 minutes to 1 hour longer, or until the batter does not look wet. The cake will still appear wobbly, but that is okay.

8. Remove the cake to a wire rack and cool it to room temperature in the pan. Unlock the springform and lift out the cake, but leave it on the metal base. Chill the cake in the refrigerator for at least 4 hours before serving.

STORAGE: Keep in the refrigerator, wrapped airtight in plastic, for up to 5 days. Remove the cheesecake 30 minutes before serving. You can also freeze this cake for a couple of months.

**Berry White Chocolate Cheesecake

This amazingly delicious cake is made with fresh berries and white chocolate. It smells divine while baking and tastes extraordinary when served slightly warm from the oven. Chill the cake to store it, but bring it back to room temperature before serving. The ricotta cheese makes the texture of this cheesecake coarser than those made only with cream cheese.

Makes one
9-inch cake

Serves 12

Level of difficulty ★

22 (5 ounces) 2-inch-square graham crackers

4 tablespoons (2 ounces) unsalted butter, melted

½ cup plus 2 tablespoons (4.75 ounces) granulated sugar

¼ pound cream cheese, at room temperature

2 cartons (15 to 16 ounces each) whole-milk ricotta cheese, at room temperature

2 teaspoons grated lemon zest

3 tablespoons bleached all-purpose flour

4 large eggs

10 ounces white chocolate, melted and cooled

1 cup fresh raspberries

1 cup fresh blueberries

Very Berry Compote (page 372), optional

Additional berries and confectioners' sugar, optional

1. Position a rack in the center of the oven and preheat to 350°F. Lightly butter the bottom only of a 9 × 3-inch springform pan and wrap the outside of the pan with foil to prevent leakage.

2. In a food processor fitted with the steel blade, pulverize the graham crackers into crumbs. (You'll have about 1¼ cups.) Transfer the crumbs to a mixing bowl, add the melted butter and 2 tablespoons of the sugar, and mix with a rubber spatula. With your fingers, press the crumb mixture over the bottom of the springform pan, reaching all the way to the sides so it forms a bit of a seal against leakage. Bake for 10 minutes and set it aside. Lower the heat to 325°F.

3. With an electric mixer (or a stationary mixer fitted with the paddle attachment) on low speed, beat the cream cheese and the remaining ½ cup sugar until blended. Add the ricotta cheese, lemon zest, flour, and eggs, one at a time, beating well after each addition. Fold in the white chocolate.

4. Combine the raspberries and blueberries in a bowl. Fold ½ the berries into the cheese mixture and pour the batter into the pan, spreading it evenly over the crust. Scatter the remaining berries over the top, and with a table knife or a rubber spatula, gently push the berries halfway down into the batter (you should still see them clearly on top).

5. Bake for 1 hour and 30 to 45 minutes, or until the cake is golden brown and has barely set (the batter will still be a bit wobbly when you remove it from the oven, but it will firm as it cools). Turn off the oven and leave the cake inside with the door ajar, for 45 minutes longer.

6. Remove the cake to a wire rack and cool it to room temperature in the pan. Run a knife around the cake to loosen it from the pan, and unlock the springform. Remove the cake from the springform, but leave it on the metal base.

7. Serve the cake at room temperature, either plain, with a small portion of Very Berry Compote on the side, or topped with more berries with confectioners' sugar sifted over the top.

STORAGE: Keep in the refrigerator, wrapped airtight, for up to 3 days.

BUTTER AND SHORTENED CAKES

$\mathcal{C}$AKES FALL INTO two broad categories: the high-in-fat, "shortened" group of cakes like pound, tea, and layer cakes, and the low-in-fat "egg-foam" cakes like sponge and angel food cakes. What distinguishes the high-fat cakes from the lean ones is that they are rich in butter, shortening, or oil as well as in sugar, and are usually leavened with baking powder or baking soda. These high-fat cakes feel like velvet on the tongue, are light in crumb, moist, and are put together by what we call the "creaming" technique.

Grouped together at the beginning of this chapter is a lovely collection of plain pound and tea cakes, some baked in loaf tins, others in Bundt pans; some are pure chocolate, others are marbled, and some are chock-full of spices, nuts, and even booze. Most are served plain, others need the kiss of a glaze, and all are perfect candidates for plated dessert presentations.

Recipes for stacked and frosted layer cakes follow the more austere pound cakes. At the front of this section are recipes for basic chocolate cake layers that are the building blocks for filled cakes. There is an astonishing variety of basic chocolate layer recipes, so I have included a selection that covers just about every way of making them. There are buttermilk and sour cream chocolate layers, cocoa and melted chocolate layers, chocolate nut layers, and white chocolate layers. To help you make a choice, the most chocolate-tasting of these recipes are the cakes made with cocoa powder, not melted chocolate. You'll also find a couple of recipes for yellow and white cake layers because in the South of the United States, a chocolate cake is a yellow cake filled with chocolate frosting.

These chocolate cake layers assume unique identities if you eat the cake on its own, without icing, but their differences diminish quite a bit after the layers are filled and frosted. For each of the basic chocolate cake layers, I suggest the icing I like best. But to give you more flexibility, almost all the different basic cake recipes are baked in 9-inch round pans so you can mix and match different frostings with different cakes.

After the recipes for basic layers are recipes for cakes matched with specific frostings, like the Boston "Blackout" Cake, Aztec Devil's Food Cake, and Michele's German Chocolate Cake.

Layer cakes are so rich and filling, you should serve them unadorned or, at most, on plates decorated with a dusting of cocoa powder or a few artistic squiggles of chocolate sauce.

BUILDING THE CAKES

Creaming Method

The technique used to mix these shortened cakes, called the creaming method, makes the cakes delicate, high, and light. The purpose of the creaming process is to create an emulsion and develop small air bubbles that are uniformly distributed throughout the batter.

Creaming also lays the foundation upon which the cake rises. In creaming the fat and sugar, the facets of the sugar crystals cut into the fat, providing microscopic openings into which air gets trapped. When the cake hits the oven, the steam (created by heat) causes the air to expand, and this lifts the cake to its desired height. In some pound cakes, where no

chemical leavener is used, a complete and thorough creaming process is essential because it is the only way to get air into the batter and, ultimately, volume into the cake. But even when you add baking powder or baking soda to a cake batter, the creaming process is still essential because the gases created by these chemical leaveners don't create the air pockets; they merely enlarge the ones already set in place by the creaming process.

Assembling the Batter

For the proper emulsion to take place, all the ingredients must be between 68° and 70°F. Fat that is too cold isn't malleable enough to wrap around the air bubbles and tends to break them, whereas fat that is too warm melts, and the air bubbles dissolve.

It is best and easiest to use an electric mixer to make these cakes, preferably a stationary one fitted with the paddle attachment. The paddle attachment beats in just enough air to create small air cells without drawing an excess of air, which can cause too much aeration, which translates into big holes in your cakes. Begin on low speed, because the first air cells are fragile and break easily. You can increase the speed to medium after you have added some of the sugar, but if you beat the ingredients at too high a speed, the heat generated by the added friction will melt the butter and break the air bubbles.

During the mixing process, an electric mixer will throw some of the batter against the sides of the bowl, and the beaters will get clogged with fat. So that you are guaranteed a homogeneously mixed batter, stop the machine every now and then, scrape down the sides of the bowl and the beaters, and then resume mixing.

Creaming the Fat

Begin by beating the softened fat for about 1 minute, so it begins to draw in air and get ready to absorb the sugar. If you are using shortening that was stored in the refrigerator, remove it a couple of hours ahead of time so it is at the right temperature. Even though I prefer the flavor of butter and use it almost exclusively, it is not as good an emulsifier as solid vegetable shortening. Shortening is a great emulsifier because it melts at a higher temperature than butter and so keeps its shape long enough before melting for the flour and other ingredients to set up around the air cells. (For cakes especially high in sugar and liquids, professionals use a "high-ratio" shortening, which contains emulsifiers that hold even greater amounts of liquid.)

Adding the Sugar

The next step is to add the sugar. Superfine rather than granulated sugar is recommended because it helps develop a finely woven, airy texture in the finished cake. The small crystals of superfine sugar have more facets that cut more, smaller air pockets in the fat. Add the sugar slowly, about 2 tablespoons at a time, so that a good cell structure begins to take shape and the batter will be strong enough to hold in the liquid. Add the next amount of sugar only after the first amount has disappeared into the fat. Depending on how much sugar you are adding, this process can take from 2 to 3 minutes. I have worked in professional kitchens where creaming pounds of butter with pounds of sugar took me 20 to 30 minutes, and even longer during the dead of winter when the kitchen was cold.

Adding the Eggs

Eggs are another key ingredient in these butter cakes because the yolk itself is a natural emulsifier. Remove the eggs from the refrigerator about 20 minutes before you are ready to assemble the batter. If you forget to do this, set the eggs in their shells in a bowl of warm water, and they will be ready to use within minutes. If your batter curdles, as it can with some of the pound cakes, which call for so many eggs, mix 1 to 2 tablespoons of the flour into the batter and continue beating. If your batter curdles because the room or the eggs are too cold, warm the bowl, with the ingredients in it. To do this, hold the mixing bowl over an open flame for just a few seconds, rotating it constantly so the ingredients don't get too hot. When the bowl feels warm, resume mixing.

Adding the Flour

The last part of the mixing process that affects the structure of the cake is the kind of flour you add, how you mix it in, and how you combine it with the liquids.

Use cake or pastry flour, made from soft wheat, because it develops less gluten and is high in starch, which allows the cake to absorb more liquid, which means it will be moist. Some of these cakes—those that have nuts or dried fruits added to the batter—need a stronger all-purpose or bread flour to hold up the weight of these ingredients.

Because cake flour tends to lump, it must be sifted before you add it to the creamed butter and sugar. If you are using chemical leaveners, the flour must also be sifted with these so the leaveners are evenly distributed throughout the flour and won't clump in one spot, possibly leaving your cakes with unsightly holes.

When you are ready to combine the dry sifted ingredients with the liquid ones, don't dump all the liquids in at once and mix. Instead, gradually add the flour alternately with the liquid, beginning and ending with the flour. This is so that the liquid ingredients have something to adhere to in the batter and the batter can be homogeneously mixed.

To develop just the right amount of gluten so the

cake has structure, but not so much that it becomes tough and chewy, begin by blending the flour and liquids by hand, then switch back to the electric mixer and beat for a couple of minutes.

Two-Stage Mixing

Cakes that are higher in sugar and liquid call for a slightly different method of mixing, an easier one that resembles the mix-and-dump batter cakes from the first chapter. This is called the two-stage method of mixing. Combine and mix the dry ingredients and then blend in the fat until it is broken down into small particles. The liquid ingredients are combined with each other and slowly added to the dry ones. The unbaked batter is quite runny, and the baked cake is extremely moist. This method is used for cakes made with solid vegetable shortening or for cakes that don't contain quite enough fat to use the creaming method.

OVEN HEAT AND BAKING

Most high-fat cakes are baked at 350°F, which is hot enough so that the moisture in the batter turns to steam quickly and the cake rises as much as possible before the proteins and starches set its structure. However, when there is a large volume of batter in the pan, begin baking at 350° so the proteins set, but after a while, lower the temperature to 325° to allow the interior to cook through without overbaking the outside.

If the temperature of the oven is set too low, it takes too long for the batter to bake through and the cake will be dry. Conversely, if the oven is set too high, the cake will set unevenly, a dome might develop in its center, or it might be flat because the proteins have set before the cake had enough time to expand fully.

CHECKLIST FOR CREAMED BUTTER CAKES

- Have the ingredients at room temperature; butter is softened.
- Beat fat slowly for a moment, or until light, before adding the sugar.
- Add sugar slowly, not faster than about 2 tablespoons at a time.
- Be patient with the creaming process; do it slowly and methodically.
- Add eggs one at a time, adding the next only after the first is absorbed into the butter and sugar.
- Every now and then scrape down the beaters and the sides of the bowl to make sure all the ingredients get mixed.
- Incorporate the dry and liquid ingredients alternately into the batter, always beginning and ending with the dry ingredients.

BEFORE YOU BEGIN, READ ABOUT

- Preheating the oven and positioning of racks (page 52)
- How to measure ingredients (page 51)
- Preparing pans (page 52)
- How to melt chocolate (page 33)
- How to sift (page 16)
- How to whip egg whites (page 11)
- Testing for doneness (page 54)
- Cooling cakes (page 55)
- How to slice cakes (page 339)
- How to fill and frost two and three cake layers (page 341)
- How to decorate whole cakes (page 335)
- About plated desserts (page 351)

Dependable Chocolate Pound Cake

This pound cake is infinitely satisfying and dependably right for all occasions. In years past, a pound cake was composed of equal weights—1 pound each—of butter, eggs, flour, and sugar. The only leavener in the cake was the air whipped into the batter by some poor housewife who beat these heavy ingredients together by hand. Today, thanks to the electric mixer, a pound cake is no longer such a big deal to make. You can serve this basic chocolate cake plain or dusted with confectioners' sugar, with whipped cream or ice cream, glazed or with fruit, and, of course, it is the perfect candidate for just about any and all plated dessert presentations.

Makes one 9 × 5-inch loaf cake

Serves 10 to 12

Level of difficulty ★

1¾ cups plus 1 tablespoon (8 ounces) cake flour

Scant ⅔ cup (2 ounces) unsweetened, Dutch-processed cocoa powder

1 teaspoon baking powder

¼ teaspoon salt

2 sticks (8 ounces) unsalted butter, softened

1 generous cup (8 ounces) superfine sugar

4 large eggs

2 teaspoons vanilla extract

¼ cup water or milk

---

1. Position a rack in the lower third of the oven and preheat to 350°F. Grease a 9 × 5 × 3-inch loaf pan, dust it with flour, and tap out the excess. Line the bottom with parchment or greased and floured waxed paper.

2. Sift the flour with the cocoa, baking powder, and salt twice, and set it aside.

3. With an electric mixer on low speed (or with a stationary mixer fitted with the paddle attachment), beat the butter for about 1 minute, or until light. Slowly add the sugar, about 2 tablespoons at a time (this should take 2 to 3 minutes). When all the sugar is added, continue to beat on medium speed for 2 to 3 minutes longer, scraping down the beaters and sides of the bowl as needed. Beat until the mixture looks fluffy, like something between mayonnaise and whipped cream.

4. Add the eggs, one at a time, beating for 10 seconds between additions, or until each egg is absorbed by the butter. Scrape down the beaters and sides of the bowl and beat for another minute, then add the vanilla.

5. With a large rubber spatula, fold the sifted ingredients into the batter in three additions, alternating with the water in two additions. Once the ingredients are combined, beat the batter with the electric mixer on low speed for another minute, or until smooth.

6. Transfer the batter to the prepared pan, smooth the top, and rap the pan sharply on the counter a couple of times to break up any large air bubbles. Bake for about 1 hour and 10 minutes, or until a tester inserted in the center comes out dry.

7. Cool the cake in the pan on a wire rack for 30 minutes. Lightly coat the wire rack with nonstick vegetable spray. Tip the pan on its side, ease out the cake, and cool to room temperature on the greased wire rack, right side up. Peel off the paper after the cake is cool.

STORAGE: Keep at room temperature, wrapped airtight in plastic, for up to 3 days; refrigerate after that.

GLAZED CHOCOLATE POUND CAKE

After cooling, glaze the top only with ½ cup of Maria's Best Chocolate Glaze (page 331), Chocolate Satin Glaze (page 330), or Midnight Icing (page 326).

SPICY CHOCOLATE POUND CAKE

Add and sift into the flour, cocoa, and baking soda, ½ to 1 teaspoon ground spices such as allspice, cinnamon, mace, or nutmeg.

CHIPPED CHOCOLATE POUND CAKE

Just before transferring the batter to the pan, fold in 1 cup bittersweet, milk, or white chocolate chips, or peanut butter chips, previously tossed in ½ teaspoon unsweetened cocoa powder.

NUTTY CHOCOLATE POUND CAKE

Just before transferring the batter to the pan, fold in 1 cup (3 to 4 ounces) chopped toasted walnuts, pecans, or hazelnuts.

CHEWY CHOCOLATE POUND CAKE

Just before transferring the batter to the pan, fold in 1 cup plumped currants, raisins, dried currants, cherries, or cut-up apricots.

COCONUT CHOCOLATE POUND CAKE

Just before transferring the batter to the pan, fold in 1 cup sweetened shredded coconut.

POPPY SEED CHOCOLATE POUND CAKE

Just before transferring the batter to the pan, fold in ¼ cup poppy seeds.

"ANTIQUE" CHOCOLATE POUND CAKE

Old-fashioned pound cakes were flavored with rose water, which I like with chocolate. If this appeals to you, substitute 1 teaspoon rose water or orange flower water for the vanilla extract.

"CRAZY QUILT" CHOCOLATE POUND CAKE

Come up with your own combination, such as spices with chocolate chips, nuts, or dried fruit; however, don't add more than 1½ cups of these "add-in" ingredients. A lovely "Crazy Quilt" combination is ½ teaspoon allspice, ½ cup chopped walnuts, and ½ cup semisweet chocolate morsels.

continued on next page

Dependable Chocolate Pound Cake

continued from previous page

PLATED DESSERT SUGGESTION (per portion)

1 slice of cake
¼ cup of
Vanilla or Flavored
Custard Sauce (pages 358 and 359) or
Melted ice cream or
Deadly Delicious Chocolate Sauce
(page 362) or
Raspberry Squeeze Sauce
(page 368) or

Passion Fruit Sauce (page 366)
Chocolate Shavings made from
bittersweet, milk, or white
chocolate (page 380) or
A handful of raspberries
Whipped cream in a pastry bag
fitted with a star tip

Center the slice of cake on a 10-inch plate and pour the sauce of choice around the cake. Scatter the chocolate shavings or raspberries over the sauce, and pipe a rosette of whipped cream in the center of the cake.

For more ideas, see plated dessert suggestions for unfrosted cakes (page 352).

Light Chocolate Pound Cake

This is a lovely cake to have in your repertoire for those times when you want something that is like a chocolate pound cake but not as dense. This pound cake is as buttery as the others, with an airier texture created by the beaten egg whites.

Makes one 8.5 × 4.5-inch loaf cake

Serves 8 to 10

Level of difficulty ★

---

4 ounces semisweet or bittersweet chocolate, finely chopped

½ cup heavy cream

1½ cups (7 ounces) bleached all-purpose flour

---

1 teaspoon baking powder

¼ teaspoon salt

¾ stick (3 ounces) unsalted butter, softened

¾ cup (5.5 ounces) superfine sugar

---

2 large eggs, separated

¼ teaspoon almond extract

½ teaspoon vanilla extract

Confectioners' sugar, optional

Whipped cream (page 318), optional

Fresh berries or Very Berry Compote (page 372), optional

---

1. Position a rack in the lower third of the oven and preheat to 350°F. Grease an 8.5 × 4.5 × 2.75-inch loaf pan, dust it with flour, and line the bottom with parchment or greased and floured waxed paper.

2. Place the chocolate in a mixing bowl. In a small saucepan, bring the cream to just under a boil and pour it over the chocolate. Let the mixture stand for 30 seconds, then, with a small whisk, blend the cream and chocolate until smooth and set it aside to cool to room temperature.

3. Sift the flour, baking powder, and salt twice, and set it aside.

4. With an electric mixer on low speed (or with a stationary mixer fitted with the paddle attachment), beat the butter for 1 minute, or until light. Slowly add the sugar, about 2 tablespoons at a time (this should take about 3 minutes). When all of the sugar is added, continue to beat on medium speed for about 5 minutes, scraping down the beaters and sides of the bowl as needed. The mixture should look fluffy, like something between mayonnaise and whipped cream.

5. Add the egg yolks and beat until absorbed by the butter, then beat in the almond and vanilla extracts.

6. With a large rubber spatula, fold the sifted ingredients into the batter in three additions, alternating with the melted chocolate in two additions. Once the ingredients are combined, beat the batter with the electric mixer on low speed for another minute, or until smooth.

7. In a clean bowl, with an electric mixer, whip the egg whites until they are stiff and glossy, and fold them into the batter with a rubber spatula.

8. Transfer the batter to the prepared pan and smooth the top. Bake for 15 minutes, then lower the heat to 325°F and bake for 50 minutes to 1 hour more, or until a tester inserted in the center comes out dry. Cool the cake in the pan on a wire rack for 30 minutes. Lightly coat the wire rack with nonstick vegetable spray. Tip the pan on its side and ease the cake out of the pan. Cool to room temperature on the greased wire rack, right side up. Peel off the paper after the cake is cool.

9. Center a 2-inch-wide strip of paper down the length of the pound cake, then sift some confectioners' sugar over the top and carefully lift up the paper. Serve with whipped cream and berries or compote on the side.

STORAGE: Keep at room temperature, wrapped airtight in plastic, for up to 5 days; refrigerate after that.

Marbled Chocolate Pound Cake

This is a fabulous buttery cake and a good keeper. It is rich and best served plain.

Makes one 10-inch
tube cake

Serves 16 to 18

Level of difficulty ★

4 cups (18 ounces) cake flour

2 tablespoons unsweetened,
Dutch-processed cocoa powder

1 teaspoon baking powder

¾ teaspoon baking soda

½ teaspoon salt

4 sticks (1 pound) unsalted
butter, softened

3 cups (22.5 ounces) superfine
sugar

9 large eggs

3 ounces unsweetened
chocolate, melted and cooled

2 teaspoons vanilla extract

1. Position a rack in the lower third of the oven and preheat to 325°F. Butter and flour a 10-inch tube pan. You can line the bottom with a special tube-cake parchment liner.

2. Sift the flour, cocoa, baking powder, baking soda, and salt twice and set it aside.

3. With an electric mixer on low speed (or with a stationary mixer fitted with the paddle attachment), beat the butter for about 1 minute, or until light.

4. Slowly add the sugar, about 2 tablespoons at a time (this should take 3 to 4 minutes). When all the sugar is added, continue to beat on medium speed for about 6 minutes, scraping down the beaters and sides of the bowl as needed. The mixture will look fluffy, like something between mayonnaise and whipped cream.

5. Add the eggs one at a time, beating for 10 seconds between additions, or until each egg is absorbed by the butter. (Toward the end, if the batter looks curdled, add 1 to 2 tablespoons of the flour mixture, continue to beat, and things will be okay.) Scrape down the beaters and sides of the bowl and beat for another minute, or until the mixture looks smooth and creamy.

6. With a large rubber spatula, fold in the sifted ingredients in three additions. Remove ½ the batter to a separate bowl. Fold the melted chocolate into one half of the batter and the vanilla extract into the other.

7. In a random pattern, spoon some light batter into the prepared pan, leaving spaces where you will spoon some of the darker batter. For the second layer, spoon some light batter over the dark batter underneath and spoon some dark batter over the light batter. Continue until all the batter is used up. Draw a knife or wooden skewer in large swirls around the middle of the two batters to create the marbled effect. Take care not to overdo this step, or you'll blend the batters. Rap the pan sharply on the counter a couple of times to break up any large air bubbles.

8. Bake for 45 minutes, then lower the heat to 300°F and bake for 45 minutes longer, or until a tester inserted in the center comes out dry. Cool the cake in the pan on a wire rack for 45 minutes. Lightly coat the wire rack with non-stick vegetable spray. Run a long thin spatula or a knife around the cake and around the inner tube to loosen the cake from the pan. Invert the cake and cool it to room temperature upside down on the greased wire rack.

STORAGE: Keep at room temperature, wrapped airtight in plastic, for up to 5 days; refrigerate after that.

Super Rich Chocolate Pound Cake

This is how a chocolate pound cake ought to be—super-rich with a dense velvety crumb and a chocolate flavor reinforced by the addition of chocolate morsels.

Makes one 8.5 × 4.5-inch loaf cake

Serves 8 to 10

Level of difficulty ★

1½ cups (7 ounces) cake flour

½ teaspoon baking powder

¼ teaspoon baking soda

¼ teaspoon salt

1¾ sticks (7 ounces) unsalted butter, softened

1 cup plus 3 tablespoons (9.25 ounces) superfine sugar

4 large eggs

3 ounces unsweetened chocolate, melted and cooled

½ cup (3 ounces) semisweet or milk chocolate morsels

½ teaspoon unsweetened cocoa powder

---

1. Position a rack in the lower third of the oven and preheat to 350°F. Butter and flour an 8.5 × 4.5 × 2.75-inch loaf pan and line the bottom with parchment or greased and floured waxed paper.
2. Sift the flour, baking powder, baking soda, and salt twice over parchment or waxed paper and set it aside.
3. With an electric mixer on low speed (or with a stationary mixer fitted with the paddle attachment), beat the butter for about 1 minute, or until light. Slowly add the sugar, about 2 tablespoons at a time (this should take about 3 minutes), and when all of it has been added, continue to beat on medium speed for about 5 minutes, scraping down the beaters and sides of the bowl as needed. The mixture will look fluffy, like something between mayonnaise and whipped cream.
4. Add the eggs one at a time, beating for 10 seconds between additions, or until each egg is absorbed by the butter. Scrape down the beaters and sides of the bowl and beat for another minute. Add the melted chocolate and beat until the mixture is smooth.
5. With a large rubber spatula, fold the sifted ingredients into the batter in four additions. Beat the batter with the electric mixer on low speed for another minute, or until smooth. Toss the chocolate morsels with the cocoa and fold them into the batter.
6. Transfer the batter to the prepared pan, smooth the top, and rap the pan sharply on the counter a couple of times to break up any large air bubbles. Bake for 15 minutes. Lower the heat to 325° and bake for about 1 hour longer, or until a tester inserted in the center comes out dry.
7. Cool the cake in the pan on a wire rack for 30 minutes. Lightly coat the wire rack with nonstick vegetable spray. Tip the pan on its side and ease the cake out of the pan. Cool to room temperature right side up on the greased wire rack. Peel off the paper after the cake is cool.

STORAGE: Keep at room temperature, wrapped airtight in plastic, for up to 5 days; refrigerate after that.

Almond Chocolate Cake with Ganache

The honey adds a melt-in-your-mouth quality to this cake.

Makes one 9 ×
13-inch sheet cake

Serves about 15

Level of difficulty ★

2 cups (9.5 ounces) bleached all-purpose flour

½ teaspoon baking soda

¼ teaspoon salt

1 cup (3.5 ounces) blanched almonds, finely ground

½ stick (2 ounces) unsalted butter

13 tablespoons (6 ounces) superfine sugar

2 large eggs

4 ounces bittersweet chocolate, melted and cooled

½ cup (6 ounces) clover honey

1 cup buttermilk

½ recipe Ganache (page 324)

1. Position a rack in the center of the oven and preheat to 350°F. Grease and flour a 9 × 13 × 2-inch pan.
2. Sift the flour, baking soda, and salt into a large mixing bowl. Add the almonds, combine with a whisk, and set it aside.
3. With an electric mixer on low speed (or with a stationary mixer fitted with the paddle attachment), beat the butter for about 1 minute, or until light. Slowly add the sugar, about 2 tablespoons at a time. When all of the sugar is added, continue to beat for 2 to 3 minutes, scraping down the beaters and sides of the bowl as needed. The mixture will look fluffy, like something between mayonnaise and whipped cream.
4. Add the eggs one at a time, beating for 10 seconds between additions, or until each is absorbed by the butter. Add the melted chocolate and honey, and beat for a few seconds, or until smooth.
5. With a rubber spatula, fold the sifted ingredients into the batter in three additions, alternating with the buttermilk in two additions. Beat with an electric mixer on low speed for 1 minute, or until the mixture looks smooth.
6. Transfer the batter to the prepared pan and smooth the top. Bake for about 30 minutes, or until a tester inserted in the center comes out dry.
7. Cool the cake in the pan on a wire rack. Frost the top only with the ganache while the cake is still warm, and serve it from the pan.

STORAGE: Keep in the refrigerator, wrapped airtight, for up to 4 days, but serve at room temperature.

Chocolate Banana Tea Cake

Banana and chocolate, a favorite American combination, come together in this lovely tea cake, which is fabulous for breakfast or an afternoon snack.

Makes one 8.5 × 4.5-inch loaf cake

Serves 8 to 10

Level of difficulty ★

1¾ cups (8.25 ounces) bleached all-purpose flour, sifted

¼ cup (0.75 ounce) unsweetened cocoa powder

1 teaspoon baking powder

¼ teaspoon baking soda

¼ teaspoon salt

1 stick (4 ounces) unsalted butter, softened

⅔ cup (5 ounces) granulated sugar

2 large eggs

1 cup mashed ripe banana (about 3 medium)

Generous ½ cup (2 ounces) walnuts or pecans, coarsely chopped

¼ cup (1 ounce) chopped dried California apricots, cranberries, or cherries

½ cup (3 ounces) bittersweet or milk chocolate mini-morsels

1. Position a rack in the center of the oven and preheat to 350°F. Grease an 8.5 × 4.5 × 2.75-inch loaf pan, dust it with flour, and line the bottom with parchment or greased and floured waxed paper.

2. Sift the flour with the cocoa, baking powder, baking soda, and salt, and set it aside.

3. With an electric mixer on low speed (or with a stationary mixer fitted with the paddle attachment), beat the butter for 1 minute, or until light. Slowly add the sugar, about 2 tablespoons at a time, and when all of it has been added, continue to beat on medium speed for about 2 minutes, scraping down the beaters and sides of the bowl as needed. The mixture will look like fluffy mayonnaise.

4. Add the eggs one at a time, beating for 10 seconds between additions, or until each one is absorbed by the butter. Scrape down the beaters and sides of the bowl, and continue to beat for 1 minute, or until smooth.

5. With a large rubber spatula, fold the sifted ingredients into the batter in three additions, alternating with the mashed bananas in two additions. Beat the batter with an electric mixer on low speed for 1 minute, or until smooth. Fold in the nuts, apricots, and mini chocolate chips.

6. Transfer the batter to the prepared pan, smooth the top, and rap the pan sharply on the counter to break up any large air bubbles. With the edge of a spatula, make an indentation running down the length of the cake so that when it splits open during baking, it will split along the straight seam rather than breaking open in random places. Bake for 50 minutes to 1 hour, or until a tester inserted in the center comes out dry.

7. Cool the cake in the pan on a wire rack for 15 minutes. Ease the cake out of the pan and cool it to room temperature on the paper liner and on the wire rack. Remove the paper when the cake is cool.

STORAGE: Keep at room temperature, wrapped airtight in plastic, for up to 3 days.

**Chocolate Chocolate Tea Cake

This cake tastes intensely of chocolate, has a velvety crumb, slices beautifully, and is perfect for brunch.

Makes one 8.5 × 4.5-inch loaf cake

Serves 8 to 10

Level of difficulty ★

Scant 1½ cups (7 ounces) unbleached all-purpose flour, sifted

½ cup (1.5 ounces) unsweetened, Dutch-processed cocoa powder

1 teaspoon baking powder

¼ teaspoon baking soda

¼ teaspoon salt

1 stick (4 ounces) unsalted butter, softened

1 cup (7.5 ounces) granulated sugar

2 large eggs

½ cup sour cream

4 ounces extra-bittersweet chocolate, finely chopped (preferably Lindt 70% or Valrhona 71%)

1. Position a rack in the center of the oven and preheat to 350°F. Lightly grease and flour an 8.5 × 4.5 × 2.75-inch loaf pan and line the bottom with parchment or greased and floured waxed paper.

2. Sift the flour with the cocoa, baking powder, baking soda, and salt, and set it aside.

3. With an electric mixer on low speed (or with a stationary mixer fitted with the paddle attachment), beat the butter for 1 minute, or until light. Slowly add the sugar, about 2 tablespoons at a time, and continue to beat on medium speed for another 2 minutes, scraping down the beaters and sides of the bowl as needed. The mixture will look fluffy, like something between mayonnaise and whipped cream.

4. Add the eggs one at a time, beating for 10 seconds between additions, or until each is absorbed by the butter.

5. With a large rubber spatula, fold the sifted ingredients into the batter in three additions, alternating with the sour cream in two additions. Beat the batter for 1 minute with the electric mixer on low speed, or until smooth, then fold in the chopped chocolate.

6. Transfer the batter to the prepared pan and rap the pan sharply on the counter once to break up any large air bubbles. Smooth the top with a rubber spatula and bake for 55 minutes to 1 hour, or until a tester inserted in the center comes out dry.

7. Cool the cake in the pan on a wire rack for 20 minutes, then ease it out of the pan. Cool the cake to room temperature, right side up, on the paper liner and on the wire rack. Remove the paper when the cake is cool.

STORAGE: Keep at room temperature, wrapped airtight in plastic, for up to 3 days.

Deep-Dish Chocolate Cake with Sour Cream Icing

This is the perfect cake to serve when you want a sweet, moist cake without too much icing.

Makes one 9 × 13-inch sheet cake

Serves 15 to 18

Level of difficulty ★

2½ cups (12 ounces) bleached all-purpose flour, sifted

1 teaspoon baking powder

½ teaspoon baking soda

½ teaspoon salt

1¾ sticks (7 ounces) unsalted butter, softened

2¾ cups (20 ounces) granulated sugar

5 large eggs

7 ounces unsweetened chocolate, melted and cooled

1 teaspoon vanilla extract

1¾ cups milk

Sour Cream Chocolate Icing (page 326)

1. Position a rack in the center of the oven and preheat to 350°F. Lightly grease a 9 × 13 × 2-inch baking pan.
2. Sift the flour with the baking powder, baking soda, and salt, and set it aside.
3. With an electric mixer on low speed (or with a stationary mixer fitted with the paddle attachment), beat the butter for 1 minute, or until light. Slowly add the sugar, about 2 tablespoons at a time, and when all of it has been added, continue to beat on medium speed for 2 minutes, scraping down the beaters and sides of the bowl as needed. The mixture will look like wet sand.
4. Add the eggs one at a time, beating for 10 seconds between additions, or until each one has been absorbed by the butter. Beat for 2 minutes longer, or until light, scraping down the beaters and sides of the bowl as needed. Add the cooled chocolate and the vanilla, and beat for 1 minute more, or until smooth and well mixed.
5. With a large rubber spatula, fold the sifted ingredients into the batter in four additions, alternating with the milk in three additions. When all the ingredients are combined, beat the batter with the electric mixer on low speed for about 1 minute, or until smooth.
6. Transfer the batter to the prepared pan, smooth the top, and rap the pan sharply on the counter a couple of times to break up any large air bubbles. Bake for 50 minutes to 1 hour, or until a tester inserted in the center comes out dry and the cake begins to pull away from the sides of the pan.
7. Cool the cake to room temperature in the pan on a wire rack. Frost the top when the cake is cool; cut and serve it from the pan.

STORAGE: Keep in the refrigerator, lightly covered, for 3 to 4 days, but bring back to room temperature before serving.

Cherry and Hazelnut Chocolate Cake

This cake, lovely to give as a Christmas gift, is full of tangy rum-soaked dried cherries, toasted hazelnuts, and bits of chocolate. Because the cake contains so many added ingredients, it needs a stronger flour than most pound cakes to hold them, and it needs to cook slowly and for a long time to be baked through.

Makes one 9-inch tube cake

Serves 12 to 14

Level of difficulty ★★

---

1 cup (3.5 ounces) dried cherries

2 tablespoons dark rum

1 cup (3.5 ounces) skinned and roasted hazelnuts (see Note below)

2½ cups (12 ounces) unbleached all-purpose or bread flour, sifted

⅓ cup (1 ounce) unsweetened, nonalkalized cocoa powder

¾ teaspoon baking soda

½ teaspoon salt

⅛ teaspoon ground nutmeg

2 sticks (8 ounces) unsalted butter, softened

1½ cups (11.25 ounces) superfine sugar

3 large eggs

½ cup sour cream

1 cup (6 ounces) semisweet chocolate mini-morsels

---

1. Position a rack in the lower third of the oven, and preheat to 350°F. Marinate the cherries in the rum; toss them every now and then to make sure they are absorbing the liquid. Coarsely chop the hazelnuts.

2. Lightly butter a 9-inch tube or Bundt pan and dust it with flour or cocoa powder. Tap out the excess and set the pan aside. Lightly coat a wire rack with nonstick vegetable spray.

3. Sift the flour with the cocoa, baking soda, salt, and nutmeg twice and set it aside.

4. With an electric mixer on low speed (or with a stationary mixer fitted with the paddle attachment), beat the butter for 1 minute, or until light. Slowly add the sugar, about 2 tablespoons at a time (this takes about 3 minutes), and when all the sugar has been added, beat for 5 minutes longer, scraping down the beaters and sides of the bowl as needed. The mixture will look fluffy, like something between mayonnaise and whipped cream.

5. Add the eggs one at a time, beating for 10 seconds between additions, or until each one has been absorbed by the butter. Scrape down the bowl as needed and beat for 1 minute longer, or until creamy and light.

6. With a large rubber spatula, fold the sifted ingredients into the batter in three additions, alternating with the sour cream in two additions. Fold in the cherries and the rum they were soaking in, along with the chopped hazelnuts and chocolate morsels.

7. Transfer the batter to the prepared pan and smooth the top. Bake for 45 minutes, lower the heat to 325°, and bake 30 to 40 minutes longer, or until a tester inserted in the center comes out dry (if the tester hits a pocket of melted chocolate from the morsels, it will appear wet, so test it in several places).

8. Cool the cake in the pan on a wire rack for 30 minutes, then run a table knife around the cake and the inner tube to loosen it from the mold. Invert the cake onto the greased wire rack and cool it to room temperature, right side up.

STORAGE: Keep at room temperature, wrapped airtight in plastic, for up to 5 days.

NOTE: You can buy skinned and toasted hazelnuts from some grocery stores or from King Arthur's *Baker's Catalogue*, but they still need 10 minutes or so of roasting to fully develop their aroma.

**Chocolate Pain de Gênes

Pain de Gênes *is a French pound cake, luxuriously moist and intensely flavored with almond paste. Never one to leave good enough alone, I decided to experiment with this classic by adding chocolate to the batter. The result is a deliciously rich cake, made especially tender by replacing part of the flour with cornstarch.*

Makes one 9-inch, single-layer cake

Serves 8 to 10

Level of difficulty ★

2 tablespoons sliced blanched almonds

¾ cup (3.5 ounces) bleached all-purpose flour

¼ cup (1 ounce) cornstarch

⅛ teaspoon salt

¼ teaspoon baking soda

8 ounces almond paste

1¼ sticks (5 ounces) unsalted butter, softened

⅔ cup (5 ounces) granulated sugar

4 large eggs

1 tablespoon dark rum

1 teaspoon vanilla extract

2½ ounces unsweetened chocolate, melted and cooled

2 teaspoons superfine or vanilla sugar, optional

1. Position a rack in the center of the oven and preheat to 325°F. Generously butter a 9 × 2-inch round cake pan and scatter the sliced almonds on the bottom.
2. Sift the flour with the cornstarch, salt, and baking soda, and set it aside.
3. With an electric mixer on low speed (or with a stationary mixer fitted with the paddle attachment), beat the almond paste for about 1 minute, or until smooth. Add the butter and beat for 2 to 3 minutes, or until blended. Add the granulated sugar and continue to beat on medium speed for 2 to 3 minutes, scraping down the beaters and sides of the bowl as needed. The mixture will look aerated but somewhat grainy because of the almond paste.
4. Add the eggs one at a time, beating for 10 seconds between additions, or until each one is absorbed by the butter. Add the rum, vanilla, and chocolate, and beat the batter for 1 minute longer, scraping down the sides of the bowl as needed.
5. Sift the dry ingredients, in two additions, over the mixture and fold them into the batter with a rubber spatula.
6. Transfer the batter to the prepared pan, smooth the top, and rap the pan sharply on the counter to level the batter. Bake for 35 to 40 minutes, or until a tester inserted in the center comes out dry.
7. Cool the cake in the pan on a wire rack for 20 minutes. Lightly coat the wire rack with nonstick vegetable spray. Run a table knife around the cake to loosen it from the pan. Invert the cake onto the greased wire rack and cool it to room temperature upside down so the almonds are on top. Just before serving, sprinkle the top with sugar over the almonds.

STORAGE: Keep at room temperature, wrapped airtight in plastic, for up to 3 days; refrigerate after that.

PLATED DESSERT SUGGESTION (per portion)

1 slice of cake
Raspberry Squeeze Sauce
(page 368), in a squeeze bottle

Melted and cooled bittersweet
chocolate in a paper cone or a
heavy-duty plastic bag (pages 33, 349)

Center the slice of cake on a 10-inch plate. Squeeze nickel-size rounds of raspberry sauce randomly on the plate and then squeeze tiny dots of melted chocolate in between.

Hazelnut Chocolate Cake

This cake is wonderful for a luxurious breakfast or brunch because it is not too sweet. It is lovely spread with red currant jelly or served at tea time with clotted cream.

Makes one 9 × 5-inch loaf cake

Serves 12

Level of difficulty ★

2½ cups plus 1 tablespoon (12 ounces) unbleached all-purpose flour

1 teaspoon baking soda

½ teaspoon salt

1 stick (4 ounces) unsalted butter, softened

1 cup packed (7.5 ounces) light brown sugar

4 large eggs, lightly beaten

4 ounces unsweetened chocolate, melted and cooled

1 cup buttermilk

Generous 1½ cups (6 ounces) roasted skinned hazelnuts, coarsely chopped (see page 27)

---

1. Position a rack in the center of the oven and preheat to 350°F. Lightly grease and flour a 9 × 5 × 3-inch loaf pan and line the bottom with parchment or greased and floured waxed paper.
2. Sift the flour with the baking soda and salt twice, and set it aside.
3. With an electric mixer on low speed (or with a stationary mixer fitted with the paddle attachment), beat the butter for 1 minute, or until light. Slowly add the sugar, about 2 tablespoons at a time, and when all of it has been added, continue to beat on medium speed for about 2 minutes, scraping down the beaters and sides of the bowl as needed. The mixture will look like fluffy mayonnaise.
4. Add the eggs one at a time, beating for 10 seconds between additions, or until absorbed by the butter. Scrape down the beaters and sides of the bowl and continue to beat for 1 minute, or until smooth. Fold in the melted chocolate.
5. With a large rubber spatula, fold the sifted ingredients into the batter in four additions, alternating with the buttermilk in three additions. Beat the batter for a moment, or until smooth, scraping down the beaters and sides of the bowl as needed. Fold in the nuts.
6. Transfer the batter to the prepared pan, smooth the top, and rap the pan sharply on the counter to break up any large air bubbles. With the edge of a spatula, make an indentation running down the length of the cake so that it will split along the straight seam during baking, rather than breaking open in random places.
7. Bake for 35 to 45 minutes, or until a tester inserted in the center comes out dry.
8. Cool the cake in the pan on a wire rack for 20 minutes. Ease it out of the pan, remove the paper, and cool to room temperature, on its side, on the wire rack.

STORAGE: Keep at room temperature, wrapped airtight in plastic, for up to 3 days; refrigerate after that.

Mocha Tea Cake

This lovely, not-too-sweet tea cake has a tightly knit crumb yet feels light on the tongue. It is the perfect choice for a brunch.

Makes one 8.5 × 4.5-inch loaf cake

Serves 8

Level of difficulty ★

1½ cups (7 ounces) bleached all-purpose flour

¼ teaspoon baking soda

⅛ teaspoon salt

¾ stick (3 ounces) unsalted butter, softened

13 tablespoons (6 ounces) superfine sugar

2 large eggs

3 ounces unsweetened chocolate, melted and cooled

¾ cup double-strength coffee (or 2 teaspoonfuls instant espresso coffee powder dissolved in ¾ cup boiling water)

---

1. Position a rack in the center of the oven and preheat to 350°F. Lightly butter and flour an 8.5 × 4.5 × 2.75-inch loaf pan and line the bottom with parchment or greased and floured waxed paper.
2. Sift the flour with the baking soda and salt twice, and set it aside.
3. With an electric mixer (or a stationary mixer fitted with the paddle attachment) on low speed, beat the butter for 1 minute, or until light. Slowly add the sugar, about 2 tablespoons at a time, and when all of it is in, beat on medium speed for about 3 minutes, scraping down the beaters and sides of the bowl as needed. The mixture will look fluffy, like something between mayonnaise and whipped cream.
4. Add the eggs one at a time, beating for 10 seconds between additions, or until each has been absorbed by the butter. Scrape down the beaters and sides of the bowl, add the cooled chocolate, and beat on low speed to just combine.
5. With a rubber spatula, add the sifted ingredients to the batter in three additions, alternating with the coffee in two additions. With the electric mixer on low speed, combine the ingredients, beating for 1 minute, or until smooth.
6. Transfer the batter to the prepared pan, smooth the top, and rap the pan sharply on the counter to get rid of any large air bubbles. Bake for 50 minutes to 1 hour, or until a tester inserted in the center comes out dry.
7. Cool the cake to room temperature in the pan on a wire rack.

STORAGE: Keep at room temperature, wrapped airtight in plastic, for up to 3 days; refrigerate after that.

Midnight Cake

This cake, with its tightly woven crumb, is as dense and dark as night. It is a fabulous example of how the texture of a chocolate cake batter, baked in a water bath, comes out remarkably different from a batter baked straight in the oven. What you get is a divinely unctuous flat cake. What is fun, too, is that the cake is firm enough so you can cut it into unusual shapes—like triangles, stars, or circles—and present the shapes as centerpieces of gorgeous plated desserts (see plated dessert suggestions for unfrosted cakes, page 352).

Makes one 8-inch square cake

Serves 8 to 10

Level of difficulty ★

1¾ cups (8.25 ounces) bleached all-purpose flour

½ teaspoon baking powder

⅛ teaspoon salt

1 stick (4 ounces) unsalted butter, softened

½ cup packed (3.75 ounces) light brown sugar

½ cup (3.75 ounces) granulated sugar

2 large eggs

4 ounces unsweetened chocolate, melted and cooled

1 teaspoon vanilla extract

¾ cup hot tap water, tea, or prepared coffee

1. Lightly butter an 8-inch square baking pan. Lay two long strips of microwavable plastic wrap, perpendicular to one another, in the pan so you can lift the cake out of the pan after it is done. The plastic wrap should stick up only 1 inch above the rim of the pan. Position the rack in the center of the oven and preheat to 350°F.

2. Sift the flour with the baking powder and salt twice, and set it aside.

3. With an electric mixer on low speed (or with a stationary mixer fitted with the paddle attachment), beat the butter for 1 minute, or until light. Slowly add the brown and granulated sugars, and when all the sugar is added, continue to beat for about 3 minutes, scraping down the beaters and sides of the bowl as needed. The mixture will look fluffy, like something between mayonnaise and whipped cream.

4. Add the eggs one at a time, beating for 10 seconds between additions, or until each is absorbed by the butter; then add the chocolate and vanilla, and mix until blended.

5. With a large rubber spatula, fold the sifted ingredients into the batter in three additions, alternating with the water in two additions. Beat with an electric mixer on low speed for 1 minute, or until the mixture is smooth.

6. Transfer the batter to the prepared pan. Set the pan in a larger baking pan. Pour very hot tap water into the larger pan so it reaches halfway up the sides of the pan with the batter. Bake for 35 to 40 minutes, or until a tester inserted in the center comes out dry. Remove the pan from the water bath and cool it on a wire rack for 30 minutes. Lift the cake out of the pan with the help of the plastic wrap. Cut and serve warm.

STORAGE: Keep in the refrigerator, wrapped airtight in plastic, for up to 3 days; reheat for 30 seconds in a microwave oven before serving.

PLATED DESSERT SUGGESTION (per portion)

¼ cup melted mint, coffee, or chocolate ice cream

or

Vanilla or Flavored Custard Sauce (pages 358 and 359)

1 slice of cake

Chunk of bittersweet chocolate

Pour the ice cream or custard sauce in the center of a plate; place the cake in the middle. With a vegetable peeler, shave the chocolate over the sauce.

Pecan Bourbon Chocolate Cake

This bourbon-drenched delight is an amazing cake, rich in chocolate and chock-full of pecans. It mellows and improves with age and is so high in alcohol that it keeps for a long time. It is incredibly rich, so a sliver goes a long way.

Makes one 10-inch tube cake

Serves 16 to 20

Level of difficulty ★

---

5 cups (24 ounces) bleached all-purpose flour, sifted

Scant 1 cup (3 ounces) unsweetened, Dutch-processed cocoa powder, sifted

1½ teaspoons baking powder

½ teaspoon baking soda

1 teaspoon salt

3 sticks (12 ounces) unsalted butter, softened

4¼ cups (2 pounds) packed light brown sugar

5 large eggs

2 cups good-quality bourbon whiskey

1 pound pecans, coarsely chopped

Whipped Cream (page 318) or ice cream, optional

---

1. Position a rack in the lower third of the oven and preheat to 350°F. Generously butter a 10-inch tube pan and dust the inside with flour; tap out the excess and set it aside.

2. Sift the flour with the cocoa, baking powder, baking soda, and salt twice, and set it aside.

3. With an electric mixer on low speed (or with a stationary mixer fitted with the paddle attachment), beat the butter for 1 minute, or until light. Add the sugar slowly, about 2 tablespoons at a time (this should take 3 to 4 minutes). When all the sugar is added, beat on medium speed for 5 to 6 minutes, scraping down the beaters and sides of the bowl as needed. The mixture will look fluffy, like something between mayonnaise and whipped cream.

4. Add the eggs one at a time, beating for 10 seconds between additions, or until each one is absorbed by the butter. Scrape down the beaters and sides of the bowl and beat for another minute, or until smooth and creamy.

5. With a large rubber spatula, fold the sifted ingredients into the batter in four additions, alternating with the bourbon in three additions. When all the ingredients are combined, beat the batter with an electric mixer on low speed for 1 minute, or until the mixture looks smooth.

6. With a large rubber spatula, fold the pecans into the batter and transfer the batter to the prepared pan. Smooth the top and rap the pan sharply on the counter a few times to get rid of any large air bubbles.

7. Bake for 1 hour. Lower the heat to 325°F and bake for about an hour longer, or until a tester inserted in the center comes out a little bit moist, the way it would in a brownie.

8. Cool the cake in the pan on a wire rack for 1 hour. Run a long thin knife around the outside of the cake and around the inside tube. Turn the cake out of the pan and cool it to room temperature, right side up, on a wire rack.

9. Serve with a dollop of whipped cream or a small scoop of ice cream, if you wish.

STORAGE: Keep at room temperature, wrapped airtight in plastic, for up to 1 week; refrigerate after that.

PECAN BOURBON FUDGE CAKE

Follow the recipe with these changes: Use 4 cups (1 pound plus 3 ounces) of flour and 1 cup of bourbon. This variation has a fudgelike interior and, like a brownie, develops a sugary cracked crust as the cake cools.

Glazed Cocoa Coconut Cake

Unsweetened coconut milk and lightly toasted coconut flakes are the secret to this cake's exquisite flavor.

Makes one 9-inch tube cake

Serves 12

Level of difficulty ★★

CAKE

2½ cups loosely packed (7.5 ounces) sweetened coconut flakes

2 cups (9 ounces) cake or pastry flour

½ cup (1.5 ounces) unsweetened, Dutch-processed cocoa powder, sifted

¼ teaspoon baking powder

½ teaspoon baking soda

¼ teaspoon salt

2 sticks (8 ounces) unsalted butter, softened

1¼ cups (9.5 ounces) superfine sugar

3 large eggs

1 large egg yolk

½ cup canned unsweetened coconut milk

GLAZE

4 ounces bittersweet chocolate, finely chopped

⅓ cup canned unsweetened coconut milk

½ cup toasted coconut flakes, reserved from cake

TO MAKE THE CAKE

1. Heat a 9-inch nonstick skillet over medium-low heat for 1 minute. Add the coconut flakes and cook, stirring with a wooden spoon or heatproof rubber spatula for 3 to 4 minutes, or until steam begins to rise from the pan, the coconut begins to smell toasty, and the color begins to turn a light golden. The coconut toasts unevenly, so it's okay if some pieces are slightly browner or more golden than others. Remove the skillet from the heat and transfer the toasted coconut to a bowl to cool.

2. Position a rack in the lower third of the oven and preheat to 325°F. Lightly butter a 9-inch Bundt or tube pan, dust it with flour, and tap out the excess.

3. Sift the flour with the cocoa, baking powder, baking soda, and salt twice and set it aside.

4. With an electric mixer on low speed (or with a stationary mixer fitted with the paddle attachment), beat the butter for 1 minute, or until light. Slowly add the sugar, about 2 tablespoons at a time (this will take about 3 minutes), and when all of it has been added, continue to beat on medium speed for about 5 minutes, scraping down the beaters and sides of the bowl as needed. The mixture will look fluffy, like something between mayonnaise and whipped cream.

5. Add the eggs and the yolk, one at a time, beating for 10 seconds between additions, or until each egg is absorbed by the butter; then beat for 1 minute, or until smooth, scraping down the beaters and sides of the bowl as needed.

6. With a large rubber spatula, fold the sifted ingredients into the batter in three additions, alternating with the coconut milk in two additions. Remove and set aside ½ cup of the toasted coconut and fold the rest into the batter.

7. Transfer the batter to the prepared pan, smooth the top, and bake for 1 hour to 1 hour and 10 minutes, or until a tester inserted in the center comes out dry. Cool the cake in the pan on a wire rack for 30 minutes. Lightly coat the wire rack with nonstick vegetable spray. Run a knife around the cake and inner tube to loosen the cake from the pan, ease the cake out of the pan, and cool to room temperature, right side up, on the greased wire rack.

Set the chocolate in a bowl. In a small skillet over low heat, bring the coconut milk to just under a boil and pour it over the chocolate. Let the mixture stand for a minute, then whisk until smooth with a small wire whip. With an offset spatula, spread the glaze over the sides and top of the cake, then loosely pat the reserved toasted coconut around the sides and over the top. The glaze will show beneath the coconut flakes.

STORAGE: Keep at room temperature, lightly covered with foil, for 2 to 3 days.

PLATED DESSERT SUGGESTION (per portion)

1 slice of cake
Fresh or Canned Mango Sauce
   or Passion Fruit Sauce
   (pages 365 and 366)

Raspberry Squeeze Sauce
   (page 368)
Coconut flakes, optional

Center a slice of cake on a 10-inch plate. Spoon or squeeze alternating 1-inch circles of mango and raspberry sauces next to one another toward the outside edge of the plate. Run the blunt end of a wooden skewer in a circle in the middle of the sauces so they run into each other slightly, forming heart shapes. Scatter coconut flakes over the slice of cake.

Orange and Chocolate Bundt Cake

The taste and aroma of this cake derive from the concentrated frozen orange juice rein-forced by the orange extract.

Makes one 8.5-inch tube cake

Serves 12 to 14

Level of difficulty ★

2 cups (9.5 ounces) bleached all-purpose flour

½ teaspoon baking soda

½ teaspoon salt

1 stick (4 ounces) unsalted butter, softened

½ cup (4 ounces) solid vegetable shortening, at room temperature

1½ cups (11.25 ounces) superfine sugar

4 large eggs

1 teaspoon orange extract or ¼ teaspoon orange oil

½ cup thawed frozen orange juice concentrate

3 ounces unsweetened chocolate, melted and cooled

1. Position a rack in the lower third of the oven and preheat to 350°F. Butter and flour an 8.5-inch Bundt pan (8-cup capacity) and tap out the excess flour.
2. Sift the flour with the baking soda and salt twice, and set it aside.
3. With an electric mixer on low speed (or with a stationary mixer fitted with the paddle attachment), beat the butter with the vegetable shortening for 1 minute, or until light. Slowly add the sugar, about 2 tablespoons at a time, and when all of it has been added, continue to beat on medium speed for about 5 minutes, scraping down the beaters and sides of the bowl as necessary. The mixture will look fluffy, like something between mayonnaise and whipped cream.
4. Add the eggs one at a time, beating for 10 seconds between additions, or until each egg is absorbed by the butter. Scrape down the beaters and sides of the bowl and beat for another minute; add the orange extract or oil.
5. With a large rubber spatula, fold the sifted ingredients into the batter in three additions, alternating with the orange juice concentrate in two additions. Remove 1½ cups of batter to a separate bowl and fold the melted chocolate into the larger quantity.
6. With a large spoon, drop some orange batter into the pan, leaving small spaces into which you should drop the chocolate batter. For the second layer, drop some light batter over the chocolate and chocolate over the light (this does not have to be exact, but you get the idea). Continue for about three layers, or until all the batter is used up. Rap the pan sharply on the counter once to level it, then smooth the top.
7. Bake for 30 minutes, lower the temperature to 325°F, and bake for 35 to 40 minutes longer, or until a tester inserted in the center comes out dry.
8. Cool the cake in the pan on a wire rack for 30 minutes. Lightly coat the wire rack with a nonstick vegetable spray. Run a thin spatula or table knife around the inside of the pan and the inner tube to loosen the cake from the mold. Invert the cake and cool it, right side up, to room temperature on the greased wire rack.

STORAGE: Keep at room temperature, wrapped airtight in plastic, for up to 3 days; refrigerate after that.

PLATED DESSERT SUGGESTION (per portion)

1 slice of cake
Orange or Peppered Custard
Sauce (page 359), in a
squeeze bottle
Deadly Delicious Chocolate
Sauce (page 362), in a
squeeze bottle

Chopped orange "supremes"
(page 65), optional

Center the slice of cake on a 10-inch plate. Squeeze alternating nickel-size dots of the custard and chocolate sauces around the outside edge of the plate, and run a skewer through the center of the dots in a circle around the plate to create heart shapes. Set a clump of orange segments to one side of the cake.

**Potato Chocolate Chip Cake

This cake is remarkable, primarily for its taste but also because it is made with riced boiled potatoes! Initially I wanted to include it because it is such a novelty item, but it proved to be delicious as well. While I have no hard facts to back me up, my theory about how this recipe evolved is simply that someone added leftover boiled potatoes to a batter and came up with a very moist and delicious cake.

Makes one 10-inch, single-layer cake

Serves 12

Level of difficulty ★

CAKE

2 medium (12 ounces) baking potatoes, skinned and boiled

¾ cup (3 ounces) blanched almonds, finely ground

8 ounces bittersweet chocolate, grated or pulverized in a food processor

2 cups (15 ounces) superfine sugar

1½ cups (7 ounces) cake flour

1½ teaspoons baking powder

½ teaspoon ground cinnamon

¼ teaspoon ground coriander

¼ teaspoon plus a pinch of salt

2 sticks (8 ounces) unsalted butter, softened

4 large eggs, separated

½ cup milk

GLAZE

Chocolate Satin Glaze
(page 330)

12 whole blanched almonds

Bittersweet chocolate shavings
(page 380)

TO MAKE THE CAKE

1. Rice the potatoes or grate them through the large holes of a box grater. Combine the potatoes with the ground almonds and grated chocolate, and set aside. Set aside ½ cup of the sugar for whipping the egg whites later on.

2. Position a rack in the center of the oven and preheat to 350°F. Lightly butter and flour a 10 × 3-inch springform pan, tap out the excess, and line the bottom with a parchment or greased and floured waxed paper circle.

3. Sift the flour, baking powder, cinnamon, coriander, and ¼ teaspoon of the salt twice, and set it aside.

4. With an electric mixer on low speed (or with a stationary mixer fitted with the paddle attachment), beat the butter for 1 minute, or until light. Slowly add the remaining 1½ cups sugar, about 2 tablespoons at a time, and when all of it has been added, continue to beat on medium speed for 2 to 3 minutes, scraping down the beaters and sides of the bowl as needed. The mixture will look fluffy, like something between mayonnaise and whipped cream.

5. Add the egg yolks two at a time, beating for 10 seconds between additions, or until absorbed by the butter. Scrape down the beaters and sides of the bowl and beat for a minute longer, or until smooth. Beat in the grated potato mixture and mix until just combined.

6. With a large rubber spatula, fold the sifted ingredients into the batter in three additions, alternating with the milk in two additions. Beat with an electric mixer on low speed for 1 minute, or until the mixture looks smooth.

7. With an electric mixer, beat the egg whites with a pinch of salt until they form soft peaks. With the machine running, slowly add the reserved ½ cup sugar, about 2 tablespoons at a time, and beat until stiff and glossy. Fold the beaten whites into the batter.

8. Spoon the batter into the prepared pan and smooth the top with a rubber or offset spatula. Set the springform pan on a larger baking sheet (to catch the drips) and bake for about 50 minutes to 1 hour, or until a tester inserted in the center comes out dry.

9. Cool the cake to room temperature in the pan on a wire rack. Run a knife around the cake to loosen it from the sides and unlock the springform. Lift the cake up and out of the form and invert it onto a plate or cardboard round. Remove the bottom of the pan and peel off the paper circle.

TO GLAZE

Set the cake, on the cardboard, on a wire rack and set waxed paper underneath the wire rack to catch the drips from the glaze. Pour the glaze over the top of the cake and spread it toward and over the edges so it drips down the sides. Spread the glaze around the sides and drag a decorating comb around the sides. Decorate the top of the cake with 12 whole almonds set in a circle around the edge, and scatter the chocolate shavings inside the circle of almonds.

STORAGE: Keep at room temperature, under a cake dome or an inverted large mixing bowl, for up to 2 days. Refrigerate after that, but bring back to room temperature before serving.

Raspberry-Scented Cocoa Cake

The raspberry purée adds moistness to the cake as well as subtle overtones of flavor that are echoed in the lovely raspberry-scented icing.

Makes one 10-inch tube cake

Serves about 16

Level of difficulty ★

CAKE

One 10-ounce package individually quick-frozen raspberries, thawed

½ cup water

2 cups (9 ounces) cake flour

½ teaspoon baking soda

Scant 1 cup (3 ounces) unsweetened, nonalkalized cocoa powder, sifted

¼ teaspoon salt

3 sticks (12 ounces) unsalted butter, softened

3 cups (22.5 ounces) superfine sugar

5 large eggs

ICING

About 1 cup (4.5 ounces) confectioners' sugar, sifted

2 teaspoons framboise liqueur or brandy

2 teaspoons or more water

¼ teaspoon Boyajian Natural Raspberry Flavor, optional

Red food coloring, optional

1 pint fresh raspberries

TO MAKE THE CAKE

1. In a food processor, purée the thawed raspberries with the water until smooth. Strain the purée through a sieve and discard the seeds; set aside the raspberry purée for later.
2. Position a rack in the lower third of the oven and preheat to 350°F. Generously butter a 10-inch tube pan, dust it with flour, and tap out the excess.
3. Sift the flour with the baking soda, cocoa, and salt twice, and set it aside.
4. With an electric mixer on low speed (or with a stationary mixer fitted with the paddle attachment), beat the butter for 1 minute, or until light. Slowly add the sugar, about 2 tablespoons at a time (this should take about 4 minutes). When all the sugar has been added, continue to beat on medium speed for 5 to 6 minutes, scraping down the beaters and the sides of the bowl as needed. The mixture will look fluffy, like something between mayonnaise and whipped cream.
5. Add the eggs one at a time, beating for 10 seconds between additions, or until each egg has been absorbed by the butter. Add the raspberry purée and beat for a few seconds; the mixture will look curdled, but that is okay.
6. With a large rubber spatula, fold the sifted ingredients in two to three additions into the batter. With an electric mixer on low speed, beat the batter for 1 minute longer, or until smooth. Spoon the batter into the prepared pan and spread it evenly with a rubber or small offset spatula.
7. Bake for 1 hour and 10 to 20 minutes, or until a tester inserted in the center comes out dry.
8. Cool the cake in the pan on a wire rack for 30 minutes. Lightly coat the wire rack with nonstick vegetable spray. Ease the cake out of the pan and cool it to room temperature, upside down, on the greased wire rack.

TO ICE

1. Sift the confectioners' sugar a second time into a mixing bowl. With your finger, make a well in the middle of the sugar and pour the framboise, 2 teaspoons water, and the raspberry flavoring into the well. With a fork, combine the ingredients by gradually pulling the sugar from the walls of the well into the center and mix until smooth.

2. Dip a toothpick in the food coloring and gradually add only as much as is needed to create a soft pink hue (bring the icing close to the cake to check on the color; if it is colored too lightly the icing will look white on the cake, not pink).

3. Transfer the icing to a 10-inch pastry bag fitted with an ⅛-inch-wide plain tip. Transfer the cake to a cardboard round cut slightly smaller than the cake, and set it on a turntable if you have one. Pipe a free-form, widely spaced filigree pattern over the top and sides of the cake. Just before serving, fill the space in the center of the cake with fresh raspberries.

STORAGE: Keep at room temperature, wrapped airtight in plastic, for up to 3 days; refrigerate after that.

PLATED DESSERT SUGGESTION (per portion)

1 slice of cake   *3 to 5 fresh raspberries*
Raspberry Squeeze Sauce
   (page 368), in a squeeze bottle

Set a slice of cake, left of center, on the plate. Squeeze a generous pool of raspberry sauce to one side and below the cake. Center the raspberries in the sauce. Randomly squeeze a few smaller dots of varying sizes onto the plate.

Spicy Chocolate Pound Cake with Brandy Glaze

This remarkably delicious, moist cake, with its quiet symphony of tastes, converted me from a spice-cake hater to a spice-cake aficionado.

Makes one 9-inch tube cake

Serves about 15

Level of difficulty ★

CAKE

2 cups (9.5 ounces) bleached all-purpose flour

Scant ⅓ cup (1 ounce) unsweetened, Dutch-processed cocoa powder

1 teaspoon baking powder

½ teaspoon baking soda

¼ teaspoon salt

½ teaspoon ground cinnamon

¼ teaspoon ground cardamom

¼ teaspoon ground cloves

¼ teaspoon ground ginger

2 sticks (8 ounces) unsalted butter, softened

1 cup (7.5 ounces) granulated sugar

¾ cup packed (5.5 ounces) light brown sugar

4 large eggs

1 teaspoon freshly grated orange zest *or* ½ teaspoon orange extract *or* ¼ teaspoon orange oil

½ cup buttermilk or sour cream

GLAZE

6 ounces semisweet or bittersweet chocolate, finely chopped

¼ cup each of brandy and water, or ½ cup water

1 tablespoon unsalted butter

Generous 1 cup (5 ounces) confectioners' sugar, sifted

TO MAKE THE CAKE

1. Position a rack in the lower third of the oven and preheat to 350°F. Generously butter a 9-inch Bundt or tube pan, lightly dust it with cocoa powder, and tap out the excess.

2. Sift the flour with the cocoa, baking powder, baking soda, salt, and spices twice, and set it aside.

3. With an electric mixer on low speed (or with a stationary mixer fitted with the paddle attachment), beat the butter for 1 minute, or until light. Slowly add the granulated and brown sugars, about 2 tablespoons at a time (this should take 2 to 3 minutes). When all the sugar has been added, continue to beat on medium speed for about 5 minutes, scraping down the beaters and sides of the bowl as needed. The mixture will look fluffy, like something between mayonnaise and whipped cream.

4. Add the eggs one at a time, beating for 10 seconds between additions, or until the egg has been absorbed by the butter; then beat in the orange zest. Scrape down the beaters and sides of the bowl and beat for a minute longer, or until homogenized.

5. With a large rubber spatula, fold the sifted ingredients into the batter in three additions, alternating with the buttermilk in two additions. Once the ingredients are combined, beat the batter with the electric mixer on low speed for another minute, or until smooth.

6. Transfer the batter to the prepared pan. Spread it evenly in the pan and smooth the top with a rubber or offset spatula. Rap the pan sharply on the counter a couple of times to break up any large air bubbles, and bake for 20 minutes. Lower the temperature to 325° and bake for 45 minutes to 1 hour longer, or until a tester inserted in the center comes out dry.

7. Cool the cake in the pan on a wire rack for 30 minutes. Lightly grease the wire rack with nonstick vegetable spray. Turn the cake out of the pan and cool it to room temperature, right side up, on the wire rack.

TO GLAZE

1. Melt the chocolate with the brandy and water in a mixing bowl or the top of a double boiler set over simmering water. When melted, add the butter, combine with a whisk, and remove from the heat. Transfer the mixture to a clean bowl.

2. Sift ½ the confectioners' sugar into the chocolate and whisk until well combined. Continue to sift in additional sugar until you achieve a consistency fluid enough to pour over the cake yet thick enough to stick.

3. Set the cake on a cardboard round cut slightly smaller than the cake. Pour the glaze over the top, letting it drizzle down the sides. Continue to pour the glaze over the top until the sides are mostly covered. If the glaze doesn't quite reach to the bottom of the cake, leave it as is or coax it down with a small spatula.

STORAGE: Keep at room temperature, loosely wrapped in foil, for up to 2 days. Refrigerate after that, but remove the cake 30 minutes before serving.

PLATED DESSERT SUGGESTION (per portion)

⅓ cup Ginger Custard Sauce (page 360)

1 slice of cake

Deadly Delicious Chocolate Sauce (page 362), in a squeeze bottle

Candied ginger, optional

Pour the custard sauce in the middle of a plate and center the cake in the sauce. Squeeze a line of chocolate sauce around the outside of the custard sauce. With a skewer, at 1- or 2-inch intervals, pull the chocolate sauce into the ginger sauce. Scatter some candied ginger over the sauce and cake, if you wish.

Streusel-Woven Chocolate Coffee Cake

Streusel is a butter, flour, and sugar mixture that is rubbed together and used as a topping for coffee cakes. Here the streusel is scattered throughout the cake as well as on top. The sour cream makes the crumb incredibly tender.

Makes one 9-inch
square cake

Serves about 15

Level of difficulty ★

STREUSEL

2 tablespoons bleached all-purpose flour

1 teaspoon ground cinnamon

2 tablespoons unsalted butter, softened

½ cup packed (3.75 ounces) light brown sugar

Generous ½ cup (2 ounces) pecans, finely chopped

½ cup (3 ounces) semisweet chocolate morsels

CAKE

1¾ cups (8.25 ounces) bleached all-purpose flour

Scant ½ cup (1.5 ounces) unsweetened, nonalkalized cocoa powder

½ teaspoon baking powder

½ teaspoon baking soda

¼ teaspoon salt

2 sticks (8 ounces) unsalted butter, softened

1 cup (7.5 ounces) superfine sugar

3 large eggs

1 teaspoon vanilla extract

1 cup sour cream

¼ cup milk or buttermilk

TO MAKE THE STREUSEL

With a fork, combine the flour with the cinnamon, then mash in the butter. With your fingers, work in the sugar. Mix in the nuts and chocolate morsels and set the mixture aside.

TO MAKE THE CAKE

1. Position a rack in the center of the oven and preheat to 350°F. Lightly grease a 9 × 9 × 2-inch baking pan and set it aside.

2. Sift the flour with the cocoa, baking powder, baking soda, and salt twice, and set it aside.

3. With an electric mixer on low speed (or with a stationary mixer fitted with the paddle attachment), beat the butter for 1 minute, or until light. Slowly add the sugar, about 2 tablespoons at a time, and when all of it has been added, continue to beat on medium speed for about 4 minutes, scraping down the beaters and sides of the bowl as needed. The mixture will look fluffy, like something between mayonnaise and whipped cream.

4. Add the eggs one at a time, beating for 10 seconds between additions, or until each has been absorbed by the butter. Add the vanilla and beat for 1 minute, scraping down the beaters and sides of the bowl as needed. Blend the sour cream and milk.

5. With a large rubber spatula, fold the sifted ingredients into the batter in three additions, alternating with the sour cream in two additions. Beat the batter with the electric mixer on low speed for another minute or until smooth.

6. Spread ½ the batter in the prepared pan and sprinkle it with ½ the streusel. Spread the remaining batter over the streusel and top that with the remaining streusel. Bake for about 45 minutes to 1 hour, or until a tester inserted in the center comes out dry.

7. Cool the cake to room temperature in the pan on a wire rack. Cut and serve it from the pan.

STORAGE: Keep at room temperature, wrapped airtight, for up to 3 days in a cool dry place.

**Tea-Infused White Chocolate Cake

This cake has a unique and delicious flavor that comes from combining white chocolate with tea. The taste of the tea reveals itself slowly and lingers on the tongue after each bite of cake. No one will be able to identify the mystery flavor, and most people will be fooled into thinking the tiny black flecks of tea are poppy seeds. This is delicious served plain or with Passion Fruit Sauce (page 366).

Makes one 9 × 5-inch loaf cake

Serves 12 to 14

Level of difficulty ★

---

4 tea bags (suggested flavors: orange pekoe, Constant Comment, jasmine, or an herbal tea)

⅓ cup boiling water

2 cups (9.5 ounces) bleached all-purpose flour

1 teaspoon baking powder

½ teaspoon salt

1¾ sticks (7 ounces) unsalted butter, softened

1⅓ cups (10 ounces) superfine sugar

4 large eggs

3 ounces white chocolate, melted and cooled

½ teaspoon grated lemon zest or ¼ teaspoon lemon extract or ⅛ teaspoon lemon oil

2 tablespoons confectioners' sugar

---

1. Empty the contents of the tea bags into a small bowl. Pour the boiling water over the tea and let it steep for as long as possible (30 minutes at least). Position a rack in the center of the oven and preheat to 350°F.
2. Lightly butter a 9 × 5 × 3-inch loaf pan and line the bottom with parchment or greased waxed paper.
3. Sift the flour with the baking powder and salt twice, and set it aside.
4. With an electric mixer on low speed (or with a stationary mixer fitted with the paddle attachment), beat the butter for 1 minute, or until light. Slowly add the granulated sugar, about 2 tablespoons at a time, and when all of it has been added, continue to beat on medium speed for 4 minutes, scraping down the beaters and sides of the bowl as needed. The mixture will look fluffy, like something between mayonnaise and whipped cream.
5. Add the eggs one at a time, beating for 10 seconds between additions, or until each one has been absorbed by the butter. Add the cooled melted chocolate, the lemon zest, and the steeped tea leaves along with any liquid in the bowl, and combine. Beat for 1 minute, or until smooth and creamy.
6. With a large rubber spatula, in two or three additions, fold the sifted ingredients into the batter, then beat with an electric mixer on low speed for 1 minute.
7. Transfer the batter to the prepared pan, smooth the top, and rap the pan sharply on the counter a couple of times to break up any large air bubbles.
8. Bake for 45 minutes, then lower the temperature to 325° and bake for 30 to 45 minutes longer, or until a tester inserted in the center comes out dry.
9. Cool the cake in the pan on a wire rack for 20 minutes. Lightly grease the wire rack with nonstick vegetable spray. Invert the cake onto the greased wire rack, remove the paper, and cool to room temperature right side up.
10. Just before serving, sift the confectioners' sugar over the top.

STORAGE: Keep at room temperature, wrapped airtight, for up to 3 days in a cool dry place.

Tunnel of Fudge Cake

I couldn't write a book on chocolate cakes without including this famous recipe, originally developed for a Pillsbury Bake-Off contest. What is so special about this cake is that after baking and cooling, there remains a puddinglike, soft interior. The original recipe used a package of Pillsbury Frosting mix, no longer available, so the test kitchen at Pillsbury redeveloped the recipe, which stood until 1998 when, still not satisfied, they gave it another round of testing and reinventing and came up with this cake, the most updated version of the old classic. Pillsbury has generously allowed me to reprint the recipe below. I have changed some of the language so it conforms with the editorial style of this book.

Makes one 10-inch
tube cake

Serves 12 to 14

Level of difficulty ★

FILLING

1½ cups milk

1 (3.4-ounce) package chocolate fudge pudding and pie filling mix (not instant)

1 cup (6 ounces) semisweet chocolate chips

CAKE

1⅓ cups (10 ounces) granulated sugar

1½ sticks (6 ounces) unsalted butter, softened

½ cup (4 ounces) solid vegetable shortening, at room temperature

1 teaspoon vanilla extract

4 large eggs

2 cups (9.5 ounces) Pillsbury BEST™ bleached all-purpose flour

½ cup (1.5 ounces) unsweetened cocoa powder

½ teaspoon baking powder

½ teaspoon salt

1 cup milk

2 cups chopped walnuts

GLAZE

¾ cup (4 ounces) confectioners' sugar

¼ cup (0.75 ounce) unsweetened cocoa powder

4 to 6 teaspoons milk

TO MAKE THE FILLING

1. In a medium saucepan, combine the milk and pudding mix, and cook as directed on the package. Remove the saucepan from the heat, add the chocolate chips, and stir until melted. Set aside.

TO MAKE THE CAKE

1. Position a rack in the lower third of the oven and preheat to 350°F. Lightly grease and flour a 10-inch Bundt or tube pan.
2. In a large bowl, combine the sugar, butter, and shortening; beat until light and fluffy. Add the vanilla and eggs, and mix well.
3. Lightly spoon the flour into a measuring cup and level it off. Add the flour, cocoa, baking powder, salt, and milk. Beat at low speed until moistened. Beat for 3 minutes at medium speed. Stir in the walnuts.
4. Reserve 2 cups of the batter. Pour the remaining batter into the prepared pan. Spoon the filling in a ring on top of the batter, making sure it does not touch the sides of the pan. Spoon the reserved batter over the filling.
5. Bake for 50 to 60 minutes, or until the cake springs back when touched lightly in the center. (You can't gauge this with a cake tester because the inside "tunnel of fudge" remains moist.) Cool 1 hour; remove from the pan. Cool 1½ hours, or until completely cooled.

TO MAKE THE GLAZE

1. In a small bowl, blend the glaze ingredients, adding enough milk for the desired drizzling consistency. Spoon it over the top of the cake, allowing some to run down the sides. Use a very sharp or serrated knife to slice the cake.

STORAGE: Best served the day it is made; store any remaining cake in the refrigerator, wrapped airtight in plastic.

Walnut-Chocolate Filled Kugelhopf

What makes this so delicious is the band of grated chocolate, mixed with walnuts and sugar, that is distributed throughout the cake and melts into an almost puddinglike consistency.

Makes one 10-inch tube cake

Serves about 16

Level of difficulty ★

---

3 cups (14.25 ounces) bleached all-purpose flour

¾ cup (2.5 ounces) unsweetened, Dutch-processed cocoa powder

1 teaspoon baking powder

½ teaspoon baking soda

¾ teaspoon ground cinnamon

½ teaspoon ground cardamom

½ teaspoon salt

Generous 1 cup (4 ounces) walnuts, finely chopped

1 cup grated (6 ounces) bittersweet or semisweet chocolate (or semisweet chocolate morsels)

2¼ cups packed (18 ounces) light brown sugar

4 sticks (1 pound) unsalted butter, softened

5 large eggs

1 tablespoon vanilla extract

2 cups sour cream, at room temperature

---

1. Position a rack in the center of the oven and preheat to 350°F. Generously butter a 10-inch tube pan and set it aside.

2. Sift the flour with the cocoa, baking powder, baking soda, ½ teaspoon of the cinnamon, ¼ teaspoon of the cardamom, and the salt twice. In a small bowl, combine the walnuts, grated chocolate, ¼ cup of the brown sugar, the remaining ¼ teaspoon cinnamon, and the remaining ¼ teaspoon cardamom, and set it aside.

3. With an electric mixer on low speed (or with a stationary mixer fitted with the paddle attachment), beat the butter for 1 minute, or until light. Slowly add the remaining 2 cups sugar, about 2 tablespoons at a time, and when all of it has been added, continue to beat on medium speed for 3 to 4 minutes, scraping down the beaters and sides of the bowl as needed. The mixture will look fluffy, like something between mayonnaise and whipped cream.

4. Add the eggs one at a time, beating for 10 seconds between additions, or until each one has been absorbed by the butter. Add the vanilla, scrape down the beaters and sides of the bowl, and beat for another minute.

5. With a large rubber spatula, fold the sifted ingredients into the batter in four additions, alternating with the sour cream in three additions. Once the ingredients are combined, beat the batter with the electric mixer on low speed for another minute, or until smooth.

6. Spoon ⅓ of the batter into the prepared pan, spread it evenly with a spatula, and sprinkle ½ the chocolate and walnut mixture over that. Spoon and spread ⅓ of the batter over the nuts, sprinkle the remaining chocolate and walnut mixture over that, and spread the last of the batter over the nuts. Smooth the top with a rubber or small offset spatula and bake for 1 hour to 1 hour and 15 minutes, or until a tester inserted in the center comes out dry.

7. Cool the cake in the pan on a wire rack for 30 minutes. Lightly grease the wire rack with nonstick vegetable spray. Ease the cake out of the pan and cool it to room temperature, right side up, on the wire rack.

STORAGE: Keep at room temperature, wrapped airtight, for up to 3 days; refrigerate after that.

Chocolate Apricot Upside-Down Cake

In this pretty cake, the apricots provide a tangy counterpoint to the sweetness of the chocolate. The cake is best served warm, with a generous spoonful of whipped cream on the side.

Makes one 9-inch, single-layer cake

Serves 8

Level of difficulty ★

TOPPING

1 (30-ounce) can apricot halves, drained

½ stick (2 ounces) unsalted butter

⅓ cup packed light brown sugar

2 tablespoons light corn syrup

1 cup whole pecans

CAKE

1 cup (4.5 ounces) cake or pastry flour

¼ cup (0.75 ounce) unsweetened, nonalkalized cocoa powder

¼ teaspoon baking powder

½ teaspoon baking soda

¼ teaspoon salt

¾ stick (3 ounces) unsalted butter, softened

¾ cup (5.5 ounces) superfine sugar

2 large eggs

⅓ cup milk

TO MAKE THE TOPPING

1. Position a rack in the center of the oven and preheat to 350°F. Lightly butter a 9 × 2-inch round cake pan. Blot the apricots between several layers of paper towels to absorb any excess liquid.
2. In a small saucepan, melt the butter over low heat. Add the brown sugar and corn syrup, stir, and heat until melted into the butter. Remove from the heat and pour into the prepared cake pan. Place a pecan in each apricot half and place the apricots, pecan side down, in the pan. Wedge more pecans between the apricots and set the pan aside.

TO MAKE THE CAKE

1. Sift the flour with the cocoa, baking powder, baking soda, and salt twice, and set it aside.
2. With an electric mixer on low speed (or with a stationary mixer fitted with the paddle attachment), beat the butter for 1 minute, or until light. Slowly add the sugar, about 2 tablespoons at a time, and when all of it has been added, continue to beat for about 3 minutes, scraping down the beaters and sides of the bowl as needed. The mixture will look fluffy.
3. Add the eggs one at a time, beating for 10 seconds between additions, and beat for another minute, or until smooth.
4. With a large rubber spatula, fold the sifted ingredients into the batter in three additions, alternating with the milk in two additions. Spoon the batter over the fruit and spread it evenly with a rubber spatula. Bake for 45 to 50 minutes, or until the top feels springy and a cake tester inserted in the center of the cake part comes out dry.
5. Cool the cake in the pan on a wire rack for 15 minutes. Run a knife around the cake to loosen it from the sides. Place a platter over the pan, invert the cake, and leave it for 5 minutes without moving it. The cake should drop out of the pan with the help of gravity. If not, tap it once and the cake will fall out. If any fruit or nuts stick to the pan, simply place them back on the cake.

STORAGE: This tastes best served the day it was made. Keep at room temperature, wrapped airtight, for 1 day; refrigerate leftovers after that.

Chocolate Cake Pudding

"Unbelievably rich and delicious" is how my daughter Alessia describes this pudding, made from cubes of leftover cake baked in a cream and egg custard. This extraordinarily fabulous dessert is like bread pudding—only better.

Makes one 9-inch square cake

Serves 8

Level of difficulty ★

3 cups heavy cream

½ cup (3.75 ounces) granulated sugar

4 large eggs

4 cups (12 ounces) 1-inch cubes of unfrosted pound cake such as:
Dependable Chocolate Pound Cake (page 104)
Light Chocolate Pound Cake (page 107)
Super Rich Chocolate Pound Cake (page 109)
Chocolate Chocolate Tea Cake (page 112)
Hazelnut Chocolate Cake (page 116)

Chunk of bittersweet chocolate, optional

1. Position a rack in the center of the oven and preheat to 350°F. Generously butter a 6-cup-capacity ovenproof glass casserole, or 9 × 9-inch square pan.
2. In a medium saucepan, over low heat, bring the cream and ¼ cup of the sugar to a simmer, and remove it from the heat.
3. In a large mixing bowl, whisk the remaining ¼ cup sugar with the eggs, then drizzle the hot cream into the eggs. Add the cake cubes and toss them with the egg and cream mixture.
4. Spoon the cake and custard into the prepared pan. Set the pan in a larger baking pan. Pour boiling water into the larger pan so it comes halfway up the sides of the smaller pan, and bake for 45 minutes, or until the edges begin to set. Remove the pan from the water and cool until warm.
5. Serve in small bowls, with freshly grated chocolate shavings over the top, if you wish.

STORAGE: Store leftovers, wrapped airtight in plastic, in the refrigerator for up to 3 days; rewarm them in the microwave oven before serving.

LAYER CAKES

WHEN I STARTED on the research for this book, I had no idea I would discover so many recipes for chocolate cake; I think I found a dozen or so different recipes for devil's food cake alone! My goal in determining which recipes to include was to make sure I offered the reader a terrific selection of the best and that each cake was distinctive. After eliminating recipes that were dull or tasted too much alike, I was left with a dozen or so great recipes for chocolate cake layers.

To help me decide which were the best of the best, I conducted a rather informal tasting with eight eager souls. I baked the cake layers, left them unfrosted, and got my taste-testers to evaluate each one in terms of texture, moistness, and chocolate flavor. The results were predictable: Those cake layers that tasted most of chocolate and were the moistest were the winners and are included in this book.

MATCHING LAYER TO FROSTING

The layer cakes in this chapter are butter cakes, which means they are heavier than sponge cakes and need fillings and frostings that can support the weight of the cake itself. The frostings should also be thick enough to glue the layers together while camouflaging the seams where layers join with frosting. The best are American confectioners' sugar frostings and boiled icings; whipped cream and other fluffy, mousselike fillings; as well as the French buttercreams and ganache icings.

Although there are both European- and American-style frostings that have the right consistency for these layer cakes, because the majority of the stacked cakes in this chapter are quintessentially American, I liked pairing them with frostings that are also American in style.

If you prefer to fill the layers with frostings different from the ones I suggest, take a look at the Creative Combinations that follow.

CREATIVE COMBINATIONS
FOR LAYER CAKES

1. Single-Layer Cakes:

Halve the recipe for one of the butter chocolate layer cakes and bake it in a single cake pan.
Glaze the outside with
Ganache (page 324) or
White Chocolate Glaze (page 331)
Split the single layer in two
Fill the inside with raspberry, red currant, or apricot jam
Glaze the outside with
Ganache (page 324) or Maria's Best Chocolate Glaze (page 331)

2. Two-Layer Cakes:

Split each of two layers in half; soak the layers with Simple Syrup (page 370)
Fill and frost with
Classic French Buttercreams (page 302) or
Chocolate Mousse Filling (page 314) or
Fruit Mousse Filling (page 316)

3. Three-Layer Cakes:

Fill the layers with one type of frosting, such as
Orange Chocolate Frosting (page 298) or
Peanut Butter Chocolate Frosting (page 301) or
Minted Cream Cheese Frosting (page 299) or
Chocolate Malted Frosting (page 299)
Frost the top and sides with
Classic American Chocolate Frosting (page 298) or
Wicked Chocolate Frosting (page 298) or
Chocolate Water Icing (page 325)
Fill the layers with
Classic American Chocolate Frosting (page 298) or
Wicked Chocolate Frosting (page 298)
Frost the top and sides with
Butterscotch Frosting (page 300) or
Mocha Frosting (page 300) or
Seven-Minute Icing (page 313) or
Boiled Icing (page 312)
For textural contrast, sprinkle chopped nuts or coconut on the inside layers only, or carry the theme throughout by sprinkling them on top and around the outside as well.

4. Four-Layer Cakes:

Fill the layers with
Vanilla Pastry Cream (page 322), or
flavored pastry creams (page 322)
Frost the top and sides with
Real Fudge Icing (page 327) or
Fudge Caramel Icing (page 329)
Fill the layers with

Ganache (page 324) of one type of chocolate

Frost the top and sides with
  Whipped Ganache (page 321) of a contrasting chocolate

Fill the layers only, or fill the inside and frost the top and sides with
  Whipped Cream (page 318) and imbed a fine dice of fresh orange or berries inside

Fill the layers with
  Seven-Minute Icing (page 313) or
    Whipped Cream (stabilized or not)
      (pages 318 and 320) or
  Whipped Ganache (page 321)

Leave the top and sides plain

Classic Devil's Food Cake Layers

I consider this the perfect recipe for devil's food cake because the layers come out springy and have an intense chocolate taste that is not too sweet. I tested many different recipes for devil's food cake, and many of them were surprisingly light in both chocolate flavor and color. This one, though, reminds me of the 1950s layer cakes sold at country fairs, bakeries, drugstores, and diners. It is made by the two-stage method, and I think it is what cake mixes try to emulate. I love a real fudge frosting with this, but if that's too hard for you to make, sandwich the layers and ice the cake with another type of all-American frosting.

Makes one 8-inch,
2- or 4-layer cake

Serves 12

Level of difficulty ★ ★

1½ cups (7 ounces) cake flour

Scant ½ cup (1.5 ounces) unsweetened, Dutch-processed cocoa powder

¾ teaspoon baking soda

¼ teaspoon salt

½ cup (4 ounces) solid vegetable shortening, at room temperature

1⅓ cups (10 ounces) superfine sugar

1 cup milk

2 large eggs, lightly beaten

1 teaspoon vanilla extract

SUGGESTED FROSTINGS

Real Fudge Icing (page 327)

Classic American Chocolate Frosting (page 298)

Wicked Chocolate Frosting (page 298)

Boiled Icing (page 312)

Seven-Minute Icing (page 313)

1. Position a rack in the center of the oven and preheat to 350°F. Lightly grease and flour two 8 × 1.5-inch round cake pans and line the bottoms with parchment or greased and floured waxed paper circles. Tap out excess flour.
2. Sift the flour with the cocoa, baking soda, and salt twice into a mixing bowl. Add the vegetable shortening to the sifted ingredients. With an electric mixer on low speed, beat for 1 minute, or until the ingredients are combined and the fat is broken down into small pieces. Add the sugar and blend with a fork until combined.
3. Drizzle ½ the milk into the flour and beat on low speed for 1 minute, scraping down the sides of the bowl as needed.
4. Combine the remaining milk with the eggs and vanilla and, with the beaters running on low speed, slowly add this to the batter in three additions. Scrape down the beaters and sides of the bowl and beat for 1 minute longer or until velvety smooth.
5. Transfer the batter (it will be runny) to the prepared pans. Rap the pans sharply a couple of times on the counter to break up any large air bubbles. Bake for 25 to 30 minutes, or until the cake begins to shrink from the sides of the pan and a tester inserted in the center comes out dry.
6. Remove the cakes from the oven and cool them in their pans on a wire rack for 5 minutes. Run a table knife or a spatula around the cakes to loosen them from the sides of the pan so they don't tear as they shrink during cooling. Finish cooling the cakes to room temperature in their pans.
7. Unmold and peel off the paper circles just before frosting, and frost when the layers are completely cool.

STORAGE: Keep under a cake dome or an inverted large mixing bowl at room temperature in a cool, dry place, for a couple of days; refrigerate after that. Bring the cake back to room temperature so the icing softens before serving.

Classic Devil's Food Cake Layers

continued from previous page

continued on next page

VARIATION: 9-inch, 3-layer Classic Devil's Food Cake

Make the same recipe with the following changes: Prepare three 9 × 1.5-inch round cake pans. Use the following quantities: 2¼ cups (10 ounces) cake flour, ¾ cup (2.5 ounces) cocoa powder, 1 teaspoon baking soda, ½ teaspoon salt, ¾ cup (4.5 ounces) solid vegetable shortening, 2 cups (15 ounces) superfine sugar, 1½ cups milk, 3 large eggs, and 1½ teaspoons vanilla.

Devil's Food

The origin of the name *Devil's Food* appears murky. John F. Mariani in *The Dictionary of American Food and Drink* (New York: Hearst Books, 1994) says the name comes from the fact that cakes made with dark chocolate are "sinful" because they are so rich. I prefer the theory laid out in Jean Anderson's *American Century Cookbook* (New York: Clarkson Potter, 1997), which explains that the name *Devil's Food* came about to contrast the cake's denseness and dark color to the texture and color, as well as the name, of a cake called "Angel Food."

Custard Devil's Food Cake Layers

I cannot count the number of cookbooks in which this recipe appears. Many a cookbook author claims it was her or his mother's favorite, which is not surprising given that it is in early editions of both The Joy of Cooking *and* The Settlement Cookbook.

What makes this recipe distinctive and so recognizable is that it is made with a custard, which is then blended into the batter. When I asked Dieter Schorner—former chairman of the pastry department at the French Culinary Institute—how he thought this method would affect the cake, he said he thought it would help to create a very moist cake, which indeed it does.

For a long time I thought the recipe was a Pillsbury original because Jean Anderson, in her American Century Cookbook *(New York: Clarkson Potter, 1997), says it was published by Pillsbury in their 1905* A Book for Cooks. *I have since discovered earlier versions of a recipe very much like it, namely one in Mrs. Moritz and Adele Kahn's* The Twentieth Century Cook Book, *published in 1898.*

Makes one 9-inch, 2-layer cake

Serves 12 to 14

Level of difficulty ★★

---

1 cup milk

1½ cups (11.25 ounces) granulated sugar

4 ounces unsweetened chocolate, finely chopped

1 large egg yolk

2 teaspoons vanilla extract

2 cups (9 ounces) cake flour

1 teaspoon baking powder

½ teaspoon baking soda

¼ teaspoon salt

1 stick (4 ounces) unsalted butter

2 large eggs

SUGGESTED ICINGS

Seven-Minute Icing (page 313)

Whipped Cream, plain or flavored (page 318)

---

1. In a small saucepan over medium heat, combine ½ cup of the milk and ½ cup of the sugar and bring to a simmer, stirring. Add the chocolate and bring back to a simmer, stirring. Remove the saucepan from the heat, add the egg yolk, and stir for a few seconds, or until the mixture thickens to custardlike consistency. Transfer the mixture to a bowl to cool to room temperature. Stir in the vanilla.

2. Position a rack in the center of the oven and preheat to 350°F. Lightly grease and flour two 9 × 1.5-inch round cake pans and tap out the excess. Line the bottoms with parchment or greased and floured waxed paper circles.

3. Sift the flour with the baking powder, baking soda, and salt twice, and set it aside.

4. With an electric mixer on low speed (or with a stationary mixer fitted with the paddle attachment), beat the butter for 1 minute, or until light. Slowly add the remaining cup of sugar, about 2 tablespoons at a time, and when all of it has been added, continue to beat on medium speed for 3 to 4 minutes, scraping down the beaters and sides of the bowl as needed. The mixture will look like whipped mayonnaise.

5. Add the eggs one at a time, beating for 10 seconds between additions, or until absorbed by the butter. Add the cooled chocolate custard and beat for a minute on low speed, or until the mixture is smooth and blended.

6. With a large rubber spatula, fold the sifted ingredients into the batter in three additions, alternating with the remaining ½ cup milk in two additions. Beat with the electric mixer on low speed for 1 minute longer, or until smooth.

continued on next page

Custard Devil's Food Cake Layers

continued from previous page

7. Transfer the batter to the prepared pans. Spread the batter evenly and smooth the tops with a rubber or offset spatula. Bake for 25 to 30 minutes, or until a tester inserted in the center comes out dry.

8. Remove the cakes from the oven. Immediately run a knife around the cakes to loosen them from the sides of the pan, so the cakes don't tear as they shrink. Cool the cakes to room temperature in their pans on a wire rack.

9. Unmold the cakes, peel off the paper circles, and ice.

STORAGE: Keep in the refrigerator, under a cake dome or an inverted mixing bowl, for up to 3 days.

**Aztec Devil's Food Cake

In reading about the history of chocolate, I learned that thousands of years ago the Aztecs and Mayans flavored their bitter chocolate drinks with flowers, hot chiles, and numerous exotic spices, unlike the ones we use to flavor chocolate today. Inspired, I came up with this exotic variation on devil's food cake. It is flavored with freshly ground black pepper, providing an extraordinary counterpoint to the boiled icing, which is flavored with rose water and almond extract.

Makes one 9-inch, 2-layer cake

Serves 12 to 14

Level of difficulty ★★

CAKE

Custard Devil's Food Cake Layers batter (page 141)

1 to 2 teaspoons freshly ground black pepper

1 tablespoon vanilla extract

¼ teaspoon rose water extract

ICING

½ teaspoon rose water

½ teaspoon almond extract

Boiled Icing (page 312)

TO MAKE THE CAKE

After making the cake batter, add the pepper, vanilla, and rose water. Bake the cake layers and cool completely as directed in the recipe.

TO ICE

Fold the rose water and almond extract into the icing and taste; add more of either if you want, then ice the cake.

STORAGE: Keep at room temperature, loosely covered with a cake dome or an inverted mixing bowl, in a cool dry place. After a couple of days the icing will wilt or bead up; if so, refrigerate the cake.

Mocha Devil's Food Cake

Coffee in the cake batter and in the icing makes this a java-lover's dream.

Makes one 9-inch,
4-layer cake

Serves 12

Level of difficulty ★

CAKE

Custard Devil's Food Cake
Layers batter (page 141)

1 tablespoon instant espresso
coffee powder

FILLING AND FROSTING

1½ sticks (6 ounces) butter,
softened

About 5 cups (1.5 pounds)
confectioners' sugar, sifted

¼ cup (0.75 ounce)
unsweetened cocoa powder,
sifted

2 tablespoons instant espresso
coffee powder

2 tablespoons boiling water

1 teaspoon vanilla extract

4 to 6 tablespoons heavy cream

TO MAKE THE CAKE

In the first step of making the cake batter, simmer the espresso powder coffee with the milk and sugar. When the cake is baked through, split the cooled layers in half.

TO FILL AND FROST

1. With an electric mixer (or a stationary mixer fitted with the paddle attachment), beat the butter for 1 minute, or until soft. Sift the sugar with the cocoa into the butter, and beat until well mixed.
2. Dissolve the espresso in the boiling water. Add the vanilla and 2 tablespoons of the heavy cream and beat until blended; then add enough additional cream to achieve a spreadable consistency.
3. With an electric mixer on low speed (use the paddle attachment if you have one), beat the frosting until light. If the consistency is too loose, add more sugar; if too stiff, add more cream.
4. Fill and frost the cake.

STORAGE: Keep in the refrigerator, under a cake dome or an inverted large bowl, for up to 3 days.

Sweet Devil's Food Cake Layers

This devil's food cake layer was my taste-testers' favorite. It is sweeter than others be-cause of the brown sugar, which, along with the sour cream, also contributes to its moist, tender, and fudgy texture. The layers slice like a dream and marry best with creamy whipped fillings.

Makes one 9-inch, 4-layer cake

Serves 12 to 14

Level of difficulty ★

2 cups (9 ounces) cake flour

½ teaspoon baking powder

½ teaspoon baking soda

¼ teaspoon salt

1 stick (4 ounces) chilled unsalted butter, cut into tablespoon-size pieces

1¼ cups (9.5 ounces) superfine sugar

1 cup packed (7.5 ounces) light brown sugar

4 ounces unsweetened chocolate, melted and cooled

1 cup sour cream

3 large eggs

1 teaspoon vanilla extract

SUGGESTED FILLINGS AND ICINGS

Whipped Cream, cocoa-, coffee-, or mocha-flavored (page 318)

Whipped Ganache, dark or milk chocolate (page 321)

Boiled Icing, plain, chocolate, or zebra (page 312)

Seven-Minute Icing, plain or orange (page 313)

TO MAKE THE CAKE

1. Position a rack in the center of the oven and preheat to 350°F. Lightly grease and flour two 9 × 2-inch round cake pans, tap out the excess, and line the bottoms with parchment or greased and floured waxed paper circles.

2. Sift the flour with the baking powder, baking soda, and salt into a mixing bowl (or the bowl of a stationary mixer fitted with the paddle attach-ment). Add the butter to the sifted ingredients and with an electric mixer beat on low speed for 1 minute, or until the ingredients are combined and the fat is broken down into the flour in small pieces. Add the super-fine sugar and blend with a fork until combined.

3. Mix in the brown sugar, then add the chocolate and sour cream and mix again, on medium speed, scraping down the beaters and sides of the bowl as needed.

4. (If you are using the paddle attachment, switch now to the wire whip.) Combine the eggs with 1 cup water and the vanilla. With the machine running on low speed, slowly drizzle the liquids into the dry ingredients in three additions, scraping down the beaters and sides of the bowl as needed. When all the liquid has been added, beat for a couple of minutes, or until velvety smooth.

5. Transfer the batter to the prepared pans and spread it evenly with a rub-ber spatula (it is runny so it spreads easily). Rap the pans sharply on the counter to break up any large air bubbles and bake for 40 to 45 minutes, or until a tester inserted in the center comes out dry.

6. Cool the cakes to room temperature in their pans on a wire rack (they will shrink quite a bit). Unmold and peel off the paper circles just before frosting.

TO FILL AND ICE

Split each cake layer in half. Set one layer, split side down, on a cardboard round cut slightly larger than the diameter of the cake. Spread the frost-ing between the layers and over the top. Frost the sides or leave them un-frosted if you are filling the cake with whipped cream.

STORAGE: Keep in the refrigerator, covered with a cake dome or an inverted mixing bowl, for 2 to 3 days (2 for whipped cream filling).

Linda's Quintessential Devil's Food Cake

This is a recipe given to me by Linda Dann, the administrative assistant of the New York Culinary Center, which is a terrific cooking school located in New York City. Before she was administrative assistant, Linda ran a small specialty cake business, and this was the cake her clients requested most often. Linda describes it as what we expect a devil's food cake to be: "rich, dark, and moist." While the layers can stand up to all types of fillings and frostings, I've assembled the cake the way Linda recommends: with mocha buttercream between the layers and a chocolate icing poured on top. You can also bake the batter in three 8-inch pans, and if you do, bake the cakes for 10 minutes' less time.

Makes one 9-inch,
2-layer cake

Serves 12 to 14

Level of difficulty ★★

CAKE

2 cups (9.5 ounces) bleached all-purpose flour

1 cup (3.25 ounces) unsweetened, Dutch-processed cocoa powder

2 teaspoons baking powder

2 teaspoons baking soda

1 stick (4 ounces) unsalted butter, softened

2 cups (15 ounces) superfine sugar

2 large eggs

1¼ teaspoons vanilla extract

FILLING AND ICING

1⅓ cups Classic French Buttercream, mocha or orange (page 302)

Chocolate Water Icing (page 325)

TO MAKE THE CAKE

1. Position a rack in the center of the oven and preheat to 350°F. Lightly grease and flour two 9 × 2-inch round cake pans, then line the bottoms with parchment or greased and floured waxed paper circles.
2. Sift the flour with the cocoa, baking powder, and baking soda twice, and set it aside.
3. With an electric mixer (or with a stationary mixer fitted with the paddle attachment) on low speed, beat the butter for 1 minute, or until light. Slowly add the sugar, about ¼ cup at a time, and when all of it has been added, continue to beat on medium speed for 2 minutes, scraping down the beaters and sides of the bowl as needed. The mixture will look like fluffy wet sand.
4. Add the eggs one at a time, beating for 10 seconds between additions, or until absorbed by the butter, then beat in the vanilla. Scrape down the beaters and sides of the bowl and beat for 1 minute more, or until fluffy, light, and smooth.
5. With a large rubber spatula, fold the sifted ingredients into the batter in three additions, alternating with 1 cup water in three additions. Add 1 cup water in small additions, beating it in thoroughly with a whisk after each addition. When all the water is added, beat the ingredients together with an electric mixer on low speed until the mixture looks smooth.
6. Pour the batter (it is fairly wet) into the prepared pans and rap them sharply on the counter to break up any large air bubbles. Bake for about 30 minutes, then turn the heat down to 325° and bake for another 10 to 15 minutes, or until a tester inserted in the center comes out dry.
7. Cool the cakes to room temperature in their pans on a wire rack. Unmold and peel off the paper circles just before frosting.

1. Set one of the layers on a cardboard round cut slightly larger than the cake. Fill the layers with the buttercream and spread a very thin "crumb coating" of buttercream around the top and sides of the cake. Refrigerate for 1 hour.

2. Set the cake on a wire rack with waxed paper underneath to catch the drips. Using a metal spatula, spread the icing over the top and around the sides of the cake. Any icing that drips off the cake onto the waxed paper can be reused to fill in spots that need more coverage. Refrigerate, unwrapped, until the icing sets.

STORAGE: Keep in the refrigerator, wrapped airtight in plastic, for up to 3 days.

Buttermilk Chocolate Cake Layers

The generous amount of cocoa powder imparts a deep chocolate flavor to these layers, and the buttermilk adds a distinctive tang. Because there is so much cocoa, the layers don't rise quite as much as other layers, and they are a tad drier as well. There is enough batter here for three layers, which makes this an awesome-looking cake. I like filling the layers with an icing that contrasts with the chocolate, such as a butterscotch, chocolate malted, or peanut butter frosting. But my chocoholic taste-testers insisted I suggest something richer and more luxurious like Ganache or Wicked Chocolate Frosting.

Makes one 9-inch, 3-layer cake

Serves 14 to 16

Level of difficulty ★

¾ cup (2.5 ounces) unsweetened, Dutch-processed cocoa powder, sifted

1 cup buttermilk

2½ cups (11.25 ounces) cake flour

1 teaspoon baking powder

½ teaspoon baking soda

½ teaspoon salt

1½ sticks (6 ounces) unsalted butter, softened

1 cup packed (7.5 ounces) light brown sugar

1 cup (7.5 ounces) superfine sugar

4 large eggs

2 teaspoons vanilla extract

SUGGESTED FROSTINGS

Ganache (page 324)

Wicked Chocolate Frosting (page 298)

---

1. Bring ¾ cup water to a boil, pour it over the cocoa powder, and, with a small whisk, mix until smooth. Cool to room temperature and whisk in the buttermilk.

2. Position a rack in the center of the oven and preheat to 350°F. Lightly grease and flour three 9 × 1.5-inch round cake pans and tap out the excess. Line the bottoms with parchment or greased and floured waxed paper circles.

3. Sift the flour with the baking powder, baking soda, and salt twice, and set it aside.

4. With an electric mixer on low speed (or with a stationary mixer fitted with the paddle attachment), beat the butter for 1 minute, or until light. Slowly add the sugars, about 2 tablespoons at a time, and when all the sugar has been added, continue to beat on medium speed for 3 to 4 minutes longer, scraping down the beaters and sides of the bowl as needed. The mixture will look fluffy, like something between mayonnaise and whipped cream.

5. Add the eggs one at a time, beating for 10 seconds between additions, or until absorbed by the butter, then beat in the vanilla. Scrape down the beaters and sides of the bowl and beat for 2 minutes longer, or until smooth.

6. With a large rubber spatula, fold the sifted ingredients into the batter in three additions, alternating with the chocolate and buttermilk mixture in two additions. Beat with an electric mixer on low speed for 1 minute, or until the mixture is smooth.

7. Spread the batter evenly in the prepared pans, smooth the tops, and rap the pans sharply on the counter to break up any large air bubbles. Bake for 25 to 30 minutes, or until a tester inserted in the center comes out dry.

8. Remove the cakes from the oven, cool them for a couple of minutes, then run a knife around the cakes to loosen them so they don't tear as they shrink. Cool the cakes to room temperature in their pans on a wire rack.

9. Unmold, peel off the paper circles, and frost when the cakes are completely cool.

STORAGE: Keep under a cake dome or mixing bowl at room temperature in a cool dry place for up to 3 days, or cover with plastic wrap and refrigerate. Remove from the refrigerator 30 minutes before serving.

Light Chocolate Cake Layers

This cake has a subtle chocolate flavor that many people prefer to other, more intensely chocolate cakes. It is not too sweet and has a real "cakey" texture.

Makes one 9-inch,
2-layer cake

Serves 12 to 14

Level of difficulty ★

2¼ cups (10 ounces) cake flour

Generous ⅓ cup (1.25 ounces) unsweetened, nonalkalized cocoa powder

1 teaspoon baking powder

½ teaspoon baking soda

½ teaspoon salt

1 stick plus 2 tablespoons (5 ounces) unsalted butter, softened

1¼ cups (9.5 ounces) superfine sugar

4 large eggs

1 teaspoon vanilla extract

¾ cup milk

SUGGESTED FROSTINGS

Wicked Chocolate Frosting (page 298)

Classic American Chocolate Frosting, or brandy variation (page 298)

1. Position a rack in the center of the oven and preheat to 350°F. Lightly grease and flour two 9 × 1.5-inch round cake pans, and line the bottoms with parchment or greased and floured waxed paper circles.
2. Sift the flour with the cocoa, baking powder, baking soda, and salt twice, and set it aside.
3. With an electric mixer on low speed (or with a stationary mixer fitted with the paddle attachment), beat the butter for 1 minute, or until light. Slowly add the sugar, about 2 tablespoons at a time, and when all of it has been added, continue to beat on medium speed for 3 to 4 minutes, scraping down the beaters and sides of the bowl as needed. The mixture will look fluffy, like something between mayonnaise and whipped cream.
4. Add the eggs one at a time, beating for 10 seconds between additions, or until each is absorbed by the butter, then add the vanilla. Scrape down the beaters and sides of the bowl and beat for 1 minute longer, or until smooth and fluffy.
5. With a large rubber spatula, fold the sifted ingredients into the batter in three additions, alternating with the milk in two additions. Beat with an electric mixer on low speed for 30 seconds, or until the mixture looks creamy.
6. Transfer the batter to the prepared pans. Spread it evenly and smooth the tops with a rubber or small offset spatula. Rap the pans sharply on the counter a couple of times to break up any large air bubbles and bake for 25 to 30 minutes, or until a tester inserted in the center comes out dry.
7. Remove the cakes from the oven and cool them to room temperature in their pans on a wire rack. Run a knife around the cakes to loosen them from the pans, invert them onto a cardboard round, remove the paper circles, and frost.

STORAGE: Keep under a cake dome or an inverted mixing bowl in a cool dry place for up to 3 days. Or keep loosely covered with plastic wrap in the refrigerator. Remove from the refrigerator 30 minutes before serving.

Silky Chocolate Cake Layers

This layer is sweeter than most, with a silky, buttery chocolate taste. Its dense, rich tex-ture marries best with airy fillings like whipped cream, pastry cream, or boiled icing.

Makes one 9-inch, 2-layer cake

Serves 12 to 14

Level of difficulty ★

2 cups (9 ounces) cake flour
Scant ¾ cup (2.25 ounces) unsweetened, Dutch-processed cocoa powder, sifted
1½ teaspoons baking powder
½ teaspoon salt
2 sticks (8 ounces) unsalted butter, softened
2 cups (15 ounces) superfine sugar
2 large eggs
2 teaspoons vanilla extract
1⅓ cups milk

SUGGESTED ICINGS

Boiled Icing or Old-Fashioned Marshmallow Icing (page 312)
Whipped Ganache (page 321)
Whipped Cream, plain or flavored (page 318)
Vanilla, Praline, or Gianduja Pastry Cream (page 322)

1. Position a rack in the center of the oven and preheat to 350°F. Lightly grease and flour two 9 × 2-inch round cake pans and line the bottoms with parchment or greased and floured waxed paper circles.
2. Sift the flour with the cocoa, baking powder, and salt twice, and set it aside.
3. With an electric mixer on low speed (or with a stationary mixer fitted with the paddle attachment), beat the butter for 1 minute, or until light. Slowly add the sugar, about 2 tablespoons at a time, and when all of it has been added, continue to beat on medium speed for 3 to 4 minutes, scrap-ing down the beaters and sides of the bowl as needed. The mixture will look fluffy and almost white, like something between mayonnaise and whipped cream.
4. Add the eggs one at a time, beating for 10 seconds between additions, or until absorbed by the butter, then beat in the vanilla. Scrape down the beaters and sides of the bowl and beat for 1 minute, or until smooth.
5. With a large rubber spatula, fold the sifted ingredients into the batter in three additions, alternating with the milk in two additions. Beat with an electric mixer on low speed for 1 minute, or until the mixture is well combined.
6. Transfer the batter to the prepared pans, smooth the tops with a rubber or small offset spatula, and rap the pans sharply on the counter to break up any large air bubbles. Bake for 35 to 45 minutes, or until a tester in-serted in the center comes out dry.
7. Cool the cakes to room temperature in their pans on a wire rack. Unmold them, peel off the paper circles, and ice. If you are spreading the layers with pastry cream, leave the sides uniced.

STORAGE: Keep in the refrigerator, under a cake dome or an inverted mixing bowl, for up to 3 days.

Classic Devil's Food Cake (PAGE 139) WITH *Vanilla Frosting* (PAGE 301) AND

One, Two, Three, Four Golden Cake (PAGE 155)

WITH *Wicked Chocolate Frosting* (PAGE 298)

ABOVE: *Michele's Fantasy Cupcakes* WITH *Midnight Icing* (PAGE 281) AND
Fudge Nut Cupcakes (PAGE 280) AND *Best Brownies* (PAGE 69)
RIGHT: *Checkerboard Cake* WITH *Wicked Chocolate Frosting* (PAGE 159)

LEFT: *White and Black Chocolate Cheesecake* (PAGE 98)

ABOVE: *Sacher Torte* (PAGE 174)

ABOVE: *Filled Angel Food Cake* (PAGE 228) AND
Dark Chocolate Swiss Roll (PAGE 222)
RIGHT: *Chocolate Apricot Upside-Down Cake* (PAGE 134)

Hawaiian Coconut Cake with White Chocolate Ganache (PAGE 166)

AND *Michele's German Chocolate Cake* (PAGE 170)

Sin City Cake Layers

This cake layer recipe is used in the Sin City Cake (next page) so called because it tastes more of chocolate, is denser, richer, and definitely more "sinful" than any other cake layer in this book. It needs to be paired with an equally sinful frosting, such as the ones I suggest below.

Makes one 9-inch, 3-layer cake

Serves 16

Level of difficulty ★

2½ cups (11.25 ounces) cake flour

2 teaspoons baking powder

¼ teaspoon baking soda

¼ teaspoon salt

2 sticks (8 ounces) unsalted butter, softened

2 cups plus 1 tablespoon (1 pound) superfine sugar

4 large eggs

8 ounces unsweetened chocolate, melted and cooled

2 cups water or prepared coffee (regular, not double-strength)

SUGGESTED FROSTINGS

Classic American Chocolate Frosting (page 298)

Peanut Butter Chocolate Frosting (page 301)

Cream Cheese Chocolate Frosting or mint variation (page 299)

1. Position a rack in the center of the oven and preheat to 325°F. Lightly grease and flour three 9 × 1.5-inch round cake pans, tap out the excess, and line the bottoms with parchment or greased and floured waxed paper circles.
2. Sift the flour with the baking powder, baking soda, and salt twice, and set it aside.
3. With an electric mixer on low speed (or with a stationary mixer fitted with the paddle attachment), beat the butter for 1 minute, or until light. Slowly add the sugar, about 2 tablespoons at a time, and when all of it has been added, continue to beat on medium speed for about 2 minutes, scraping down the beaters and sides of the bowl as needed. The mixture will look like fluffy wet sand.
4. Add the eggs one at a time, beating for 10 seconds between additions, or until absorbed by the butter. Add the chocolate, scrape down the beaters and sides of the bowl, and beat for 1 minute longer, or until light and smooth.
5. With a large rubber spatula, fold the sifted ingredients into the batter in four additions, alternating with the water in three additions. Beat with an electric mixer on low speed for 1 minute, or until the mixture looks smooth.
6. Transfer the batter to the prepared pans, smooth the tops with a rubber or small offset spatula, and rap the pans sharply on the counter to break up any large air bubbles. Bake for 25 to 30 minutes, or until a tester inserted in the center comes out dry.
7. Remove the cakes from the oven and cool them to room temperature in their pans on a wire rack. Unmold, peel off the paper circles, and frost when the cakes are cool.

STORAGE: Keep in the refrigerator, under a cake dome or an inverted mixing bowl, for up to 3 days; remove 30 minutes before serving.

Sin City Cake

One bite of this luscious confection will leave you in a blissful daze and feeling a little sinful. The cake layers have twice as much chocolate as any other layer cake, and, as if that were not enough, the filling and icing are also intensely rich and chock-full of chocolate.

Makes one 9-inch, 3-layer cake

Serves 16

Level of difficulty ★★

1½ sticks (6 ounces) unsalted butter, softened

3 ounces unsweetened chocolate, melted and cooled

2½ cups (12 ounces) confectioners' sugar

1¼ cups heavy cream

3 Sin City Cake Layers (page 151), baked and cooled

8 ounces bittersweet chocolate, finely chopped

---

1. In a mixing bowl, combine 1 stick of the butter with the unsweetened chocolate, then add the sugar and ¼ cup of the cream. Beat with an electric mixer on low speed for a few seconds, until blended. Increase the speed to medium and beat until light and "spreadable." If the filling is too stiff, add more cream. Measure and set aside ½ cup of this filling.

2. Set one cake layer on a cardboard round cut slightly larger than the cake, and spread it thinly with ¾ cup of the filling. Set the second cake layer upside down over this, and spread it with the remaining filling. Set the last layer right side up over the filling.

3. Look carefully at the cake "seams" where filling and layers meet, and patch up any gaping holes between the layers so that the sides are nice and straight. Refrigerate the cake, uncovered, for 1 hour so the filling hardens a bit.

4. Set the bittersweet chocolate in a heatproof bowl. In a small saucepan, bring the remaining 1 cup cream to a simmer over low heat, then remove it from the heat. Pour the cream over the chopped chocolate and let it sit for 30 seconds, then whisk it into the chocolate and mix until smooth. Whisk in the remaining ½ stick butter and refrigerate for 1 hour, or until stiff enough to spread.

5. Set the filled cake on a turntable, if you have one. With a straight edge or offset spatula, spread the chilled icing over the top of the cake all the way to and slightly over the edges. Spread more icing around the sides of the cake and keep on turning the cake on the turntable to spread the icing evenly around the sides.

6. Add any leftover icing to the reserved ½ cup of filling and whisk until smooth. Transfer this to a 12-inch pastry bag fitted with a ⅜-inch-wide star tip. Pipe a small "shell" border around the bottom edge of the cake and a wreath of 16 small rosettes around the top. Refrigerate the cake, unwrapped, until the frosting sets.

STORAGE: Keep in the refrigerator, loosely wrapped in foil, for up to 3 days; bring the cake to room temperature before serving.

Sour Cream Chocolate Cake Layers

The sour cream makes this layer remarkably tangy, tender, and moist. The cake is absolutely delicious with the suggested peanut butter frosting, but like many of these basic layer cakes, it also takes perfectly well to many other frostings, buttercreams, and whipped cream fillings.

Makes one 9-inch, 2-layer cake

Serves 12

Level of difficulty ★

---

2 cups (9 ounces) cake flour

¼ teaspoon baking powder

½ teaspoon baking soda

¼ teaspoon salt

1 stick (4 ounces) unsalted butter, softened

1½ cups (11.25 ounces) superfine sugar

2 large eggs

4 ounces unsweetened chocolate, melted and cooled

1 teaspoon vanilla

1¼ cups sour cream

2 tablespoons dark rum, optional

SUGGESTED FROSTING

Peanut Butter Chocolate Frosting (page 301)

---

1. Position a rack in the center of the oven and preheat to 350°F. Lightly grease and flour two 9 × 1.5-inch round cake pans, tap out the excess, and line the bottoms with parchment or greased and floured waxed paper circles.
2. Sift the flour with the baking powder, baking soda, and salt twice, and set it aside.
3. With an electric mixer on low speed (or with a stationary mixer fitted with the paddle attachment), beat the butter for 1 minute, or until light.
4. Add the sugar slowly, about 2 tablespoons at a time, and when all of it has been added, continue to beat on medium speed for about 2 minutes, scraping down the beaters and sides of the bowl as needed. The mixture will look like fluffy wet sand.
5. Add the eggs one at a time, beating for 10 seconds between additions, or until absorbed by the butter, then beat in the chocolate and vanilla. Scrape down the beaters and sides of the bowl and beat for 1 minute longer, or until light and smooth.
6. With a large rubber spatula, fold the sifted ingredients into the batter in three additions, alternating with the sour cream in two additions. Beat with an electric mixer on low speed for 1 minute, or until the mixture is smooth.
7. Transfer the batter to the prepared pans, spread it evenly, smooth the tops with a rubber or small offset spatula, and rap the pans sharply on the counter to break up any large air bubbles. Bake for 30 to 35 minutes, or until a tester inserted in the center comes out dry.
8. Remove the cakes from the oven and cool them in their pans for 5 minutes. Run a knife around the edges to loosen the cakes from the sides of the pans so they don't tear as they shrink. Cool to room temperature in their pans on a wire rack.
9. Unmold the cakes, peel off the paper circles, and frost when they are cool. If you want, brush each layer with dark rum before frosting.

STORAGE: Keep in the refrigerator, wrapped airtight in plastic, for up to 3 days.

White Chocolate Cake Layers

A chocolate ganache is the best icing to pair with these velvety rich, white chocolate layers. The combination will make for a stupendously rich cake with gorgeous flavor. People who love their cake very moist will be enchanted with these layers.

Makes one 9-inch, 3-layer cake

Serves 12 to 14

Level of difficulty ★

---

2 cups (9 ounces) cake flour

1½ teaspoons baking powder

¼ teaspoon salt

1 stick (4 ounces) unsalted butter, softened

1 cup (7.5 ounces) superfine sugar

3 large eggs

1 teaspoon freshly grated orange zest *or* 1 teaspoon orange extract *or* ¼ teaspoon Boyajian orange oil

3 ounces white chocolate, melted and cooled

⅔ cup milk

SUGGESTED ICING

Ganache (page 324) made with 10 ounces extra-bittersweet or 70% bittersweet chocolate and 10 ounces (1¼ cups) heavy cream

---

1. Position a rack in the center of the oven and preheat to 350°F. Lightly grease and flour two 9 × 1.5-inch round cake pans and line the bottoms with parchment or greased and floured waxed paper circles.
2. Sift the flour with the baking powder and salt twice, and set it aside.
3. With an electric mixer on low speed (or with a stationary mixer fitted with the paddle attachment), beat the butter for 1 minute, or until light. Slowly add the sugar, about 2 tablespoons at a time, and when all of it has been added, continue to beat on medium speed for 4 to 5 minutes, scraping down the beaters and sides of the bowl as needed. The mixture will look fluffy, like something between mayonnaise and whipped cream.
4. Add the eggs one at a time, beating for 10 seconds between additions, or until each is absorbed by the butter. Add the orange zest and white chocolate, and beat until just blended. Scrape down the beaters and sides of the bowl and beat for 1 minute longer, or until light and smooth.
5. With a large rubber spatula, fold the sifted ingredients into the batter in three additions, alternating with the milk in two additions. Beat with an electric mixer on low speed for 1 minute, or until the mixture looks creamy.
6. Transfer the batter to the prepared pans, spread it evenly, smooth the tops with a rubber or small offset spatula, and rap the pans sharply on the counter to break up any large air bubbles. Bake for 30 to 35 minutes, or until a tester inserted in the center comes out dry.
7. Remove the cakes from the oven. Run a knife around the edges to loosen the cakes from the sides of the pans so they don't tear as they shrink and cool. Cool the cakes to room temperature in their pans on a wire rack. Unmold and peel off the paper circles just before frosting.
8. With a serrated knife, split only one of the cake layers in half, and set one of the split layers on a cardboard circle cut slightly smaller than the cake. Set the cake on a wire rack with waxed paper underneath to catch the drips.
9. Spread ⅓ cup of the ganache over the thin layer. Top with the unsplit cake layer, spread it with another ⅓ cup of ganache, top that with the other split layer set cut side down, and spread it with at least ½ cup of ganache.
10. Drizzle more ganache around the edges of the cake so it drips down the sides. With a small offset spatula, spread the ganache around the sides. Pour whatever remaining ganache you have around the top so it drizzles down the sides of the cake. Refrigerate to set the icing.

STORAGE: Keep in the refrigerator, wrapped airtight in plastic, for up to 2 days; bring back to room temperature before serving.

One, Two, Three, Four Golden Cake Layers

In the South of the United States, a yellow layer cake with chocolate frosting qualifies as chocolate cake. I have concluded that this is a great idea because the buttery flavor of the cake brings the taste of the chocolate frosting to the fore. This is my favorite among yellow cake recipes because of its exquisite velvety texture and closely woven crumb. The reason they call this classic recipe a "One, Two, Three, Four Cake" is that it calls for 1 cup butter, 2 cups sugar, 3 cups flour, and 4 eggs. It couldn't be simpler. If you bake this in 8-inch pans, the cake will be toweringly tall.

Makes one 8-inch,
3-layer cake, or one
9-inch, 2-layer cake

Serves 12

Level of difficulty ★

---

3 cups (13.5 ounces) cake flour

1 tablespoon baking powder

½ teaspoon salt

2 sticks (8 ounces) unsalted butter, softened

2 cups (15 ounces) superfine sugar

4 large eggs

2 teaspoons vanilla extract

1 cup milk

SUGGESTED FROSTINGS

Classic American Chocolate Frosting (page 298)

Wicked Chocolate Frosting (page 298)

Cream Cheese Chocolate Frosting (page 299)

---

1. Position a rack in the lower third of the oven and preheat to 350°F. Lightly butter and flour three 8 × 2-inch or two 9 × 2-inch round cake pans and line the bottoms with parchment or greased and floured waxed paper circles.

2. Sift the flour with the baking powder and salt twice, and set it aside.

3. With an electric mixer on low speed (or with a stationary mixer fitted with the paddle attachment), beat the butter for 1 minute, or until light. Slowly add the sugar, about 2 tablespoons at a time, and when all of it is added, continue to beat on medium speed for 4 to 5 minutes, scraping down the beaters and sides of the bowl as needed. The mixture will look fluffy and almost white, like something between mayonnaise and whipped cream.

4. Add the eggs one at a time, beating for 10 seconds between additions, or until absorbed by the butter, then beat in the vanilla. Scrape down the beaters and sides of the bowl and beat for 1 minute longer, or until smooth.

5. With a large rubber spatula, fold the sifted ingredients into the batter in three additions, alternating with the milk in two additions. Beat with an electric mixer on low speed for 1 minute, or until the mixture looks creamy.

6. Transfer the batter to the prepared pans, smooth the tops, and rap the pans sharply on the counter a couple of times to break up any large air bubbles. Bake for 30 to 35 minutes (25 to 30 minutes for 9-inch layers), or until a tester inserted in the center comes out dry.

7. Remove the cakes from the oven and cool them for a moment. Run a knife around the edges to loosen the cakes from the sides of the pans so they don't break as they cool and shrink. Cool the cakes to room temperature in their pans on a wire rack.

8. Unmold, peel off the paper circles, and frost when the cakes are completely cool. Refrigerate, uncovered, until the frosting sets up.

STORAGE: Keep in the refrigerator, loosely covered with plastic wrap, for up to 3 days; remove 30 minutes before serving.

Yellow Cake Layers

This cake is almost identical to the white cake layer that follows but looks golden because it is made with whole eggs. The cake is lighter than the One, Two, Three, Four recipe, and it is a great choice if you want a 2-layer rather than a 3-layer yellow cake.

Makes one 9-inch, 2-layer cake

Serves 12

Level of difficulty ★

2 cups (9 ounces) cake flour

2 teaspoons baking powder

½ teaspoon salt

1 stick (4 ounces) unsalted butter, softened

1¼ cups (9.5 ounces) superfine sugar

3 large eggs

2 teaspoons vanilla extract

⅔ cup milk

SUGGESTED FROSTINGS

Classic American Chocolate Frosting (page 298)

Wicked Chocolate Frosting (page 298)

Beginner's Chocolate Buttercream Frosting (page 309)

1. Position a rack in the center of the oven and preheat to 350°F. Lightly grease and flour two 9 × 1.5-inch round cake pans, tap out the excess, and line the bottoms with parchment or greased and floured waxed paper circles.
2. Sift the flour with the baking powder and salt twice, and set it aside.
3. With an electric mixer on low speed (or with a stationary mixer fitted with the paddle attachment), beat the butter for 1 minute, or until light. Slowly add the sugar, about 2 tablespoons at a time, and when all of it is added, continue to beat on medium speed for 4 to 5 minutes, scraping down the beaters and sides of the bowl as needed. The mixture will look fluffy and almost white, like something between mayonnaise and whipped cream.
4. Add the eggs one at a time, beating for 10 seconds between additions, or until each is absorbed by the butter, then beat in the vanilla. Scrape down the beaters and sides of the bowl and beat for 1 minute longer, or until smooth.
5. With a large rubber spatula, fold the sifted ingredients into the batter in three additions, alternating with the milk in two additions. Beat with an electric mixer on low speed for 1 minute, or until blended.
6. Transfer the batter to the prepared pans, smooth the tops, and rap the pans sharply on the counter a couple of times to break up any large air bubbles. Bake for 25 to 35 minutes, or until a tester inserted in the center comes out dry.
7. Remove the cakes from the oven and cool them for a moment. Run a knife around the edges to loosen the cakes from the sides of the pans so they don't crack as they cool and shrink. Cool the cakes to room temperature in their pans on a wire rack.
8. Unmold, peel off the paper circles, and frost when the layers are completely cool. Set the cake in the refrigerator, uncovered, until the frosting sets up.

STORAGE: Keep in the refrigerator, loosely covered with plastic wrap, for up to 3 days; remove 30 minutes before serving.

White Cake Layers

This simple, delicious cake is a good foil for the cream cheese frosting, which is sweet yet not too cloying.

Makes one 9-inch, 4-layer cake

Serves 12 to 14

Level of difficulty ★

2¼ cups (10 ounces) cake flour

1½ teaspoons baking powder

½ teaspoon salt

¾ cup packed (4.5 ounces) solid vegetable shortening

1½ cups (11.25 ounces) superfine sugar

½ cup milk

6 large egg whites

1 teaspoon vanilla extract

¼ teaspoon almond extract

SUGGESTED FROSTING

Cream Cheese Chocolate Frosting (page 299)

1. Position a rack in the center of the oven and preheat to 350°F. Lightly grease and flour two 9 × 1.5-inch round cake pans and tap out the excess. Line the bottoms with parchment or greased and floured waxed paper circles.
2. Sift the flour with the baking powder and salt twice.
3. Combine the sifted ingredients with the vegetable shortening in the bowl of a stationary electric mixer fitted with the paddle attachment (or do this with a handheld electric mixer at very low speed). Beat at low speed for 1 minute, or until the ingredients are combined and the fat is broken down into small particles.
4. Add the sugar and mix with a fork to combine. With the electric mixer running on low speed, slowly add the milk, making sure the batter is absorbing it.
5. Combine the egg whites with the vanilla and almond extracts and, with the machine running on low speed, slowly add this mixture to the batter. Beat for 2 to 3 more minutes, scraping down the beaters and sides of the bowl as needed.
6. Transfer the batter to the prepared pans, smooth the tops, and rap the pans sharply on the counter a couple of times to break up any large air bubbles. Bake for 25 to 30 minutes, or until the cakes begin to shrink from the sides of the pans, the tops begin to look lightly golden, and a tester inserted in the center comes out dry.
7. Remove the cakes from the oven and cool them for a moment. Then run a knife around the edges to loosen the cakes from the sides of the pans so they don't tear as they cool and shrink. Cool the cakes to room temperature in their pans on a wire rack.
8. Unmold and peel off the paper circles just before frosting. Split each layer in half horizontally before filling.

STORAGE: Keep in the refrigerator, loosely wrapped, for up to 3 days; remove 15 minutes before serving.

Boston Blackout Cake

This cake combines elements of a Boston cream pie with those of a blackout cake. A Boston cream pie isn't a true pie at all, but a yellow layer cake filled with pastry cream and glazed with a chocolate icing. A blackout cake was a popular confection of the late 1960s created by the now defunct Ebinger's bakery in Brooklyn. It was a chocolate layer cake filled and frosted with a gooey icing and finished with a cake crumb coating. What I have developed here is better than either one of those cakes on their own. This is a moist chocolate layer cake filled with a rich chocolate pastry cream, and finished with a chocolate topping and cake crumbs.

Makes one 9-inch, 3-layer cake

Serves 12

Level of difficulty ★★

CAKE

Silky Chocolate Cake Layers (page 150), baked and cooled, or Sour Cream Chocolate Cake Layers, baked and cooled (page 153)

½ recipe Chocolate Pastry Cream (page 322)

TOPPING

1 cup milk

1 cup (7.5 ounces) granulated sugar

2 ounces unsweetened chocolate, finely chopped

2 tablespoons cornstarch

2 tablespoons unsalted butter, cut into pieces

1 teaspoon vanilla extract

TO MAKE THE CAKE

1. With a serrated knife, cut each cake layer in half horizontally. With your hands, pulverize one of the halved layers into cake crumbs. Set aside.
2. Set one of the remaining layers on a cardboard circle cut slightly larger than the diameter of the cake, and spread it thinly with ½ the pastry cream. Top the cream with a second cake layer, and spread it thinly with the remaining pastry cream. Set the third cake layer, cut side down, over the pastry cream, and refrigerate the cake for 30 minutes, or until the filling is firm.

TO TOP

1. In a small saucepan, combine ¾ cup of the milk with the sugar and chocolate. Bring to a simmer, stirring with a whisk. With a fork, blend the cornstarch with the remaining ¼ cup milk and add this to the saucepan. Bring back to a simmer over low heat, whisking all the while. As the milk comes to a boil, the mixture will thicken. As it thickens, whisk more vigorously, making sure to get into the corners of the pan.
2. Remove the saucepan from the heat, add the butter and vanilla, and transfer the mixture to a clean bowl to cool to room temperature.
3. Pour the topping over the cake and, with an offset spatula, spread it from the center to the edges, letting it drip down the sides. Press the reserved cake crumbs around the sides of the cake and scatter more on top.

STORAGE: Keep in the refrigerator, under a cake dome or an inverted mixing bowl, and eat within 2 days.

Checkerboard Cake

This is an amusing creation of cake layers that are composed of alternating bands of chocolate and yellow batter. The layers are stacked on top of each other in such a way that when the cake is sliced, each piece is patterned like a checkerboard. You can buy special pans for this so the batters don't run into each other, but if you follow my instructions carefully, you can get a pretty good looking cake without investing in special equipment. Keep in mind that no matter how imperfect it looks, the cake will be absolutely delicious.

Makes one 9-inch, 3-layer cake

Serves 12

Level of difficulty ★★

One, Two, Three, Four Golden Cake Layers batter (see page 155)

3 tablespoons unsweetened, Dutch-processed cocoa powder

SUGGESTED FROSTINGS

Classic American Chocolate Frosting (page 298)

Wicked Chocolate Frosting (page 298)

1. Position a rack in the lower third of the oven and preheat to 350°F. Butter and flour three 9-inch round cake pans. Cut out 3 parchment circles to line the pans, and on each one draw a 3-inch circle in the center and another around that which is 6 inches in diameter. These marks will guide where to place the batter so that the bands of cake come out more evenly.

2. Make the batter and when it is done, transfer ½ (a generous 3 cups) to another bowl and whisk in the cocoa powder.

3. You will get a better-looking cake if you carefully measure how much batter you are going to put in each cake pan. Start by spooning (in 2-tablespoonful batches) ½ cup of chocolate batter dead center into two of the prepared cake pans, then spoon ½ cup of yellow batter dead center into the third cake pan (work as carefully as possible within the lines you have drawn). Spoon a 1½-inch-wide band of yellow batter, about ¾ inch deep, around each of the chocolate circles and follow that with a chocolate band of the same dimensions on the outside edge of pan. For the third pan with the yellow center, reverse the procedure, spooning a chocolate band around the center and ending with a band of yellow batter spooned around the outside edge.

4. Bake the cakes for 30 to 35 minutes, or until a tester inserted in the center comes out dry. Remove the cakes from the oven and immediately run a knife around the edges to loosen the cakes from the sides of the pans so they don't tear as they cool and shrink. Cool the cakes to room temperature in their pans on a wire rack. Unmold and peel off the paper circles just before frosting.

5. Set one of the layers with an outside chocolate band on a cardboard circle cut slightly larger than the diameter of the cake. Spread the cake with just enough frosting so the next layers will stick (you don't want the frosting to be too thick or you won't see the checkerboard pattern). Set the second cake layer, with the yellow outer band of batter, over the first layer, frost thinly, and top with the last cake layer, which has an outside chocolate band. Spread the top and sides with frosting and refrigerate uncovered until the frosting sets.

STORAGE: Keep in the refrigerator, wrapped airtight in plastic, for up to 3 days; bring back to room temperature before serving.

**Chocolate Blitz Torte

Makes one 8-inch,
2-layer cake

Serves 8

Level of difficulty ★★

This fabulous recipe is my adaptation of what I believe to be an old German recipe. I found it in my mom's 1943 edition of Joy of Cooking *and in her 1949 edition of* The Settlement Cookbook. *What makes this so unusual is how it is assembled: The cake batter is spread with a meringue topping and sliced almonds dusted with cinnamon sugar. One layer is set meringue side down, filled, and topped with a second layer, meringue side up. To make this fit into the* Chocolate Cake *way of thinking, I have added chocolate to the layers and filled the cake with a mocha pastry cream. It is unbelievably delicious and the perfect end to a lovely dinner party. Unfortunately, it does not keep well, so you must eat it on the day it is baked.*

CAKE

1 cup (4.5 ounces) cake flour

⅓ cup (1 ounce) unsweetened, Dutch-processed cocoa powder

1 teaspoon baking powder

¼ teaspoon salt

1½ cups (11.25 ounces) superfine sugar

1 stick (4 ounces) unsalted butter, softened

4 large eggs, separated

1 teaspoon vanilla extract

⅓ cup milk

½ cup sliced blanched almonds

1 tablespoon sugar

¼ teaspoon ground cinnamon

FILLING

½ recipe Chocolate or Mocha Pastry Cream (page 322)

½ cup toasted sliced almonds (page 25)

TO MAKE THE CAKE

1. Position a rack in the center of the oven and preheat to 325°F. Lightly butter two 8 × 2-inch round cake pans and line the bottoms with parchment or greased waxed paper circles.

2. Sift the flour with the cocoa, baking powder, and salt twice, and set it aside. Set aside ¼ cup of the sugar.

3. With an electric mixer on low speed (or with a stationary mixer fitted with the paddle attachment), beat the butter for 1 minute, or until light. Slowly add the remaining 1 cup sugar, about 2 tablespoons at a time, and when all of it has been added, continue to beat on medium speed for 2 to 3 minutes longer, scraping down the beaters and sides of the bowl as needed. The mixture will look fluffy, like something between mayonnaise and whipped cream.

4. Add the egg yolks two at a time, beating for 10 seconds between additions, or until absorbed by the butter. Add the vanilla and beat until just combined.

5. With a large rubber spatula, fold the sifted ingredients into the batter in three additions, alternating with the milk in two additions. Beat with an electric mixer on low speed for 30 seconds, or until well mixed. Divide the cake batter between the prepared pans.

6. In a clean bowl with an electric mixer, whip the egg whites until beginning to hold soft peaks. One tablespoon at a time, beat in the reserved ¼ cup sugar, and beat until the egg whites are stiff and glossy. Divide the meringue between the two cake rounds and spread it carefully over the batter. Sprinkle the almonds over the meringue. Mix the tablespoon of sugar with the cinnamon and sprinkle over the almonds. Bake for about 30 minutes, or until a tester inserted in the center comes out dry.

7. Cool the cakes in their pans on a wire rack for 20 minutes. Lightly grease the wire rack with nonstick vegetable spray. Run a knife around the out-

side edge of each cake to loosen it from the pan. Carefully unmold the cakes by flipping them with the aid of a plate or cardboard round (they are delicate). Cool to room temperature on the greased rack, meringue side up. Remove the paper circles just before filling and frosting.

TO FILL

Set one of the layers, meringue side down, on a cardboard circle cut slightly larger than the cake. With a small offset spatula, spread the layer with all but ¼ cup of the pastry cream. Place the second layer, meringue side up, over the pastry cream. Spread the sides of the cake with the reserved ¼ cup pastry cream and pat the toasted almonds around the sides. Refrigerate, uncovered, until ready to serve.

STORAGE: Best eaten immediately. Keeps in the refrigerator, loosely covered with foil, for up to 2 days.

Chocolate Chip Cake

The addition of chocolate chips to the batter makes this cake a bit richer than others. It is fabulous paired with Classic American Chocolate Frosting.

Makes one 9-inch, 2-layer cake

Serves 10 to 12

Level of difficulty ★

1¾ cups (8.25 ounces) bleached all-purpose flour

3 tablespoons unsweetened, Dutch-processed cocoa powder

½ teaspoon baking powder

¼ teaspoon baking soda

¼ teaspoon salt

1 stick (4 ounces) unsalted butter, softened

1 generous cup (8 ounces) superfine sugar

2 large eggs

1 teaspoon vanilla extract

⅔ cup milk

1 cup (6 ounces) semisweet chocolate morsels *or* grated bittersweet chocolate

SUGGESTED FROSTING

Classic American Chocolate Frosting (page 298)

1. Position a rack in the center of the oven and preheat to 350°F. Lightly grease and flour two 9 × 1.5-inch round cake pans, tap out the excess, and line the bottoms with parchment or greased and floured waxed paper circles.
2. Sift the flour with the cocoa, baking powder, baking soda, and salt twice, and set it aside.
3. With an electric mixer on low speed (or with a stationary mixer fitted with the paddle attachment), beat the butter for 1 minute, or until light. Slowly add the sugar, about 2 tablespoons at a time, and when all of it has been added, continue to beat on medium speed for 3 to 4 minutes, scraping down the beaters and sides of the bowl as needed. The mixture will look fluffy, like something between mayonnaise and whipped cream.
4. Add the eggs one at a time, beating for 10 seconds between additions, or until absorbed by the butter; then beat in the vanilla. Scrape down the beaters and sides of the bowl and beat for 1 minute longer, or until smooth.
5. With a large rubber spatula, fold the sifted ingredients into the batter in three additions, alternating with the milk in two additions. Beat with an electric mixer on low speed for 1 minute, or until the mixture is blended. Fold in ½ the chocolate morsels.
6. Transfer the batter to the prepared pans. Sprinkle the remaining morsels over the batter, smooth the tops, and rap the pans sharply on the counter a couple of times to break up any large air bubbles. Bake for 35 to 40 minutes, or until a tester inserted in the center comes out dry (the chocolate chips make the tops of the cakes look dimpled).
7. Remove the cakes from the oven and cool them for a moment. Run a knife around the edges to loosen the cakes from the sides of the pans so they don't tear as they shrink. Cool the cakes to room temperature in their pans on a wire rack. Unmold, peel off the paper circles, and frost when the cakes are completely cooled.

STORAGE: Keep at room temperature, under a cake dome or an inverted large mixing bowl, for a couple of days; refrigerate after that. Bring back to room temperature before serving, or the morsels will be too hard.

Cinnamon-Chocolate-Walnut Cake

The walnuts add a delightfully subtle texture to this cake, which marries wonderfully with the icing. If the icing is too hard for you to do, substitute a rum-spiked Spirited Whipped Cream (page 318), which would also be delicious.

Makes one 9-inch,
2-layer cake

Serves 12

Level of difficulty ★ ★ ★

---

2 cups (9 ounces) cake flour

½ teaspoon baking powder

½ teaspoon baking soda

½ teaspoon salt

¾ teaspoon ground cinnamon

1½ cups (5.25 ounces) walnuts

1⅓ cups (10 ounces) superfine sugar

1 stick (4 ounces) unsalted butter, softened

4 large eggs, separated

4 ounces bittersweet chocolate, melted and cooled

1 cup buttermilk

SUGGESTED FROSTING

Fudge Caramel Icing (page 329)

---

1. Position a rack in the center of the oven and preheat to 375°F. Lightly grease and flour two 9 × 1.5-inch round cake pans, tap out excess, and line bottoms with parchment or greased and floured waxed paper.

2. Sift the flour with the baking powder, baking soda, salt, and cinnamon into a mixing bowl. In a food processor, pulverize the nuts with 2 tablespoons of the sugar until finely ground and stir this into the flour. Set aside ¼ cup of the remaining sugar.

3. With an electric mixer on low speed (or with a stationary mixer fitted with the paddle attachment), beat the butter for 1 minute, or until light. Slowly add the remaining 7 tablespoons sugar, about 2 tablespoons at a time, and when all of it has been added, continue to beat on medium speed for about 4 minutes, scraping down the beaters and sides of the bowl as needed. The mixture will look fluffy, like something between mayonnaise and whipped cream.

4. Add the egg yolks two at a time, beating for 10 seconds between additions, or until they are absorbed by the butter. Add the cooled chocolate and beat for 1 minute longer, or until smooth, scraping down the sides of the bowl as needed.

5. With a large rubber spatula, fold the flour and nut mixture into the batter in three additions, alternating with the buttermilk in two additions. Beat with an electric mixer on low speed for 1 minute, or until the mixture looks well blended.

6. In a clean bowl with clean beaters, beat the egg whites until soft peaks form. With the machine running, add the reserved ¼ cup sugar, 1 tablespoon at a time, and beat until the egg whites are stiff and glossy. Fold the egg whites into the batter.

7. Transfer the batter to the prepared pans, spread it evenly, and smooth the tops with a rubber or small offset spatula. Bake for 15 minutes. Lower the temperature to 350°F and bake for 15 to 20 minutes more, or until a tester inserted in the center comes out dry.

8. Cool the cakes in their pans on a wire rack for 20 minutes. Lightly grease the wire rack with nonstick vegetable spray. Run a knife around each cake to loosen it from the pan, and invert it onto the greased rack. Cool to room temperature upside down, and remove the paper circles just before filling and frosting. Frost the cake while the icing is still warm.

STORAGE: Keep at room temperature, under a cake dome or an inverted mixing bowl, in a cool dry place for up to 3 days.

Fudge Cake

Select this cake when you're in the mood for something that tastes intensely of chocolate.

Makes one 9-inch,
single-layer cake

Serves 12

Level of difficulty ★

1½ cups (7 ounces) cake flour

¼ teaspoon baking powder

¼ teaspoon baking soda

⅛ teaspoon plus a pinch of salt

1 cup (7.5 ounces) superfine sugar

1 stick (4 ounces) unsalted butter, softened

1 cup packed (7.5 ounces) light brown sugar

4 large egg yolks

4 ounces unsweetened chocolate, melted and cooled

½ cup buttermilk or sour cream

3 large egg whites

Confectioners' sugar, for dusting

---

1. Position a rack in the center of the oven and preheat to 350°F. Lightly butter the bottom and sides of a 9 × 3-inch springform pan and line the bottom with a parchment or greased waxed paper circle.
2. Sift the flour with the baking powder, baking soda, and ⅛ teaspoon salt twice, and set it aside. Set aside ⅓ cup of the superfine sugar.
3. With an electric mixer on low speed (or with a stationary mixer fitted with the paddle attachment), beat the butter for 1 minute, or until light. Slowly add the brown sugar and the remaining ⅔ cup superfine sugar, about 2 tablespoons at a time, and when all the sugar has been added, continue to beat on medium speed for 1 minute, scraping down the beaters and sides of the bowl as needed. The mixture will look like fluffy wet sand.
4. Add the egg yolks two at a time, beating for 10 seconds between additions, or until absorbed by the butter. Scrape down the beaters and sides of the bowl and beat for 1 minute longer, or until smooth. Add the melted chocolate and beat until just combined.
5. With a large rubber spatula, fold the sifted ingredients into the batter in three additions, alternating with the buttermilk in two additions. Beat with an electric mixer on low speed for 1 minute, or until the mixture looks smooth.
6. Whip the egg whites with a pinch of salt until foamy, then continue to beat until soft peaks form. With the machine running, add the reserved ⅓ cup superfine sugar, 1 tablespoon at a time, and beat until the egg whites are stiff and glossy; then fold them into the batter.
7. Transfer the batter to the prepared pan. Smooth the top and set the pan on a larger baking sheet. Bake for 50 minutes to 1 hour, or until a tester inserted in the center comes out dry.
8. Cool the cake to room temperature in the pan on a wire rack. Unlock the springform and lift the cake up and out of the pan. Invert the cake, peel off the paper, and set right side up. Serve at room temperature, lightly dusted with confectioners' sugar.

STORAGE: Keep in the refrigerator, wrapped airtight in plastic, for up to 3 days.

¼ cup Coffee Custard Sauce,
   medium thickness (page 359)
or
¼ cup melted coffee ice cream

1 slice of cake
Deadly Delicious Chocolate
   Sauce (page 362)

Spoon the custard sauce or ice cream in the center of a 10-inch plate and rotate the plate to spread the sauce to the edges. Center the slice of cake in the middle of the sauce. Squeeze some chocolate sauce over the cake, letting it drip down into the custard sauce or ice cream below.

**Hawaiian Coconut Cake with White Chocolate Ganache

This cake should be made with fresh coconut because the unsweetened coconut is too dry and the sweetened coconut too sweet. I call this divine confection "Hawaiian" because of the addition of macadamia nuts, which add just the right texture.

Makes one 9-inch,
3-layer cake

Serves 12 to 14

Level of difficulty ★ ★

CAKE

1 fresh coconut (2 pounds),
opened and peeled (page 26)

2⅔ cups (12 ounces) cake flour

1 tablespoon baking powder

½ teaspoon salt

½ cup (2 ounces) macadamia
nuts, preferably unsalted

1½ cups (11.25 ounces)
superfine sugar

1½ sticks (6 ounces) unsalted
butter, softened

3 large eggs, separated

4 ounces white chocolate,
melted and cooled

1 teaspoon vanilla extract

1 cup unsweetened coconut milk

FILLING

1½ recipes Whipped Ganache,
made with white chocolate
(page 321)

4 cups freshly grated coconut

1 cup finely chopped macadamia
nuts, preferably unsalted

TO MAKE THE CAKE

1. Cut the coconut into chunks, grate it with the shredding disk of a food processor, and set it aside.
2. Position a rack in the lower third of the oven and preheat to 350°F. Lightly grease and flour three 9 × 1.5-inch round cake pans, tap out the excess, and line the bottoms with parchment or greased and floured waxed paper circles.
3. Sift the flour with the baking powder and salt twice, and set it aside.
4. In a food processor, finely chop 1 cup of the freshly grated coconut with the macadamia nuts and 2 tablespoons of the sugar. The mixture will be somewhat sticky because of the natural oils in the nuts and coconut. Set aside 2 tablespoons of the remaining sugar. Reserve remaining fresh coconut for the filling.
5. With an electric mixer on low speed (or with a stationary mixer fitted with the paddle attachment), beat the butter for 1 minute, or until light. Slowly add the remaining 1¼ cups sugar, about 2 tablespoons at a time, and when all of it has been added, continue to beat on medium speed for 2 to 3 minutes longer, scraping down the beaters and sides of the bowl as needed. The mixture will look fluffy, like something between mayonnaise and whipped cream.
6. Add the egg yolks and beat until absorbed by the butter. Add the melted chocolate and beat for a few seconds, or until blended, then add the vanilla along with the ground coconut and macadamia mixture. Beat until combined.
7. With a large rubber spatula, fold the sifted ingredients into the batter in four additions, alternating with the coconut milk in three additions. Beat with an electric mixer on low speed for 30 seconds, or until well mixed.
8. In a clean bowl, with an electric mixer, whip the egg whites until beginning to hold soft peaks. Slowly beat in the reserved 2 tablespoons sugar, and whip until the egg whites are stiff and glossy. With a rubber spatula, fold the egg whites into the batter.
9. Transfer the batter to the prepared pans (about 2 cups of batter per pan). Spread it evenly and smooth the tops with a rubber or small offset spatula. Bake for 20 minutes. Lower the heat to 325° and bake for 15 minutes longer, or until a tester inserted in the center comes out dry.
10. Run a knife around the outside edge of each cake to loosen it from the pan, and cool the cakes to room temperature in their pans on a wire rack.

Invert and remove the paper circles before filling and frosting.

TO FILL AND FROST

Set one of the layers on a cardboard circle cut slightly larger than the diameter of the cake, and spread it with ganache, ¼ cup of fresh coconut, and 2 tablespoons of chopped macadamia nuts. Repeat with the second cake layer, ganache, coconut, and nuts. Top with the last of the cake layers, turned upside down. Spread the top and sides with the remaining whipped ganache. Press the remaining fresh coconut and chopped macadamia nuts around the sides and top of the cake.

STORAGE: Keep in the refrigerator, under a cake dome or an inverted bowl, and eat within 3 days.

PLATED DESSERT SUGGESTION (per portion)

1 slice of cake	*Raspberry Squeeze Sauce (page 368)*
3 slices of star fruit	*or Fruit Plate Sauce (page 369),*
3 fresh whole raspberries	*in a squeeze bottle, optional*

Center the slice of cake in the middle of a 10-inch plate. Set the slices of star fruit to one side of the cake and center a raspberry on each of the slices of star fruit. Squeeze tiny dots of sauce randomly on the other side of the cake.

Linda's "Comfort Food" Chocolate Cake

This recipe was given to me by my friend Linda Dann. While the cake layers can be frosted with just about anything, Linda likes them best with a boiled icing, covered with oodles of shredded coconut. I have cut down slightly on the amount of salt she adds, and I've changed the language of the recipe to conform to the style of this book.

Makes one 9-inch,
2- or 4-layer cake

Serves 12

Level of difficulty ★

CAKE

4 ounces unsweetened chocolate, finely chopped

1 stick (4 ounces) unsalted butter, cut into 1-inch chunks

1½ teaspoons baking soda

1 cup sour cream

2 cups (9.5 ounces) bleached all-purpose flour

½ teaspoon salt

2 cups (15 ounces) superfine sugar

2 large eggs

1 teaspoon vanilla extract

FILLING AND ICING

Boiled Icing (page 312)

2 packages (7 ounces each) sweetened flaked coconut

2 ounces unsweetened chocolate, optional

TO MAKE THE CAKE

1. In a small saucepan, combine the chocolate, 1 cup water, and the butter. Slowly bring to a simmer over low heat, stirring continuously with a whisk. Transfer the mixture to a clean bowl and cool it to room temperature (this can take 30 minutes). In a small bowl, mix the baking soda with the sour cream and set it aside for 15 to 20 minutes, or until the mixture increases in volume by about half.

2. Position a rack in the center of the oven and preheat to 350°F. Lightly butter and flour two 9 × 2-inch round cake pans, tap out the excess, and line the bottoms with parchment or greased and floured waxed paper circles.

3. In a large bowl, combine the flour, salt, and sugar with a whisk. Add the cooled chocolate and beat with an electric mixer on low speed for about 1 minute, or until blended.

4. Add the eggs one at a time, beating for 10 seconds between additions, or until each is thoroughly absorbed into the batter. Add the vanilla and sour cream mixture, and beat until blended and smooth.

5. Pour the batter (it's very runny) into the prepared pans and rap the pans sharply on the counter a couple of times to break up any large air bubbles. Bake for 35 to 40 minutes, or until a tester inserted in the center comes out dry.

6. Cool the cakes to room temperature in their pans on a wire rack. Run a knife around the cakes to loosen them from the sides of the pans. Unmold and peel off the paper circles just before frosting.

TO FILL AND ICE

1. Set one of the layers on a cardboard circle cut slightly larger than the cake. Spread the layer with about 1 cup of icing and scatter ½ cup of coconut over that. Top with the second layer, turned upside down, and coat the top and sides with icing. Pat as much coconut as is possible around the sides and top.

2. A slightly different way of finishing this cake is to split each layer in half and fill the layers with icing and coconut. Frost the top and sides with

boiled icing; pat the coconut just around the sides, not over the top. Melt and cool the unsweetened chocolate and, with a small offset spatula, spread a thin coating of chocolate over the top of the cake, on top of the boiled icing. Refrigerate the cake until the chocolate hardens.

STORAGE: Keep at room temperature, under a cake dome or an inverted mixing bowl, but eat within a couple of days.

What fascinates me about this cake is how it defies the rules about baking soda. In this recipe, you stir the baking soda into the sour cream and let the mixture stand for 20 minutes (I presume to see if the baking soda is alive). In theory, this is not a good idea because the strength of baking soda dissipates upon standing. However, perhaps because the baking soda does sit around for 20 minutes, the recipe calls for three times as much as I would recommend. Despite these rule-defying eccentricities, the recipe works perfectly, the cake is beautifully moist, and I wouldn't dream of changing it.

Michele's German Chocolate Cake

One of my fondest college memories is of having afternoon tea with my friend Iris. On those weekly occasions she would buy cookies or bake a German chocolate cake.

German chocolate cake is not part of any Teutonic culinary repertoire. Rather, the cake is named after Mr. Sam German, an American who developed a bittersweet chocolate, called German's Sweet Chocolate. This chocolate is still marketed under that name, and the recipe for the cake appears on the package. This cake became "Michele's German Chocolate Cake" because I added espresso powder to make the layers less sugary, used unsweetened coconut milk in the cake batter, and completely changed the filling. The cake is so delicious that it has become one of the few my husband and daughter (tasting, at one point, an average of ten cakes a week) refused to let me give away.

Makes one 9-inch, 3-layer cake

Serves 12

Level of difficulty ★★

CAKE

4 ounces German's Sweet Chocolate or bittersweet chocolate, finely chopped

½ cup milk

1 tablespoon instant espresso coffee powder

2¼ cups (10 ounces) cake flour

1 teaspoon baking powder

½ teaspoon baking soda

½ teaspoon salt

2 sticks (8 ounces) unsalted butter, softened

2 cups (15 ounces) superfine sugar

4 large egg yolks

1 teaspoon vanilla extract

1 cup unsweetened coconut milk

TO MAKE THE CAKE

1. In a small saucepan, combine the chocolate with the milk and espresso coffee. Over low heat, bring the mixture to a simmer, stirring. Remove from the heat and transfer it to a bowl to cool to room temperature.

2. Position the oven racks so they are both as close to the center of the oven as possible. Preheat the oven to 350°F. Lightly butter and flour three 9 × 2-inch round cake pans, tap out the excess, and line the bottoms with parchment or greased and floured waxed paper circles.

3. Sift the flour, baking powder, baking soda, and salt twice, and set it aside.

4. With an electric mixer on low speed (or with a stationary mixer fitted with the paddle attachment), beat the butter for 1 minute, or until light. Slowly add the sugar, about 2 tablespoons at a time, and when all of it has been added, continue to beat on medium speed for 2 minutes, scraping down the beaters and sides of the bowl as needed. The mixture will look fluffy, like something between mayonnaise and whipped cream.

5. Add the egg yolks one at a time, beating for 10 seconds between additions, then add the vanilla and cooled chocolate and beat for a few minutes longer, or until the mixture is smooth.

6. With a rubber spatula, fold the sifted ingredients into the batter in three additions, alternating with the coconut milk in two additions. Beat with an electric mixer on low speed for 1 minute, or until blended.

7. Transfer the batter to the prepared pans, smooth the tops, and rap the pans sharply on the counter to break up any large air bubbles. Bake for 35 to 45 minutes, or until a tester inserted in the center comes out dry. (After the first 20 minutes of baking, rotate the pans from back to front and top to bottom so they bake evenly.)

8. Cool the cakes to room temperature in their pans on a wire rack. Run a knife around the edges to loosen the cakes from the sides of the pans. The layers shrink quite a bit once they cool down. Unmold and peel off the paper circles just before filling.

TO FILL AND FROST

1. Set aside ¼ cup of the brown sugar. In a small saucepan, combine the remaining ¾ cup brown sugar with the cream, butter, and espresso and bring to a simmer, stirring. Remove from the heat.

2. Combine the egg yolks with the reserved ¼ cup brown sugar. Slowly drizzle some of the hot cream and sugar into the yolks, whisking constantly so the eggs don't curdle. Add about half the hot liquid to the yolks, then return the yolk mixture to the saucepan. Stirring continuously with a wooden spoon, bring the liquid to a simmer and cook over very low heat until it has thickened and steam rises from the pan.

3. Pour the filling through a sieve into a clean bowl and whisk in the chopped chocolate until it melts. Cool to room temperature, then add the coconut and pecans.

4. Center one cake layer, upside down, on a cardboard round cut slightly larger than the cake. Frost it with ⅓ of the filling. Set the second layer turned upside down over the filling and frost it with ⅓ more of the filling. Top with the last layer, set upside down and spread with the last of the filling, leaving the sides unfrosted.

STORAGE: Keep in the refrigerator, wrapped airtight in plastic, and eat within 3 days.

FILLING

1 cup packed (7.5 ounces) light brown sugar

1 cup heavy cream

1 stick (4 ounces) unsalted butter

1 tablespoon instant espresso coffee powder

3 large egg yolks

4 ounces German's Sweet Chocolate or bittersweet chocolate, finely chopped

1½ cups sweetened coconut flakes

1½ cups (6 ounces) toasted pecans, finely chopped

Minted Chocolate Cake

My daughter is a great fan of mint–chocolate chip ice cream, and she absolutely adores this cake. For St. Patrick's Day, you can color the frosting a pastel shade of green.

Makes one 9-inch,
2-layer cake

Serves 12 to 14

Level of difficulty ★

CAKE

2¼ cups (10 ounces) cake flour

1 teaspoon baking powder

½ teaspoon baking soda

½ teaspoon salt

2 sticks (8 ounces) unsalted butter, softened

1¾ cups (13 ounces) superfine sugar

3 large eggs

4 ounces unsweetened chocolate, melted and cooled

1 teaspoon Boyajian peppermint oil or other mint flavoring

1 cup milk

FROSTING

Cream Cheese Chocolate Frosting, minted variation (page 299)

2 tablespoons crushed peppermint candy *or* Bittersweet chocolate shavings (page 380)

TO MAKE THE CAKE

1. Position a rack in the center of the oven and preheat to 350°F. Lightly grease and flour two 9 × 2-inch round cake pans, tap out the excess, and line the bottoms with parchment or greased and floured waxed paper circles.

2. Sift the flour with the baking powder, baking soda, and salt twice, and set it aside.

3. With an electric mixer on low speed (or with a stationary mixer fitted with the paddle attachment), beat the butter for 1 minute, or until light. Slowly add the sugar, about 2 tablespoons at a time, and when all of it has been added, continue to beat for about 4 minutes, scraping down the beaters and sides of the bowl as needed. The mixture will look fluffy, like something between mayonnaise and whipped cream.

4. Add the eggs one at a time, beating for 10 seconds between additions, or until each is absorbed by the butter, then beat for 1 minute, or until smooth. Add the cooled chocolate and the peppermint, and mix until combined.

5. With a large rubber spatula, fold the sifted ingredients into the batter in three additions, alternating with the milk in two additions. Beat with an electric mixer on low speed for 1 minute, or until the mixture looks smooth.

6. Transfer the batter to the prepared pans (about 3 cups per pan), smooth the tops, and rap the pans sharply on the counter a couple of times to break up any large air bubbles. Bake for 35 to 45 minutes, or until a tester inserted in the center comes out dry.

7. Remove the cakes from the oven and cool them for a moment. Run a knife around the edges to loosen the cakes from the sides of the pans so they don't tear as they shrink during cooling. Cool the cakes to room temperature in their pans on a wire rack. Unmold and peel off the paper circles just before frosting.

TO FILL AND FROST

Frost the cakes and pat some candy or chocolate shavings around the outside edge of the cake, and center a small clump on top. (Add the peppermint candy at the last minute because it eventually melts into the frosting.) Refrigerate, uncovered, until the frosting sets.

STORAGE: Keep loosely covered in the refrigerator for up to 3 days.

Red Velvet Cake

This delicious cake, with its bright red layers and crumbly, airy texture, is perfect for Valentine's Day. I first ate it in 1972 when one of my coworkers brought it to work. I was so taken with this novelty cake that I asked for the recipe, and have kept it all these years. The "red" in the name comes from the fact that cocoa powder, in reaction with buttermilk and vinegar, turns a reddish hue. Over time, however, I am sure, someone decided to enhance the natural reddish hue by adding red food coloring.

Makes one 9-inch, 2-layer cake

Serves 12 to 14

Level of difficulty ★

2¼ cups (10 ounces) cake flour

Scant ½ cup (1.5 ounces) unsweetened, nonalkalized cocoa powder

1 teaspoon baking powder

½ teaspoon baking soda

½ teaspoon salt

½ cup solid (4 ounces) vegetable shortening, at room temperature

2 cups (15 ounces) superfine sugar

3 large eggs

1 teaspoon vanilla extract

2 to 3 teaspoons red food coloring

1 tablespoon white or cider vinegar

1 cup buttermilk

1¾ cups (6 ounces) pecans, finely chopped

Cream Cheese Chocolate Frosting, vanilla variation (page 299)

---

1. Position a rack in the center of the oven and preheat to 350°F. Lightly grease and flour two 9 × 2-inch round cake pans, tap out the excess, and line the bottoms with parchment or greased and floured waxed paper circles.
2. Sift the flour with the cocoa, baking powder, baking soda, and salt twice, and set it aside.
3. With an electric mixer on low speed (or with a stationary mixer fitted with the paddle attachment), beat the shortening for 1 minute, or until light. Slowly add the sugar, about 2 tablespoons at a time, and when all of it has been added, continue to beat on medium speed for 1 minute, or until the mixture has the consistency of wet sand.
4. Add the eggs one at a time, beating for 10 seconds between additions; then beat for 2 minutes, or until smooth. Beat in the vanilla and red food coloring. Stir the vinegar into the buttermilk.
5. With a large rubber spatula, fold the sifted ingredients into the batter in three additions, alternating with the buttermilk in two additions. Beat with an electric mixer on low speed for 1 minute, or until the mixture is smooth.
6. Transfer the batter to the prepared pans, smooth the tops, and rap the pans sharply on the counter a couple of times to break up any large air bubbles. Bake for 35 to 45 minutes, or until a tester inserted in the center comes out dry.
7. Cool the cakes to room temperature in their pans on a wire rack. Unmold and peel off the paper circles just before frosting.
8. Fold 1 cup of the pecans into the frosting. Frost the cake and sprinkle the remaining ¾ cup pecans over the top.

STORAGE: Keep in the refrigerator, under a cake dome or an inverted large mixing bowl, for up to 4 days; bring back to room temperature before serving.

Sacher Torte

There are many stories and myths about the origins of this famous cake. The version I know was told to me by Jurgen David, one of my pastry teachers at the French Culinary Institute. He is Austrian and worked for a few years at the Sacher Hotel, making countless numbers of Sacher tortes, and he swears this is the only authentic recipe for Sacher torte.

Sometime in the 1830s, Emperor Franz Josef, of the Austro-Hungarian empire, asked his pastry chef, Eduard Sacher, to create a less filling cake than the whipped cream–filled ones then in vogue. At the time, Mr. Sacher was working at Demel's pastry shop in Vienna, where he created for the emperor the jam-filled cake we know today as Sacher torte. However, after he left Demel's pastry shop and established his own establishment—the Sacher Hotel—he continued to bake his cake. This is how a dispute arose between Demel's and the Sacher Hotel about which was the authentic cake. Eventually the dispute was settled and laws were put into place about which ingredients are allowed in an authentic Sacher torte and how it must be prepared. Today, only Demel's and the Sacher Hotel in Vienna are allowed, by law, to inscribe the name Sacher on their cakes. The only change I have made is to substitute unsweetened chocolate (which Europeans do not use) for the bittersweet chocolate so that the glaze is less cloying.

Makes one 9-inch, 2-layer cake

Serves 12

Level of difficulty ★★

CAKE

7 tablespoons (3.5 ounces) unsalted butter, softened

Scant ½ cup (2 ounces) confectioners' sugar, sifted

6 large eggs, separated

3.5 ounces bittersweet chocolate, melted and cooled

Pinch of salt

7 tablespoons (3.5 ounces) superfine sugar

¾ cup plus 1 tablespoon (3.5 ounces) cake flour

FILLING

¼ cup granulated sugar

3 tablespoons dark rum

1 cup (12-ounce jar) apricot preserves

TO MAKE THE CAKE

1. Position a rack in the center of the oven and preheat to 350°F. Butter a 9 × 2.5-inch springform pan and line the bottom with a parchment or greased waxed paper circle.
2. With an electric mixer on low speed (or with a stationary mixer fitted with the paddle attachment), beat the butter for 1 minute, or until light. Add the confectioners' sugar and beat for 2 minutes longer.
3. Add the egg yolks two at a time, beating for 10 seconds between additions, or until absorbed by the butter. Scrape down the beaters and sides of the bowl and beat for 1 minute longer, or until smooth. Add the melted chocolate and mix until combined.
4. Whip the egg whites with a pinch of salt until they form soft peaks. With the machine running, add the superfine sugar, about 2 tablespoons at a time, and beat until the egg whites are stiff and glossy. With a rubber spatula, fold ½ the egg whites into the batter. Transfer the flour to a strainer and sift it over the batter as you fold it in along with the remaining beaten egg whites.
5. Transfer the batter to the prepared cake pan, smooth the top, and set the pan on a larger baking sheet (to catch the drips). Bake for 40 to 45 minutes, or until a tester inserted in the center comes out dry.

6. Cool the cake to room temperature in the pan on a wire rack. Run a knife around the cake to loosen it from the sides, then unlock the springform and lift the cake out of the ring.

TO MAKE THE FILLING

1. Turn the cooled cake upside down onto a cardboard round cut slightly smaller than the diameter of the cake. Remove the metal base and peel off the paper. With a serrated knife, split the cake horizontally in two and set aside the top layer.
2. In a small saucepan, combine the sugar with ¼ cup water and bring to a boil, stirring. Remove from the heat and add 2 tablespoons of the rum.
3. Purée the apricot preserves in a blender with 1 tablespoon of water and strain out the chunks by passing the purée through a small sieve. Transfer the preserves to a small saucepan and bring them to a boil over low heat, stirring. Boil for 2 minutes, or until thickened, then remove from the heat and add the remaining tablespoon of rum.
4. With a pastry brush, soak the cake layer on the cardboard with ½ the sugar syrup (be generous or the cake will be dry). Spread ⅓ of the warm apricot preserves over the syrup and top it with the second cake layer. Brush the second layer with the remaining sugar syrup and brush the top and sides with the remaining apricot preserves. Set the cake on a cooling rack or an icing grid set over waxed paper to catch the drips.

TO GLAZE

1. Bring the sugar and ½ cup water to a boil in a small saucepan and cook until a candy thermometer registers 220°F. Add the chocolate, stir, and cook until a candy thermometer registers 230°F (the "thread" stage). Remove the saucepan from the heat and stir until smooth.
2. Pour the hot glaze back and forth over the top and sides of the cake. Be generous as you pour so that the sides get covered, because the glaze can't be moved once it is on the cake. If there are any unglazed patches on the sides of the cake, use a small offset spatula to patch the nude spots with more glaze. Let the cake stand for 1 hour before transferring it to a plate or platter.

STORAGE: Keep at room temperature, under a cake dome or an inverted large mixing bowl. Refrigerate only after a couple of days, but bring the cake back to room temperature before serving.

NOTE: If you are so inclined, write the name *Sacher* on top of the cake with piping chocolate (page 345). Or cover the top with crystallized flowers.

SACHER GLAZE

1 cup plus 2 tablespoons (8.75 ounces) granulated sugar

7 ounces unsweetened chocolate, finely chopped

Yeasted Chocolate Cake

This highly original way of making chocolate cake is an adaptation of a recipe I found in Woman's Day Collector's Cookbook *(New York: Simon & Schuster, 1970). This recipe takes time but it is so unique I wanted to include it. The small amount of yeast in the batter gives the cake a peculiar firm and porous texture, which makes the layers easy to handle and good candidates for absorbing sugar syrups. The original recipe paired the layers with a dense confectioners' sugar frosting, but I think the cake, which is somewhat dry, does better with whipped cream fillings.*

Makes one 9-inch,
3-layer cake

Serves 12 to 14

Level of difficulty ★★

1¼ teaspoons dry yeast

⅓ cup plus ¼ cup warm water

2¾ cups (13 ounces) unbleached all-purpose flour

¼ teaspoon salt

2 sticks (8 ounces) unsalted butter, softened

2 cups (15 ounces) superfine sugar

3 large eggs

2 teaspoons vanilla extract

3 ounces unsweetened chocolate, melted and cooled

¾ cup milk

1 teaspoon baking soda

Whipped Cream (page 318), plain or flavored

---

1. Dissolve the yeast in the ⅓ cup of warm water and set it aside. Sift the flour with the salt and set it aside.

2. With an electric mixer on low speed (or with a stationary mixer fitted with the paddle attachment), beat the butter for 1 minute, or until light. Slowly add the sugar, about 2 tablespoons at a time, and when all of it has been added, continue to beat on medium speed for 3 to 4 minutes, scraping down the beaters and sides of the bowl as needed. The mixture will look fluffy, like something between mayonnaise and whipped cream.

3. Add the eggs one at a time, beating for 10 seconds between additions, or until each is absorbed by the butter. Add the vanilla and cooled chocolate and beat for 1 minute, or until the mixture is smooth and blended.

4. With a large rubber spatula, fold the sifted ingredients into the batter in three additions, alternating with the milk in two additions. Beat the mixture with an electric mixer on low speed for 1 minute longer, or until smooth; then blend in the dissolved yeast.

5. Cover the bowl with plastic wrap and set it aside in a cool place for 4 hours, then refrigerate overnight.

6. Remove the dough from the refrigerator and let it come back to room temperature. Position a rack in the center of the oven and preheat to 350°F. Lightly butter three 9 × 1.5-inch round cake pans and line the bottoms with parchment or greased waxed paper circles.

7. Stir the baking soda into the ¼ cup of warm water and blend this into the batter. Transfer the batter to the prepared cake pans and bake for 30 to 35 minutes, or until a tester inserted in the center comes out dry and the cakes begin to pull away from the sides of the pans.

8. Cool the cakes to room temperature in their pans on a wire rack. Unmold and peel off the paper circles just before frosting. Fill the layers and spread the top and sides with whipped cream. Chill for a couple of hours before serving.

VARIATION

Brush each of the layers first with ¼ cup Simple Syrup flavored with rum (page 370), then spread the layers with whipped cream and sprinkle 1 cup chopped pecans and 3 ounces shaved chocolate (page 380) over the whipped cream. Keep the sides of the cake simply frosted with whipped cream.

STORAGE: Keep in the refrigerator, under a cake dome or an inverted large mixing bowl. Eat within 2 days.

FOAM CAKES

*F*OAM CAKES, OR "sponge" cakes as they are commonly known, are essential in the creation of the kind of elegant cakes you see in pastry shops and form the basis of petits fours and other classic confections as well.

What distinguishes foam cakes from butter cakes is that they are low in fat and are leavened primarily by the air beaten into the eggs. Because these cakes are virtually fat-free, they don't have the melt-in-your-mouth quality of butter cakes. Instead, they are neutral in character, with a spongy quality and a firm cell structure that make them supple enough to roll up or to slice into the thinnest of layers. These unique properties make them great partners for rich buttercream, mousse, and whipped cream fillings.

There are two categories of foam cakes: the whole egg sponge and the separated egg sponge. Whole egg foam cakes without butter are known as sponge cakes, whereas whole egg foam cakes with butter are known as butter sponge cakes, or *genoise* in French. Both are made by warming and whipping up whole eggs and sugar into a light airy foam and folding in the flour and other sifted ingredients.

The separated egg sponge cake, or *biscuit*, as it is known in French, is made by folding one egg foam made of egg yolks and sugar into another one made of egg whites and sugar, and folding flour into the combined egg foams.

Finally, there are the American angel food and chiffon cakes, which are in a class by themselves and are included in this chapter because they are made like an egg foam cake. For an angel food cake, you fold flour into a meringue, whereas for chiffon cake you fold flour into a separated egg foam batter to which vegetable oil has been added.

WHOLE EGG SPONGE CAKES

To make a sponge cake whip whole eggs and sugar over simmering water. This warming dissolves the sugar and makes the eggs elastic enough to stretch to their maximum volume and incorporate as much air as possible. Cake flour, which is low in gluten, or sometimes a mix of cake flour and cornstarch is then gently folded into the eggs along with flavorings.

At the beginning of the whole egg recipes, I have grouped a few basic recipes for sponge cake. These basic cakes can then be paired with any icing or filling you like. Following the basics are recipes for well-known classics like Black Forest Cake, and after that come a few of my own creations like Michele's Marvelous Mistake.

SEPARATED EGG SPONGE CAKES

In this method, the yolks are beaten with a portion of the sugar and are folded into the whites, which have been beaten separately with another portion of sugar. Cake flour is sifted and folded into the combined egg foams, and some flavorings are added as well. In this separated egg category are included the well-loved jelly roll or Swiss roll cakes as well as a number of uniquely European specialties, known as biscuit cakes. Biscuit is basically a separated egg sponge batter, feathery light in nature and used for piping into ladyfingers or cake disks, or for spreading in sheet pans to become the basis for rectangular or square cakes as well as for jelly rolls. Sometimes ground nuts are added to the biscuit batter for flavor and texture.

At the beginning of the separated egg cake section come the basic cake recipes, which you can fill as you please, and after that come recipes for cakes matched with specific fillings and icings.

ANGEL FOOD AND CHIFFON CAKES

Angel food, a uniquely American cake, is made by folding flour into an egg white meringue. It is a virtually fat-free cake and a lovely dessert for those who love sweets but need to watch their cholesterol. Chiffon cake, also an American original, is made like a separated egg sponge, but oil is added to the batter, which accounts for the cake's moist crumb. Both cakes can be served plain, glazed, or with a fruit garnish. If you wish, you can gussy up the cakes by splitting them into layers and filling the layers with mousse or whipped cream.

PUTTING THE BATTER TOGETHER

Sponge cakes are almost the direct opposite of pound and layer cakes. Sponge cakes are lean, have a small proportion of flour in relation to eggs and sugar, and are leavened almost exclusively with the air you beat into the egg foam. In theory, one should not add any chemical leavener to the batter, but I have found that a tiny pinch of baking soda or baking powder helps them rise. The heat of the oven turns the moisture in the batter to steam, which then rises through and pushes up the batter and causes the air cells to expand.

Basically, sponge cakes are easy to prepare, but you need to be organized and work fast so as to not deflate the precious air bubbles you have worked so hard to develop. Read through the recipe at least once and assemble all your ingredients before you begin. Be sure to use the ingredients specified, measure them out, and have them at room temperature.

Prepare the cake pans. For most sponge cake batters you want to butter and flour the bottoms of the pans or simply line them with waxed paper, but you must leave the sides ungreased so the fragile cake batter has a rough surface to cling to as it climbs up the sides of the pan.

The Ingredients

Cake flour is recommended in these cakes because it yields a more tender crumb.

Superfine sugar is recommended because it dissolves quickly and the fine sugar crystals produce the smoothest of meringues.

It is better to sift the flour and cocoa powder at least once, before sifting it again with other dry ingredients, to minimize the possibility of small undissolved lumps of flour or cocoa showing up in your finished cake.

In the case of angel food cakes, sift the sugar as well so that it is entirely lump-free.

Whipping the Eggs

Eggs whip to a higher volume if they are warm (however, you should separate them while cold because it is easier to do), which is why the French have come up with the technique of warming whole eggs over simmering water. When directed to beat the eggs over heat, you should set the eggs and sugar in a large, wide bowl and set the bowl over a pan of simmering water. The bowl should be wide enough so that it contains the ingredients comfortably and so that the bottom does not come in direct contact with the simmering water below. If the bottom of the bowl touches the water, you risk scrambling the eggs. With a handheld electric mixer on low speed, or with a whisk, stir the eggs and sugar, keeping them moving constantly so they don't scramble. You want to warm the eggs enough so that when you poke your finger into them, they actually feel hot (about 110° to 115°F on an instant-read thermometer).

Remove the bowl from the heat and, with a whip attachment, continue to beat the eggs until they triple in volume and are feathery light and pale in color. With a stationary mixer, this can take from 3 to 5 minutes, depending on the quantity of eggs, whereas with a handheld electric mixer, it can take from 7 to 10 minutes. You know you have whipped the eggs to the proper stage if, when you lift the beaters, the egg foam falls in "ribbon" shapes on top of the foam and sits there for several seconds before sinking back into the foam. If you are adding melted butter, remove a small amount of the egg foam to another bowl and fold it into the melted butter, then fold this back into the batter after you have folded in the dry ingredients.

The procedure for separated egg foams is similar to that for sponge cakes. The difference is that the whites are beaten into a meringue with part of the sugar and the yolks are beaten separately with the other part of the sugar. The two egg foams are then folded together along with the flour.

Angel food cakes are made somewhat differently again. Here you whip the egg whites with some of the sugar into a stiff moist meringue. Then you fold sifted flour and sugar into the meringue. Even though you want to incorporate as much air as possible into the egg whites, you must take care not to overbeat them. If the egg whites are overbeaten and dry, your cake might collapse, because the whites will have been stretched to the maximum and won't have the capacity to expand further in the oven.

Adding the Flour

For all these types of cakes, the tricky part of the operation comes when you fold the sifted dry ingredients into the fluffy egg foam. This part is difficult because these two mixtures are of different textures and weights and the flour tends to lump and sink to the bottom of the bowl. While you can use a rubber spatula to fold the ingredients together, I urge you to do as professional bakers do and use your hand instead as a spatula. This way you can press between your fingers any undissolved lumps of flour and break them up as you fold. (Don't worry about bacteria on your hands; it gets destroyed by the heat of the oven.)

So as to not deflate the fragile air cells you worked so hard to develop, carefully and quickly transfer the batter to the pans, and give the pans one sharp rap on the counter to get rid of any large air bubbles. Get the pans in the oven immediately before the cells lose air.

OVEN HEAT AND BAKING

Most sponge cakes are baked at a higher temperature than the butter cakes because they need more heat to quicky convert the moisture in the cakes into steam. The steam then expands the air cells and this provides the crucial lift that is needed to give these cakes volume.

On the other hand, it is important to bake angel food cakes at a slightly lower temperature, because the cake has more volume and takes longer to bake through. Too high a heat can cause the air cells to expand too quickly, and the entire cake might collapse.

FROSTING THE CAKE

Sponge cakes are lean, which means they can taste dry unless handled properly after baking. To compensate for the leanness, it is essential that you moisten the layers with a flavored sugar syrup before spreading them with filling. If you have baked the batter in a round pan, it is important that you slice the finished cake into layers that are as thin as possible so you can introduce as much moisture as possible with the sugar syrups and fillings between the layers of cake. If you leave the cake in one big layer, it will taste dry no matter how rich and lovely the icing.

Unlike butter cakes, which are themselves moist and rich, lean sponge cakes beg for contrasting rich buttercreams, mousses, and whipped cream fillings. The buttercream layers, however, should not be too thick, or you'll get too big a bite of it in your mouth when you eat the cake.

ROLL CAKES

Roll cakes, also known as jelly rolls, Swiss rolls, or *roulades* in French, are sponge batters baked in sheet pans. The cake is unmolded and rolled around jam or an airy filling like whipped cream. The key to a successful jelly roll is to prepare and fill the pans correctly, to not overbake the cake, and to unmold it right away so it remains pliable enough to roll up.

To make it easier to unmold this rather sticky dough, you must line the bottom of the pan with a greased baking parchment or a nonstick baking mat. However, do not grease the sides of the pan because you want a rough surface to which the batter can adhere as it rises.

When you fill the pan with batter, make sure to level it and spread it into the corners. If you don't, the cake will bake unevenly, and it will crack where spread too thin. The best way to spread the batter evenly is to use a long offset spatula.

The next crucial step is to make sure you don't bake the cake for too long a time. You can tell it is done when the cake looks puffy, feels somewhat resistant when you press it lightly, and a tester inserted in the center comes out dry.

Next you must make sure to unmold the cake properly. First, lightly dust a cotton cloth or parchment paper with a fine coating of confectioners' sugar or cocoa powder (this is so that the cake doesn't stick to the surface when you try to roll it up). Then, grab a corner of the parchment paper or baking mat on which the sponge was baked and pull the cake, still on the paper, off the baking pan. If you have used a baking mat, leave the cake on it until cool enough to fill, then fill and roll it up. If you have baked the sponge on parchment, invert the cake onto the dusted cloth or paper and peel off the baking parchment. If the paper sticks to the cake, brush it with warm water and try to peel off the paper a few minutes later.

These sheet cakes are so thin that they are at room temperature within 20 to 30 minutes of coming out of the oven. I prefer to fill and roll them up when they have been just baked, because they are most pliable at this stage. However, if you want to make them in advance, you can roll them up, unfilled, in the cloth or paper and refrigerate them overnight in a plastic bag to keep them moist. The next day, you unroll and fill them up. People claim that the roll "takes its shape" this way and won't crack, but I have not found that to be true. Because these rolls contain chocolate or cocoa powder, which is drying, they tend to crack a bit upon rolling. This should not concern you, however, because you can hide the cracks with powdered sugar or cocoa.

Whether you roll the cake around the filling from the long or short end depends on the filling. Fluffy fillings like whipped cream and mousses are spread thickly, and it is easier to enclose them if you roll the cake up from a long end. This way requires fewer "turns," with less room for the filling to ooze out. Were you to roll the cake around the filling from a short end,

you would also end up with an incredibly fat cake. When you fill a roll with a thin layer of jam or ganache, it is better to roll up the cake from a short end.

Don't be intimidated by the rolling process. Grab hold of the parchment or cloth towel and begin to roll up the cake by pushing it with the paper or towel and lifting it up slightly from the surface. It is important to tuck in this first turn tightly. Once you get going, the cake will roll onto itself. Then, at the end, again with the help of the paper or towel, roll the wrapped cake onto a baking sheet or platter, making sure it is seam side down. With a serrated knife, trim off the ends on a diagonal, and with a pastry brush, wipe off any excess cocoa powder or confectioners' sugar from the top. Refrigerate the filled cake for several hours or overnight to firm up the filling and make it easier to slice.

Transfer the jelly roll from the work surface to a platter by supporting it at both ends with two wide spatulas or a "cake lifter." To finish the cake and camouflage any cracks, sift a fine dusting of confectioners' sugar or cocoa powder over the top. Slice the cake with a serrated knife so the filling doesn't get squashed.

CHECKLIST FOR EGG FOAM CAKES

- Have ingredients ready at room temperature
- Properly prepare the pan
- Sift flour and cocoa powder
- Sift sugar for angel food cakes
- For whole egg sponge cakes, beat the eggs and sugar over simmering water
- For whole egg sponge cakes, after the eggs and sugar are warm, beat the batter long enough so it triples in volume and is almost white
- Sift the dry ingredients over the foam in several additions

- Fold with your hands rather than a rubber spatula
- Get filled pans into the oven as quickly as possible

BEFORE YOU BEGIN, READ ABOUT

- Preheating the oven and positioning of racks (page 52)
- How to measure ingredients (page 51)
- Preparing pans (page 52)
- How to melt chocolate (page 33)
- How to sift flour (page 16)
- How to whip egg whites (page 11)
- Testing for doneness (page 54)
- Cooling cakes (page 55)
- How to slice cakes (page 340)
- How to fill and frost two and three cake layers (page 341)
- How to decorate whole cakes (page 335)
- About plated dessert suggestions for frosted cakes (page 354)

CREATIVE COMBINATIONS FOR FOAM CAKES

Here are some ideas for combining egg foam cakes with various fillings and icings.

1. Butter Sponge Cake, raspberry variation, sliced into 3 layers (page 184)

   Moisten with Simple Syrup (page 370) flavored with framboise

   Fill with Ganache made with bittersweet chocolate (page 324)

   Spread Whipped Cream (page 318) on the top and sides, and cover with fresh raspberries

2. Butter Sponge Cake, orange variation, sliced into 2 layers (page 184)

   Moisten with Simple Syrup flavored with orange liqueur (page 370)

   Fill with Classic French Buttercream, orange variation (page 302)

   Spread the top and sides with Classic French Buttercream, chocolate variation (page 302)

3. Chocolate Biscuit, baked in a 16 × 12 × 1-inch sheet pan, sliced into 4 rectangular layers (page 208)

   Moisten the layers with Simple Syrup flavored with vanilla (page 370)

   Make Classic French Buttercream (page 302) and flavor 1 cup with 1 teaspoon instant espresso coffee powder dissolved in 1/2 teaspoon water , 1 cup with 2 ounces melted and cooled bittersweet chocolate, and 2 cups with 4 ounces melted and cooled white chocolate.

   After moistening the layers with syrup, spread one of them with 1 cup of the white chocolate buttercream, one with the chocolate buttercream, one with the coffee buttercream, and the top and sides (if you have enough) with the remaining 1 cup white chocolate buttercream. Garnish the top with white chocolate shavings.

4. Dark Chocolate Swiss Roll (page 222)

   Moisten with Simple Syrup flavored with rum (page 370) Fill with Chocolate Sabayon Mousse (page 317) or Vanilla Pastry Cream, chocolate variation (page 322)

5. Cocoa Puff (page 226), sliced into 3 layers

   Hollow out a channel of cake and fill it with Raspberry or Passion Fruit Mousse Filling (page 316)

   Serve with Deadly Delicious Chocolate Sauce (page 362)

Butter Sponge Cake Layers (Genoise)

Butter sponge cake is the workhorse of pastry shops and restaurant kitchens. This supple cake is so simple and plain that it works beautifully with all flavors and innumerable fillings. The reason for its popularity among professionals is that once you get the hang of it, it is the quickest, most reliable, versatile, and cheapest of all cakes to prepare. You can bake this batter in a variety of cake pans. A cake baked in an 8-inch pan should be sliced into three layers, whereas a 9-inch cake is only thick enough to be sliced into two layers. If you like rectangular cakes, then bake the batter in a sheet pan and cut it into strips before icing. Please read How to Glaze, Ice, Fill, Frost, and Assemble Cakes (page 339); Planning the Design (page 337); and Buttercream and American Frosting Designs (page 344).

Makes one 8-inch 3-layer cake, or

one 9-inch, 2-layer cake or

one 10 × 15-inch sheet cake, which can be rolled or cut into strips

Serves 8

Level of difficulty ★★

CAKE

1 cup (4.5 ounces) cake flour, sifted

⅛ teaspoon baking powder, optional

¼ teaspoon salt

5 large eggs

½ cup plus 1½ tablespoons (4 ounces) superfine sugar

2 tablespoons (1 ounce) unsalted butter, melted

MOISTENING SYRUP

¼ or ⅓ cup water

¼ or ⅓ cup sugar

1 to 3 tablespoons brandy, cognac, whiskey, or dark rum

SUGGESTED BUTTERCREAMS AND FILLINGS

Classic French Buttercream, chocolate or Gianduja variations (page 302), or Linda Dann's Swiss Meringue Buttercream, mocha variation (page 307) or Vanilla Pastry Cream, chocolate variation (page 322)

Whipped Ganache, made with bittersweet chocolate (page 321) or Chocolate Mousse Filling, made with bittersweet chocolate (page 314)

TO MAKE THE CAKE

1. Position a rack in the center of the oven and preheat to 375°F (or 400° if you are baking a sheet cake). Butter the bottom only of an 8 or 9 × 2-inch round cake pan and line it with a parchment or greased waxed paper circle, leaving the sides ungreased. (For a sheet cake, line a 10 × 15 × 1-inch jelly roll pan with baking parchment, or waxed paper brushed with butter.)

2. Sift the flour together with the baking powder and salt and set it aside.

3. In a mixing bowl, with a whisk or a handheld electric mixer on low speed, beat the eggs with the sugar until combined. Set the bowl over a saucepan of simmering water, making sure the bottom of the bowl does not come in contact with the water below. Continue to beat on low speed until hot to the touch (110° to 115°F on an instant-read thermometer).

4. Remove the bowl from the heat, and with the electric mixer (fitted with the whip attachment) on high speed, beat the egg mixture for 2 to 3 minutes, or until tripled in volume, pale in color, and thick. (With a handheld electric mixer, this will take 7 to 8 minutes.) Some of the batter, when lifted with the beaters, will keep its shape for several seconds on the surface before sinking back into the batter.

5. Fold ½ cup of the batter into the melted butter and set it aside. In four additions, sift and fold the flour into the eggs, then fold in the lightened melted butter.

6. Pour the batter into the prepared pan. Tap the pan on the counter *once* to level the batter and break up any large air bubbles. Bake for 25 to 30 minutes, or until the top is golden brown, feels firm when pressed lightly in the middle, and a tester inserted in the center comes out dry. (For a sheet cake, bake for about 15 minutes, or until the top feels firm and the cake begins to shrink from the sides.)

7. Cool a round cake in the pan for 5 minutes. Then invert the cake onto a wire rack but do not remove the paper circle. Turn the cake right side up and cool it to room temperature on the wire rack. Remove the paper circle just before frosting.

8. To cool a sheet cake, run a knife around the sides to loosen it from the pan. Grab hold of the parchment paper underneath the cake to help you slide it from the pan onto a rectangular wire rack. Cool the cake on the paper to keep it moist. When ready to frost, invert the cake over a clean piece of parchment and carefully lift off the top paper. With a serrated knife, cut away the crusty edges of the cake before rolling it up or cutting it into strips.

TO FILL AND FINISH

1. To make the moistening syrup, bring the water and sugar to a boil (use the larger amounts for a 3-layer cake) in a small saucepan. Remove from the heat, transfer the moistening syrup to a clean bowl, and add brandy to taste.

2. Slice the cake horizontally into two or three layers, each about ⅜ inch thick. Set one layer on a cardboard round cut slightly larger than the diameter of the cake. With a pastry brush, moisten the first layer with ⅓ or ½ of the syrup (depending on how many layers you have), then spread the layer with ½ (or ¾) cup of the buttercream or other filling. Top the filling with the second layer, moisten it with ⅓ (or ½) of the syrup, and spread with the same amount of buttercream or filling. Top the filling with the last layer (if you have one), and moisten it with the remaining syrup. Spread the top and sides with buttercream or filling (if you are using a buttercream, give the cake a "crumb coating" first—coat with a thin layer of buttercream and let it set before applying the final frosting).

3. Smooth and level the top and sides of the cake with an offset spatula and finish the top with decorative touches if you like.

STORAGE: Unfrosted cake layers keep, wrapped airtight in plastic, at room temperature for a few days or in the freezer for up to 3 months.

Cakes frosted with buttercream should be kept in the refrigerator, wrapped airtight in plastic, for a few days, or in the freezer for 1 month.

Cakes frosted with mousse or whipped cream should be kept in the refrigerator, under an inverted bowl or a cake dome, and eaten within 2 days.

CAKE BATTER VARIATIONS

Orange Butter Sponge: Add 1 teaspoon orange extract or ¼ teaspoon orange oil to the melted butter before you fold it into the batter.

continued on next page

Butter Sponge Cake Layers (Genoise)

continued from previous page

Raspberry Butter Sponge: Reduce the sugar by 2 tablespoons and add ¼ cup raspberry jelly or strained raspberry jam to the melted butter before you fold it into the batter.

Nut Butter Sponge: Instead of 1 cup (4.5 ounces) cake flour, use only 2.5 ounces sifted with ½ cup (2 ounces) sifted cornstarch. Grind 2 ounces (generous ½ cup) of nuts, such as walnuts, toasted pecans, or toasted hazelnuts, and fold them into the batter after you have folded in the flour.

Chocolate Butter Sponge Cake Layers (Chocolate Genoise)

This is the chocolate version of a sponge cake. I have added one extra egg to the batter because cocoa powder weighs the batter down. Because it is flatter than a sponge cake without cocoa powder, this cake is easier to slice into two rather than three layers.

Makes one 8- or 9-inch, 2-layer cake or one 10 × 15-inch sheet cake, which can be rolled or cut into strips

Serves 8

Level of difficulty ★★

CAKE

1 cup (4.5 ounces) cake flour, sifted

3½ tablespoons (0.75 ounce) unsweetened cocoa powder, sifted

⅛ teaspoon baking soda, optional

¼ teaspoon salt

6 large eggs

½ cup plus 1½ tablespoons (4 ounces) superfine sugar

2 tablespoons (1 ounce) unsalted butter, melted

MOISTENING SYRUP

¼ cup water

¼ cup sugar

1 to 2 tablespoons brandy, cognac, whiskey, dark rum, or other alcoholic flavoring of choice

SUGGESTED BUTTERCREAMS AND FILLINGS

½ recipe Classic French Buttercream, chocolate or any other flavor (page 302) or Dione Lucas's Chocolate Buttercream (page 310)

½ recipe Whipped Ganache, made with milk or white chocolate (page 321) or ½ recipe Chocolate Mousse Filling, made with milk chocolate (page 314)

TO MAKE THE CAKE

1. Position a rack in the center of the oven and preheat to 375°F. Butter the bottom only of an 8 or 9 × 2-inch round cake pan and line it with a parchment or greased waxed paper circle, leaving the sides ungreased. (For a sheet cake, line a 10 × 15 × 1-inch jelly roll pan with baking parchment, or waxed paper brushed with butter.)

2. Sift the flour together with the cocoa, baking soda, and salt and set it aside.

3. In a mixing bowl, with a whisk or a handheld electric mixer on low speed, beat the eggs with the sugar until combined. Set the bowl over a saucepan of simmering water, making sure the bottom of the bowl does not come in contact with the water below. Continue to beat on low speed until hot to the touch (110° to 115°F on an instant-read thermometer).

4. Remove the bowl from the heat, and with the electric mixer (fitted with the whip attachment) on high speed, beat the egg mixture for 2 to 3 minutes, or until tripled in volume, pale in color, and thick. (With a handheld electric mixer, this will take 7 to 8 minutes.) Some of the batter, when lifted with the beaters, will keep its shape for several seconds on the surface before sinking back into the batter.

5. Fold ½ cup of the batter into the melted butter and set it aside. In four additions, sift and fold the dry ingredients into the eggs, then fold in the lightened melted butter.

6. Pour the batter into the prepared pan. Tap the pan on the counter *once* to level the batter and break up any large air bubbles. Bake for 25 to 30 minutes, or until the top feels firm when pressed lightly in the middle and a tester inserted in the center comes out dry. (For a sheet cake, bake for about 15 minutes, or until the top feels firm and the cake begins to shrink from the sides.)

TO FILL AND FINISH

To cool, split, moisten, fill, decorate, and store, see Butter Sponge Cake Layers (pages 184–186).

continued on next page

Chocolate Butter Sponge Cake Layers (Chocolate Genoise)

continued from previous page

CAKE BATTER VARIATIONS

Mocha Sponge: Add 2 teaspoons instant espresso coffee powder to the melted butter while it is still warm.

Mocha Nut Sponge: Make the mocha sponge and, after you fold in the flour, fold in ⅓ cup (1.5 ounces) ground nuts.

Chocolate Nut Sponge: After you fold in the flour, fold in ⅓ cup (1.5 ounces) nut flour or finely ground blanched almonds, walnuts, toasted pecans, or toasted hazelnuts.

Chocolate Nut Sponge Cake Layers

To compensate for the weight of the ground nuts and melted chocolate, this cake requires more eggs than a simple sponge to give it enough volume. The nuts add a delightful texture but make it hard to slice the cake into more than two layers.

Makes one 9-inch,
2-layer cake

Serves 12 to 14

Level of difficulty ★★

CAKE

1 cup minus 2 tablespoons
(4 ounces) cake flour, sifted

½ teaspoon salt

¼ teaspoon baking powder

Generous ½ cup (3 ounces)
blanched almonds, hazelnuts, or
pecans, ground in the food
processor

7 large eggs

Generous ¾ cup (6 ounces)
superfine sugar

¼ stick (2 ounces) unsalted
butter, melted

½ teaspoon vanilla or orange
extract

2 ounces bittersweet chocolate,
melted and cooled

MOISTENING SYRUP

¼ cup water

¼ cup sugar

2 tablespoons brandy, cognac,
whiskey, or dark rum

SUGGESTED FILLINGS

Any of the chocolate
buttercreams or variations (see
pages 309–311)

TO MAKE THE CAKE

1. Position a rack in the center of the oven and preheat to 375°F. Butter the bottom of a 9 × 2.5-inch springform pan, leaving the sides ungreased, and line the bottom with a parchment or greased waxed paper circle.

2. Sift the flour with the salt and baking powder into a mixing bowl and, with a whisk, combine it with the ground nuts.

3. In a mixing bowl, with a whisk or a handheld electric mixer on low speed, beat the eggs with the sugar until combined. Set the bowl over a saucepan of simmering water, making sure the bottom of the bowl does not come in contact with the water below. Continue to beat on low speed until hot to the touch (110° to 115°F on an instant-read thermometer).

4. Remove the bowl from the heat and, with the electric mixer (fitted with the whip attachment) on high speed, beat the egg mixture for 5 minutes, or until tripled in volume, pale in color, and thick. (With a handheld electric mixer, this will take about 10 minutes.) Some of the batter, when lifted with the beaters, will keep its shape for several seconds on the surface before sinking back into the batter.

5. Stir the butter and vanilla into the chocolate, then fold about ¾ cup of the egg foam into the chocolate mixture. In three additions, sift and fold the dry ingredients into the remaining egg foam, then fold in the chocolate and butter mixture.

6. Pour the batter into the prepared pan. Tap the pan on the counter *once* to level the batter and break up any large air bubbles. Bake for about 20 minutes, then lower the heat to 350° and bake for 10 to 15 minutes longer, or until a tester inserted in the center comes out dry.

7. Cool the cake to room temperature in the pan on a wire rack. Run a knife around the cake to loosen it from the sides of the pan, then unlatch the springform and lift the cake up and out of the form.

TO FILL AND FINISH

To split, moisten, fill, decorate, and store, see Butter Sponge Cake Layers (pages 184–186).

Chocolate Sponge Sheet Cake

Baking a sponge batter in a sheet pan gives the baker the flexibility of creating a rolled or rectangular cake. The cake cracks minimally when you roll it up because it is free of butter and contains just a bit of cocoa powder. If you don't want to make a rolled cake, then slice it into three or four strips and fill.

Makes one 10 × 15-inch sheet cake, which can be rolled or cut into strips

Serves 8

Level of difficulty ★★

CAKE

About 3 tablespoons unsweetened cocoa powder or confectioners' sugar, for dusting the cloth, plus additional for top

¾ cup (3.5 ounces) cake flour, sifted

¼ cup (1 ounce) cornstarch, sifted

3 tablespoons unsweetened cocoa powder, sifted

½ teaspoon baking soda

¼ teaspoon salt

4 large eggs

⅔ cup (5 ounces) superfine sugar

MOISTENING SYRUP

3 tablespoons sugar

1 to 2 tablespoons brandy or other alcohol for flavoring

SUGGESTED FILLINGS

2 to 3 cups of Italian Meringue Buttercream (page 308) or

Whipped Cream (page 318) or

Whipped Ganache (page 321) or

Chocolate Mousse Filling (page 314) or

Raspberry Mousse Filling (page 316)

TO MAKE THE CAKE

1. Position a rack in the center of the oven and preheat to 375°F. Line the bottom of a 10 × 15 × 1-inch jelly roll pan with parchment or buttered waxed paper. Sift the cocoa powder through a fine mesh strainer over a piece of parchment or a cloth towel that is slightly larger than the dimensions of the jelly roll pan. Set it aside.

2. Sift the flour with the cornstarch, cocoa, baking soda, and salt, and set it aside.

3. In a mixing bowl with a whisk or a handheld electric mixer on low speed, beat the eggs with the sugar until combined. Set the bowl over a saucepan of simmering water, making sure the bottom of the bowl does not come in contact with the water below. Continue to beat on low speed until hot to the touch (110° to 115°F on an instant-read thermometer).

4. Remove the bowl from the heat and, with the electric mixer (fitted with the whip attachment) on high speed, beat the egg mixture for 2 to 3 minutes, or until tripled in volume, pale in color, and thick. (With a handheld electric mixer, this will take 7 to 8 minutes.) Some of the batter, when lifted with the beaters, will keep its shape for several seconds on the surface before sinking back into the batter.

5. In three additions, sift the dry ingredients over the eggs and gently fold them in.

6. Pour the batter into the prepared pan and level it with an offset spatula, making sure you spread it evenly all the way into the corners. Bake for 14 to 15 minutes, or until the cake feels firm when pressed in the center and the sides begin to pull away from the pan.

7. Cool the cake in the pan for 5 minutes on a wire rack. Run a knife around the cake to loosen it from the sides of the pan. Flip the pan over the cocoa-dusted parchment or cloth towel, and peel off the parchment paper.

8. If you are not ready to fill and frost the cake, roll it up (along the short or long end, as you prefer) around the parchment, so it develops a shape that will hold later on when you fill it. Set the rolled-up cake in a plastic bag and refrigerate it until ready to use.

1. Bring 3 tablespoons water and the sugar to a boil in a small saucepan. Remove it from the heat, transfer it to a clean bowl, and add the brandy.

2. Unroll the cake, leaving it on the piece of parchment or cloth (if the cake cracks in places, don't worry; it will be "patched together" again with the filling). With a pastry brush, moisten the cake with the sugar syrup and spread it with the filling of your choice, leaving about ¼ inch unfilled around the edges.

3. Roll up the cake, using the parchment or towel to guide you. With a sharp knife, trim both edges on a diagonal. Choose a platter long enough to accomodate the roll, cut the roll in half again, on a diagonal, and serve it in two pieces.

4. Transfer the filled cake to the platter. Dust the top, through a strainer, with cocoa powder or confectioners' sugar, depending on what you used on the surface when you first unmolded it.

STORAGE: Refrigerate the platter, loosely covered with plastic wrap. Eat within 2 days.

**Chocolate Praline Cake

This sponge cake is moister and tastes more of chocolate than most because it contains brown sugar, which holds in moisture; more butter; and melted bittersweet chocolate as well.

Makes one 8-inch, 4-layer cake

Serves 10 to 12

Level of difficulty ★★★

CAKE

1 stick (4 ounces) unsalted butter, cut into 1-inch pieces

4 ounces bittersweet or semisweet chocolate, finely chopped

1 cup (4.5 ounces) cake flour

Scant ⅓ cup (1.25 ounces) cornstarch

½ teaspoon baking powder

¼ teaspoon salt

7 large eggs

1 cup packed (7.5 ounces) light brown sugar

MOISTENING SYRUP AND FILLING

⅓ cup sugar

2 tablespoons (or to taste) cognac or brandy

Classic French Buttercream, praline variation (page 302)

GLAZE AND FINISHING

Ganache, made with bittersweet chocolate (page 324)

½ cup (2 ounces) finely chopped, toasted skinned hazelnuts

12 whole toasted skinned hazelnuts

TO MAKE THE CAKE

1. In a small saucepan, over low heat, heat the butter until frothy. Skim off the foam, lower the heat, and continue to cook the butter until some of the milk solids sink to the bottom of the pan, begin to turn golden brown, and emit a lovely nutty aroma. Remove the pan from the heat and transfer the butter to a clean bowl. In the same saucepan, combine the chocolate and ¼ cup water and simmer over low heat, stirring, until the chocolate is melted. Add the chocolate to the butter, whisk to combine, and set it aside.

2. Position a rack in the center of the oven and preheat to 350°F. Butter the bottom of two 8 × 1.5-inch round cake pans, leaving the sides ungreased, and line the bottoms with parchment or greased waxed paper circles.

3. Sift the flour with the cornstarch, baking powder, and salt twice, and set it aside.

4. In a mixing bowl, with a whisk or a handheld electric mixer on low speed, beat the eggs with the sugar until combined. Set the bowl over a saucepan of simmering water, making sure the bottom of the bowl does not come in contact with the water below. Continue to beat on low speed until hot to the touch (110° to 115°F on an instant-read thermometer).

5. Remove the bowl from the heat and, with the electric mixer (fitted with the whip attachment) on high speed, beat the egg mixture for 4 to 5 minutes, or until tripled in volume and thick. Fold about ⅓ of the eggs into the chocolate and butter; this is now a chocolate egg foam. In four additions, alternating with the chocolate egg foam in three additions, sift and fold the dry ingredients into the eggs.

6. Divide the batter evenly between the prepared pans. Tap the pans on the counter *once* to break up any large air bubbles, and bake for 25 to 30 minutes, or until the top is firm and a tester inserted in the center comes out dry.

7. Cool the cakes in their pans on a wire rack for 15 minutes. Run a knife around the cakes to loosen them from the sides of the pans. Unmold them, but do not remove the paper circles. Turn the cakes right side up to cool to room temperature on a wire rack. Remove the paper circles just before frosting.

TO FILL

1. In a small saucepan, bring the sugar and ⅓ cup water to a boil, remove from the heat, transfer to a clean bowl, and add the cognac.

2. With a serrated knife, split each of the cakes into 2 horizontal layers. Set one of the cake layers on a cardboard round cut exactly the same diameter as the cake. Brush the layer with about ¼ of the moistening syrup, then spread it with a thin layer of buttercream. Top with the second cake layer, moistening syrup, and buttercream, and repeat the procedure with the third and fourth cake layers. Brush the top of the cake with the remaining moistening syrup and spread the top and sides with a very thin buttercream "crumb coating." Refrigerate the cake, uncovered, to firm up the buttercream while you make the ganache.

TO GLAZE AND FINISH

Set the chilled cake on a wire rack. Spread about 1 cup of ganache over the top and let it drip down the sides. Smooth the top by passing an offset spatula across the ganache once, letting the excess drip down the sides. Evenly spread the sides with more ganache, then pass an icing comb around the sides. Pat a ½-inch border of chopped hazelnuts around the bottom edge of the cake, and set the whole hazelnuts around the top edge of the cake. Refrigerate the cake, uncovered, for 30 minutes, or until the ganache sets.

STORAGE: Keep in the refrigerator, loosely wrapped in plastic, for 2 to 3 days; remove the cake 45 minutes before serving.

ADVANCE PREPARATION TIPS

- The cake, buttercream, and nut garnish can be made 1 day ahead of serving.
- Make the ganache, fill, glaze, and finish the cake on the day of serving.
- The filled and iced cake can be assembled in advance and frozen 2 to 3 weeks ahead of serving. Thaw in the refrigerator for 24 hours before serving.

Chocolate Sponge with White Chocolate Mousse

These sponge layers are as light as air but dry quickly, so take care to moisten them thoroughly with sugar syrup.

Makes one 8-inch,
4-layer cake

Serves 12

Level of difficulty ★ ★ ★

CAKE

1 cup (4.5 ounces) cake flour, sifted

⅓ cup (1.25 ounces) cornstarch, sifted

¼ cup (0.75 ounce) unsweetened cocoa powder, sifted

¼ teaspoon baking soda

¼ teaspoon salt

7 large eggs

1 cup (7.5 ounces) superfine sugar

FILLING, FROSTING, AND FINISHING

⅓ cup granulated sugar

1 tablespoon vanilla extract

White Chocolate Mousse Filling (page 315)

2 cups (about 8 ounces) White Chocolate Shavings (page 380), chilled

TO MAKE THE CAKE

1. Position a rack in the center of the oven and preheat to 375°F. Line the bottoms of two 8 × 2-inch round cake pans with parchment or greased waxed paper circles. Leave the sides of the pans ungreased.
2. Sift the flour with the cornstarch, cocoa, baking soda, and salt twice, and set it aside.
3. In a mixing bowl, with a whisk or a handheld electric mixer on low speed, beat the eggs until blended. Slowly add the sugar and beat until combined. Set the bowl over a saucepan of simmering water, making sure the bowl does not come in contact with the water below, and continue to beat the eggs and sugar until hot to the touch (110° to 115°F on an instant-read thermometer).
4. Remove the bowl from the heat and, with the electric mixer (fitted with the whip attachment) on high speed, beat the egg mixture for 4 to 5 minutes, or until tripled in volume, ivory in color, and thick. Some of the batter, when lifted with the beaters, will keep its shape for several seconds on the surface before sinking back into the batter.
5. Sift and fold the dry ingredients into the eggs in three additions.
6. Divide the batter evenly between the prepared pans. Tap the pans on the counter *once* to break up any large air bubbles, and bake for 25 to 30 minutes, or until the cake is firm to the touch and a tester inserted in the center comes out dry.
7. Cool the cakes in their pans on a wire rack for 15 minutes. Unmold the cakes, but do not remove the paper circles. Cool them to room temperature on the wire rack. Remove the paper circles just before frosting.

TO FILL, FROST, AND FINISH

1. In a small saucepan, bring the sugar and ⅓ cup water to a boil, remove from the heat, and transfer to a clean bowl. Add the vanilla and cool to room temperature.
2. Split each of the cake layers in two horizontally. Set one of the layers on a cardboard round cut slightly larger than the diameter of the cake. Brush the layer with ¼ of the sugar syrup, and spread the cake with about 1 cup

of the mousse. Set the second layer over the mousse, brush it with ¼ of the syrup and spread it with more mousse. Repeat with the third and fourth layers. Spread the remaining mousse over the top and sides of the cake.

3. Pat the chocolate shavings around the sides of the cake and spoon more on top.

STORAGE: Keep in the refrigerator, covered with a cake dome or an inverted mixing bowl, for up to 2 days. Remove the cake 15 minutes before serving.

ADVANCE PREPARATION TIPS

- The cake and chocolate shavings can be made 1 or 2 days ahead of serving.
- Make the mousse and fill and frost the cake 1 day ahead or on the day of serving.

Dieter Schorner's Black Forest Cake

This show-stopper cake is the best version of Black Forest Cake you will ever come across. For those of you who don't know, Black Forest is a German cake confected out of sponge layers soaked in kirsch and filled with a chocolate cream, whipped cream, and cherries. As with so many classics, there are as many versions and interpretations of this cake as there are cooks and pastry chefs. What is different and remarkable about this version, taught to me by Dieter Schorner, is the heavenly chocolate mousse in the bottom layer. In order to make use of all the chocolate mousse, I spread some of it on the top layer as well, which is not how the original recipe was made. This cake requires time and patience, although it can be done in stages. But if you don't feel up to this worthwhile challenge, substitute Whipped Ganache (page 321) for the mousse.

Makes one 9-inch, 3-layer cake

Serves 14

Level of difficulty ★★★

⅓ cup sugar

¼ cup kirsch

Chocolate Butter Sponge Cake, baked in a 9-inch pan, cooled (page 187)

Chocolate Mousse Filling (page 314)

1 (14- to 16-ounce) can sour cherries, drained and patted dry

Whipped Cream, spirited variation made with kirsch (page 318)

2 cups (about 8 ounces) Bittersweet Chocolate Shavings (page 380)

---

1. In a small saucepan, bring the sugar and ⅓ cup water to a boil, stirring. Remove the syrup to a small clean bowl, add the kirsch, and set it aside.
2. Slice the cooled cake into 3 very thin horizontal layers, each about ¼ inch thick. Set one of the layers on a cardboard round cut slightly larger than the diameter of the cake. Brush the cake with ⅓ of the kirsch syrup. Spread about ⅔ of the mousse on the layer. Set aside 14 whole cherries for garnish and imbed the rest in the mousse. Top the cherries with the second cake layer, moisten it with ⅓ of the syrup, and spread it with a layer of whipped cream. Top the whipped cream with the last cake layer, brush it with the remaining syrup, and spread the remaining mousse over the top. Refrigerate the cake and the remaining whipped cream for 30 minutes to firm up the cake.
3. Rewhip the cream with an electric mixer if it has deflated. Set aside in the refrigerator 1 cup of the whipped cream for garnish. Generously spread the sides and top of the cake with the remaining whipped cream, and don't worry if some of the mousse shows through, because it will be covered by the chocolate shavings.
4. Transfer the whipped cream you set aside to a 12-inch pastry bag fitted with a ⅜-inch-wide star tip. Pipe 14 rosettes around the top edge of the cake and top each of the rosettes with one of the cherries you set aside.
5. Pat chocolate shavings around the sides of the cake and spoon the remaining shavings in the middle of the cake, inside the wreath of rosettes.

STORAGE: Keep in the refrigerator, loosely covered with a cake dome or an inverted mixing bowl, for up to 2 days.

- The cake, mousse, and chocolate shavings can be made 1 day ahead of serving.
- Make the whipped cream and kirsch syrup, and assemble the cake on the day of serving.

I have worked in the restaurant and food industry for more than twenty-five years, and Dieter Schorner is among the most gifted pastry chefs I have ever met. What I admire most is his unerring sense of taste; everything he touches tastes exquisite and looks beautiful and soberly elegant. In addition, Dieter is so well trained and has worked in pastry and confectionery for so many years that his experience alone has brought him to culinary heights few of us can reach. From the age of fourteen, he worked in baking, beginning in a bread bakery in Germany, where he was born. Then he moved on to studying the art of chocolate and confectionery in Switzerland. He continued in one of Germany's finest pastry shops, making 140 different types of chocolate, then moved on to working in Sweden, in the country's oldest pastry shop, which supplied pastries to the king of Sweden. He worked on cruise ships and in London, where he worked under his mentor, executive chef Silvano Trompetto. He then became a pastry chef in some of the most illustrious three-star restaurants in New York City, including La Cote Basque and Le Cirque, where he developed what has become the most renowned and best crème brûlée in the city.

Dieter Schorner's Chocolate Gateau

Dieter Schorner, formerly the chairman of the pastry department of the French Culinary Institute, is an extraordinary pastry chef. Among his innumerable contributions to the field is this delicious cake he developed in the 1970s when he was pastry chef at Le Chantilly Restaurant in New York City. What makes this cake so extraordinary is the filling, which is a whipped ganache with much more chocolate than usual.

Makes one 9-inch,
2-layer cake

Serves 12

Level of difficulty ★★

2 cups heavy cream

12 ounces bittersweet or semisweet chocolate, finely chopped

¼ cup sugar

2 tablespoons dark rum

Chocolate Butter Sponge Cake, baked in a 9-inch pan, cooled (page 187)

Cocoa powder, for dusting

1. In a small saucepan over low heat, bring the heavy cream to just under a boil and pour it over the chocolate. Wait 30 seconds, then blend the cream and chocolate together with a whisk and mix until smooth. Chill, stirring occasionally, over a bowl of ice until the mixture feels cold yet is still fluid.

2. Meanwhile, bring ¼ cup water and the sugar to a boil in a small saucepan. Remove from the heat and transfer to a clean bowl, then whisk in the rum.

3. With an electric mixer fitted with the whip attachment, beat the cream and chocolate on medium speed for a few minutes, or until lightened in color and whipped (it will never be as fluffy as whipped cream).

4. With a serrated knife, slice the cake horizontally into 2 layers. Set one of the layers on a cardboard round cut slightly larger than the diameter of the cake. With a pastry brush, moisten the layer with ½ the rum syrup, then spread it with a layer of the whipped chocolate. Top with the second layer, moisten it with the remaining rum syrup, and spread the top and sides with the remaining ganache.

5. If there is enough ganache, transfer it to a pastry bag fitted with a ½-inch-wide star tip and pipe out a decorative border around the bottom edge of the cake. Just before serving, sift a tiny bit of cocoa powder through a strainer over the cake.

STORAGE: Keep refrigerated, loosely covered, for up to 3 days; remove the cake 20 minutes before serving.

Double Chocolate Christmas Log

A bûche de noël *(Christmas log in French) is* the *cake served on Christmas Eve in France. Most French women don't make their own but buy them from their favorite pastry shop. Classically, a Christmas log is made with a vanilla sponge cake, but I make mine with a chocolate sponge. Create little meringue mushrooms to decorate the platter and make the presentation authentic. Even though the cake is labor-intensive, you can make it in stages, or complete the* bûche *in advance and freeze it for up to 3 weeks. If you make the* bûche *in advance, reserve enough buttercream to put the mushrooms together because they should not be made more than a day ahead of serving, nor should they be stored in the refrigerator or frozen.*

Makes one 10-inch-long roll

Serves 12 to 14

Level of difficulty ★★★

¼ cup sugar

---

2 tablespoons dark rum or cognac

Chocolate Sponge Sheet Cake (page 190), cooled and rolled up

Classic French Buttercream, chocolate variation, made with 12 ounces bittersweet chocolate, softened (page 302)

Meringue Mushrooms (see page 376), optional

Holly, optional

Confectioners' sugar, optional

---

1. Bring the sugar and ¼ cup water to a boil and transfer it to a small dish, then add the rum.
2. Unroll the cake onto a sheet of parchment cut slightly larger than the cake (don't worry if there are cracks because they will be camouflaged by the buttercream). Brush the entire surface of the cake with the rum syrup.
3. If you made the buttercream in advance, rewhip it for a few minutes until it is paler in color and looks airier. Spread a thin layer of buttercream over the entire surface of the cake, leaving a ¼-inch border unfrosted around all of the sides.
4. Roll up the cake, using the parchment to help you. Again, with the help of the paper, flip the roll onto a flat surface, seam side down, so you can frost the outside. Set strips of waxed paper underneath either side of the log so you don't get buttercream on your platter. Spread the outside of the cake with buttercream, leaving the ends unfrosted. With a fork, make striations in the buttercream along the length of the log to simulate the bark of a tree.
5. Cut a 2-inch piece, on a diagonal, off one end of the log and anchor it with some buttercream somewhere on the top of the log, but not dead center. This is to make it look as if a "branch" was cut off the log. Carefully remove the waxed-paper strips from under the cake and refrigerate the log, uncovered, for about an hour, or until the buttercream firms up.
6. Decorate the top of the cake and the platter with meringue mushrooms and holly. Keep the log at room temperature for an hour before serving so the buttercream has a chance to soften. Just before bringing the platter to the table, dust the top of the log lightly with confectioners' sugar to simulate snow.

STORAGE: Refrigerate, loosely covered with plastic wrap, for 3 to 4 days; remove the cake 1 hour before serving.

Grand Marnier Chocolate Cake

This cake has a lovely subtle flavor and a terrific texture.

Makes one 9-inch, 2-layer cake

Serves 12 to 14

Level of difficulty ★★★

2 tablespoons sugar

2 to 4 tablespoons Grand Marnier, or to taste

Chocolate Nut Sponge Layer, baked in a 9-inch pan, split horizontally into 2 layers (page 189)

½ recipe Classic French Buttercream, orange variation (page 302)

Ganache, cooled but still fluid enough to spread (page 324)

1 cup Bittersweet or Semisweet Chocolate Shavings (page 380)

1. In a small saucepan, bring 2 tablespoons water and the sugar to a boil, remove from the heat, and add the Grand Marnier.
2. Set one cake layer on a cardboard round cut the same size as the diameter of the cake. Brush the layer with ½ the Grand Marnier syrup (be generous so the cake is nice and moist), and spread the layer with 1 cup orange buttercream. Top with the second layer, brush it with the remaining syrup, and give the cake a thin "crumb coating" of buttercream. Transfer the remaining buttercream to a 14-inch pastry bag fitted with a ¼-inch closed or open star tip and set it aside.
3. Set the cake on a wire rack or icing grill and spread the ganache over the top and sides. Pat a ¼-inch-thick layer of chocolate shavings around the bottom of the cake to hide the unfinished edge.
4. Set the cake on a clean surface and, using the pastry bag, pipe a border of buttercream rosettes or shells around the top edge (don't make the decorative touches too big because it is unpleasant to eat large gobs of buttercream).
5. Spoon the remaining chocolate shavings into the center of the cake, and set the cake, uncovered, in the refrigerator until the icing and decorations are set.

STORAGE: Keep in the refrigerator, loosely wrapped in plastic, for up to 3 days; remove the cake 30 minutes before serving.

Wilkinson's Chocolate Rum Cake

I made this cake for my husband, but he didn't like it because he said it had too much rum. He took it to his place of work, where his colleague Michael Wilkinson said it was fabulous and urged me not to reduce the rum. I decided to leave the cake as is and name it after someone who loves it. In addition to being delicious, this is quite an imposing-looking cake, great for festive occasions. It is a dream cake for parties because you can make and assemble it in advance and freeze it for up to 3 weeks.

Makes one 9-inch, 4-layer cake

Serves 16

Level of difficulty ★★★

¼ cup sugar

¼ cup dark rum

1½ teaspoons instant espresso coffee powder

1 recipe Linda Dann's Swiss Meringue Buttercream (page 307)

¼ cup praline paste (page 27)

6 ounces bittersweet chocolate (preferably Lindt 70%), melted and cooled

1 recipe Chocolate Butter Sponge Cake, and 1 recipe Mocha Sponge variation (page 187), each one baked in a 9-inch cake pan, cooled and split horizontally into 2 layers

1. In a small saucepan, bring the sugar and ½ cup water to a boil, stirring. Remove from the heat, transfer the syrup to a clean bowl, and add the rum.

2. Dissolve the espresso in 1 teaspoon hot tap water. In a mixing bowl, whisk 1 cup of the buttercream with the espresso, and in another mixing bowl, whisk 1 cup of buttercream with the praline paste. Combine the remaining buttercream with the chocolate.

3. Set one chocolate cake layer on a cardboard round cut slightly larger than the diameter of the cake, and brush it with about ¼ of the rum syrup. Spread the layer with the coffee buttercream and set a mocha layer on top. Brush it with ¼ of the rum syrup and spread it with about 1 cup of the chocolate buttercream. Top this with a chocolate cake layer, brush it with ¼ of the rum syrup, and spread it with the praline-flavored buttercream. Finally, top this with the mocha cake layer and brush it with the remaining rum syrup. Spread the top and sides with a very thin "crumb coating" of chocolate buttercream and refrigerate, uncovered, for 30 minutes.

4. Transfer ½ cup of the chocolate buttercream to a pastry bag fitted with a ¼-inch-wide star or plain tip. Spread the top and sides of the cake with a ¼-inch coat of the remaining chocolate buttercream, and decorate the top and bottom edges of the cake with a small border of buttercream rosettes, shells, or dots. Refrigerate, uncovered, until the buttercream is firm.

STORAGE: Keep in the refrigerator, wrapped in plastic, for up to 3 days; remove the cake 45 minutes before serving.

ADVANCE PREPARATION TIPS

- The cake layers and the meringue buttercream can be made a few days ahead of serving.
- Make the rum syrup, flavor the buttercreams, assemble the cake, and decorate it on the day of serving.

Kahlúa Chocolate Cake

Dense and delicious, rich and velvety are the best words to describe this mouth-watering cake. What accounts for its fudgelike texture is that it contains little flour but is rich in chocolate and melted butter. It is important that you saturate the cake with the Kahlúa (coffee liqueur) while it is still warm.

Makes one 9-inch, single-layer cake

Serves 10 to 12

Level of difficulty ★★

CAKE

6 ounces unsweetened chocolate, finely chopped

1 stick (4 ounces) unsalted butter, cut into 1-inch chunks

1 tablespoon instant espresso coffee powder

½ cup (2.25 ounces) cake flour, sifted

¼ teaspoon salt

6 large eggs

1⅓ cups (10 ounces) superfine sugar

¼ cup Kahlúa liqueur

GLAZING AND FINISHING

6 ounces bittersweet or semisweet chocolate, finely chopped

¾ cup heavy cream

1 tablespoon instant espresso coffee powder

½ cup Bittersweet Chocolate Shavings (page 380)

About 14 chocolate-covered espresso beans (see Note), optional

TO MAKE THE CAKE

1. Melt the chocolate with the butter in the top of a double boiler or in a mixing bowl set over simmering, not boiling, water. Be sure that the bottom of the bowl does not touch the water below. Stir occasionally and, when melted, remove from the heat. Dissolve the espresso in 2 teaspoons hot tap water. Add the coffee to the chocolate and set aside to cool to room temperature.

2. Position a rack in the lower third of the oven and preheat to 350°F. Butter the bottom of a 9 × 2.5-inch springform pan, leaving the sides ungreased, and line the bottom with a parchment or greased waxed paper circle.

3. Sift the flour with the salt and set it aside.

4. In a mixing bowl, with a whisk, combine the eggs with the sugar. Set the bowl over a saucepan of simmering water. Be sure that the bowl does not come in contact with the water below. Beat the egg mixture with an electric mixer on low speed until hot to the touch (110° to 115°F on an instant-read thermometer).

5. Remove the bowl from the heat and, with the electric mixer (fitted with the whip attachment) on high speed, beat the eggs for about 5 minutes, or until tripled in volume, pale in color, and thick.

6. Fold ¼ of the eggs into the chocolate. In three additions, sift and fold the flour into the eggs, then fold in the lightened chocolate.

7. Pour the batter into the prepared pan and tap the pan on the counter *once* to break up any large air bubbles. Set the pan on a baking sheet to catch any drips, and bake for about 25 minutes, or until it is slightly under-baked and a tester inserted in the center comes out with some moist batter clinging to it.

8. Cool the cake in the pan on a wire rack for 30 minutes. Unlatch the springform and lift the cake up and out of the form. With a skewer or a toothpick, poke holes in the top of the cake and brush the top with ½ the Kahlúa. Invert the cake over a cardboard round cut the same size or slightly smaller than the diameter of the cake. Remove the metal base and the paper circle. Poke more holes in the bottom of the cake and brush it with the remaining Kahlúa.

1. Set the cake on a wire rack set over waxed paper to catch the drips. Put the finely chopped chocolate in a bowl. In a small saucepan, bring the cream and the espresso powder to just under a boil. Pour the cream over the chocolate, let it stand for 30 seconds, then whisk until homogenized. Set aside in the refrigerator or at room temperature until the mixture has firmed up somewhat and is cool to the touch but still fluid.

2. Liberally pour the glaze over the top and sides of the cake. With an offset spatula, spread the glaze from the center of the cake toward the edges so more glaze drips down the sides. Spread the glaze around the sides and pat the chocolate shavings around the bottom ¼ inch of the cake to hide the unfinished edge.

3. Transfer the cake to a platter and either center 3 chocolate espresso beans in the middle of the cake or set 10 to 12 of them around the edges to mark the portions. Refrigerate, uncovered, until the icing sets.

STORAGE: Keep in the refrigerator, loosely wrapped in plastic, for up to 3 days; remove the cake 30 minutes before serving.

PLATED DESSERT SUGGESTION (per portion)

> 1 slice of cake
> Flavored Custard Sauce,
>   coffee variation (page 359)
> French Caramel Sauce (page 364)
> Shards of Caramel (page 374),
>   optional

Center the slice of cake on a 10-inch plate. Spoon the coffee sauce to one side of the cake and the caramel sauce to the other. Stick caramel shards in the center of the cake.

NOTE: Chocolate-covered espresso beans are available in candy stores or in the candy section of a gourmet produce store.

Michele's Marvelous Mistake

I came up with this some twenty-five years ago, when I was just starting out in the food world and was the chef of a private dining room in a corporate setting. What I set out to do was to re-create a well-loved, then famous, marble sponge cake with streusel topping, sold at the now defunct G & M pastry shop on Madison Avenue in New York City. I was in my sponge cake phase at the time, so I tried to replicate the original cake with that particular technique. I failed miserably because I included too much butter and chocolate for the delicate egg foam to hold in suspension. However, in the process I accidentally came up with this cake, which is a truly outstanding confection. In the cake, the chocolate sinks to the bottom, creating its own layer, and the sponge layer hovers around the middle, under a streusel crust. All in all, this reflects how my lack of knowledge at the time, coupled with chutzpah, *yielded something fabulous.*

Makes one 8-inch square cake

Serves 9 to 10

Level of difficulty ★★

CAKE

1⅓ cups (6.25 ounces) bleached all-purpose flour

2 tablespoons cornstarch, sifted

¼ teaspoon baking powder

¼ teaspoon salt

4 large eggs

2 large egg yolks

1 cup (7.5 ounces) superfine sugar

1 teaspoon vanilla extract

1 stick (4 ounces) unsalted butter, melted and cooled

6 ounces bittersweet chocolate, melted and cooled

TOPPING

¼ cup granulated sugar

½ teaspoon ground cinnamon

3 tablespoons unsalted butter, softened

Approximately ½ cup bleached all-purpose flour

TO MAKE THE CAKE

1. Position a rack in the center of the oven and preheat to 350°F. Butter an 8 × 2-inch square pan. Sift the flour with the cornstarch, baking powder, and salt, and set it aside.

2. In a mixing bowl, with a whisk or handheld electric mixer on low speed, beat the eggs and yolks with the sugar until combined. Set the bowl over a saucepan of simmering water, making sure the bottom of the bowl does not come in contact with the water below. Continue to beat on low speed until hot to the touch (110° to 115°F on an instant-read thermometer).

3. Remove the bowl from the heat and, with the electric mixer (fitted with the whip attachment) on high speed, beat the mixture for about 5 minutes, or until tripled in volume, pale in color, and thick. (With a handheld electric mixer this can take up to 10 minutes.)

4. In several additions, sift and fold the dry ingredients into the egg foam. Stir the vanilla into the melted butter and fold this into the batter. Divide the batter between 2 mixing bowls. Fold the melted chocolate into one of the batters.

5. Spread a layer of vanilla batter on the bottom of the pan and spoon dollops of chocolate batter over it. Repeat with a second layer of vanilla and dollops of chocolate batter, then swirl them together with a wooden skewer without overdoing this step, and bake for 25 minutes.

TO MAKE THE TOPPING

1. While the cake is baking, blend the sugar with the cinnamon; then, with a wooden spoon, blend this into the butter. With your fingertips, pinch just enough flour into the mixture to make it crumbly.

2. Crumble this topping over the batter and bake for 25 minutes longer, or until a tester inserted in the center comes out dry. Cool the cake in its pan on a wire rack; cut and serve it from the pan.

STORAGE: Keep at room temperature, wrapped airtight in foil, for 2 days; refrigerate after that but serve at room temperature.

Raspberry Cake

This is a lovely summer chocolate cake. Raspberry sponge cake layers are filled with raspberry jam and chocolate ganache and iced with a white chocolate whipped cream. For a crowd-pleasing finish, blanket the top with fresh raspberries.

Makes one 8-inch, 3-layer cake

Serves 8 to 10

Level of difficulty ★★

Butter Sponge Cake, raspberry variation, baked in an 8-inch pan, cooled and sliced horizontally into 3 layers (page 184)

6 tablespoons raspberry jam or jelly

½ recipe Ganache (page 324)

½ recipe Whipped Ganache, made with white chocolate (page 321), chilled but not whipped

2 to 3 cups whole fresh raspberries

---

1. Set one of the cake layers on a cardboard round cut slightly larger than the diameter of the cake.
2. Spread the layer with 2 tablespoons of the raspberry jam and top that with ½ the ganache. Set the second cake layer on top and spread it with 2 tablespoons of raspberry jam and the remaining ganache. Top that with the last cake layer and spread it with the remaining 2 tablespoons jam.
3. In a chilled bowl, beat the whipped ganache until it just forms peaks, and spread it over the top and sides of the cake.
4. To garnish the cake, blanket the top with the most gorgeous of the fresh raspberries, or for a more modest look, set a border of raspberries, 2 layers deep, around the top outside edge of the cake.

STORAGE: Keep in the refrigerator, covered with a cake dome or an inverted mixing bowl, for up to 2 days.

ADVANCE PREPARATION TIPS

Begin making the parts of this cake at least a day ahead of serving.
- The raspberry sponge cake layers and the whipped ganache mix can be made 1 day ahead of serving.
- Make the ganache and assemble the cake on the day of serving.

BISCUIT CAKES

*I*N FRENCH THE word *biscuit* generally means "cookie," but in pastry language it describes a sponge cake made by the separated egg method. Biscuit, like sponge cake, has a good firm texture but a not terribly exciting flavor, which makes it great for jelly rolls, or as a structural support for mousse and refrigerated icebox cakes, or as the cake base for bite-sized, iced petits fours.

The batter is airy and can be shaped by piping it into rounds or ladyfingers, or by spreading it on a sheet pan. Biscuit bakes up firmer than whole egg sponge cake because it includes more flour. A biscuit batter that includes nuts yields a cake that is firmer still.

If you want to use a biscuit as you would any other cake layer, spread the batter in a sheet pan, cut the finished cake into three or four rectangular strips, then fill and stack the strips with the appropriate fillings. Given that the texture of a biscuit is so spongy and light, it is best to pair it with an equally airy filling such as pastry cream, custard buttercream, whipped cream, or mousse. And like most sponge cakes, biscuit is lean, so be sure to brush each layer with a sugar syrup before spreading it with filling.

Chocolate Biscuit

This biscuit batter doesn't have much pizzazz, which is okay because its main function is to play the supporting role to the rich mousselike and whipped cream fillings.

Makes one 12 × 16-inch sheet cake, or two 9-inch or three 7-inch disks, or 2½ to 3 dozen ladyfingers

Level of difficulty ★★

½ cup (2.25 ounces) cake flour, sifted

3 tablespoons cornstarch, sifted

3 tablespoons unsweetened cocoa powder, sifted

5 large egg whites, at room temperature

¼ teaspoon salt

½ cup (3.75 ounces) superfine sugar

4 large egg yolks, at room temperature

TO PREPARE THE PANS

1. *For a sheet cake:* Line a 12 × 16 × 1-inch half-sheet pan with buttered baking parchment or line it with a nonstick baking mat.
2. *For disks:* Line 2 baking sheets with baking parchment or waxed paper. On each paper, in pencil, draw a 9-inch circle. Turn the paper over so the pencil marks face the bottom of the pan and won't come off on your cake. Butter the paper. (For 7-inch disks, draw two 7-inch circles on one baking parchment and one 7-inch circle on the other.) Set out an 18-inch pastry bag fitted with a ½-inch-wide plain tip.
3. *For ladyfingers:* Line 2 baking pans with buttered baking parchment and set out an 18-inch pastry bag fitted with a ¾-inch-wide plain tip.

TO MAKE THE CAKE BATTER

1. Position a rack in the center of the oven (or if using two levels, set one in the top third of the oven and the other in the bottom third) and preheat to 350°F.
2. Sift the flour with the cornstarch and cocoa, and set the mixture aside.
3. With an electric mixer on low speed, beat the egg whites with the salt until frothy. Increase the speed to medium and whip the whites until semi-stiff. Gradually add the sugar, about 2 tablespoons at a time, and beat until the whites are stiff and glossy. Transfer the egg whites to a clean bowl.
4. Beat the yolks with a fork, pour them over the whites, and, with a rubber spatula, fold them together until partially mixed. Sift the dry ingredients over the eggs and gently fold them together until homogenized.

TO SHAPE THE BATTER AND BAKE

1. *For a sheet cake:* With an offset spatula, spread the batter evenly in the prepared pan, reaching carefully into the corners and making sure the batter is level. Bake the cake for 15 to 20 minutes, or until the top feels firm and the edges begin to draw away from the sides of the pan. Remove the cake from the oven and cool it in the pan on a wire rack for a few minutes. Pull the paper, with the cake still on it, off the pan.

   If you want to use this as a jelly roll, lightly dust a piece of waxed paper, parchment, or a cloth towel with cocoa powder and invert the cake over the paper. Pull off the top paper and roll the cake up in the paper or cloth to "set" the jelly roll shape. Cool the cake, rolled up.

If you want to use this for a rectangular cake, after you invert the cake and pull off the top paper, cut it into three or four 12-inch-long strips.

2. *To pipe out disks:* Transfer the batter to the prepared pastry bag and pipe out the batter in the traced circles, holding the pastry bag about 1 inch above the pan so the batter flows evenly. Pipe the batter in concentric circles, beginning with the outside edge, and place them ¼ inch apart. With a small offset spatula, spread the batter evenly within the pencil marks to level it. Bake for about 15 minutes. Pull the paper, with the disks still on them, off the pan and cool them on a wire rack.

Once the disks are cool, peel them off the paper. If the batter spread during baking and the outside edge is uneven, trim the rounds with scissors or a knife to make even circles.

3. *To pipe out ladyfingers:* Transfer the batter to the prepared pastry bag and pipe it out in "fingers," about 3 inches long. Hold the pastry bag about 1 inch above the baking pan so the batter flows evenly. Bake for about 15 minutes. Pull the paper, with the ladyfingers still on it, off the pan and cool them on a wire rack. When the ladyfingers are cool, peel them off the paper.

BLONDE BISCUIT

This is made the same way as the chocolate biscuit but with the ingredients in different proportions.

Omit the cocoa powder. Use 5 eggs separated, ⅔ cup (5 ounces) superfine sugar, and ¾ cup (3.5 ounces) cake flour. Bake in the same way. When done, the cake will be a deep golden color.

STORAGE: Use right away or keep the cake strips, disks, or ladyfingers tightly wrapped in plastic in the freezer for up to 3 months.

Chocolate Nut Biscuit

The nuts give this biscuit additional flavor and better texture. You can shape it pretty much as you would any biscuit, except that you can't use this for a jelly roll because the cake is too firm and will crack when you try to roll it up.

Makes one 10 × 15-inch sheet cake, or two 9-inch or three 7-inch disks

Level of difficulty ★★

½ cup (2.25 ounces) cake flour, sifted

2½ tablespoons unsweetened, nonalkalized cocoa powder, sifted

⅛ teaspoon baking soda

½ cup (2 ounces) ground toasted blanched almonds, toasted skinned hazelnuts, or walnuts

5 large eggs, separated

¼ teaspoon salt

½ cup (3.75 ounces) superfine sugar

½ stick (2 ounces) unsalted butter, melted and cooled

Cocoa powder or confectioners' sugar, for cooling cakes

TO PREPARE THE PANS

1. *For a sheet cake:* Line a 10 × 15 × 1-inch jelly roll pan with buttered baking parchment.

2. *For disks:* Line 2 baking sheets with baking parchment or waxed paper. On each paper, in pencil, draw one 9-inch circle. Turn the paper over so the pencil marks face the bottom of the pan and won't come off on your cake. Butter the paper. (For 7-inch disks, draw two 7-inch circles on one baking parchment and one 7-inch circle on the other.) Set out an 18-inch pastry bag fitted with a ½-inch-wide plain tip.

TO MAKE THE CAKE BATTER

1. Position a rack in the center of the oven (or if using two levels, set one in the top third of the oven and the other in the bottom third) and preheat to 350°F.

2. Sift the flour with the cocoa powder and baking soda into a mixing bowl, then blend in the ground nuts with a whisk.

3. With an electric mixer on low speed, beat the egg whites with the salt until frothy. Increase the speed to medium and whip the whites until they are semistiff. Add about ⅔ of the sugar, about 2 tablespoons at a time, and beat on high speed until the whites are stiff and glossy. Transfer the whipped egg whites to another bowl. In the same bowl, with the same beaters, whip the egg yolks with the remaining sugar until they are pale and thick. Beat in the melted, cooled butter; the mixture will look a little bit like Hollandaise sauce. With a rubber spatula, fold the egg yolks into the egg whites, then fold in the dry ingredients.

TO SHAPE THE BATTER AND BAKE

1. *For a sheet cake:* With an offset spatula, spread the batter evenly in the prepared pan, reaching carefully into the corners and making sure the batter is level. Bake the cake for about 18 minutes, or until the top feels firm and the edges begin to draw away from the sides of the pan. Remove the cake from the oven and cool in the pan on a wire rack for a few minutes. Pull the paper with the cake still on it, off the pan.

   Lightly dust a piece of waxed paper, parchment, or a cloth towel with cocoa powder and invert the cake over the paper. Pull off the top paper and cut the cake into strips.

2. *To pipe out disks:* Transfer the batter to the prepared pastry bag and pipe out the batter in the traced circles, holding the pastry bag about 1 inch above the pan so the batter flows evenly. Pipe the batter in concentric circles, beginning with the outside edge. Place them close together. With a small offset spatula, spread the batter evenly within the pencil marks to level it, and bake for about 15 minutes. Pull the paper, with the disks still on them, off the pan and cool them on a wire rack.

   Once the disks are cool, peel them off the paper. If the batter spread during baking and the outside edge is uneven, trim the rounds with scissors or a knife to make even circles.

STORAGE: Use the strips or disks right away to create a cake, or keep them tightly wrapped in plastic in the freezer for up to 2 months.

Chocolate Almond Biscuit

This deliciously moist biscuit is intensely flavored with almond paste and superb as a cake base for iced petits fours.

½ cup (4 ounces) almond paste

¼ stick (1 ounce) unsalted butter, melted

¾ cup (4 ounces) confectioners' sugar, sifted

4 large egg yolks

2 large eggs

½ cup (2 ounces) cornstarch, sifted

Scant ⅓ cup (1 ounce) unsweetened, nonalkalized cocoa powder

5 large egg whites

¼ teaspoon salt

⅓ cup (2.5 ounces) superfine sugar

1 tablespoon granulated sugar

1. Position a rack in the center of the oven and preheat to 375°F. Line the bottom of a 12 × 16 × 1-inch half-sheet pan with buttered baking parchment or line it with a nonstick baking mat.
2. In an electric mixer (preferably fitted with a paddle attachment), beat the almond paste with the butter and confectioners' sugar until smooth. Add the egg yolks and whole eggs and beat for a couple of minutes, or until light and airy; then beat in the cornstarch and cocoa powder.
3. With an electric mixer on low speed, beat the egg whites with the salt until frothy; increase the speed to medium and whip them until semistiff. Gradually add the superfine sugar, about 2 tablespoons at a time, and beat until the egg whites are stiff and glossy.
4. With a rubber spatula, fold the whipped egg whites into the almond paste mixture. With an offset spatula, spread the batter evenly in the prepared pan, reaching carefully into the corners and making sure the batter is level.
5. Bake for 18 to 20 minutes, or until the top feels firm and the edges begin to draw away from the sides of the pan.
6. Cool the cake in the pan on a wire rack. Sprinkle a piece of parchment, a nonstick baking mat, or a cloth towel, larger than the cake, with the granulated sugar. Invert the cake onto the paper or cloth, then remove the pan and peel off the paper. The cake is now ready to be cut into strips or other shapes.

STORAGE: If you don't use this immediately, keep it wrapped airtight in the freezer for up to 2 months.

Glorious Amaretto Cake

This divinely flavored cake is an almond-lover's dream. It is fashioned out of an almond paste cake layer and filled with crushed amaretto cookies and white chocolate whipped ganache.

Makes one 4 × 12-inch, 4-layer cake

Serves 12

Level of difficulty ★★

Chocolate Almond Biscuit (page 212), cut into 4 strips, each about 4 × 12 inches long

32 small amaretto cookies

¼ cup sugar

1 to 2 tablespoons amaretto liqueur, optional

Whipped Ganache, made with white chocolate (page 321)

¼ cup toasted sliced or slivered almonds

1. Set one of the cake layers on a cookie sheet or platter that is long enough to hold it comfortably. Place the cookies in a plastic bag. Close the bag loosely and crush the cookies into crumbs with a rolling pin. Set the crumbs aside.
2. In a small saucepan, bring ¼ cup water and the sugar to a boil. Remove it from the heat and cool to room temperature, then add the amaretto.
3. With a pastry brush, moisten the first cake layer with about ¼ of the amaretto syrup, and spread it with about ¾ cup of the whipped ganache. Sprinkle some cookie crumbs over that. Top with the second cake layer and repeat with the moistening syrup, filling, and cookie crumbs. Continue with the third layer, repeat the procedure, and finish with the last cake layer, which you should brush with the last of the moistening syrup.
4. Spread the remaining ganache over the top and sides of the cake, leaving the ends unfrosted. Pat the remaining cookie crumbs over the sides of the cake. Sprinkle a 1-inch band of cookie crumbs along the top edge of the cake and sprinkle the almonds in the center.

STORAGE: Keep refrigerated, loosely covered, for up to 2 days.

ADVANCE PREPARATION TIPS

- Make the cake and the whipped ganache mixture 1 day ahead of serving.
- Make the moistening syrup, whip the ganache, toast the almonds, and put the cake together on the day of serving.

Alessia's Banana Chocolate Cream Cake

Much to my surprise, my daughter Alessia pronounced this fancy cake among her favorites. It is composed of a walnut sponge batter folded into an Italian meringue, and this particular technique makes the cake as springy as an angel food cake. The layers are then heavily soaked with a cognac syrup and layered with jam, sliced fresh bananas, and a milk chocolate whipped ganache. If the cake itself is too hard to make, substitute Chocolate Nut Sponge Layer (page 189), cut it into two layers, and fill it as you would this cake.

Makes one 9-inch,
2-layer cake

Serves 12

Level of difficulty ★★★

CAKE

½ cup (2.25 ounces) cake flour

½ cup (2 ounces) cornstarch, sifted

Scant ¼ cup (0.75 ounce) unsweetened, nonalkalized cocoa powder, sifted

½ teaspoon baking powder

½ cup (2 ounces) walnuts or pecans, finely ground

1 cup (7.5 ounces) superfine sugar

6 large eggs, separated

1 teaspoon light corn syrup

¼ teaspoon salt

⅛ teaspoon cream of tartar

FILLING AND FINISHING

¼ cup sugar

1 to 2 tablespoons cognac or brandy

Whipped Ganache, made with milk chocolate, not whipped (page 321)

2 medium bananas

¼ cup raspberry jam, strained

1 cup Bittersweet Chocolate Shavings (page 380)

TO MAKE THE CAKE

1. Position a rack in the center of the oven and preheat to 350°F. Line the bottoms of two 9 × 2-inch round cake pans with buttered parchment or greased waxed paper circles, but leave the sides of the pans ungreased.

2. Sift the flour with the cornstarch, cocoa, and baking powder into a small mixing bowl, then add the walnuts and combine with a whisk. Set ¼ cup of the sugar aside. Place the egg whites in the bowl of a stationary mixer.

3. In a heavy 1-quart saucepan, over low heat, bring the remaining ¾ cup sugar, the corn syrup, and ¼ cup water to a boil, stirring. Dip a pastry brush in cold water and brush down the sides of the pot to dissolve any sugar crystals. Without stirring, let the syrup come to 200°F on a candy thermometer.

4. When the syrup is at that temperature, lower the heat and begin to whip the egg whites with the salt until frothy. Add the cream of tartar and beat until the egg whites are semistiff. Gradually, with the mixer running, add the reserved ¼ cup sugar and beat until the whites form firm peaks.

5. Increase the heat under the syrup and let it reach 234° to 236°F on a candy thermometer. Start the electric mixer again. Rewhip the whites on medium speed, and slowly, in one spot at the edge of the mixing bowl, pour the hot syrup into the egg whites, whipping as you pour. (If you pour the sugar syrup in the center of the bowl and the syrup hits the beaters, it will splatter against the sides of the mixing bowl rather than being integrated into the egg whites.) Once all the syrup is incorporated, continue to beat until the outside of the bowl in which you are whipping the egg whites feels warm to the touch but not scalding hot. You have now formed an Italian meringue.

6. Blend the egg yolks with a whisk. With a rubber spatula, fold 1 cup of the Italian meringue into the yolks, then fold this back into the remaining meringue. When the mixtures are combined, sprinkle the sifted dry ingredients over the top and continue to fold until blended.

7. Divide the mixture evenly between the prepared pans and bake for 25 to 30 minutes, or until a tester inserted in the center comes out dry. Cool the cakes to room temperature in their pans on a wire rack.

TO FILL AND FINISH

1. In a small saucepan, bring the sugar and ¼ cup water to a boil. Remove the saucepan from the heat, transfer the syrup to a clean bowl, and add the cognac.

2. Run a knife around the cakes to loosen them from the pans, then unmold them and peel off the paper circles. Set one cake layer on a cardboard round cut slightly larger than the diameter of the cake. In a chilled bowl, beat the whipped ganache until it just forms soft peaks. Peel one of the bananas and cut it into thin slices.

3. Brush the cake layer with ½ the cognac syrup and spread ½ the jam over that. Spread about 1 cup of the whipped ganache over the jam and embed the sliced bananas into the cream. Top the cream with the second cake layer and repeat with the syrup and jam. Spread the top and sides of the cake with the remaining ganache and refrigerate, uncovered, for at least 30 minutes to firm up the ganache. When the ganache is firm, pat the chocolate shavings around the sides of the cake, leaving the top plain (reserve any leftover shavings for the top of the cake). Set the finished cake on a clean platter and refrigerate, uncovered, until serving time.

4. Just before serving, slice the second banana into 20 slices and set them in a circle around the top outside edge of the cake. Spoon a tiny bit more of the chocolate shavings over each banana slice and serve immediately.

STORAGE: Keep in the refrigerator, covered with a cake dome or an inverted bowl, for up to 2 days.

ADVANCE PREPARATION TIPS

- The cake layers, whipped ganache mixture, and chocolate shavings can be made 1 day ahead of serving.
- Make the moistening syrup, whip the ganache, and assemble and decorate the cake on the day of serving.

Austrian Dobos Torte

A classic Hungarian Dobos Torte is composed of thin layers of yellow sponge cake filled with chocolate or coffee buttercream. The top is covered with a glasslike caramel flat top scored with marks so that it is easy to cut into portions. I learned this Austrian version from Jurgen David, one of my pastry teachers at the French Culinary Institute, and it differs from the original because the caramel top is first cut into sections, which are angled, like little hats, across the buttercream rosettes.

Makes one 6-inch,
5-layer cake

Serves 8

Level of difficulty ★ ★ ★

CAKE

Generous ¾ cup (3.5 ounces) cake flour

4 large egg whites

¼ teaspoon salt

½ cup (3.75 ounces) superfine sugar

5 large egg yolks

3 tablespoons sour cream

FILLING AND FINISHING

2½ cups Classic French Buttercream, chocolate or mocha variation (page 302)

¼ cup granulated sugar

TO MAKE THE CAKE

1. Position two racks in the upper and lower thirds of the oven and preheat to 350°F. Fit a 16-inch pastry bag with a ⅜-inch-wide plain tip and set it aside. Line two 12 × 16 × 1-inch half-sheet pans with baking parchment. On each sheet of parchment, draw in pencil three 6-inch circles, then turn the paper over so the pencil lines don't come off on your cake.

2. Sift the flour once and set it aside. With an electric mixer on low speed, beat the egg whites with the salt until frothy. Increase the speed to high and whip until they form soft peaks. Add ½ the sugar, about 1 tablespoon at a time, and whip until the egg whites are stiff and glossy; then transfer them to another bowl.

3. In the same bowl in which you whipped the egg whites, beat the egg yolks with the remaining sugar for a couple of minutes, or until light. With a rubber spatula, fold the yolks into the sour cream and then pour this mixture into the whipped egg whites and fold together along with the flour.

4. Transfer ½ the batter to the pastry bag and pipe the mixture in a spiral shape within the outline of the three circles traced on the parchment paper. Repeat this with the other ½ of the batter on the other three circles.

5. Bake for 10 minutes, then reverse the positions of the baking sheets and bake for 10 minutes longer, or until the center of the disks are firm when pressed and the edges begin to turn crisp.

6. Remove the disks from the oven. Slide each of the papers onto a wire rack and cool the disks to room temperature. Peel them off the paper when they are cool.

TO FILL AND FINISH

1. Set one cake disk on a 6-inch cardboard round. Spread ¼ cup of the buttercream between each of the five disks of cake, setting aside the sixth disk to be caramelized later.

2. Spread ¼ cup of buttercream on top of the cake and spread ⅓ cup of buttercream around the sides. Refrigerate the cake for 30 minutes to firm up the buttercream. Spread a final thin layer of buttercream around the sides of the cake and ridge the sides with an icing comb.

3. With the tip of a knife, lightly score the top of the cake to mark 8 portions. Fill a 12-inch pastry bag, fitted with a ⅜-inch-wide star tip, with about ½ cup of the buttercream and pipe 8 rosettes around the edge of the cake between the scoring lines. Refrigerate, uncovered, as you make the caramel layer.

4. Set the sixth cake layer upside down, so the flat part is on top on a non-stick baking mat, a piece of baking parchment, or on the back of a cookie sheet or baking pan. In a heavy-bottomed 1-quart saucepan (or an unlined copper pot), bring the sugar and 2 tablespoons water to a boil, stirring. Brush down the insides of the pot a couple of times with a pastry brush dipped in cold water to prevent the sugar from crystallizing. Stop stirring. Let the mixture cook until it turns golden amber, smells of caramel, and registers 320°F on a candy thermometer. Immediately remove the caramel from the heat and quickly pour it over the top of the cake layer. Very rapidly, before the caramel sets, spread it evenly and let it set until hard and cold.

5. You are now going to cut the caramel-coated sponge into 8 pie-shaped wedges. Take a beat-up, old chef's knife and heat the blade over an open flame. When the blade appears hot, cut the layer in half, but first score the caramel with the hot knife to melt the sugar, then press down and through the caramel and cake. Rinse the knife in very hot water and heat it up again over an open flame. Cut the halves in half again. Proceed this way until you have 8 pie-shaped caramel cake wedges.

6. Angle the caramel wedges over the rosettes, with the points facing in so that each person gets a portion of caramel-coated cake with each slice. Refrigerate the cake, uncovered, until serving time.

STORAGE: Keep leftovers in the refrigerator, loosely covered with plastic wrap, for 3 to 4 days.

ADVANCE PREPARATION TIPS

• Make the cake layers and the buttercream the day before serving.
• Assemble and make the caramel sponge layer on the day of serving.

The Lorenzini

This recipe was given to me by Francis Lorenzini, head of the baking and pastry department of New York City Technical College. It is the recipe he chose when I asked him, "What comes to mind when I say the words chocolate cake?" He was right to select this recipe because, after one bite, my daughter pronounced this to be "the most chocolate of chocolate cakes!" In the original recipe the cake was round. I decided to bake the batter in a sheet pan because it is easier for the home cook.

Makes one 4 ×
12-inch, 4-layer cake

Serves 16

Level of difficulty ★★★

CAKE

½ cup plus 1 tablespoon (2.75 ounces) cake flour

Scant ⅓ cup (1 ounce) unsweetened cocoa powder

⅛ teaspoon baking powder

⅛ teaspoon baking soda

5 large eggs, separated

¼ teaspoon salt

½ cup (3.75 ounces) superfine sugar

GLAZE

6 ounces semisweet chocolate, finely chopped

6 ounces heavy cream

FILLING AND FINISHING

8 ounces semisweet chocolate, finely chopped

2 cups heavy cream

½ cup sugar

2 tablespoons dark rum

TO MAKE THE CAKE

1. Position a rack in the center of the oven and preheat to 375°F.
2. Line the bottom of a 12 × 16 × 1-inch half-sheet pan with buttered baking parchment or a nonstick baking mat.
3. Sift the flour with the cocoa, baking powder, and baking soda twice, and set it aside.
4. With an electric mixer on low speed, beat the egg whites with the salt until frothy. Increase the speed to medium and whip the whites until they are semistiff. Slowly add the sugar, about 2 tablespoons at a time, and beat until the egg whites are stiff and glossy. Transfer them to a clean bowl.
5. Beat the yolks with a fork, pour them over the whites, and with a rubber spatula, fold the two together until partially mixed. Gradually sift the dry ingredients over the eggs and fold them in.
6. With a long offset spatula, spread the batter in the prepared pan, reaching carefully into the corners and making sure the batter is level.
7. Bake for about 15 minutes, or until the top feels firm and the cake begins to pull away from the sides of the pan. Cool the cake to room temperature in its pan on a wire rack. Pull the cake off the pan with the paper and flip it over onto a clean piece of parchment or a cotton cloth. Peel off the top paper. Cut the sheet of cake into 4 rectangular strips, each about 4 inches wide and 12 inches long.

TO MAKE THE GLAZE

Set the chocolate in a small bowl, bring the heavy cream to just under a boil, and pour it over the chocolate. Let the mixture stand for 30 seconds, then blend it with a rubber spatula until smooth. Set it aside to cool to room temperature.

TO FILL AND FINISH

1. Set the chocolate in a bowl, bring the heavy cream to just under a boil, and pour it over the chocolate. Let the mixture stand for 30 seconds, then blend it with a whisk until smooth. Set this bowl in a larger bowl filled with ice and cool the mixture, stirring occasionally, until it feels cold but

Francis Lorenzini

Francis is an enormously talented, classically trained, and incredibly accomplished French pastry chef who is not well known outside the rarefied world of professionals. He worked as a pastry chef in some of the more illustrious New York City restaurants of the 1970s, and during that era, chefs were not the celebrities they are today.

Born in Alsace, Francis made his way to New York, where he became the first full-time pastry chef at Le Cygne Restaurant. After that, for a brief time, he operated his own business, then worked for Guy Pascal and opened the glorious Les Delices de la Côte Basque pastry shop. After that he returned to work in top-rated restaurants such as La Caravelle Restaurant. Since 1989, he has taught at New York City Technical College, where his expertise and knowledge are much appreciated by his eager students.

is still fluid enough to whip. (If you cool it in the refrigerator for too long, it will be too stiff to whip.)

2. When the mixture feels cold, whip it with a handheld whisk or an electric mixer on medium-low speed for a few seconds, or until the mixture looks airier and has doubled in volume. Don't overdo this step or the mixture can turn grainy. Refrigerate until the glaze is cool.

3. Bring ½ cup water and the sugar to a boil in a small saucepan, remove from the heat, transfer to a clean bowl, and add the rum.

4. Set one cake strip on a cookie sheet or on a piece of cardboard cut the same size as the strip of cake. Rewhip the filling for just a few turns of the beaters. Brush the cake with ¼ of the rum syrup, then spread it with ⅓ of the filling. Cover the filling with the second strip of cake, set upside down, making sure the edges are lined up, and repeat with brushing the syrup and filling until the last strip of cake, set upside down, which you should brush with the remaining syrup. If you wish, you can refrigerate the cake, uncovered, to firm it up.

5. When the glaze feels cool to the touch, spread it with a small offset spatula over the top and around the sides of the cake, leaving the ends uniced. Refrigerate the cake a few minutes, then give it a second coating of glaze.

6. If you wish, ridge the sides and top of the cake with an icing comb. Refrigerate, uncovered, until the glaze sets.

STORAGE: Keep in the refrigerator, loosely covered, for up to 3 days; remove the cake 45 minutes before serving.

Rigo Jancsi

This is my adaptation of my mother-in-law's recipe for Rigo Jancsi, a Hungarian choco-late pastry made of sponge cake layers sandwiching a thick layer of whipped cream. This sponge cake is not easy to handle because it is higher in sugar, which means it's stickier than most. There is some doubt as to whether or not the original recipe included gelatin in the whipped cream filling, but I decided to include it so that the filling won't collapse under the weight of the cake.

Makes twelve 2-inch square cakes

Serves 12

Level of difficulty ★ ★ ★

CAKE

⅓ cup (1.75 ounces) cake flour, sifted

⅓ cup (1 ounce) unsweetened cocoa powder, sifted

6 large eggs, separated

¼ teaspoon salt

¾ cup (5.5 ounces) superfine sugar

GLAZE AND FILLING

Cocoa powder, for dusting

6 ounces bittersweet chocolate, finely chopped

¼ stick (1 ounce) unsalted butter, chilled

1 envelope unflavored gelatin

½ cup (2.75 ounces) confectioners' sugar, sifted

3 tablespoons unsweetened cocoa powder, sifted

2 cups chilled heavy cream

TO MAKE THE CAKE

1. Position a rack in the center of the oven and preheat to 350°F. Line the bottom of a 12 × 16 × 1-inch half-sheet pan with buttered baking parch-ment or a nonstick baking mat.
2. Sift the flour with the cocoa and set it aside.
3. With an electric mixer on low speed, beat the egg whites with the salt un-til frothy. Increase the speed to medium and whip the whites until they are semistiff. Slowly add ½ cup of the sugar, about 2 tablespoons at a time, and beat until the whites are stiff and glossy. Transfer the egg whites to a clean bowl.
4. In the same bowl, with the same beaters, whip the egg yolks with the re-maining ¼ cup sugar until light and thick. With a rubber spatula, fold ⅓ of the whipped egg whites into the yolks, then fold this mixture back into the remaining egg whites. When the eggs are partially blended, grad-ually sift and fold in the flour mixture.
5. With a long offset spatula, spread the batter in the prepared pan, making sure the batter is level and evenly distributed into the corners. Bake for 18 to 20 minutes, or until the top feels firm.
6. Cool the cake in the pan for 5 minutes. Run a knife around the edges of the cake to loosen it from the sides of the pan; slide it, still on the paper, out of the pan to cool to room temperature on a wire rack.

TO GLAZE, FILL, AND FINISH

1. Set out a piece of waxed paper or baking parchment slightly larger than the dimensions of the cake and sprinkle it with 1 teaspoon cocoa powder. Better yet, sprinkle the cocoa powder on the rough side, facing up, of a second nonstick baking mat.
2. Cut the cake in half so you have 2 rectangles, each about 8 × 12 inches. Slide one of these rectangles, right side up, onto a baking sheet or a piece of cardboard. Then invert the second piece of the cake (this will become the top of your cake, which you will glaze) onto another cookie sheet or cardboard rectangle.

3. In a small saucepan over low heat, melt the chocolate with ⅓ cup water, stirring occasionally. When the chocolate has melted, whisk in the butter and transfer the mixture to a mixing bowl to cool to room temperature. When the glaze is cool, spread it over the piece of cake that is upside down and refrigerate it for 5 minutes. Remove it from the refrigerator, spread it with a second coat of glaze, and return it to the refrigerator for 15 minutes, or until somewhat firm. Then cut this glazed piece into twelve 2-inch squares.

4. Pour ¼ cup water into a small skillet, sprinkle the gelatin over the water, and let the mixture stand until thickened, about 1 minute. Set the skillet over very low heat and stir until the gelatin is just liquefied. Pour into a clean cup or a small bowl and set aside.

5. Sift the confectioners' sugar with the cocoa powder a couple of times and set it aside.

6. With an electric mixer on low speed, begin to whip the cream, then increase the speed to medium and beat until the cream is softly whipped. With the machine running, drizzle in the liquefied gelatin, then stop the machine. Sift the cocoa powder mixture over the cream and resume beating for a few more seconds, or until the whipped cream is stiff.

7. Spread a ¾-inch-thick layer of this filling over the unglazed piece of cake. Remove the glazed chocolate squares from the refrigerator and, with a spatula, lift and place them over the whipped cream filling.

8. Refrigerate until ready to serve. Just before serving, cut the cake, between the squares, all the way through to the bottom.

STORAGE: Store in the refrigerator, loosely covered, for up to 3 days.

Dark Chocolate Swiss Roll

This cake is so puffy it should be spread with the thinnest layer of filling or it will be too fat to roll up. Sometimes I like to fill the cake with jelly or ganache, and sometimes with both, as in this version. While you can make the cake one day, then fill and roll it up on the next, I urge you to fill and roll it up right away because the cake will be more pliable and easier to work with when it is freshly baked.

Makes one 15-inch roll

Serves 12 to 14

Level of difficulty ★★

CAKE

½ cup (2.25 ounces) cake flour, sifted

Scant ¼ cup (0.75 ounce) unsweetened, Dutch-processed cocoa powder, sifted

¼ teaspoon baking powder

½ teaspoon salt

6 large eggs, separated

⅛ teaspoon cream of tartar

1 cup (7.5 ounces) superfine sugar

¾ teaspoon vanilla extract

3 to 4 tablespoons unsweetened cocoa powder or confectioners' sugar, sifted, for unmolding the cake

FILLING AND FINISHING

4 ounces semisweet or milk chocolate, finely chopped

½ cup heavy cream

3 tablespoons sugar

1 to 2 tablespoons cognac or brandy

½ cup strained raspberry or apricot jam

Confectioners' sugar, for finishing

TO MAKE THE CAKE

1. Position a rack in the center of the oven and preheat to 375°F. Line the bottom of an 12 × 16 × 1-inch half-sheet pan with a buttered baking parchment or a nonstick baking mat.
2. Sift the flour with the cocoa, baking powder, and ¼ teaspoon of the salt and set it aside.
3. With an electric mixer on low speed, beat the egg whites with the remaining ¼ teaspoon salt and the cream of tartar until frothy. Increase the speed to medium and whip until the whites are semistiff. Slowly add ¾ cup of the sugar, about 2 tablespoons at a time, and whip until the egg whites are stiff and glossy; then transfer them to a clean bowl.
4. In the same bowl you whipped the whites, beat the egg yolks with the remaining ¼ cup sugar and the vanilla for 1 minute, or until thick and somewhat lighter in color. Pour the yolks over the whites and fold them together with a rubber spatula until partially mixed. Sift the dry ingredients over the eggs and fold them in.
5. Spoon dollops of the batter into the prepared pan. With a long offset spatula, spread the batter, reaching carefully into the corners and making sure the batter is level. Bake for about 15 minutes, or until the top looks puffy, feels somewhat firm, and begins to draw away from the sides of the pan. (Take care not to overbake the cake or it will be too brittle to roll up.)
6. While the cake is baking, sift the cocoa powder over a clean cotton tea towel or piece of parchment that is larger than the dimension of the pan. When the cake comes out of the oven, let it cool for 5 minutes in the pan. Then run a knife around the cake to loosen it from the sides of the pan. Pull the cake out of the pan by grabbing a corner of baking parchment or mat, and invert it over the tea towel. Peel off the parchment and cool another 5 minutes.

1. Set the chocolate in a mixing bowl. In a small saucepan, over low heat, bring the cream to just under a boil and pour it over the chocolate. Let the mixture stand for 30 seconds, then whisk it together and refrigerate until somewhat thick.

2. Bring the sugar and 3 tablespoons water to a boil in a small saucepan, remove from the heat, and add the cognac.

3. Brush the cake with the cognac syrup, spread a very thin layer of jam over the surface, then spread the chocolate and cream mixture over that. From a short end, roll up the cake as tightly as possible, trim off the untidy ends, and flip it onto a platter, seam side down. Brush off any excess cocoa powder from the top, and refrigerate the cake until ready to eat. Just before serving, sift confectioners' sugar over the top.

STORAGE: Keep in the refrigerator, wrapped airtight in plastic, for up to 2 days; remove the cake 30 minutes before serving.

Dione Lucas's Chocolate Swiss Roll

I adore this lovely recipe from Dione Lucas, grande dame of the 1960s culinary world. I have seen this recipe in many 1970s cookbooks but never attributed to the author. It is a lighter-than-air vanilla sponge cake that is filled, rolled up, and iced with a chocolate glaze. The only change I have made is to alter the chocolate glaze so that it is easier to work with. In addition to its elegant simplicity, the cake takes precious little time to make, is the lightest sponge roll you could ever hope to prepare, and the finished cake is the perfect size for an intimate dinner party.

Makes one 10 × 3-inch roll

Serves 4 to 6

Level of difficulty ★★

CAKE

4 large eggs, separated

⅛ teaspoon salt

⅛ teaspoon cream of tartar

⅓ cup (2.5 ounces) superfine sugar

½ teaspoon vanilla extract

3 tablespoons cake flour

1 tablespoon granulated sugar

FILLING AND FINISHING

6 ounces semisweet chocolate (morsels will do)

¼ cup heavy cream

1 tablespoon unsalted butter

2 teaspoons dark rum

½ cup Chocolate Shavings, made of dark, milk, or white chocolate (page 380)

Confectioners' sugar, for dusting

TO MAKE THE CAKE

1. Position a rack in the center of the oven and preheat to 350°F. Line the bottom of a 10 × 15 × 1-inch jelly roll pan with buttered waxed paper or baking parchment.
2. With an electric mixer on low speed, beat the egg whites, salt, and cream of tartar until frothy. Increase the speed to medium and beat until semi-stiff. With the machine running, add ½ the superfine sugar, about 2 tablespoons at a time, and beat until the egg whites are stiff and glossy.
3. In a separate bowl, whip the egg yolks with the remaining superfine sugar for 1 minute, or until light, then add the vanilla. With a rubber spatula, fold ¼ of the whites into the yolks, then fold the lightened egg yolks back into the remaining egg whites; sift and fold in the flour.
4. With an offset spatula, spread the batter into the prepared pan, reaching carefully into the corners and making sure the batter is level.
5. Bake for 15 minutes, or until the batter begins to smell like an omelet and the surface begins to turn golden brown. Remove the pan from the oven and run a knife around the cake to loosen it from the sides of the pan.
6. Set out a piece of baking parchment or a clean cotton tea towel that is slightly larger than the size of the cake. Sprinkle the granulated sugar over the parchment, lift the cake up by the corners of the waxed paper, and invert it over the sugared parchment. Because the cake is fragile and delicate, very carefully peel off the top paper. From a short end, roll up the cake in the parchment and set it aside while you make the glaze.

1. Combine the chocolate and cream in the top of a double boiler set over simmering water. When melted, remove the pan from the heat, stir in the butter and rum, and cool to room temperature. Unroll the cake and spread it with ½ the chocolate. Roll up the cake tightly and place it on a cookie sheet, seam side down.

2. Slip strips of waxed paper halfway under the cake to catch any drips and pour the remaining glaze over the top. With a small offset spatula, spread the glaze evenly on the outside of the cake, leaving the ends unglazed. Sprinkle the chocolate shavings down the length of the top of the cake and refrigerate until ready to serve. Dust the top of the cake with confectioners' sugar just before serving. Serve each person 3 thin slices of cake.

STORAGE: Keep in the refrigerator, loosely wrapped in plastic, for up to 2 days; remove the cake 30 minutes before serving.

Cocoa Puff

Cocoa Puff is my name for an angel food cake prepared with cocoa powder. It is a cake without saturated fat and is designed to satisfy cholesterol-minded sweet lovers. Angel food cakes are confected out of few ingredients—egg whites, sugar, and flour with a dash of flavorings. The air trapped in the whipped whites gives the cake its characteristic cloudlike quality, and the quantity of sugar in the batter makes it sticky as well. Serve the cake plain, or with a side of whipped cream or melted ice cream, or a spoonful of fruit sauce or compote. You can also slice the cake into two layers and stack them with whipped cream or mousse in between.

Makes one 10-inch tube cake

Serves 12

Level of difficulty ★★

---

12 large (1½ cups) egg whites

11 tablespoons (3.25 ounces) cake flour, sifted

Scant ¼ cup (0.75 ounce) unsweetened cocoa powder

1½ cups plus 1 tablespoon (12 ounces) superfine sugar

¼ teaspoon salt

¼ teaspoon cream of tartar

Confectioners' sugar, for dusting

---

1. Separate the eggs while cold, but leave the whites out to come to room temperature.

2. Position a rack in the lower third of the oven and preheat to 325°F. Set out a 10-inch angel food pan, preferably one with "feet" and a removable bottom. Do not grease the pan, but you can line the bottom with a doughnut-shaped parchment round, if you wish.

3. Sift the flour with the cocoa and ⅓ cup of the sugar a couple of times and set it aside.

4. Beat the egg whites on low speed until frothy. Add the salt and cream of tartar, increase the speed to medium, and whip until the whites are semi-stiff. Increase the speed to high and, with the mixer running, add the remaining sugar, about 2 tablespoons at a time. Beat until the egg whites are stiff and glossy. (In a KitchenAid 5-quart mixer, the volume of the beaten whites will reach almost to the top of the mixing bowl.) If you think it will be awkward to fold the dry ingredients into the egg whites, transfer the whites to a larger bowl.

5. In four or five additions, sift the dry ingredients through a strainer over the beaten egg whites, then fold them into the whites, using a rubber spatula or, preferably, your hand.

6. Spoon the batter into the pan and level the top with a rubber spatula. Rap the pan sharply on the counter a couple of times to break up any large air bubbles, and bake for 45 to 50 minutes, or until the top is springy and a tester inserted in the center comes out dry.

7. Immediately remove the pan from the oven and invert it onto its feet, or hang it upside down over the neck of a bottle or funnel. Allow it to hang upside down until completely cool.

8. To remove the cake, slide a long, thin metal spatula or knife around the sides and the inner tube to loosen it from the pan. Work carefully, and angle the spatula toward the pan so you don't tear the cake. With your fin-

gers, ease the cake out of the pan and set it, right side up, on a plate or cardboard round. Just before serving, dust the top with confectioners' sugar.

ANGEL FOOD CAKE

Omit the cocoa powder and make the cake as above but with 14 tablespoons (4 ounces) cake flour, sifted. Fold 1 teaspoon vanilla extract into the egg whites before you fold in the flour.

STORAGE: Keep at room temperature, under a cake dome or lightly wrapped in foil, for up to 3 days.

Filled Angel Food Cake

The simplicity of an angel food cake makes it the perfect partner for a rich filling like whipped ganache, and the addition of fruit or nuts adds textural interest.

Makes one 10-inch,
3-layer tube cake

Serves 12

Level of difficulty ★★

Cocoa Puff, baked and cooled
(page 226)

2 to 4 cups Whipped Ganache,
made with bittersweet or 70%
extra-bittersweet chocolate
(page 321)

1 cup raspberries *or*
1 cup chopped nuts, such as
toasted pecans, hazelnuts, or
almonds, optional

1. With a serrated knife, cut the cake horizontally into 3 layers. Set the bottom layer on a cardboard round cut the same diameter as the cake.
2. Spread 4 cups of ganache between the layers as well as on top and around the sides of the cake. Or spread 2 cups of ganache between the layers and on the top, but leave the sides plain. Scatter the berries or nuts between the layers and over the top.

STORAGE: Keep in the refrigerator, under a cake dome or an inverted large mixing bowl, for up to 5 days.

Chocolate Pudding–Filled Angel Food Cake

Hollowing out an angel food cake and replacing the insides with a chocolate pudding is an effective way of embellishing what might otherwise be too plain a cake. The rich filling is starch-free and more like a thick custard sauce than a pudding, so make it at least 4 hours in advance to give it time to firm up in the refrigerator. If you don't like this filling, substitute a Chocolate Pudding Filling (page 323) or Chocolate Sabayon Mousse (page 317).

Makes one 10-inch tube cake

Serves 12

Level of difficulty ★★

¾ cup heavy cream

3 tablespoons granulated sugar

6 large egg yolks

6 ounces semisweet chocolate, melted and cooled

Cocoa Puff, angel food variation, baked and cooled (page 226)

Confectioners' sugar

Candied Violets or Roses or Sugared Flowers, optional (page 378)

---

1. In a small saucepan, over low heat, bring the cream and sugar to just under a boil, stirring. With a rubber spatula, stir the egg yolks into the chocolate. Slowly drizzle the hot cream into the yolks and chocolate, stirring continuously.

2. Set the bowl with the chocolate mixture over a saucepan of simmering water, making sure the bottom of the bowl is not in contact with the simmering water below.

3. Stir the mixture continuously until it thickens or reaches 140°F on an instant-read thermometer. Strain the mixture through a sieve into a clean bowl and cool for 15 minutes. Set a piece of plastic wrap directly onto the surface of the pudding so it does not develop a skin, and refrigerate it until it is thick and spreadable.

4. With a serrated knife, slice off the top ⅓ of the cake and lift it onto another surface. Make a 1-inch-deep cut all around the cake, ½ inch from the outer edge, then make a similar cut around the inner tube of the cake. With your fingers, gently pull out a channel of cake, within the outline of the cuts, making sure you leave a shell of cake about ½ inch thick on the bottom and around the sides. Use the removed cake pieces for another purpose. Spoon the chocolate pudding into the hollowed-out tunnel and replace the top of the cake. Refrigerate, uncovered, until ready to eat.

5. Just before serving, dust the cake with confectioners' sugar, and if you wish, garnish it with candied violets.

STORAGE: Keep in the refrigerator, loosely wrapped in plastic, and eat within 2 days.

ADVANCE PREPARATION TIPS

- Make the cake and filling 1 day ahead of serving.
- Hollow out and assemble the cake on the day of serving.

Chocolate Chiffon

Chiffon cake, an American classic, is made by folding vegetable oil into a separated egg sponge batter. It is as imposingly tall as an angel food cake but more substantial in flavor and moister because of the oil. With its moist springy crumb, this cake is a great candidate for a plated dessert presentation (see Plated Dessert Suggestions for Unfrosted Cakes, page 352).

Makes one 10-inch tube cake

Serves 14 to 16

Level of difficulty ★★

2⅔ cups (12 ounces) cake flour, sifted

2 cups less 2 tablespoons (14 ounces) superfine sugar

½ cup (1.5 ounces) unsweetened, Dutch-processed cocoa powder

2 teaspoons baking powder

¾ teaspoon salt

5 large egg yolks

½ cup neutral-flavored vegetable oil

1 teaspoon vanilla extract

¼ teaspoon cream of tartar

7 large egg whites, at room temperature

Confectioners' sugar or Chocolate Satin Glaze (page 330)

---

1. Position a rack in the lower third of the oven and preheat to 325°F. Set out a 10-inch angel food pan, preferably one with "feet" and a removable bottom. Leave the sides and bottom ungreased, but line the bottom, if you wish, with a doughnut-shaped parchment round.

2. Sift the flour with ¾ cup of the sugar, the cocoa, baking powder, and ½ teaspoon of the salt, and set it aside.

3. With an electric mixer on low speed, beat the egg yolks with the oil, ½ cup water, and the vanilla until combined. Add ½ the sifted ingredients and beat on medium speed for 1 minute, or until homogenized.

4. In a separate bowl, with an electric mixer on low speed, whip the egg whites until frothy. Add the remaining ¼ teaspoon salt and the cream of tartar, increase the speed to medium, and beat until the whites are semistiff. With the machine running, add the remaining 1 cup plus 2 tablespoons sugar and beat until the whites are stiff and glossy.

5. With a rubber spatula, fold the egg whites into the egg yolk batter as you sift and fold in the remaining dry ingredients.

6. Pour the batter into the angel food pan and bake for 50 minutes. Increase the heat to 350° and bake for 20 minutes longer, or until a tester inserted in the center comes out dry and the top springs back when lightly pressed.

7. Immediately remove the pan from the oven and invert it onto its feet, or if you are using a tube pan without feet, turn it upside down over the neck of a bottle or funnel. Hang the cake, inverted, until completely cool.

8. To remove the cake, slide a long, thin metal spatula or a knife around the sides and the inner tube to loosen it from the pan. Work carefully, and angle the spatula toward the pan so you don't tear the cake. With your fingers, ease the cake out of the pan and remove the paper circle.

9. Set the cake on a cardboard round cut the same diameter as the cake. Dust the top with the confectioners' sugar or spread the glaze around the top and sides of the cake.

STORAGE: Store at room temperature, under a cake dome, for up to 3 days.

Pink Pear Sauce, warm
(page 367)
1 slice of cake, unglazed

White and dark Chocolate
Shavings, page 380
3 fresh whole raspberries

Spoon ¼ cup of sauce in the middle of a 10-inch plate. Rotate the plate so the sauce spreads to the edges. Center the slice of cake, set upright, in the middle of the sauce. Scatter the white and dark chocolate shavings and the raspberries over the sauce.

Tips for Angel Food Cakes

- Read through the recipe once and assemble the ingredients before you begin to prepare the batter because you must work quickly once the egg whites are whipped.

- Do not grease the cake pan so the batter has a rough surface to cling to as it rises up the sides.

- It is easier to separate the eggs while they are cold, but then let them come to room temperature so the whites will incorporate as much air as possible.

- Even though you want to incorporate as much air as possible into the batter, don't overbeat the egg whites or they will be dry and cottony and won't have room to expand in the oven.

- It is easier to fold the sifted ingredients into the beaten egg whites with your hands than with a rubber spatula so you can feel the little flour lumps and break them up as you fold.

- Get the cake in the oven immediately or the precious air cells will begin to deflate.

- Rather than cut the cake with a knife, which tamps it down, slice it with a cake divider ("cake breaker") or pull it apart with two forks inserted in the cake back to back.

FLOURLESS CAKES

*I*N THIS CHAPTER you'll find an amazing selection of cakes and cakelike confections made entirely, or almost entirely, without flour. To give the cakes texture, the flour has been replaced by another ingredient, usually ground nuts, or sometimes by a more surprising one, such as grated apples, a purée of beans, potatoes, chestnuts, cake crumbs, ground poppy seeds, cornstarch, or potato starch. Included here as well are the voluptuous French flourless confections consisting of melted chocolate, butter, eggs, and sugar. And some cakes, which I call meringue cakes, are confected out of an egg white and sugar meringue folded into ground nuts.

The characteristics and look of these cakes differ greatly from most other cakes because they are flourless and thus gluten-free, they are higher in sugar, and the only leavening comes from the whipped egg whites. All of this translates into fairly flat cakes that have a dense, fudgelike, and sometimes chewy texture.

As these cakes are so gloriously rich in and of themselves, they need little more to finish them off than a light dusting of confectioners' sugar or a thin chocolate glaze.

Ann Rothschild's Cake

My friend Ann Rothschild contributed this recipe. Its origin is unknown. It is much like Souffléed Chocolate Cake (page 254), but is a little lighter in taste because of the milk chocolate. It tastes best served on the day you bake it.

Makes one 9-inch, single-layer cake

Serves 8 to 10

Level of difficulty ★★

6 ounces milk chocolate, finely chopped

6 ounces semisweet chocolate, finely chopped

1½ sticks (6 ounces) unsalted butter, cut into 1-inch chunks

5 large eggs, separated

¼ teaspoon salt

⅛ teaspoon cream of tartar

¾ cup (5.5 ounces) granulated sugar

2 tablespoons cake flour

Confectioners' sugar, for dusting

Whipped Cream, optional (page 318)

1. Melt the milk and semisweet chocolates in a mixing bowl or in the top of a double boiler set over simmering water. Stir occasionally and, when just melted, transfer to a large, clean mixing bowl, whisk in the butter, and set aside to cool to room temperature.

2. Position a rack in the center of the oven and preheat to 350°F. Lightly butter a 9 × 2.5-inch springform pan, leaving the sides ungreased.

3. With an electric mixer on medium speed, whip the egg whites with the salt until frothy. Add the cream of tartar and whip until soft peaks form. With the machine running, add ½ cup of the sugar, about 2 tablespoons at a time, and beat until the whites are stiff and glossy. Transfer the egg whites to a clean bowl. In the same bowl you whipped the egg whites, beat the egg yolks with the remaining ¼ cup sugar until light and thick, and fold them into the egg whites, using a rubber spatula. Spoon the egg mixture over the melted butter and chocolate, sift the flour over the top, and fold until the mixture is homogenized.

4. Pour the batter into the prepared pan, set the pan on a baking sheet to catch the drips, and bake for 25 minutes. Lower the heat to 325° and bake for 25 to 30 minutes longer, or until the center of the cake barely jiggles when you shake the pan. You can't test whether or not this is done, so just remove it from the oven and set it to cool to room temperature in its pan on a wire rack. As the cake cools, the top cracks, so push it gently back together; this side will become the bottom anyway, so don't worry.

5. Run a knife around the edge of the cake to loosen it from the sides. Unlatch the springform, lift the cake up and out of the mold, remove the metal base, and invert it over a cardboard round cut the same dimension or slightly smaller than the cake. Just before serving, sift confectioners' sugar through a sieve over the top and serve at room temperature, with sweetened whipped cream, if you wish.

STORAGE: Keep in the refrigerator, wrapped airtight in plastic, for up to 5 days; remove the cake 45 minutes before serving.

Apple Pecan Chocolate Cake

The grated apples make this cake moist and give it intriguing flavor as well. It is delicious with a caramel or butterscotch sauce.

Makes one 10-inch, single-layer cake

Serves 10 to 12

Level of difficulty ★★

CAKE

1 pound Granny Smith or other tart apples

6 ounces (about 1⅔ cups) whole pecans

6 ounces (about 13 tablespoons) superfine sugar

¼ cup (1 ounce) cornstarch, sifted

¼ teaspoon freshly ground nutmeg

6 large eggs, separated

¼ teaspoon salt

⅛ teaspoon cream of tartar

3 ounces bittersweet chocolate, melted and cooled

GLAZE AND FINISHING

Jurgen's Chocolate Glaze (page 330)

½ cup toasted and finely ground pecans

12 whole pecans

French Caramel Sauce (page 364), optional, or Butterscotch Sauce (page 364), optional

TO MAKE THE CAKE

1. Core, peel, and grate the apples with a food processor or on a box grater. Transfer the grated apples to a strainer set over a bowl and let them drain for 15 minutes. Press the juice out of the apples (reserve the juice to drink), then transfer the apples to a double thickness of cheesecloth and squeeze out the excess moisture; set the apples aside.

2. Position a rack in the center of the oven and preheat to 325°F. Butter a 10 × 2.5-inch springform pan and line the bottom with a buttered parchment circle.

3. In a food processor, grind the pecans with ¼ cup of the sugar. Transfer the pecans and sugar to a mixing bowl and, using a whisk, combine them with the cornstarch and nutmeg. Add the grated apples and mix until they are well distributed throughout the pecan mixture; set aside.

4. With an electric mixer on low speed, beat the egg whites with the salt until frothy. Add the cream of tartar and continue to beat on high speed until the egg whites are semistiff. With the machine running, add the remaining ½ cup plus 1 tablespoon sugar, about 2 tablespoons at a time, and beat until the egg whites are stiff and glossy. Transfer the whites to another bowl.

5. Break up the yolks with a fork, pour them over the whites, and fold them together with a rubber spatula. Fold 1 cup of the egg mixture into the chocolate, then fold this lightened mixture back into the whipped egg mixture along with the pecan and apple mixture. Fold until homogenized.

6. Pour the batter into the prepared pan, set the pan on a baking sheet to catch the drips, and bake for 45 to 55 minutes, or until a tester inserted in the center comes out clean. Cool the cake in its pan on a wire rack until it is at room temperature. The top of the cake will crack and lift up a bit, so just gently press it back into the cake. Run a knife around the cake to loosen it from the sides of the pan. Open the springform and lift the cake up and out of the form.

1. Invert the cake onto a cardboard round cut the same diameter as the cake, remove the metal base, and peel off the paper circle. Place the cake on a wire grid set over a large piece of waxed paper to catch the drips from the glaze. While the glaze is still warm, spread a little bit of it around the sides of the cake with a small offset spatula. Pour a light coating over the top and spread it to the edges, where it will drip over the sides. Spread the glaze around the sides.

2. Very carefully, because the glaze smudges easily, pick up the cake with one hand and, with the other hand, pat the ground pecans around the sides of the cake. Set 12 whole pecans around the top edge of the cake to mark the portions. Refrigerate, uncovered, until ready to serve.

3. If you want to serve this with the sauce, spoon 2 to 3 tablespoons in the center of a dessert plate and position a slice of cake over the sauce.

STORAGE: Keep in the refrigerator, loosely covered, for up to 4 days; remove the cake 30 minutes before serving.

Autumn Chestnut Cake

This marvelously moist cake consists simply of a purée of chestnuts, chocolate, and butter blended into an egg white meringue. The cake is then hidden under a blanket of rum-scented whipped cream and garnished with candied chestnuts. It is best to make this in late fall or early winter, around Christmas, when it is easier to find canned and candied chestnuts. If you can't find marrons glacés, *make Sugared Chestnuts and garnish the top of the cake with spoonfuls of these in lieu of the whole candied chestnuts.*

Makes one 10-inch,
single-layer cake

Serves 10

Level of difficulty ★

CAKE

1½ cups (about 8 ounces) unsweetened whole chestnuts packed in water, drained

6 ounces bittersweet chocolate, finely chopped

1 stick (4 ounces) unsalted butter, softened

1 cup less 2 tablespoons (6 ounces) granulated sugar

6 large eggs, separated

1 tablespoon vanilla extract

¼ teaspoon salt

FROSTING AND FINISHING

1½ cups chilled heavy cream

¼ cup confectioners' sugar, sifted

2 tablespoons dark rum

10 whole *marrons glacés* or Sugared Chestnuts (page 373)

TO MAKE THE CAKE

1. Position a rack in the center of the oven and preheat to 375°F. Butter and flour a 10 × 2.5-inch springform pan and line the bottom with a buttered parchment or greased and floured waxed paper circle. Tap out the excess flour. Pat the chestnuts dry and, in a food processor fitted with the steel blade, purée them until smooth.

2. Melt the chocolate in the top of a double boiler or in a mixing bowl set over simmering water. Stir occasionally until melted, then transfer to a clean mixing bowl and set aside to cool to room temperature.

3. With an electric mixer on medium speed (fitted with the paddle attachment if you have one), cream the butter with about ½ the sugar for 2 minutes, or until the mixture has an ivory hue and the texture of mayonnaise. Scrape down the sides of the bowl and beat for a few seconds longer, then add the chestnut purée and beat until smooth. Add the egg yolks, two at a time, and continue to beat until the mixture looks light. With a rubber spatula, fold in the melted chocolate and the vanilla.

4. In a separate bowl, with an electric mixer on low speed, whip the egg whites with the salt until frothy, then increase the speed to high and beat until they are semistiff. With the machine running, add the remaining sugar, about 2 tablespoons at a time, and beat until the egg whites are stiff and glossy.

5. With a rubber spatula, fold the egg whites into the chocolate and chestnut mixture, then pour the batter into the prepared cake pan. Tap the pan on the counter once to break up any air bubbles, set it on a baking sheet to catch the drips, and set the cake in the oven. Immediately turn the oven down to 350° and bake for 15 minutes. Turn the oven down to 325° and bake for another 35 to 45 minutes, or until a tester inserted in the center comes out dry and the cake begins to pull away from the sides. Turn off the heat and leave the cake in the oven with the door ajar for 30 minutes.

6. Remove the cake from the oven and cool it for 10 minutes on a wire rack. Run a metal spatula or table knife around the cake to loosen it from the sides of the pan. Open the springform lock, lift the cake up and out of the form, and cool it to room temperature.

TO FROST AND FINISH

1. Invert the cake onto a cardboard cake round cut slightly larger than the diameter of the cake. Remove the metal base and carefully peel off the paper circle.

2. In a chilled bowl and with chilled beaters, begin to whip the cream on low, then on medium speed until it holds soft peaks. Sift the confectioners' sugar over the top, add the rum, and beat on high speed until the cream is stiffly whipped.

3. Spread the whipped cream over the top and sides of the cake, and ridge the top and sides with an icing comb. Set the *marrons glacés* around the top edge of the cake to mark the portions.

STORAGE: Keep refrigerated, under a cake dome or an inverted mixing bowl, for up to 5 days.

Chile Chocolate Peanut Torte

This cake is designed for gingerbread or other spice cake aficionados. It combines an intriguing mix of chocolate, peanuts, and chile powder, which introduces a mysteriously spicy undertone. The addition of ancho chile powder, which is not fiery hot, was inspired by the way the Aztecs flavored their chocolate drinks. People who are allergic to peanuts can substitute cashews or pecans. This cake has a marvelous texture, with a crunchy meringue top that contrasts with the moist velvety interior. It tastes best served plain or at most with a scoop of vanilla ice cream.

Makes one 9-inch, single-layer cake

Serves 12

Level of difficulty ★

---

6 ounces semisweet chocolate, finely chopped

1½ sticks (6 ounces) unsalted butter, melted and cooled

1 cup (3.5 ounces) roasted unsalted peanuts

1 tablespoon cornstach

2 teaspoons ground pure ancho chile powder

½ teaspoon ground cinnamon

5 large eggs, separated

¼ teaspoon salt

14 tablespoons (6 ounces) superfine sugar

Confectioners' sugar, for dusting

---

1. Position a rack in the center of the oven and preheat to 350°F. Lightly butter a 9 × 2.5-inch springform pan. Melt the chocolate in a mixing bowl or in the top of a double boiler set over simmering water. Stir occasionally and, when melted, whisk in the butter, then set aside to cool.

2. In a food processor fitted with the steel blade, process the peanuts with the cornstarch until finely ground. Add the chile powder and cinnamon, and process until combined.

3. In a mixing bowl, with an electric mixer on medium speed, whip the egg whites with the salt until they form soft peaks. With the machine running, add the sugar, 2 tablespoons at a time, and beat until the egg whites are stiff and glossy. Break up the yolks with a fork and then fold them into the egg whites, using a rubber spatula. Fold in the chocolate and butter, and finally add the peanut-spice mixture.

4. Pour the batter into the prepared pan and set it on a baking sheet to catch the drips. Bake for 45 to 55 minutes; the interior should remain moist.

5. Remove the cake to a wire rack and cool to room temperature in the pan. As the cake is cooling, the crunchy meringue top crust will sink and crack, which is okay. When the cake is cool, slide a metal spatula or a table knife around the cake to loosen it from the sides of the pan. Open the springform lock and lift the cake up and out of the form. Serve the cake on its metal base and, just before serving, dust the top with confectioners' sugar.

STORAGE: Keep in the refrigerator, wrapped airtight in plastic, for up to 5 days; remove the cake 45 minutes before serving.

Chocolate Bean Torte

People I have served this cake to never guess its secret ingredient—a purée of white beans blended with walnuts and rum. The beans add moistness and a slightly crunchy texture rather than flavor.

Makes one 10-inch, single-layer cake

Serves 12

Level of difficulty ★

---

8 ounces semisweet chocolate, finely chopped

---

2 cups (7 ounces) walnuts

---

1 cup (7.5 ounces) granulated sugar

1½ cups cooked (one 15-ounce can, drained) white beans, patted dry

---

2 tablespoons dark rum

---

1 tablespoon vanilla extract

---

6 large eggs, separated

Pinch of salt

Confectioners' sugar, for dusting

---

1. Position a rack in the center of the oven and preheat to 350°F. Lightly butter a 10 × 2.5-inch springform pan.

2. Melt the chocolate in the top of a double boiler or in a mixing bowl set over simmering water. Stir occasionally until melted, then transfer to a clean mixing bowl and set aside until cool to the touch. In a food processor, grind the walnuts with ¼ cup of the sugar and transfer to a mixing bowl. Purée the beans in the food processor with the rum and vanilla. Add the egg yolks to the purée and process until smooth. Add the chocolate and process again until smooth; set aside.

3. With an electric mixer on low speed, whip the egg whites with the salt until frothy. Increase the speed to medium-high and beat until soft peaks form. With the machine running, add the remaining ¾ cup sugar, about 2 tablespoons at a time, and beat until the egg whites are stiff and glossy.

4. With a rubber spatula, fold the bean and chocolate purée into the egg whites, and when halfway mixed, fold in the ground nuts.

5. Pour the batter into the prepared pan, set the pan on a baking sheet to catch the drips, and bake for 50 minutes to 1 hour, or until the top is firm, a tester inserted in the center comes out dry, and the cake begins to pull away from the sides of the pan.

6. Cool the cake to room temperature in its pan on a wire rack. Run a metal spatula or table knife around the cake to loosen it from the sides of the pan. Open the springform lock and lift the cake up and out of the form. Let any loose pieces of cake from the sides and top fall away naturally. Serve the cake on its metal base and, just before serving, lightly dust the top with confectioners' sugar.

STORAGE: Keep the cake at room temperature, loosely covered, for up to 2 days; refrigerate after that but serve at room temperature.

Chocolate Pumpernickel Torte

Among the countless wonderful experiences I had writing this book was discovering the infinite ways of creating cakes that combine chocolate with unusual tastes and ingredients. The spiciness of this cake, which blends nuts, pumpernickel crumbs, spices, pepper, and port wine, reminds me of a German spice cake or an American gingerbread. The pumpernickel crumbs add a mysterious quality to the cake without overwhelming it. I like serving this in thin slices with whipped cream or orange sorbet on the side.

Makes one 10-inch, single-layer cake

Serves 14 to 16

Level of difficulty ★

CAKE

6 ounces bittersweet chocolate, finely chopped

6 slices (6 ounces) pumpernickel bread (see Note), crusts removed

½ cup ruby port wine

1 cup plus 2 tablespoons (4 ounces) walnuts, almonds, or pecans

1 teaspoon freshly ground black pepper, optional

1 teaspoon ground cinnamon

8 large eggs, separated

¼ teaspoon salt

1½ cups (11.25 ounces) granulated sugar

ICING AND FINISHING

½ cup red currant jelly

Midnight Icing (page 326)

TO MAKE THE CAKE

1. Position a rack in the center of the oven and preheat to 350°F. Butter a 10 × 3-inch springform pan. Line the bottom with a buttered parchment or greased and floured waxed paper circle.

2. Melt the chocolate, stirring, in a mixing bowl or the top of a double boiler set over simmering water, and set it aside to cool.

3. In a food processor fitted with the steel blade, pulverize the bread into crumbs (you should have about 2⅓ cups) and transfer the crumbs to a mixing bowl. Pour the port wine over the crumbs and mix until the crumbs are damp. In the same food processor, grind the nuts until ground and transfer them to another mixing bowl. With a rubber spatula, blend the pepper, if using, and cinnamon into the nuts, then combine this with the soaked bread crumbs, egg yolks, and chocolate and mix thoroughly.

4. With an electric beater on medium speed, whip the egg whites with the salt until they are semistiff. With the machine running, add the sugar, about 2 tablespoons at a time, and beat until the egg whites are stiff and glossy.

5. With a rubber spatula, in three or four batches, fold the beaten egg whites into the nut and chocolate mixture, then transfer the batter to the prepared cake pan. Set the pan on a baking sheet to catch the drips and bake for 30 minutes. Turn the heat down to 325° and bake for 45 minutes to 1 hour longer, or until the top feels firm and a tester inserted in the center comes out dry. Turn off the heat and leave the cake in the oven, with the door ajar, for 30 minutes longer.

6. Cool the cake to room temperature in the pan on a wire rack. Press the cracked top back down onto the cake. Run a metal spatula or a table knife around the cake to loosen it from the sides of the pan. Open the springform lock and lift the cake up and out of the ring. Refrigerate for 3 to 4 hours.

TO ICE AND FINISH

1. Invert the cake onto a cardboard round cut the same diameter or slightly smaller than the cake. Remove the metal base and peel off the paper circle. If the cake is larger on top than on the bottom, straighten the sides with a serrated knife.

2. Heat the red currant jelly in a small saucepan or a microwave oven until just warm to the touch. Spread the jelly on top and around the sides of the cake. Set the cake on a wire rack with waxed paper underneath to catch the drips.

3. While the icing is still warm, pour it over the top. With a metal spatula, spread it across the cake so it drips over the sides, then spread it around the sides. Refrigerate, uncovered, until the icing sets.

STORAGE: Keep in the refrigerator, loosely covered, for up to 5 days, and serve cold.

NOTE: Use packaged sliced pumpernickel bread from the supermarket because anything more authentic will simply overpower the cake.

The Java

This marvel of a cake is a velvety rich coffee-lover's dream. When you take the cake out of the oven, it looks as if it has risen quite a bit, but as it cools, it flattens so much that it looks like a pancake. It needs nothing more than a spoonful of whipped cream on the side, along with a drizzle of caramel sauce on the plate.

Makes one 9-inch, single-layer cake

Serves 12 to 14

Level of difficulty ★

8 ounces milk chocolate, finely chopped

1 stick (4 ounces) unsalted butter, softened

¼ cup Kahlúa

2 teaspoons instant espresso coffee powder

2 tablespoons cornstarch

2 tablespoons unsweetened cocoa powder

5 large eggs, separated

¼ teaspoon salt

⅛ teaspoon cream of tartar

½ cup (3.75 ounces) superfine sugar

Confectioners' sugar, for dusting

2 cups Whipped Cream (page 318)

French Caramel Sauce (page 364), optional

1. Position a rack in the center of the oven and preheat to 350°F. Butter a 9 × 2.5-inch springform pan.

2. Melt the chocolate in a mixing bowl or in the top of a double boiler set over simmering water. Stir occasionally and when the chocolate has just melted, transfer it to a clean mixing bowl and whisk in the butter, then add the Kahlúa. Dissolve the coffee in 2 teaspoons hot water, add to the chocolate, and set it aside. Sift the cornstarch together with the cocoa and set it aside.

3. With an electric mixer on medium speed, whip the egg whites with the salt until frothy. Add the cream of tartar and whip until the whites are semistiff. With the machine running, add the sugar, about 2 tablespoons at a time, and beat until the egg whites are stiff and glossy. In another mixing bowl, stir the egg yolks with a fork, then pour them over the egg whites and fold the two together with a rubber spatula. Fold ¼ of the egg whites into the chocolate and butter mixture to lighten it, then fold this back into the remaining egg whites. Sift and fold in the cocoa mixture at the same time.

4. Pour the batter into the prepared pan, set the pan on a baking sheet to catch the drips (or wrap the outside of the pan with foil), and bake for 35 to 40 minutes. The top will look a bit crusty but the inside should remain slightly underbaked.

5. Remove the cake from the oven and set it to cool to room temperature in its pan on a wire rack. The cake will sink in the middle. Slide a knife or a metal spatula around the cake to loosen it from the sides of the pan. Unlock the springform and lift the cake up and out of the form. Serve the cake on its metal base, at room temperature, lightly dusted with confectioners' sugar. Spoon whipped cream on the sides and, with a squeeze bottle, drizzle the caramel sauce, if using, over the cake, whipped cream, and plate.

STORAGE: Keep in the refrigerator, wrapped airtight in plastic, for up to 5 days; remove the cake 45 minutes before serving.

Rehrucken (Chocolate Saddle of Venison)

This bizarrely named, oddly shaped cake is nothing more than a spicy chocolate almond cake baked in a long, ribbed, semicircular mold. The shape of the cake is meant to simulate the look of a tied roasted saddle of venison, and the icing, pricked with slivered almonds, is meant to look like strips of lard running through the roast! For people who don't care to invest in this special mold, the cake can also be baked in a 9-inch spring-form pan. The mold can be purchased in professional baking supply houses such as Bridge Kitchenware (see Appendix C, page 389).

Makes one
12-inch-long cake

Serves 10

Level of difficulty ★

---

3 ounces bittersweet chocolate, finely chopped

2 cups (7 ounces) unblanched almonds, finely ground

⅛ teaspoon ground cinnamon

⅛ teaspoon ground cloves

Grated zest of 1 lemon

5 large eggs, separated

½ cup (3.75 ounces) granulated sugar

Pinch of salt

Maria's Best Chocolate Glaze (page 331)

⅓ cup slivered almonds

Whipped Cream (page 318)

---

1. Position a rack in the center of the oven and preheat to 350°F. Butter a nonstick, 12-inch-long tinned Rehrucken pan, taking care to be generous with the butter in order to get into all the nooks and crevices (or use a 9-inch springform pan). Dust with granulated sugar and tap out the excess.

2. Melt the chocolate in a mixing bowl or the top of a double boiler set over simmering water. Stir occasionally and, when melted, set aside to cool. In a mixing bowl, combine the almonds with the cinnamon, cloves, and lemon zest and set aside. With an electric mixer on medium speed, beat the egg yolks with about ¼ cup sugar for 2 minutes, or until the mixture looks light, then fold in the chocolate with a rubber spatula.

3. In a separate bowl, with an electric mixer on medium speed, whip the egg whites with the salt until they are semistiff. With the machine running, slowly add the remaining ¼ cup sugar, 2 tablespoons at a time, and beat until the egg whites are stiff and glossy.

4. With a rubber spatula, fold the egg yolk and chocolate mixture into the egg whites, then fold this into the almond mixture. Pour the batter into the prepared pan and bake for 40 to 45 minutes, or until a tester inserted in the center comes out dry. Cool the cake in the pan for 10 minutes, then unmold it onto a wire rack and cool to room temperature.

5. Pour ½ the chocolate glaze over the cake and chill the cake for 20 minutes, then spread the other ½ on top. Transfer the cake to a platter and stud it randomly with 3 rows of slivered almonds, pointing upward. Serve with whipped cream.

STORAGE: Keep in the refrigerator, loosely covered, for up to 5 days; bring the cake back to room temperature before serving.

Karen's Chocolate Hazelnut Torte

I met Chef Karen Fohrhaltz and her husband Michael Miele when my husband and I became devoted fans of their restaurant, Amsterdam's, on the Upper West Side of Manhattan. The restaurant, right around the corner from where we lived, was known for Karen's intensely flavored, unpretentious bistro fare. When I asked Karen if she wanted to contribute to this book, she replied graciously by sharing this fabulous recipe. The only change I have made is to recommend milk chocolate rather than the bittersweet chocolate Karen prefers, because I think it allows the flavor of the hazelnut to shine through more forcefully.

Makes one 10-inch, single-layer cake

Serves 12 to 14

Level of difficulty ★

CAKE

9 ounces milk chocolate, finely chopped

2 sticks less 1 tablespoon (7.5 ounces) unsalted butter, softened

1 cup (7.5 ounces) superfine sugar

8 large eggs, separated

½ teaspoon instant espresso coffee powder

1 teaspoon vanilla extract

¼ teaspoon salt

Generous 2¼ cups (9 ounces) toasted skinned hazelnuts, finely ground

GLAZE AND FINISHING

1½ cups heavy cream, plus more if necessary

1 cup toasted skinned hazelnuts, coarsely chopped

8 ounces bittersweet chocolate, finely chopped

TO MAKE THE CAKE

1. Butter a 10 × 3-inch springform pan and line the bottom with a buttered parchment or greased waxed paper circle.
2. Melt the chocolate in a mixing bowl or in a double boiler set over very hot or barely simmering water. Stir occasionally and, when melted, set the chocolate aside to cool to room temperature.
3. Position a rack in the center of the oven and preheat to 350°F. With an electric mixer on medium speed, beat the butter with ¼ cup of the sugar for about 2 minutes, or until the mixture has an ivory hue and is light. Scrape down the sides of the bowl, beat a few seconds longer, then add the egg yolks two at a time, and continue to beat until the mixture looks airy. Dissolve the coffee in ½ teaspoon hot water. Add the vanilla, coffee, and chocolate to the egg mixture, and mix until blended.
4. In a separate bowl, with an electric mixer on medium speed, whip the egg whites with the salt until they are semistiff. With the machine running, add the remaining ¾ cup sugar, about 2 tablespoons at a time, and beat until the whites are stiff and glossy.
5. With a rubber spatula, fold the hazelnuts into the egg whites, then pour the butter and chocolate mixture over the whites and fold the ingredients together. Pour the batter into the prepared pan and set it on a baking sheet to catch the drips. Bake for 1 hour. Turn the heat down to 325° and bake for 20 to 30 minutes longer, or until the cake feels firm on top and begins to shrink away from the sides of the pan. The interior will not be quite dry, so the cake remains moist and fudgy when cool. Turn off the oven and leave the cake in the oven for 30 minutes with the door ajar.
6. Cool the cake to room temperature in the pan on a wire rack. It will sink in the middle as it cools, but the sides will remain stuck at a slightly higher level. When the cake is cool, cut away the ¼ inch of cake that has stuck to the sides of the pan so that the top is flat. Open the springform lock and lift the cake up and out of the ring.

Karen's Chocolate Hazelnut Torte

I met Chef Karen Fohrhaltz and her husband Michael Miele when my husband and I became devoted fans of their restaurant, Amsterdam's, on the Upper West Side of Manhattan. The restaurant, right around the corner from where we lived, was known for Karen's intensely flavored, unpretentious bistro fare. When I asked Karen if she wanted to contribute to this book, she replied graciously by sharing this fabulous recipe. The only change I have made is to recommend milk chocolate rather than the bittersweet chocolate Karen prefers, because I think it allows the flavor of the hazelnut to shine through more forcefully.

Makes one 10-inch,
single-layer cake

Serves 12 to 14

Level of difficulty ★

CAKE

9 ounces milk chocolate, finely chopped

2 sticks less 1 tablespoon (7.5 ounces) unsalted butter, softened

1 cup (7.5 ounces) superfine sugar

8 large eggs, separated

½ teaspoon instant espresso coffee powder

1 teaspoon vanilla extract

¼ teaspoon salt

Generous 2¼ cups (9 ounces) toasted skinned hazelnuts, finely ground

GLAZE AND FINISHING

1½ cups heavy cream, plus more if necessary

1 cup toasted skinned hazelnuts, coarsely chopped

8 ounces bittersweet chocolate, finely chopped

TO MAKE THE CAKE

1. Butter a 10 × 3-inch springform pan and line the bottom with a buttered parchment or greased waxed paper circle.

2. Melt the chocolate in a mixing bowl or in a double boiler set over very hot or barely simmering water. Stir occasionally and, when melted, set the chocolate aside to cool to room temperature.

3. Position a rack in the center of the oven and preheat to 350°F. With an electric mixer on medium speed, beat the butter with ¼ cup of the sugar for about 2 minutes, or until the mixture has an ivory hue and is light. Scrape down the sides of the bowl, beat a few seconds longer, then add the egg yolks two at a time, and continue to beat until the mixture looks airy. Dissolve the coffee in ½ teaspoon hot water. Add the vanilla, coffee, and chocolate to the egg mixture, and mix until blended.

4. In a separate bowl, with an electric mixer on medium speed, whip the egg whites with the salt until they are semistiff. With the machine running, add the remaining ¾ cup sugar, about 2 tablespoons at a time, and beat until the whites are stiff and glossy.

5. With a rubber spatula, fold the hazelnuts into the egg whites, then pour the butter and chocolate mixture over the whites and fold the ingredients together. Pour the batter into the prepared pan and set it on a baking sheet to catch the drips. Bake for 1 hour. Turn the heat down to 325° and bake for 20 to 30 minutes longer, or until the cake feels firm on top and begins to shrink away from the sides of the pan. The interior will not be quite dry, so the cake remains moist and fudgy when cool. Turn off the oven and leave the cake in the oven for 30 minutes with the door ajar.

6. Cool the cake to room temperature in the pan on a wire rack. It will sink in the middle as it cools, but the sides will remain stuck at a slightly higher level. When the cake is cool, cut away the ¼ inch of cake that has stuck to the sides of the pan so that the top is flat. Open the springform lock and lift the cake up and out of the ring.

Rehrucken (Chocolate Saddle of Venison)

This bizarrely named, oddly shaped cake is nothing more than a spicy chocolate almond cake baked in a long, ribbed, semicircular mold. The shape of the cake is meant to simulate the look of a tied roasted saddle of venison, and the icing, pricked with slivered almonds, is meant to look like strips of lard running through the roast! For people who don't care to invest in this special mold, the cake can also be baked in a 9-inch springform pan. The mold can be purchased in professional baking supply houses such as Bridge Kitchenware (see Appendix C, page 389).

Makes one
12-inch-long cake

Serves 10

Level of difficulty ★

---

3 ounces bittersweet chocolate, finely chopped

2 cups (7 ounces) unblanched almonds, finely ground

⅛ teaspoon ground cinnamon

⅛ teaspoon ground cloves

Grated zest of 1 lemon

5 large eggs, separated

½ cup (3.75 ounces) granulated sugar

Pinch of salt

Maria's Best Chocolate Glaze (page 331)

⅓ cup slivered almonds

Whipped Cream (page 318)

---

1. Position a rack in the center of the oven and preheat to 350°F. Butter a nonstick, 12-inch-long tinned Rehrucken pan, taking care to be generous with the butter in order to get into all the nooks and crevices (or use a 9-inch springform pan). Dust with granulated sugar and tap out the excess.

2. Melt the chocolate in a mixing bowl or the top of a double boiler set over simmering water. Stir occasionally and, when melted, set aside to cool. In a mixing bowl, combine the almonds with the cinnamon, cloves, and lemon zest and set aside. With an electric mixer on medium speed, beat the egg yolks with about ¼ cup sugar for 2 minutes, or until the mixture looks light, then fold in the chocolate with a rubber spatula.

3. In a separate bowl, with an electric mixer on medium speed, whip the egg whites with the salt until they are semistiff. With the machine running, slowly add the remaining ¼ cup sugar, 2 tablespoons at a time, and beat until the egg whites are stiff and glossy.

4. With a rubber spatula, fold the egg yolk and chocolate mixture into the egg whites, then fold this into the almond mixture. Pour the batter into the prepared pan and bake for 40 to 45 minutes, or until a tester inserted in the center comes out dry. Cool the cake in the pan for 10 minutes, then unmold it onto a wire rack and cool to room temperature.

5. Pour ½ the chocolate glaze over the cake and chill the cake for 20 minutes, then spread the other ½ on top. Transfer the cake to a platter and stud it randomly with 3 rows of slivered almonds, pointing upward. Serve with whipped cream.

STORAGE: Keep in the refrigerator, loosely covered, for up to 5 days; bring the cake back to room temperature before serving.

together and set it aside in the refrigerator, stirring occasionally, until it is cool to the touch yet still fluid enough to spread.

3. In a double boiler or in the microwave oven, melt the white chocolate and cool it to room temperature. Whip the remaining cup of cream until stiff; working rapidly, fold it into the white chocolate along with the orange extract. Refrigerate it until you are ready to assemble the cake.

4. Set one strip of cake on a cookie sheet or on a cardboard rectangle cut slightly larger than the strip of cake. Spread the strip with ⅓ of the dark chocolate filling. Top it with a second layer of cake, set upside down, and spread that with 1 cup of the white chocolate filling, making sure it is evenly spread and level. Top with the third strip of cake and spread it with ⅓ of the dark chocolate filling. Turn the last strip of cake upside down so that the flat side is facing up, and spread it with the last of the dark chocolate filling. With an icing comb, ridge the top and refrigerate the cake for 15 minutes along with the remaining white chocolate filling.

5. With a small offset spatula, spread the remaining white chocolate filling all around the sides of the cake, then pat the sliced almonds around the sides. Refrigerate, uncovered, for 1 hour, or until the fillings are set.

STORAGE: Keep refrigerated, wrapped loosely in foil, for up to 5 days; remove the cake 30 minutes before serving.

ADVANCE PREPARATION TIPS

• Make the cake 1 day ahead of serving.
• Make the fillings and assemble the cake on the day of serving.

**The Michele: A Pecan Extravaganza

*I absolutely adore this cake because of the multitude of flavors and textures. It is impera-
tive that you make the cake a day ahead of filling it or it won't have the right texture.*

Makes one 4 ×
12-inch, 4-layer cake

Serves 14 to 16

Level of difficulty ★ ★

CAKE

2 cups (7.5 ounces) shelled
pecans or pecan pieces

1¼ cups (9.5 ounces) granulated
sugar

¼ cup unsweetened cocoa
powder

2 tablespoons cornstarch

8 large egg whites

¼ teaspoon salt

⅛ teaspoon cream of tartar

FILLING AND FINISHING

3 ounces bittersweet chocolate,
finely chopped

1 ounce white chocolate, finely
chopped

1 cup heavy cream, whipped

8 ounces milk chocolate, melted
and cooled

½ cup of any of the chocolate
buttercreams (pages 309–311)
(see Note)

6 tablespoons raspberry or red
currant jelly

TO MAKE THE CAKE

1. In a food processor, pulverize the pecans with ¼ cup of the sugar until
finely ground, but without letting them turn oily. Add the cocoa and
cornstarch, and process again until the ingredients are well blended.
Transfer to a large bowl and set aside.

2. Position a rack in the center of the oven and preheat to 325°F. Line the
bottom of a 12 × 16 × 1-inch half-sheet pan with buttered baking parchment or a nonstick baking mat.

3. With an electric mixer on medium speed, whip the egg whites with the
salt until frothy, add the cream of tartar, and whip until they are semistiff.
With the machine running, add the remaining 1 cup sugar, about 2 tablespoons at a time, and beat until the whites are stiff and glossy. With a rubber spatula, fold the whites into the ground nut mixture. With an offset
spatula, spread the batter into the prepared baking pan, making sure it is
even and level. Bake for 40 to 45 minutes, or until the cake pulls away
from the sides of the pan and the top is crisp.

4. Remove the cake from the oven and run a knife around the edges to
loosen it from the sides of the pan. Set a piece of parchment paper over
the cake and a wire rack over that and invert the cake. Remove the paper
from the bottom of the cake. Using another wire rack or a baking sheet,
turn the cake right side up. Lift off the top parchment paper and leave the
cake at room temperature overnight so it dries out and becomes crisp.

TO FILL AND FINISH

1. With a serrated knife, trim the edges if they are uneven, then cut the cake
into 4 strips, each about 4 inches wide and 12 inches long. Set one strip
on top of the other and trim them so they are perfectly even in size.

2. Separately melt the bittersweet and white chocolates, and cool them to
room temperature. Fold the whipped cream into the milk chocolate.
With an electric mixer on low speed, whip the buttercream until smooth.

3. Set one strip of cake on a cookie sheet or on a cardboard rectangle cut the
same size as the cake. Spread the strip with 2 tablespoons of the jelly and
spread that with ½ the whipped milk chocolate cream, making sure the
filling reaches all the way to the edges. Top with a second strip of cake,
spread it with jelly, and spread the chocolate buttercream on top. Top

with the third strip of cake and spread it with the remaining jam and whipped milk chocolate cream.

4. Spread the melted bittersweet chocolate over the underside or flat side of the last strip of cake. Dip a fork or a spatula in the melted white chocolate and drizzle it back and forth over the bittersweet chocolate. Set this strip over the filling glazed side up. With the point of a paring knife, score the top into 14 or 16 portions, and refrigerate, uncovered, for 30 minutes, or until the top has set.

STORAGE: Keep in the refrigerator, wrapped airtight in plastic, for up to 3 days; remove the cake 30 minutes before serving.

ADVANCE PREPARATION TIPS

- Make the cake and buttercream 1 to 2 days ahead of serving.
- Make the filling and assemble the cake 1 day ahead or on the day of serving.

NOTE: If you don't want to bother making a buttercream for the ½ cup you need, make the milk chocolate cream filling only, increasing the chocolate to 12 ounces and the heavy cream to 1½ cups, and spread all the layers with the same filling.

Mohn Torte (Poppy Seed Cake)

When I first met my husband's family in the early 1970s, my mother-in-law, Maria, insisted that one day I would overcome my aversion to ground poppy seeds. She was convinced that I really liked this ingredient but wouldn't admit it. To make her point, one Sunday afternoon, she brought a cake to our house she claimed was an almond chocolate torte because it looked like one. I took one bite and immediately recognized the characteristic taste of ground poppy seeds. I laughed and told her that no matter how hard she tried to disguise their look, she could never convince me to like poppy seeds. However, it is true that, with age, I do find this cake more appealing than I once did, and I can see how people who love ground poppy seeds would find it a definite winner.

Makes one 9-inch,
single-layer cake

Serves 8

Level of difficulty ★

---

6 ounces semisweet chocolate, finely chopped

½ cup golden raisins

3 tablespoons dark rum

1 stick (4 ounces) unsalted butter, softened

½ cup (3.75 ounces) superfine sugar (see Note)

6 large eggs, separated

1⅓ cups (8 ounces) ground poppy seeds (see Note) or 1 (12.5-ounce) can poppy-seed filling

1 teaspoon grated lemon zest

¼ teaspoon salt

Confectioners' sugar, for dusting

---

1. Position a rack in the center of the oven and preheat to 350°F. Butter a 9 × 3-inch springform pan. Melt the chocolate in a mixing bowl or in a double boiler set over simmering water. Stir occasionally and, when melted, set the chocolate aside to cool. Soak the raisins in the rum and set them aside.

2. With an electric mixer on low speed (or with a stationary mixer fitted with the paddle attachment), beat the butter for 1 minute, or until light. Slowly add ¼ cup of the sugar and continue to beat on medium speed for about 2 minutes, scraping down the beaters and sides of the bowl as needed. The mixture will look fluffy, like something between mayonnaise and whipped cream.

3. Add the egg yolks two at a time, beating for 10 seconds between additions, or until they are absorbed by the butter. Add the cooled chocolate and beat until smooth. With a rubber spatula, blend the rum and raisins with the poppy seeds and lemon zest, and fold this mixture into the butter and chocolate.

4. In a separate bowl, with an electric mixer on medium speed, whip the egg whites with the salt until they form soft peaks. With the machine running, slowly add the remaining ¼ cup sugar and beat until the egg whites are stiff and glossy. With a rubber spatula, in three additions, fold the egg whites into the ground poppy seed and chocolate mixture.

5. Pour the batter into the prepared cake pan, set the pan on a baking sheet to catch the drips, and bake for 30 minutes. Turn the oven down to 325° and bake for another 35 to 45 minutes, or until a tester inserted in the center comes out dry and the cake begins to pull away from the sides. Turn off the heat and leave the cake in the oven, with the door ajar, for 30 minutes longer.

6. Cool the cake to room temperature in its pan on a wire rack. Run a metal spatula or a table knife around the cake to loosen it from the sides of the

pan. Open the springform lock and lift the cake up and out of the form. Just before serving, through a stencil if you wish, sift the confectioners' sugar over the top.

STORAGE: Keep the cake at room temperature, wrapped airtight in plastic, for up to 2 days; refrigerate after that.

PLATED DESSERT SUGGESTION (per portion)

1 slice of cake
Raspberry Squeeze Sauce
  (page 368)

Poppy seeds
Whipped Cream (page 318) in a
pastry bag fitted with a star tip

Center a slice of cake on a 10-inch plate and spoon the sauce around the cake. Pipe a rosette of whipped cream on the cake and sprinkle some poppy seeds over the cake, whipped cream, and sauce.

NOTE: This cake must be made with ground poppy seeds, which have a different taste from whole poppyseeds. In the early 1970s, when I first started baking my mother-in-law's Austrian and Hungarian recipes, the neighborhood she lived in bustled with Hungarian shops, including ones that ground poppy seeds for their customers. All these shops are gone today, as is the availability of poppy-seed grinders—except (of course) through King Arthur's *Baker's Catalogue,* which offers its customers an old-fashioned poppy-seed grinder. Those of you who don't care to invest $35 in a tool you might use only once can prepare the cake with a canned poppy-seed filling, but reduce the amount of sugar by 2 tablespoons.

Our Family's Favorite Chocolate Almond Cake

I never tire of the perfect balance between flavor and texture in this family favorite, which I have made dozens of times. This is the first cake I learned from my mother-in-law, who learned it from her mother, who adapted it from a recipe in the 1917 edition of the Kochbuch der Deutschen Kochschule in Prag. *It is obvious from the name of this cake that several generations of our family have baked it for every imaginable occasion—birthdays, anniversaries, and for many Sunday get-together teas. It is important you weigh all ingredients.*

Makes one 9-inch,
single-layer cake

Serves 8 to 10

Level of difficulty ★

CAKE

6 ounces bittersweet chocolate, finely chopped

¼ cup double-strength prepared coffee or 2 teaspoons instant espresso coffee powder dissolved in ¼ cup hot water

6 ounces (1½ sticks) unsalted butter, softened

6 ounces (13 tablespoons) sugar

6 large eggs, separated

¼ teaspoon salt

6 ounces (scant 2 cups) almonds, finely ground

GLAZE AND FINISHING

Maria's Best Chocolate Glaze (page 331)

⅓ cup finely chopped almonds

TO MAKE THE CAKE

1. Position a rack in the center of the oven and preheat to 375°F. Lightly butter and flour a 9 × 2.5-inch springform pan and tap out the excess. Line the bottom with a parchment or greased waxed paper circle.

2. Melt the chocolate with the coffee in a mixing bowl or a double boiler set over simmering water. Stir occasionally and, when melted, set aside to cool to room temperature.

3. With an electric mixer on medium speed (or with a stationary mixer fitted with the paddle attachment), beat the butter with ¾ cup of the sugar for about 2 minutes, or until the mixture has an ivory hue and a texture like mayonnaise. Scrape down the sides of the bowl and beat for a few seconds longer, then add the egg yolks two at a time, and continue to beat until the mixture looks airy. With a rubber spatula, fold in the melted chocolate.

4. In a separate bowl, with an electric mixer on high speed, whip the egg whites with the salt until they are semistiff. With the machine running, slowly add the remaining 2 tablespoons sugar and beat until the egg whites are stiff and glossy. With a rubber spatula, fold the almonds into the egg whites, then fold this into the creamed butter and chocolate mixture.

5. Pour the batter into the prepared cake pan and set the cake in the oven. Immediately turn the oven down to 350° and bake for 15 minutes. Turn the oven down to 325° and bake 45 minutes longer, then turn the oven down to 300° and bake 15 to 20 minutes longer, or until a tester inserted in the center comes out dry and the cake begins to pull away from the sides of the pan. Turn off the heat and leave the cake in the oven, with the door ajar, for 30 minutes longer.

6. Gently push the cracked top of the cake back down and cool the cake to room temperature in its pan on a wire rack. After the cake has cooled, if pieces of the cracked top lift off easily, remove them. Slide a metal spatula or a table knife around the cake to loosen it from the sides of the pan. Open the springform lock and lift the cake up and out of the ring.

TO GLAZE AND FINISH

Invert the cake onto a cardboard round cut the same diameter as the cake. Remove the metal base and carefully peel off the paper circle. With a small offset spatula or a table knife, spread a thin coating of glaze around the sides of the cake. Pour the rest of the glaze over the top and, with a metal spatula, spread it from the center toward the edges of the cake so that more glaze drips down the sides. Spread the glaze that dripped from the edges around the sides of the cake. Pat the chopped almonds around the bottom edge of the cake. Refrigerate, uncovered, until serving time, but remove the cake from the refrigerator about 30 minutes before serving.

STORAGE: Keep the cake in the refrigerator, covered, for up to 5 days; bring it back to room temperature before serving.

Souffléed Chocolate Cake

This cake recipe—adapted from Cooking the Nouvelle Cuisine in America *(New York: Workman Publishing, 1979)—was given to us by Bernard Loiseau, a Michelin three-star chef in France. Without a doubt, this flourless cake is my favorite of all flourless chocolate cakes because it is perfectly balanced in terms of both texture and taste.*

Makes one 9-inch, single-layer cake

Serves 8 to 10

Level of difficulty ★

---

9 ounces bittersweet chocolate, finely chopped

---

1 stick plus 1 tablespoon (4.5 ounces) unsalted butter, cut into 1-inch chunks

---

6 large eggs, separated

¼ teaspoon salt

⅛ teaspoon cream of tartar

½ cup (3.75 ounces) granulated sugar

¼ cup (1 ounce) cornstarch, sifted

Confectioners' sugar

---

1. Melt the chocolate and butter in a mixing bowl or the top of a double boiler set over barely simmering water. Stir occasionally and, when just melted, transfer the mixture to a clean bowl, whisk to combine, and set it aside to cool to room temperature.
2. Position a rack in the center of the oven and preheat to 350°F. Lightly butter a 9 × 2.5-inch springform pan.
3. With an electric mixer on medium speed, whip the egg whites with the salt until frothy. Add the cream of tartar and whip until they are semistiff. With the machine running, slowly add the granulated sugar, 2 table-spoons at a time, and beat until the egg whites are stiff and glossy. In an-other mixing bowl, break up the egg yolks with a fork, then pour them over the egg whites and fold the two together with a rubber spatula.
4. Sift the cornstarch over the mixture and fold it into the eggs, then pour this mixture over the chocolate and fold until blended. Pour the batter into the prepared pan, set the pan on a baking sheet to catch the drips, and bake for 35 to 40 minutes, or until the center jiggles slightly when you shake the pan.
5. Remove the cake from the oven and cool it to room temperature in its pan on a wire rack. Run a knife around the cake to loosen it from the sides of the pan, open the lock, and lift the cake up and out of the form, but leave the cake on the metal base.
6. Just before serving, dust the cake with confectioners' sugar passed through a sieve, or through a stencil if you wish, and serve the cake at room temperature.

STORAGE: Keep in the refrigerator, wrapped airtight in plastic, for up to 4 days; remove the cake 1 hour before serving.

PLATED DESSERT SUGGESTION (per portion)

1 slice of cake, warmed slightly
2 to 3 tablespoons Flavored
   Custard Sauce, ginger, saffron,
   szechuan pepper, or tea
   variations (pages 359–360)

Garnish to match the sauce, such
   as minced candied ginger,
   fresh mint, or peppercorns

Set the slice of cake in the middle of a 10-inch plate. Spoon the custard sauce around the cake. If it makes sense, sprinkle a garnish over the sauce.

Walnut Chocolate Torte

Walnut and almond tortes are the two types of flourless cakes ubiquitous in the Austro-Hungarian pastry repertoire. I am especially fond of this recipe, which I received from my mother-in-law, because it is deliciously light and quick to prepare. It is the perfect cake for an intimate dinner party.

Makes one 8-inch,
2-layer cake

Serves 8

Level of difficulty ★

2¼ cups (8 ounces) walnuts

¾ cup (5.5 ounces) superfine sugar

1 teaspoon instant espresso coffee powder

6 large eggs, separated

2 ounces semisweet or bittersweet chocolate, melted and cooled

¼ teaspoon salt

Beginner's Chocolate Buttercream (page 309)

9 walnut halves, plain or painted with gold dust (page 337)

---

1. Position a rack in the center of the oven and preheat to 350°F. Lightly butter and flour two 8 × 1.5-inch round cake pans and line the bottoms with buttered parchment or greased waxed paper circles. Tap out the excess flour.

2. In a food processor, pulverize the walnuts with ¼ cup of the sugar until they are finely ground. Dissolve the coffee in 1 teaspoon very hot water. With a small whisk, blend the egg yolks with the coffee and the chocolate until smooth.

3. With an electric mixer on medium speed, whip the egg whites with the salt until they are semistiff. With the machine running, slowly add the remaining ½ cup sugar, about 2 tablespoons at a time, and whip until the egg whites are stiff and glossy.

4. With a rubber spatula, fold ¼ of the whipped whites into the yolk and chocolate mixture to lighten it, then fold this back into the remaining whites as you fold in the walnuts at the same time.

5. Divide the batter evenly between the prepared cake pans and bake for 25 to 30 minutes. Cool the cakes to room temperature in their pans on a wire rack. Slide a metal spatula or a table knife around each cake to loosen it from the sides of the pan.

6. Invert one cake onto a cardboard round cut the same dimension as the cake and peel off the paper. Spread it with ½ cup of the buttercream. Invert the second cake layer over the buttercream, peel off the paper, and spread the remaining buttercream around the sides of the cake first, then over the top. Set 8 walnut halves around the edge of the cake. Break the last walnut into 3 pieces and center them on the cake.

STORAGE: Keep in the refrigerator, loosely covered, for up to 5 days; bring the cake back to room temperature before serving.

White Chocolate Flourless Cake with Lemon

This cake is a study in contrasting tastes and textures. The lemon provides a counterbalance to some of the sweetness of the white chocolate, and the crunchy, tiny poppy seeds are a lovely counterpoint to the smoothness of the cake itself. The cake is extremely easy to put together but takes a while to bake.

Makes one 9-inch, single-layer cake

Serves 8 to 10

Level of difficulty ★

---

12 ounces white chocolate, finely chopped

1 stick (4 ounces) unsalted butter, cut into 1-inch chunks, softened

5 large egg yolks

2 tablespoons freshly grated lemon zest (from 4 lemons)

¼ cup poppy seeds

4 large egg whites

¼ teaspoon salt

⅓ cup (2.5 ounces) granulated sugar

2 tablespoons cornstarch

Whipped Cream (page 318), optional

Fresh sliced strawberries, optional

---

1. Melt the chocolate in a mixing bowl or the top of a double boiler set over simmering water. Stir occasionally and, when barely melted, transfer it to a large clean mixing bowl and whisk in the butter. The mixture will appear to tighten up, but if you quickly whisk in the egg yolks, lemon zest, and poppy seeds, the batter will smooth out.

2. Position a rack in the center of the oven and preheat to 350°F. Lightly butter a 9 × 2.5-inch springform pan.

3. With an electric mixer on medium speed, whip the egg whites with the salt until they are semistiff. With the machine running, add the sugar, about 2 tablespoons at a time, and beat until the whites are stiff and glossy.

4. Fold ⅓ of the egg whites into the white chocolate batter, then fold in the rest of the whites as you sift and fold in the cornstarch at the same time.

5. Pour the batter into the prepared pan, set it on a baking sheet to catch the drips, and bake for 30 minutes. Cover the top of the pan with a buttered piece of foil to prevent the top from browning too much, and bake 30 minutes more. Lower the heat to 300° and bake for 15 minutes more.

6. Remove the cake from the oven and cool it to room temperature in the pan (the cake will sink as it cools). Open the springform lock and lift the cake out of the form. Refrigerate for several hours before eating. Serve with whipped cream and strawberries, if you wish.

STORAGE: Keep in the refrigerator, wrapped airtight in plastic, for up to 5 days.

Dione Lucas's Roulade Leontine

This absolutely scrumptious cake is yet another recipe adapted from Dione Lucas's Cordon Bleu Cookbook (New York: Little Brown & Company, 1947). Eating a slice of this cake is like eating chocolate air. It's so delicate that you must not fill it with anything more substantial than cocoa-flavored whipped cream. It is not complicated to prepare but fragile to handle and can look a little messy, but that won't interfere with its divine taste.

Makes one
15-inch-long roll

Serves 8

Level of difficulty ★ ★

CAKE

6 ounces semisweet or bittersweet chocolate, finely chopped

5 large eggs, separated

¼ teaspoon salt

⅛ teaspoon cream of tartar

¾ cup (5.5 ounces) superfine sugar

FILLING AND FINISHING

½ cup Chocolate Shavings (page 380), made with bittersweet chocolate

½ recipe Whipped Cream, cocoa variation (page 318)

Confectioners' sugar, for dusting, optional

TO MAKE THE CAKE

1. Position a rack in the center of the oven and preheat to 350°F. Line a 10 × 15 × 1-inch jelly roll pan with buttered parchment or greased waxed paper. Combine the chocolate and 3 tablespoons water in a small saucepan and bring to a simmer, stirring. Remove from the heat, stir until smooth, and transfer to a clean bowl to cool to room temperature.

2. With an electric mixer on low speed, beat the egg whites until frothy. Add the salt and cream of tartar and continue to beat on medium speed until the egg whites are semistiff. With the machine running, slowly add the sugar, about 2 tablespoons at a time, and beat until the egg whites are stiff and glossy. Break up the egg yolks with a fork, pour them over the whites, and fold the two together. When almost homogenized, fold the eggs into the chocolate in two batches.

3. With an offset spatula, spread the batter evenly in the pan, making sure that you reach into the corners and that the batter is level. Bake for 10 minutes. Lower the temperature to 325° and bake for 3 to 5 minutes longer, or until the cake is golden yet still soft on top.

4. Remove the pan from the oven and set it on a wire rack. Dampen a cotton cloth the size of the pan in cold water, wring it out, and set it flush on the cake. Cool the cake for 15 minutes, then refrigerate, with the towel, for 45 minutes.

TO FILL AND FINISH

1. On your counter, set out a piece of parchment that is slightly larger than the dimension of the pan. Remove the cake from the refrigerator and slide a knife around it to loosen the cake from the sides of the pan. Remove the towel (the cake will stick to the towel, but don't worry).

2. Scatter ½ the chocolate shavings over the cake. Set the piece of parchment paper over the cake and place another baking pan over the parchment to help you invert the cake. Remove the top pan and very gently peel off the paper. The cake is incredibly delicate, so try to handle it as little as possible.

continued on next page

3. Spread the entire surface of the cake with the whipped cream. Set out a serving platter long enough to hold the cake comfortably. Using the parchment to help you, roll up the cake from a long end and flip it onto the platter, making sure it lands seam side down.

4. Sift confectioners' sugar and the remaining chocolate shavings over the top. Refrigerate, uncovered, for 1 hour before serving.

STORAGE: Keep in the refrigerator, loosely covered, for up to 2 days.

Nut Meringue Cake

This nut meringue cake can be used as one element in a complicated, multidimensional cake (such as a Dacquoise, page 260), or it can be turned into a proper cake by filling and frosting it as you would any other layer cake. To fill and frost, you would need about 2½ to 3 cups of buttercream or another filling of your choice.

Makes one 8-inch, 3-layer cake or

one 9-inch, 2-layer cake or

one 4 × 12 inch, 4-layer cake

Level of difficulty ★★

1⅓ cups (5 ounces) whole almonds, skinned toasted hazelnuts, or a combination of the two

1 cup plus 6 tablespoons (10.5 ounces) superfine sugar

2 tablespoons cornstarch, optional

7 large egg whites

¼ teaspoon salt

⅛ teaspoon cream of tartar

---

1. Cut 2 pieces of parchment paper to fit two 12 × 16 × 1-inch half-sheet pans. On one piece of paper, trace in pencil one 8-inch circle, and on the other paper, trace two 8-inch circles. Mark the center of each circle in pencil, then turn the papers upside down so the pencil marks won't come off on your cakes. (Or if you are going to make this as a sheet cake, line a single pan with buttered parchment or with a nonstick baking mat.)

2. Position two racks as close to the center of the oven as possible and preheat to 325°F. Set out an 18-inch pastry bag fitted with a ½-inch-round plain pastry tip.

3. In the bowl of a food processor, process the nuts in a pulsing motion until coarsely chopped. Add 1 cup of the sugar and pulse until ground into a powdery flour. Transfer the ground nuts to a mixing bowl and fold in the cornstarch, if using, with a whisk; set aside for later.

4. With an electric mixer on low speed, beat the egg whites until frothy; add the salt and cream of tartar and beat on medium speed until the whites are semistiff. With the machine running on high speed, slowly add the remaining 6 tablespoons sugar and beat until the whites are stiff and glossy. In three additions, fold the ground nuts into the egg whites and transfer ⅓ of the mixture to the pastry bag.

5. To form the batter into rounds, pipe the mixture within the outline of one circle, working in a spiral pattern, beginning from the center dot you traced on the paper and working outward. Repeat with about ⅓ of the batter for each of the remaining disks. With a small offset spatula, smooth the disks if you wish to make them level.

6. If you are baking this as a sheet cake, simply spread the batter in the prepared sheet pan, making sure it is level.

7. Bake for 30 minutes, then reduce the temperature to 250° and bake for 1 hour longer to dry out the cake. (If using more than one oven rack, switch the baking sheets from top to bottom every 15 minutes so they get even distribution of heat.)

8. Remove the pans from the oven and cool them on a wire rack. When thoroughly cooled, remove the meringues from the paper.

STORAGE: Keep the unfilled disks in an airtight cookie tin with pieces of waxed paper between them. Store in a cool dry place for up to 2 weeks.

Dacquoise

Few people can agree on exactly what a dacquoise is other than a hazelnut-flavored meringue-based cake. I decided that my dacquoise would consist of pure hazelnut meringue slathered with a gianduja buttercream and garnished with crunchy toasted hazelnuts.

Makes one 8-inch,
3-layer cake

Serves 8

Level of difficulty ★★

Three 8-inch Nut Meringue Cake rounds, made with skinned toasted hazelnuts (see page 259)

2½ cups Classic French or Dione Lucas's Chocolate Buttercream, gianduja variations (page 302 or 310)

½ cup coarsely chopped, toasted skinned hazelnuts

Cocoa powder, for dusting

1. With a dab of buttercream, anchor one cake disk to a cardboard round cut a bit wider than the diameter of the cake.
2. With an offset spatula, spread ¾ to 1 cup of the buttercream on top of the layer and invert the second cake round on top. Spread the second layer with more buttercream and invert the last cake layer over the buttercream. Spread the remaining buttercream around the sides of the cake, leaving the top plain, and pat the chopped hazelnuts around the sides.
3. Lightly dust the top with cocoa powder, shaken through a fine-mesh strainer or a stencil. Refrigerate, uncovered, for 1 hour to firm up the buttercream.

STORAGE: Keep in the refrigerator, wrapped airtight in plastic, for up to 4 days; remove the cake 15 minutes before serving.

Kata Torte

This family treasure, yet another from my mother-in-law's precious repertoire, was named after her sister, Kata, because she made it often. The cake is similar in texture to a nut meringue cake but has a lot more chew.

Makes one 4 × 12-inch, 4-layer cake

Serves 12

Level of difficulty ★

Generous 2 cups (8 ounces) toasted skinned hazelnuts

¾ cup (5.5 ounces) superfine sugar

8 large egg whites

Pinch of salt

3 cups buttercream such as Beginner's Chocolate Buttercream (page 309)

1. Position a rack in the center of the oven and preheat to 325°F. Line the bottom of a 12 × 16 × 1-inch half-sheet pan with buttered parchment paper or a nonstick baking mat. In a food processor, pulverize the nuts with ¼ cup of the sugar until they are finely ground.

2. With an electric mixer on medium speed, whip the egg whites with the salt until they are semistiff. Increase the speed to high and, with the machine running, slowly add the remaining ½ cup sugar, about 2 tablespoons at a time, and beat until the egg whites are stiff and glossy. With a rubber spatula, fold the ground hazelnuts into the egg whites.

3. With an offset spatula, spread the batter into the prepared pan, making sure it is level and evenly distributed, especially in the corners. Bake for 25 to 30 minutes, or until the top feels springy and looks slightly golden. Turn off the heat and leave the cake in the oven, with the door ajar, for 30 minutes.

4. Cool the cake in the pan on a rack for 10 minutes. Run a metal spatula or a table knife around the cake to loosen it from the sides of the pan. Set another parchment paper over the cake, place a sheet pan or wire rack over that, and invert the cake. Remove the pan and carefully peel off the paper.

5. Cut the cake into four 4 × 12-inch strips. Set one layer on a baking sheet or a piece of cardboard cut to fit the dimension of the cake, and spread it with about 1 cup of the buttercream. Repeat with the second and third layers, but leave the top and sides unfrosted.

STORAGE: Keep in the refrigerator, wrapped airtight in plastic, for up to 5 days; remove the cake 20 minutes before serving.

SPECIAL, INDIVIDUAL,
AND REFRIGERATED CAKES

*T*HIS CHAPTER INCLUDES fancy, special-occasion cakes, individually portioned cakes, icebox cakes, and cakes that don't fit into any other category.

Some of the fancy cakes, like Michele's Marjolaine, are elaborate and complicated, whereas others, like the Chocolate Linzer Torte, are a snap to prepare. Individually portioned cakes include cupcakes, which are miniature versions of chocolate layer or pound cakes, as well as small cakes served warm or hot, like Mohr im Hemd and Chocolate Volcanoes. And finally, at the end of this chapter are refrigerator cakes, also known as icebox cakes, confected out of pieces of already-baked chocolate cake assembled with a mousselike filling.

**The Alessia: A Marzipan-Lover's Dream Cake

This cake was named after my daughter Alessia because she adores marzipan. The cake itself is made of ground almonds, butter, and chocolate, and the outside is enveloped in a thin layer of marzipan, which lies underneath a double layer of chocolate glaze.

Makes one 9-inch, single-layer cake

Serves 8 to 10

Level of difficulty ★★

½ cup confectioners' sugar, sifted, plus additional for dusting

1 (8-ounce) can almond paste

Green food coloring, optional

Our Family's Favorite Chocolate Almond Cake, baked and cooled (page 252)

Jurgen's Chocolate Glaze (page 330)

½ cup blanched or unskinned almonds, finely chopped

1. On a clean counter, with your hands, knead ¼ cup of the confectioners' sugar into the almond paste until blended. If the marzipan remains sticky, work in enough additional sugar so it is no longer tacky. To color the marzipan, dip a toothpick in green coloring and wipe it on the marzipan. Knead the marzipan on the counter until the color is evenly distributed.

2. Invert the cake on a cardboard round cut the same dimension as the cake. Dust the counter and a rolling pin with confectioners' sugar. Roll out the marzipan until it is ⅛ inch thick and about 12 inches around. Drape the marzipan over a rolling pin and flip it over the cake. With your hands, press the marzipan over the top and against the sides of the cake, making sure the marzipan is flush against the cake and that there are no air bubbles. With a sharp knife, trim off the excess marzipan from the bottom. Gather the scraps into a ball, wrap it in plastic wrap, and reserve to make decorations.

3. Put the cake on a wire rack set over waxed paper to catch the drips. Pour about ¾ of the glaze over the top of the cake. Carefully tilt the rack from side to side so that some of the glaze runs down the sides of the cake. With a small offset spatula, spread the glaze evenly around the sides of the cake without touching the top. Refrigerate the cake, uncovered, for 20 minutes to firm up the glaze. Repeat the procedure with a second coating of glaze. Press the chopped almonds around the side of the cake and set the cake aside while you make the marzipan decorations.

4. Between two pieces of plastic wrap, roll out the remaining piece of marzipan to about ⅛ inch thick. With a leaf cutter, or freehand with a knife, cut 14 leaves out of the marzipan. Each leaf should be about 1½ inches long and about 1 inch wide. Place the leaves around the top outside edge of the cake, setting them ¾ inch apart with the wide side of the leaf poised on the edge of the cake and the point hanging over the side.

STORAGE: Keep in the refrigerator, under a cake dome or an inverted bowl, for up to 2 days, but serve at room temperature.

Chestnut Chocolate Meringue Cake

This is a voluptuous confection of crisp meringue layers and chestnut chocolate butter-cream. The buttercream is not terribly sweet, so it provides a good contrast to the sugary meringues. You can make the various parts of the cake ahead of time but should not as-semble it more than 4 hours before serving, or the meringues will become soggy.

Makes one 8-inch,
3-layer cake

Serves 8

Level of difficulty ★ ★ ★

MERINGUE DISKS

5 large egg whites

¼ teaspoon salt

⅛ teaspoon cream of tartar

1 cup (7.5 ounces) granulated sugar

FILLING AND FINISHING

1 (10-ounce) can unsweetened chestnuts packed in water, drained and patted dry

2 tablespoons dark rum

¾ cup (5.5 ounces) granulated sugar

5 large egg yolks

2 sticks (8 ounces) unsalted butter, cut into 1-inch chunks

3 ounces bittersweet chocolate, melted

¾ cup Bittersweet Chocolate Shavings (page 380)

Cocoa powder, for dusting

Deadly Delicious Chocolate Sauce, optional (page 362)

TO MAKE THE MERINGUE DISKS

1. Line two baking sheets, one of which should be 12 × 16 × 1-inch, with baking parchment. On the larger paper, draw in pencil two 8-inch circles, and on the other, draw one 8-inch circle. Turn the paper over so the pencil marks won't come off on the meringues. Set out a 16-inch pastry bag fitted with a ¾-inch-wide plain tip. Preheat the oven to 200°F.

2. With an electric mixer on low speed, beat the egg whites with the salt until frothy, add the cream of tartar, increase the speed to high, and whip until the whites are semistiff. Slowly add the sugar, about 2 tablespoons at a time, and whip until the egg whites are stiff and glossy. Transfer the whites to the prepared pastry bag and pipe out spirals of meringue, slightly within the outline of the circles, filling the entire area. Bake for 3 hours, or until the meringues have dried out. Cool the meringues in the pans on a wire rack. Peel them off the paper when they are cold.

TO MAKE THE FILLING

1. In a food processor, purée the chestnuts with the rum until smooth, and set aside.

2. In a 1-quart saucepan, combine the sugar with ⅓ cup water and bring to a simmer, stirring. Wash down the insides of the pan with a pastry brush dipped in cold water. Boil the sugar syrup without stirring until it reaches the soft ball stage, or 236° to 238°F on a candy thermometer.

3. When the syrup reaches 230°, start to beat the egg yolks with an electric mixer (preferably a stationary machine) on medium speed until they are light and lemon colored. Leave the machine running on the lowest speed. When the syrup is at the right temperature, increase the speed to medium and pour the syrup over the egg yolks, along one interior point of the mixing bowl. Keep your eye on this point as you pour so the sugar syrup gets absorbed by the yolks. Continue to beat until the outside of the mixing bowl feels warm to the touch. Beat in the butter slowly, adding more butter to the eggs only after the first batch has been absorbed. With a wooden spoon or a rubber spatula, fold in the melted chocolate, then mix in the chestnut purée with a whisk. (If the buttercream is too soft to spread, refrigerate it until firm enough.)

TO ASSEMBLE THE CAKE

1. Set one of the meringue disks on an 8-inch cardboard round. Set aside ¾ cup of the buttercream for the outside of the cake, then spread ½ of what remains over the meringue. Cover the filling with a second meringue disk, then spread that with filling and top with the last meringue. Line up the meringues so the sides are straight. Spread a very thin coating of buttercream around the sides of the cake and chill the cake for 30 minutes. Spread the remaining buttercream around the sides and pat the chocolate shavings over the buttercream. Refrigerate the cake, uncovered, until serving time.

2. Just before serving, lightly dust the top with cocoa powder and, if you wish, serve the chocolate sauce on the side.

STORAGE: Keep in the refrigerator, loosely covered, for no longer than 4 hours.

ADVANCE PREPARATION TIPS

- Make the meringues 2 days ahead of serving.
- Make the filling, chocolate shavings, and sauce 1 day before serving.
- Assemble and refrigerate no more than 4 hours before serving.

Chocolate Mincemeat Torte

This cake, redolent with the flavor of spices and orange, is for lovers of British-style puddings and Christmas cakes. The recipe was passed on to me by Gary Goldberg, one of the founders and the director of the prestigious Culinary Center of New York cooking school. This lovely original cake was developed by the other founder of the school, Martin Johner, who was a well-known pastry chef in the 1970s. I have changed the recipe only in the way it is written so it conforms to the editorial style of this book.

Makes one 9-inch, single-layer cake

Serves 8 to 10

Level of difficulty ★

CAKE

4 ounces semisweet chocolate, finely chopped

4 ounces unsweetened chocolate, finely chopped

1 cup mincemeat (see Note)

6 tablespoons cognac

1 stick (4 ounces) unsalted butter, softened

⅓ cup granulated sugar

3 large eggs, separated

7 ounces almond paste, cut into small bits

⅓ cup bleached all-purpose flour

GLAZING AND FINISHING

3 ounces bittersweet chocolate, coarsely chopped

1 tablespoon dark corn syrup

½ stick (2 ounces) unsalted butter, cut into ¼-inch pieces, at room temperature

TO MAKE THE CAKE

1. Position a rack in the center of the oven and preheat to 350°F. Lightly butter a 9 × 2.5-inch springform pan and line the bottom with a buttered parchment or greased waxed paper circle.

2. Melt the semisweet and unsweetened chocolates in a mixing bowl or the top of a double boiler set over simmering water. Stir occasionally, and when the chocolates are barely melted, transfer them to a clean mixing bowl and set aside to cool to room temperature. In a mixing bowl, combine the mincemeat with the cognac.

3. In a food processor fitted with the steel blade, cream the butter and sugar until light. Add the egg yolks, one at a time, and process after each addition. Add the almond paste and process until smooth, then add the cooled chocolate and process until well mixed. Transfer the batter back to a mixing bowl and fold in the flour and mincemeat.

4. Beat the egg whites until stiff and glossy without being dry, and fold them into the batter. Spoon the batter into the prepared pan and tap the pan on the counter once to settle the batter.

5. Bake the cake for 30 to 35 minutes, or until it begins to pull away from the sides of the pan. (The center will remain fairly soft.) Remove the cake from the oven and let it cool to room temperature in the pan on a wire rack. Remove the sides of the springform pan, wrap the cake, and refrigerate it for at least 2 hours, or until well chilled.

TO GLAZE AND FINISH

1. In a small heavy saucepan, combine the chocolate, corn syrup, and ¼ cup water and set over moderate heat, stirring constantly until the chocolate is melted and the mixture is smooth. Remove the pan from the heat and, with a rubber spatula, stir in the butter a little bit at a time. Refrigerate the glaze for 15 to 25 minutes, or until it just begins to thicken but is still pourable. Stir gently with a rubber spatula to avoid incorporating air bubbles.

2. Invert the cake onto a cardboard round cut the same dimension or slightly smaller than the cake. Remove the metal base and peel off the pa-

per. Set the cake on a wire rack set over waxed paper to catch the drips. Slowly pour all the glaze over the top of the cake. Carefully tilt the cake and the rack from side to side so that some of the glaze runs down the sides of the cake. If the glaze is too thick, smooth it by passing a long, flat metal spatula across the top of the cake in one smooth motion. With a small offset spatula, smooth the sides, touching the top as little as possible. Transfer the cake to a plate and refrigerate it for 30 minutes, or just long enough to set the glaze.

STORAGE: Keep in the refrigerator, wrapped airtight in plastic, for up to 5 days; serve the cake at room temperature.

NOTE: Mincemeat is a pie filling consisting of beef suet, some lean minced beef, spiced preserved apples, pears, and other fruit as well as candied citrus. The mix is then heavily flavored with an array of spices. Today, few people make their own mincemeat because it is sold in jars in supermarkets and gourmet stores. The commercial variety, however, no longer includes suet or beef and is available around Thanksgiving and Christmas, the traditional time for serving mincemeat pies.

Coach House Chocolate Cake

This cake was a specialty of the Coach House, a New York City Greenwich Village restaurant and favorite hangout of James Beard in the 1970s. Some twenty years ago, a friend gave me the recipe, which I believe appeared in the New York Times, *and to which I have made some minor adjustments. I love this cake because the dough has the same texture as a cookie.*

Makes one 9-inch, 3-layer cake

Serves 12 to 14

Level of difficulty ★★

CAKE DISKS

4 cups (19 ounces) bleached all-purpose flour

½ teaspoon salt

3 sticks (12 ounces) unsalted butter, cut into 1-inch chunks, very cold

⅓ cup warm water

8 ounces bittersweet or semisweet chocolate, melted and cooled

FILLING AND FINISHING

2 cups chilled heavy cream, preferably not ultrapasteurized

¼ cup confectioners' sugar, sifted

1 pound bittersweet or semisweet chocolate, melted and cooled

A whole block (about 8 ounces) of white chocolate

TO MAKE THE CAKE DISKS

1. In the bowl of a food processor or in a stationary mixer fitted with the paddle attachment, combine the flour and salt. Add the butter and process until the butter is cut into the flour into oatmeal-size pieces. Whisk the warm water into the chocolate and add this to the flour and butter; beat until smooth. Divide the dough into 3 equal pieces (each about 13 ounces), wrap them in plastic, and refrigerate for 30 minutes.

2. Remove one of the pieces of dough from the refrigerator. Between two pieces of plastic wrap, roll it into a rectangle approximately 12 × 8 inches. It is a little bit tricky to roll out the dough because it tends to break; coax it gently with your fingertips and rolling pin until you get approximately the right size. Remove the top plastic and, with the help of the bottom plastic, lift and fold the rectangle in three, as if you were folding a business letter. (This is a "turn.") Wrap up this new rectangle, which is about 4 × 8 inches and refrigerate it for 30 minutes. Repeat this procedure with the other two pieces of dough, then repeat the process twice more for each piece of dough, resting the dough for 30 minutes between turns. (When you roll out the dough between turns, make sure you set the dough with opened folds facing right and closed fold facing left, like a book.) When you have finished the last turn, fold each piece of dough in half again so you have a little square of dough that is easier to roll out into a round. Chill the dough overnight.

3. Position a rack in the center of the oven (or if you are using two racks, position them in the upper and lower thirds of the oven) and preheat to 325°F. Lightly butter 3 cookie sheets (they must be without sides or you won't be able to slide the dough off the sheet and the dough will break), and line the sheets with parchment paper.

4. Between two pieces of plastic wrap, roll one of the pieces of dough into a circle about 9 inches in diameter. Using a 9-inch cake pan or cardboard round as a template, trim the round so that it is 9 inches even. Lift the round of dough with the plastic, and invert it onto one of the prepared cookie sheets. Repeat with the other two pieces of dough. Prick each

round with a fork. If you don't have room to bake all three rounds at once, set aside one of the rounds in the refrigerator while you bake the other two.

5. Bake the dough for 30 minutes, or until crisp. Cool the disks for 10 minutes on the pans on a wire rack, then slide the paper off the cookie sheet and cool the cake disks to room temperature.

TO MAKE THE FILLING

In a chilled bowl, whip the cream on low, then on medium speed, until it begins to hold soft peaks and is ¾ whipped. Sift the confectioners' sugar over the cream and beat for a few seconds longer, or until it holds stiff peaks. Fold the whipped cream into the melted chocolate, working rapidly so the chocolate does not seize up.

TO ASSEMBLE

1. Set a cardboard round over one of the disks and invert it. Remove and set aside 1½ cups of chocolate whipped cream filling. Spread ½ the remaining filling over the cake disk, making sure the filling is level and goes slightly beyond the edges. Set another cake disk over the filling and spread the remaining filling on top. Slide the last cake disk over the filling and spread it with about 1 cup of the reserved filling. Spread the remaining filling around the sides of the cake.

2. Hold the block of chocolate in one hand. Over the top of the cake, using a swivel-type vegetable peeler, peel the length of one side of the block of chocolate so that the it falls into "curls" on top of the cake. Keep on "peeling" the chocolate, turning the block so you work each side. Continue until the top of the cake is covered in chocolate shavings or curls.

STORAGE: Keep in the refrigerator, loosely covered with foil, for up to 3 days.

ADVANCE PREPARATION TIPS

• Make the cake dough 2 days ahead of serving.
• Roll out and bake the cake disks 1 day ahead of serving.
• Make the filling, assemble, and garnish the cake on the day of serving.

**The Gianduja

Gianduja is a term that describes a creamy concoction of praline paste and melted chocolate, used in candies mostly. I am so enamored of this taste that I have used it in both the cake and the buttercream filling.

Makes one 9-inch, 4-layer cake

Serves 14 to 16

Level of difficulty ★★

CAKE

1 stick (4 ounces) unsalted butter, softened

10 tablespoons (6 ounces) praline paste (see page 27)

6 ounces semisweet chocolate, melted and cooled

7 large eggs, separated

¼ teaspoon salt

⅓ cup (2.5 ounces) superfine sugar

1 cup (4.5 ounces) cake flour, sifted

FILLING, GLAZING, AND FINISHING

¼ cup sugar

2 tablespoons cognac or brandy

2 cups Classic French or Dione Lucas's Chocolate Buttercream, gianduja variations (page 302 or 310)

Jurgen's Chocolate Glaze (page 330)

¼ cup chopped roasted and skinned hazelnuts

16 whole roasted and skinned hazelnuts

TO MAKE THE CAKE

1. Position a rack in the center of the oven and preheat to 350°F.
2. Lightly butter two 9 × 1.5-inch round cake pans and line the bottoms with waxed paper or parchment circles; butter the paper circles as well.
3. In a stationary mixer fitted with the paddle attachment, beat the butter with the praline paste and chocolate until smooth.
4. Add the egg yolks two at a time, beating for 10 seconds between additions, or until the yolks are absorbed.
5. In a separate clean bowl, beat the egg whites with the salt until they form soft peaks. Slowly add the sugar, about 2 tablespoons at a time, and beat on medium speed until the whites are stiff and glossy. With a rubber spatula, fold the egg whites into the praline paste mixture as you sift and fold in the flour at the same time. Evenly divide the batter between the prepared pans. Bake for 25 to 30 minutes, or until a cake tester inserted in the center comes out dry and the cake begins to pull away from the sides of the pan.
6. Cool the cakes to room temperature in their pans on a wire rack. Unmold the cakes and remove the paper circles.

TO FILL, GLAZE, AND FINISH

1. In a small saucepan, bring the sugar and ¼ cup water to a boil, remove it from the heat, and add the cognac.
2. With a serrated knife, cut off the tops of each of the cakes to level them, then split each cake in two. Invert one of the layers onto a cardboard round cut the same size or slightly smaller than the diameter of the cake.
3. Brush the cake layer with ¼ of the cognac syrup (be generous so the cake is nice and moist), and spread the layer with ⅓ of the buttercream. Top with the second cake layer, brush it with ¼ of the cognac syrup, and spread it with ⅓ of the buttercream, then repeat this procedure with the third cake layer. Set the last layer, upside down, on top and brush it with the last of the cognac syrup.
4. Spread the sides of the cake with a thin "crumb coating" of buttercream, leaving the top plain. Refrigerate the cake, uncovered, while you make the glaze.

5. Set the cake on a wire rack or icing grill set over waxed paper to catch the drips. Spread about ½ the glaze over the top and sides of the cake. Refrigerate the cake for about 15 minutes to firm up the glaze. Spread the top only with the last of the glaze and, with a 12-inch offset spatula, spread it across the cake in one or two strokes so that it drips down the sides. Spread the glaze that dripped around the sides of the cake and let it firm up at room temperature for about 20 minutes.

6. Pat a ¼-inch-thick layer of chopped hazelnuts around the bottom edge of the cake. Set the whole hazelnuts around the top edge, and refrigerate the cake until serving time.

STORAGE: Keep in the refrigerator, loosely covered under a cake dome or an inverted bowl, for up to 4 days; remove the cake 45 minutes before serving.

**Michele's Marjolaine Cake

This is a cake adapted from David's Cake, a recipe that appeared in Cooking the Nouvelle Cuisine in America *(New York: Workman Publishing, 1979). David's Cake, in turn, was inspired by the Marjolaine, a famous creation of Fernand Point, the legendary chef proprietor of La Pyramide, an influential three-star restaurant in France during the late 1950s and early 1960s. In this version I have substituted a white chocolate whipped cream filling for the original vanilla buttercream. You must make this cake at least 24 hours in advance of serving so all the flavors and textures come together. This is another ideal party cake because it feeds so many people and can be made ahead of time.*

Makes one 4 ×
12-inch, 4-layer cake

Serves 20

Level of difficulty ★ ★ ★

CAKE

7 ounces blanched almonds,
toasted

5 ounces skinned hazelnuts,
toasted

1¼ cups (9.5 ounces) granulated
sugar

2 tablespoons all-purpose flour

8 large egg whites

¼ teaspoon salt

⅛ teaspoon cream of tartar

FILLINGS AND FINISHING

1 pound bittersweet or
semisweet chocolate, finely
chopped

3 cups heavy cream

6 ounces white chocolate, finely
chopped

2 tablespoons superfine sugar

7 tablespoons (4 ounces) praline
paste (page 27)

TO MAKE THE CAKE

1. In a food processor, pulverize the almonds and hazelnuts with the sugar without letting them turn oily. Add the flour, pulse the machine until the ingredients are mixed, and transfer to a mixing bowl.

2. Position a rack in the center of the oven and preheat to 350°F. Line the bottom of a 12 × 16 × 1-inch half-sheet pan with a buttered baking parchment or a nonstick baking mat.

3. With an electric mixer on medium speed, whip the egg whites with the salt until frothy; add the cream of tartar and whip until the whites are stiff and glossy. With a rubber spatula, fold the whites into the ground nuts. With a spoon, dot the baking sheet with the batter so that it is easier to spread with a spatula. Spread the batter, making sure it is even and level. Bake for 40 to 45 minutes, or until the cake is golden brown and crisp.

4. Remove the cake from the oven and run a knife around the edges to loosen it from the sides of the pan. Invert the cake over another piece of parchment and peel off the paper on which you baked the cake. Cool the cake to room temperature.

TO MAKE THE FILLINGS

1. Melt the bittersweet chocolate in a mixing bowl or the top of a double boiler set over simmering water. Stir occasionally and, when just melted, transfer to a large clean mixing bowl and whisk in 1 cup of the heavy cream; the chocolate will appear to seize up at first but will smooth out as you whisk it. Set it aside to cool to room temperature, or refrigerate it until the mixture is of spreading consistency.

2. Melt the white chocolate in a mixing bowl or the top of a double boiler set over barely simmering water. Stir occasionally and, when just melted, remove it from the heat. Set it aside until the chocolate feels cool to the touch but is still fluid. Whip 1 cup of cream with the superfine sugar until stiff and quickly fold it into the white chocolate.

3. Whip the last cup of cream until stiff and fold ¼ of it into the praline paste to loosen it up, then fold in the remaining whipped cream. Chill both the white chocolate and praline fillings until you are ready to assemble the cake.

TO ASSEMBLE THE CAKE

1. With a serrated knife, cut the cake into 4 strips, each about 4 inches wide and 12 inches long. Set one strip of cake on a rectangle of cardboard cut the same size as the strip of cake.

2. Spread the cake with 1 cup of the chocolate cream. Top with a second layer of cake and spread this with the praline cream filling. Place the third strip of cake over the praline filling and spread it with the white chocolate cream filling. Invert the fourth strip of cake over the white chocolate filling. Clean up the sides of the cake with a spatula to make sure the fillings don't ooze out, and spread the sides of the cake with a very thin layer of chocolate cream. Refrigerate the cake for 15 minutes to firm it up.

3. Spread the remaining chocolate cream over the top and sides of the cake, leaving the ends unfrosted. With an icing comb or a fork, make decorative striation marks on the top and sides of the cake, then refrigerate it, uncovered, until firm.

4. Cut off a thin slice from each end of the cake to make them even and straight. Set a piece of plastic wrap on the ends of the cake to keep them from drying out. Refrigerate the cake, uncovered, until serving time, but remove it 30 minutes before serving.

STORAGE: Keep in the refrigerator, wrapped airtight in plastic, for up to 6 days, or freeze for up to 2 months.

ADVANCE PREPARATION TIPS

- Make the cake 2 days ahead of serving.
- Make the fillings and assemble the cake 24 hours ahead of serving.

Opera Cake

Opera cake has been a favorite of mine since I first tasted one, some twenty-five years ago, from Eclair's, a now defunct pastry shop in Manhattan. It is no wonder I love it so; it combines all the flavors I adore: chocolate, praline paste, and coffee. I have changed a few things from the original recipe to make it easier for people to prepare at home. While a little difficult and delicate to assemble, this can be done in stages and over time.

Makes one 6 × 8-inch, 4-layer cake

Serves 12

Level of difficulty ★★★

CAKE

3 tablespoons (1 ounce) unbleached all-purpose flour

1½ cups plus 2 tablespoons (6.25 ounces) confectioners' sugar, sifted

7 large egg whites

⅛ teaspoon salt

½ cup plus 2 tablespoons (6 ounces) praline paste (page 27)

FILLING, GLAZING, AND FINISHING

7 ounces bittersweet chocolate, finely chopped, plus additional ½ ounce, optional

¾ cup heavy cream

Dione Lucas's Chocolate Buttercream, coffee variation (page 310)

TO MAKE THE CAKE

1. Position a rack in the center of the oven and preheat to 375°F. Line the bottom of a 12 × 16 × 1-inch half-sheet pan with a buttered baking parchment or nonstick baking mat.
2. Sift the flour with 1 cup of confectioners' sugar.
3. With an electric mixer on medium speed, whip the egg whites with the salt until they are semistiff. With the machine running, add the remaining ½ cup plus 2 tablespoons confectioners' sugar, and whip until the whites are stiff and glossy.
4. With a rubber spatula, fold 1 cup of the beaten egg whites into the praline paste to loosen it. Sift the flour and sugar mixture over the top of the remaining egg whites and fold together, preferably with your hands.
5. With an offset spatula, spread this mixture into the prepared baking pan, making sure the batter is even and level. Bake for 20 to 25 minutes, or until the cake feels firm and crisp on top and is golden brown.
6. Remove the cake from the oven and cool it in the pan on a wire rack. Run a knife around the cake to loosen it from the sides of the pan. Set a piece of parchment over the cake, then set a wire rack or baking pan over that, and invert the cake; remove the parchment the cake was baked on. If you have baked the cake long enough, you won't have trouble peeling off the paper, but if it is underbaked, the paper might stick. Invert the cake so it is right side up again and let it stand at room temperature, uncovered, for 24 hours, so it dries out a bit.

TO FILL, GLAZE, AND FINISH

1. Set 7 ounces of the bittersweet chocolate in a mixing bowl. In a small saucepan, bring the heavy cream to just under a boil. Pour it over the chocolate and let the mixture stand for 30 seconds. With a rubber spatula, blend until smooth and refrigerate until firm enough to spread. This is a crucial part of the operation; the filling must be hard enough so it won't drip down the sides, yet fluid enough to spread.
2. With an electric mixer on low speed, whip the buttercream until fluffy and smooth.

3. With a knife, cut the cake into 4 equal pieces, each about 6 × 8 inches. Set one piece of cake on a cardboard rectangle cut the same dimension as the piece of cake. If you are not using a cardboard, set one piece of cake on a cookie sheet, inserting strips of waxed paper under the sides to catch the drips of filling.

4. Spread the layer with ⅓ of the chocolate filling, making it as level as possible. Top with a second layer, pressing it down and lining up the sides of the cake as evenly as possible. Spread the layer with ½ the coffee buttercream. Top with a third layer and spread it with ⅓ of the chocolate filling. Turn the last layer upside down on the chocolate filling so the flat side is facing up, and spread it with the remaining coffee buttercream. Freeze the cake for 30 minutes so the top is very hard. Spread the remaining chocolate filling over the frozen buttercream, leaving the ends and sides of the cake unfrosted. Return the cake to the freezer for 1 hour. With a serrated knife, trim all sides of the cake so you can clearly see the levels of cake and filling. (It is easier to set a piece of waxed paper on the top of the cake as you trim the sides so the chocolate does not melt.)

5. If you wish, melt and cool the ½ ounce of bittersweet chocolate and transfer it to a paper cone. Write the word *Opera* across the top of the cake and refrigerate it, uncovered, until firm.

STORAGE: Keep in the refrigerator, wrapped airtight in plastic, for up to 4 days; remove the cake 30 minutes before serving.

ADVANCE PREPARATION TIPS

- Make the cake and coffee buttercream 1 day ahead of serving.
- Make the chocolate filling and assemble the cake on the day of serving.
- This can be made in advance and frozen for up to 3 weeks. Defrost in the refrigerator.

Special, Individual, and Refrigerated Cakes   275

Prinzregenten Torte

This extraordinary recipe is from the German repertoire and was given to me by Dieter Schorner, formerly the chairman of the pastry department of the French Culinary Institute. One of the ways I made sure I was collecting the best chocolate cake recipes for this book was to ask pastry chefs and friends which cake came to mind when I said the words chocolate cake. *When asked this question, Dieter responded without hesitation, "Prinzregenten Torte," and he promptly gave me a recipe. Traditionally, this is a round cake and the classic way of making it is to spread the batter over the back of round cake pans, baking them individually and in sequence until you have 8 or 9 layers. This procedure is too cumbersome and no longer necessary, now that we have nonstick baking mats. I adjusted the recipe so you can bake the batter in 2 sheet pans and then cut each sheet into 4 rectangles and stack the 8 layers with filling. The result is a cake that is a lot easier to make at home, but it tastes as divine, I think, as Dieter had intended.*

Makes one 4 × 12-inch, 8-layer cake

Serves 12

Level of difficulty ★★★

CAKE

1 cup (4.75 ounces) unbleached all-purpose flour

½ teaspoon baking powder

1 stick (4 ounces) unsalted butter, softened

2 tablespoons packed (1 ounce) almond paste

⅔ cup (5 ounces) superfine sugar

5 large eggs, separated

1 large egg

⅛ teaspoon salt

FILLING AND GLAZING

1 jar (12 ounces) apricot jam

2 cups Dione Lucas's Chocolate Buttercream (page 310), very soft and spreadable

Ganache made with ¾ cup (6 ounces) heavy cream and 6 ounces semisweet chocolate (page 324)

TO MAKE THE CAKE

1. Position a rack in the center of the oven and preheat to 400°F. Line the bottom of two 12 × 16 × 1-inch half-sheet pans with nonstick baking mats.
2. Sift the flour with the baking powder and set it aside.
3. In a stationary mixer fitted with the paddle attachment, beat the butter with the almond paste and ⅓ cup of the sugar until blended and smooth. Add the egg yolks two at a time, beating well after each addition, then add the whole egg and beat until the mixture is light and airy.
4. In a separate, clean bowl, beat the egg whites with the salt until they are semistiff, then slowly, about 2 tablespoons at a time, beat in the remaining ⅓ cup of sugar and whip until the whites are stiff and glossy. Fold the egg whites into the yolk mixture and, when partially folded, sift the flour mixture over the top and fold it in as well.
5. Divide the batter between the prepared pans. With a 12-inch offset spatula, spread the batter in the pans so that it is literally paper-thin. Take care to spread it into the corners where, if too thin, it will burn. Bake for about 10 minutes only, or until the batter smells "eggy," the top feels firm, and the edges begin to draw away from the sides of the pan.
6. Cool the cakes to room temperature in their pans.

TO FILL AND GLAZE

1. When the cakes are cool, turn each of them upside down over a piece of parchment paper. Carefully peel off the baking mat, and cut each cake into four strips, each strip about 4 × 12 inches. Set one of the strips on a cookie sheet or cardboard rectangle cut to fit the size of the cake strip.

2. In a small saucepan, heat the apricot jam until hot, remove it from the heat, and pass it through a strainer to remove any lumps. Cool the strained apricot jam to room temperature. With a small offset spatula, spread a very thin coating of jam on each of the strips, including the one on the cardboard.

3. Then spread the cake layer on the cardboard with buttercream and top it with a cake strip spread with jam. Keep on stacking the cake layers, spreading buttercream between the layers, ending with a cake layer set jam side up. Coat the sides, but not the ends, with a thin coating of buttercream and refrigerate the cake, uncovered, while you make the ganache.

4. Make the ganache and cool it to room temperature in the refrigerator. Spread a thin layer of ganache on the top and sides of the cake and refrigerate for 15 minutes. Spread another layer on the top and sides of the cake. Decorate the top of the cake with an icing comb.

STORAGE: Keep in the refrigerator, loosely covered, for up to 4 days; remove the cake 45 minutes before serving.

**Chocolate Linzer Torte

This is a unique recipe among my mother-in-law's contributions to this book. The cake has the texture of a cookie, is exquisitely delicious, and has the bonus of being incredibly easy to put together. It is the ideal party cake because it can be made several days ahead of time and keeps well for days after baking.

Makes one 9 × 5-inch loaf cake

Serves 10 to 12

Level of difficulty ★

---

6 ounces roasted skinned hazelnuts

1 cup minus 3 tablespoons (6 ounces) granulated sugar

1 cup plus 6 tablespoons (6 ounces) cake flour

½ teaspoon baking powder

⅛ teaspoon ground cloves, optional

¼ teaspoon ground cinnamon, optional

1½ sticks (6 ounces) unsalted butter, softened

6 ounces bittersweet chocolate, melted and cooled

1 large egg

1 large egg yolk

¾ cup seedless raspberry jam

Superfine or vanilla sugar (page 20), for dusting

---

1. Position a rack in the center of the oven and preheat to 375°F. Lightly butter a 9 × 5 × 3-inch loaf pan.

2. In a food processor, grind the hazelnuts with the sugar until the nuts are powdery. Add the flour, baking powder, cloves and cinnamon, if using, and pulse the machine several times until the ingredients are combined.

3. In a mixing bowl, with a wooden spoon (or in a stationary electric mixer fitted with the paddle attachment), beat the butter until light. Add the cooled chocolate and beat until combined, then add the egg and yolk, and beat until light and airy looking.

4. With a rubber spatula, fold the flour and nut mixture into the egg mixture and mix until the ingredients are just thoroughly combined.

5. Pat ½ the dough into the prepared loaf pan, pressing it down into the corners and against the sides. Spread the raspberry jam to within ½ inch of the edges. Spoon the rest of the dough on top of the jam and, with your fingertips, gently press and smooth it down, then smooth the top with a small offset spatula.

6. Place the cake in the oven, turn the heat down to 350°, and bake for 15 minutes, then turn the oven down to 325° and bake for 1 hour longer. Turn the oven off and leave the cake in the oven for 15 minutes with the door ajar.

7. Cool the cake to room temperature in its pan. Invert the pan and turn the cake out onto a cardboard rectangle or a platter. Just before serving, dust the top with sugar.

STORAGE: Keep at room temperature, wrapped airtight in plastic, in a cool dry place for up to 3 days; refrigerate after that.

Cupcakes

Cupcakes are miniature versions of larger cakes. They are made from a pound or layer cake batter and baked in little molds or muffin tins. In this book, you can make cupcakes from any number of the layer cake recipes, and all you need to remember is that for 24 muffin-sized cupcakes, you'll need about 6 cups of batter, or enough for two 9-inch cakes. The frostings and garnishes can be varied according to your taste.

Makes 24 cupcakes

Serves 24

Level of difficulty ★

1 OF THE FOLLOWING RECIPES

Classic Devil's Food Layer; quantity for 9-inch layers (page 139)

Light Chocolate Layer (page 149)

Linda's Quintessential Devil's Food Cake (page 146)

Sour Cream Chocolate Layer (page 153)

Yellow Layer (page 156)

2½ CUPS OF ONE OF THE FOLLOWING RECIPES*

Classic American Chocolate Frosting (page 298)

Wicked Chocolate Frosting (page 298)

Cream Cheese Chocolate Frosting (page 299)

Peanut Butter Chocolate Frosting (page 301)

Vanilla Frosting, or orange variation (page 301)

Sour Cream Chocolate Icing (page 326)

DECORATIVE TOPPINGS

Mini chocolate chips

M & M's

Chocolate or colored jimmies

1. Position a rack in the center of the oven and preheat to 350°F. Generously grease twenty-four ½-cup-capacity muffin tins or line them with paper cups.
2. Make the cake batter and spoon it into the muffin tins, filling each cup about ⅔ full. Bake for 20 to 25 minutes, or until a tester inserted in the center comes out dry. Remove the pans from the oven and cool them on a rack for about 10 minutes.
3. Loosen the cupcakes from the muffin tins and cool them to room temperature. Spread a generous tablespoon of frosting on each cupcake and press the toppings into the frosting while it is still fresh.

STORAGE: Keep in the refrigerator, wrapped airtight in plastic, for up to 4 days.

*You may need to make 1½ times the recipe of some of these to have enough.

Fudge Nut Cupcakes

These cupcakes, made of a brownielike batter, are so rich they need nothing more than a rosette of whipped cream piped out on top.

Makes 12 cupcakes

Serves 12

Level of difficulty ★

---

4 ounces unsweetened chocolate, finely chopped

2 sticks (8 ounces) unsalted butter, cut into 1-inch chunks

1 teaspoon vanilla extract

1 cup (4.75 ounces) bleached all-purpose flour

¼ teaspoon salt

1¾ cups (13 ounces) granulated sugar

4 large eggs

1½ cups (5.25 ounces) pecans, chopped

½ recipe Whipped Cream (page 318), plain or flavored, optional

---

1. Position a rack in the center of the oven and preheat to 375°F. Butter and flour twelve ½-cup capacity muffin tins or line them with paper cups. Tap out the excess flour.

2. In a small saucepan over low heat, melt the chocolate with the butter, stirring occasionally. When the chocolate and butter are melted, transfer the mixture to a clean bowl, add the vanilla, and set aside to cool to room temperature.

3. In another mixing bowl, whisk the flour together with the salt and sugar. Whisk the eggs into the chocolate, then stir in the flour mixture and pecans with a rubber spatula or a wooden spoon, stirring until blended.

4. Spoon the batter into the muffin tins and bake for 35 to 40 minutes, or until a tester inserted in the center comes out dry. Remove the pan from the oven and cool it on a wire rack. When cool, loosen the cupcakes from the muffin cups.

5. If you wish, transfer the whipped cream to a 16-inch pastry bag fitted with a ½-inch star tip and pipe a large whipped cream rosette on top of each cupcake.

STORAGE: With whipped cream, keep them in the refrigerator, loosely wrapped. Without the whipped cream, keep them at room temperature, wrapped airtight, for up to 3 days.

Michele's Fantasy Cupcakes

I was born in New York, but when I was eight years old my family moved to Belgium, where I lived until I was sixteen. While I enjoyed the fabulous food, delicious pastries, and extraordinary chocolates in Belgium, I never gave up longing for American classics like hamburgers, milkshakes, and Hostess cupcakes. When I returned to New York City, the first purchase I made was a cupcake, but after I took one bite of it, all my illusions came crashing down. The cupcake I had dreamed of bore no resemblance to reality. What I had really been fantasizing about all those years was the cupcake below: a luscious chocolate cake enveloping a whipped cream core and spread with a rich chocolate icing.

These giant cupcakes are so big you should serve them as an afternoon snack or for birthday parties rather than as dessert after a full meal.

Makes 12 jumbo cupcakes

Serves 12

Level of difficulty ★

Deep-Dish Chocolate Cake batter (page 113)

Whipped Cream, plain or flavored (page 318)

Double recipe for Midnight Icing (page 326)

---

1. Position a rack in the center of the oven and preheat to 350°F. Generously grease twelve 1-cup-capacity large-muffin tins.
2. Make the cake batter and spoon it evenly into the muffin tins, filling each one about ¾ full. Bake for 35 to 40 minutes, or until a tester inserted in the center comes out dry. Remove the pans from the oven and cool them on a rack.
3. While the cupcakes are cooling, line a baking sheet with parchment or waxed paper. When the cupcakes have cooled, loosen them from the muffin tins and place them upside down on the baking sheet.
4. With the tip of a sharp paring knife, cut out a 1-inch-wide cone from the bottom of each cupcake and reserve the cones. With a knife or your fingers, carefully scoop out as much of the inside as possible from each cupcake to make room for the whipped cream. Work carefully because the cake falls apart easily.
5. Fill a pastry bag (without a tip) with the whipped cream and pipe a generous amount into each cupcake; try to get in as much filling as possible so the cupcakes don't taste dry. Replace the reserved cones, turn the cupcakes right side up on the baking sheet, and refrigerate them while you make the icing; then ice the tops.

STORAGE: Keep in the refrigerator, loosely covered, for up to 3 days.

**Chocolate Volcanoes

In these divine little cakes, the interior becomes a molten mass of melted chocolate sur-rounded by a thin layer of chocolate cake. They are made by burying a small round of cold ganache in the cake batter. As the cakes bake, the cold ganache melts, forming the runny center. These should be made just before serving, but if this is unrealistic, make them no more than 2 hours before serving and reheat them for a few seconds in the microwave oven.

Makes 6 small cakes

Serves 6

Level of difficulty ★★

FILLING

3 ounces semisweet or bittersweet chocolate, finely chopped

6 tablespoons heavy cream

CAKE

8 ounces unsweetened chocolate, finely chopped

2 sticks (8 ounces) unsalted butter, cut into 1-inch chunks

1 teaspoon vanilla extract

5 large eggs

1⅓ cups (10 ounces) superfine sugar

½ cup (2.5 ounces) all-purpose flour, sifted

Confectioners' sugar, for dusting

TO MAKE THE FILLING

Make the filling a day ahead or at least a few hours ahead of serving. Set the chocolate in a small bowl. Bring the cream to a simmer and pour it over the chocolate. Let the mixture stand for 30 seconds, then whisk together and chill. Divide the mixture into 6 rough balls, each about 2 tablespoons, and return them to the refrigerator until you need them.

TO MAKE THE CAKE

1. In a small saucepan over low heat, melt the chocolate with the butter, stir-ring occasionally. Transfer the mixture to a clean bowl and set it aside to cool to room temperature, then add the vanilla.

2. Position a rack in the center of the oven and preheat to 350°F. Butter six 1-cup-capacity ramekins or custard dishes.

3. In a mixing bowl, with a wire whip or a handheld electric mixer, combine the eggs with the sugar. Set the bowl over a saucepan of simmering water, making sure the bottom of the bowl does not come in contact with the water. Beat the mixture at medium speed until hot to the touch (110° to 115°F on an instant-read thermometer). Remove the bowl from the heat and transfer the eggs to the bowl of a stationary mixer. Beat the eggs on medium-high speed for 2 to 3 minutes, or until tripled in volume, pale lemon in color, and thick. (This might take 7 to 8 minutes with a hand-held electric mixer.)

4. With a rubber spatula, fold the sifted flour into the egg foam, then gently fold in the melted butter and chocolate. Spoon the batter evenly into the prepared ramekins. Remove the balls of cold chocolate ganache from the refrigerator and plop one in the middle of each ramekin.

5. Set the ramekins on a baking sheet and bake for 15 to 17 minutes. Dust the cakes with confectioners' sugar and serve them immediately, in the ramekins.

    STORAGE: Keep leftovers in the refrigerator, wrapped, for up to 2 days; reheat before serving.

Chocolate Tiramisu

Tiramisu is an Italian icebox cake that consists of alcohol-soaked ladyfingers layered with a rich chocolate and mascarpone filling. This is absolutely scrumptious, can be made a couple of days ahead of serving, and is always a great hit with guests.

Makes one 9×13-inch layered dessert

Serves 16

Level of difficulty ★

---

1 cup double-strength coffee or 1½ tablespoons instant espresso powder dissolved in 1 cup boiling water

---

¼ cup granulated sugar

¼ cup dark rum

⅓ cup unsweetened cocoa powder, sifted, plus additional for dusting

---

6 tablespoons cognac or brandy

1½ cups plus 2 tablespoons heavy cream

---

1 cup (8 ounces) mascarpone cheese (see Notes)

½ cup confectioners' sugar

---

2 teaspoons vanilla extract

---

3 ounces bittersweet, milk, or white chocolate, grated or finely chopped

---

About 4 dozen (14 ounces) ladyfingers or Italian Savoiardi cookies (see Notes)

---

1. Set out a 9 × 13-inch baking dish, preferably made of glass or porcelain, so you can serve the tiramisu directly from the dish in which it is assembled. Mix the coffee with the granulated sugar and rum, and set it aside in a bowl.

2. In a mixing bowl, whisk the cocoa powder into the cognac and 2 tablespoons of heavy cream, then blend in the mascarpone cheese.

3. In a chilled bowl begin to whip the remaining 1½ cups cream on medium speed until it begins to hold soft peaks. Sift the confectioners' sugar over the cream, add the vanilla, and beat for a few seconds longer, or until the cream forms stiff billowy peaks. Fold the whipped cream into the mascarpone mixture along with the grated chocolate.

4. Dip both sides of ½ the ladyfingers in the coffee and rum, and position them on the bottom and around the sides of the baking dish. Spread them with ½ the mascarpone chocolate filling. Dip the remaining ladyfingers in the coffee and rum, and position them over the cream filling to create a second layer. Spread the remaining filling over the ladyfingers and cover the baking dish with plastic wrap. Refrigerate for at least 4 hours or, preferably, overnight.

5. Just before serving, dust the top layer with cocoa powder sifted through a fine-meshed sieve.

STORAGE: Keep in the refrigerator, wrapped airtight in plastic, for up to 3 days.

NOTES: Mascarpone is a delicious Italian cheese that tastes and looks like a cross between sour cream and cream cheese. You can get it, imported from Italy, in most fine gourmet stores. If you can't find it, substitute ¾ cup cream cheese blended with ¼ cup sour cream.

Savoiardi is the name for the Italian version of ladyfingers. They are readily available in gourmet stores.

Mohr im Hemd

This recipe was given to me by Eric Hubert, pastry chef at the four-star Jean Georges Restaurant in New York City. He is not only a very accomplished chef, but an incredibly imaginative one as well. I was impressed with his bold strokes and imaginative combinations when, in 1997, I spent some weeks working as an intern in the pastry department of the restaurant. We kept in touch and I learned of his interesting and varied work background, which explains his creativity. When I asked him to contribute a recipe to this book, he had so many possibilities, it was hard for him to choose, so I decided on this Austrian specialty, which is like a flourless soufflé-cake.

Makes 8 small cakes

Serves 8

Level of difficulty ★

---

2 tablespoons cake flour, sifted

1 cup packed (3.5 ounces) finely ground almonds or hazelnuts, or almond or hazelnut flour

1 stick (4 ounces) unsalted butter, softened

Scant ½ cup (3.5 ounces) granulated sugar

5 large eggs, separated

2 ounces bittersweet chocolate, melted and cooled

Flavored Custard Sauce, orange or peppered variation (page 359), optional

---

1. Position a rack in the center of the oven and preheat to 350°F. Lightly butter eight ½-cup-capacity ramekins or custard dishes. Line 1 or 2 baking pans (large enough to accommodate the ramekins) with newspaper or cloth towels and set them aside.

2. In a mixing bowl, with a whisk, combine the flour and ground nuts and set it aside.

3. With an electric mixer on low speed (or with a stationary mixer fitted with the paddle attachment), beat the butter for 1 minute, or until light. Slowly add ¼ cup of the sugar, about 2 tablespoons at a time, and when all of it has been added, continue to beat on medium speed for a couple of minutes longer, scraping down the beaters and sides of the bowl as needed. The mixture will look fluffy, like something between mayonnaise and whipped cream.

4. Add the egg yolks two at a time, beating for 10 seconds between additions, or until absorbed by the butter. Add the chocolate and beat until blended.

5. In a clean bowl with an electric mixer on medium speed, whip the egg whites until they are semistiff. Increase the speed to high, add the remaining ¼ cup sugar, about 2 tablespoons at a time, and beat until the egg whites are stiff and glossy.

6. With a rubber spatula, fold about ½ the egg whites into the chocolate mixture, and the other ½ into the almond-flour mixture, then fold the two mixtures together.

7. Spoon the batter into the prepared ramekins, filling them only ¾ full. Set the ramekins in the baking pan(s) and pour very hot or boiling water into the pan to come about ¾ of the way up the sides of the ramekins. Cover the ramekins, in a block rather than individually, with a piece of buttered aluminum foil and bake for 30 minutes.

8. Remove the ramekins from the water and let them stand for 2 minutes. Run a spatula or a table knife around the cakes and invert them, then set them right side up on serving plates. Spoon some of the sauce, if using, around each cake and serve immediately.

STORAGE: These can be made in advance, unmolded while warm, and refrigerated for up to 3 days. Reheat them in a microwave oven for 1 minute, or until warm.

VARIATION

Omit the flour and bake for 20 to 25 minutes, uncovered and without the water bath. These cakes will form a little crust on top. Serve them in their ramekins with the sauce on the side. Each diner breaks into the dessert and pours in the sauce.

Eric Hubert

Eric Hubert is a fascinating pastry chef with a wide range of experiences in all phases of the culinary arts. He came to the United States in 1990, having worked since the age of sixteen as chef, *charcutier*, *patissier*, and caterer in his native France, as well as in Austria, Switzerland, and Italy. What makes Eric such a fascinating chef is that he has worked all around the world, and his pastries reflect his interest in people and their culture. This curiosity about other cultures is exemplified in the "fusion" desserts he created as a pastry chef in a Japanese restaurant: a nettles pudding steamed in bamboo leaves, and a pear and figs dessert accompanied by an anise ice cream made with tofu.

American Icebox Cake

You don't really need a recipe for an icebox cake, which is the American version of a French charlotte russe or an Italian zuccotto. You line a mold with ladyfingers or pieces of cake, such as angel food, pound, or sponge, and fill the interior with a fluffy filling of your choice. Below are just some of the ways you could go about doing this.

MOLDS

Round mixing bowl

Soufflé dish

8-inch square pan

8-inch springform pan

9 × 13-inch pan

POUND CAKES

Chocolate Chocolate Tea Cake (page 112)

Chocolate *Pain de Gênes* (page 115)

Dependable Chocolate Pound Cake (page 104)

Light Chocolate Pound Cake (page 107)

Marbled Chocolate Pound Cake (page 108)

Mocha Tea Cake (page 117)

SPONGE AND BISCUIT CAKES

Any of the basic sponge or biscuit layers

3 to 4 dozen ladyfingers

Angel food cake

Cocoa Puff (page 226)

FILLINGS
(ABOUT 3 TO 4 CUPS)

Chocolate Pudding Filling (double recipe) (page 323)

Chocolate Mousse Filling (page 314)

Chocolate Sabayon Mousse (page 317)

Raspberry Mousse Filling (page 316)

Vanilla Pastry Cream, chocolate variation, and Whipped Cream (half and half) (pages 322 and 318)

Whipped Cream (page 318)

Whipped Ganache (page 321)

White Chocolate Mousse Filling (page 315)

FINISHING TOUCHES

Chocolate Glaze (pages 330–331)

Flavored Custard Sauce (page 359)

Raspberry Squeeze Sauce (page 368) or other fruit sauce (pages 368–369)

TO ASSEMBLE

1. Line the mold of choice with plastic wrap so it hangs over the sides of the mold; this will help you unmold the cake later on.

2. Cut the cake of choice into pieces that will fit the shape and size of the mold you have chosen. If you wish, although not authentically American, you can dip these cake pieces in a Simple Syrup or in one laced with alcohol (page 370).

3. Press the pieces of cake on the bottom and against the sides of the mold. Spoon the filling into the cake-lined mold, and cover the filling with more pieces of cake.

4. Refrigerate the cake for 4 to 24 hours, or long enough for the cake to absorb the moisture of the filling and, if need be, for the filling to set.

5. Invert the cake onto a plate or cardboard round, and remove the mold and plastic wrap; if you wish, glaze the cake.

6. Serve a slice with sauce, if you wish.

STORAGE: Keep in the refrigerator, wrapped airtight in plastic, for up to 3 days.

Italian Chocolate Icebox Cake

I call this an "Italian" icebox cake because the filling—sweetened ricotta cheese, orange zest, raisins, and chopped chocolate—reminds me of the filling for cannolis. You can make this with a homemade cake or a commercially prepared 9-inch sponge cake.

Makes one 9-inch, 3-layer cake

Serves 12 to 14

Level of difficulty ★

½ cup dark rum

⅓ cup very hot water

3 Buttermilk Chocolate Layers, baked and cooled (page148)

2 cups (15 ounces) whole milk ricotta cheese

½ cup (3.75 ounces) superfine sugar

½ cup golden raisins

1 tablespoon grated orange zest

4 ounces bittersweet chocolate, coarsely chopped and chilled

Confectioners' sugar *or* Maria's Best Chocolate Glaze, without the butter, cooled (page 331)

1. Mix the rum with the hot water and brush the liquid on each of the cake layers with a pastry brush.
2. In a mixing bowl, with a rubber spatula, combine the cheese with the sugar, raisins, and orange zest. Place the chocolate in a food processor and chop until it is reduced to small pieces. Add the chocolate to the cheese.
3. Set out a large sheet of plastic wrap and center one of the biscuit layers on the plastic. Spread ½ the cheese mixture over the first layer, place another cake layer on top, and spread that with the remaining cheese filling. Top the filling with the third cake layer, and wrap the cake airtight in plastic. Refrigerate for at least 4 hours or, preferably, overnight.
4. When ready to serve, dust the top with confectioners' sugar or spread the top and sides with glaze.

STORAGE: Keep in the refrigerator, wrapped airtight, for up to 3 days.

Chocolate Velvet

Chocolate Velvet is an obscenely rich dessert developed by the legendary pastry chef Albert Kumin in the 1970s for the Four Seasons Restaurant in Manhattan. It is confected of a voluptuous chocolate mousse enveloped by a thin layer of cake and glazed with chocolate icing. I found the recipe in the New York Times *some twenty years ago and have kept it all these years. However, for this book, I modified a couple of things: The original recipe called for a plain sponge cake, which I changed to a chocolate biscuit, and I have used a chocolate mousse made with cooked egg yolks rather than one made with raw eggs. This is the ideal party recipe because it serves at least sixteen and can be made in stages and finished several days ahead of serving.*

Makes one 8-cup dome cake

Serves 16

Level of difficulty ★★★

CAKE

Chocolate Biscuit baked in a 12 × 16 × 1-inch pan, cooled (page 208)

12 ounces semisweet or bittersweet chocolate, finely chopped

¼ cup packed (2.5 ounces) praline paste (page 27)

3 tablespoons crème de cacao liqueur

3 tablespoons dark rum

1½ teaspoons instant espresso coffee powder dissolved in 1 teaspoon hot water

3 tablespoons (1.5 ounces) unsalted butter, melted and cooled

2 cups heavy cream

½ cup (3.75 ounces) granulated sugar

1 teaspoon light corn syrup

1 large egg

4 large egg yolks

ICING

5 ounces semisweet or bittersweet chocolate, finely chopped

⅓ cup boiling water

TO MAKE THE CAKE

1. Line a round mixing bowl of about 2-quart capacity, or 4 inches deep and 7 inches wide, with plastic wrap and let the plastic drape over the sides of the bowl.

2. Cut a round out of the biscuit to fit the bottom of the bowl and cut out strips to line the sides of the bowl. Press the strips of cake against the inside of the bowl, making sure the entire inner surface of the bowl is covered with cake; if not, stuff little pieces of cake where needed.

3. In a mixing bowl or the top of a double boiler set over simmering water, melt the chocolate, stirring. When the chocolate is melted, remove the pan from the heat and set it aside to cool to room temperature.

4. Dissolve the coffee in 1 teaspoon hot water. In a mixing bowl, with a small whisk, blend the praline paste with the crème de cacao, rum, butter, and coffee and set aside.

5. In a chilled bowl, whip the cream with an electric mixer on low, then at medium speed until it begins to hold softly firm peaks. Set it aside in the refrigerator.

6. In a 1-quart saucepan, combine the sugar with the corn syrup and ¼ cup water and bring to a simmer, stirring. Wash down the insides of the pan with a pastry brush dipped in cold water. Boil the sugar syrup without stirring until it reaches the soft ball stage at 236° to 238°F on a candy thermometer. When the syrup reaches 230°, start to beat the egg and egg yolks with an electric mixer fitted with the whip attachment until light and lemon colored. When the syrup is at the right temperature, with the machine running, pour the hot syrup into the eggs, alongside one point of the mixing bowl. Whip until the mixture is light, fluffy, lemon colored, and tepid. Whisk this into the praline mixture and then into the chocolate. The chocolate will look as if it is about to seize up when you blend it in, but keep on whisking vigorously and the mixture will come together.

7. If the whipped cream has deflated somewhat, rewhip it until it holds soft peaks again, then, in a couple of batches, fold it into the chocolate and egg mixture.

8. Spoon the filling into the cake-lined mold. Cut out more pieces of cake to fit the top of the mold, making sure the entire top surface is covered. Pick up the sides of the plastic wrap and cover the top, then wrap the cake in more plastic so it is well sealed, and refrigerate for at least 4 hours or, preferably, 24 hours.

TO MAKE THE ICING

1. Melt the chocolate in the top of a double boiler or a mixing bowl set over simmering water, stirring occasionally. When melted, remove it from the heat and immediately whisk in the boiling water, beating vigorously. Set the bowl back over the water and finish blending the chocolate with a wooden spoon until it is smooth. Cool to room temperature.

2. Invert the cake over a cardboard round, and remove the bowl and the plastic wrap. Set the cake on a wire rack set over waxed paper. Pour some of the icing over the top and let it drip down the sides of the cake. Repeat until the sides are covered. Use a small spatula to spread more icing over any patches that need it. Refrigerate until ready to serve.

STORAGE: Keep in the refrigerator, wrapped airtight in plastic, for up to 4 days.

ADVANCE PREPARATION TIPS

- Bake the biscuit 2 days ahead of serving.
- Make the filling and assemble the cake 1 day ahead of serving.
- Ice the cake the day of serving.

About Charlotte Russe

What is a "charlotte russe"? It is a French type of icebox cake made by lining a charlotte mold with alcohol-soaked ladyfingers and filling the center with a Bavarian cream, which is a gelatin-set mousse. A charlotte is a tall, round metal mold, about 4 inches high (the length of a ladyfinger), which narrows at the bottom to 6 to 7 inches in diameter. You can purchase these molds in restaurant supply houses such as J. B. Prince or Bridge Kitchenware. (See appendix C, page 389.)

Rob Russe

I named this cake after Rob Carmella, a colleague of my husband's, because he insisted I include a charlotte russe type of cake and that I name it after him.

Makes one 4-cup dome cake

Serves 6

Level of difficulty ★ ★

⅓ cup Grand Marnier

2 to 3 dozen soft ladyfingers or Savoiardi (Italian ladyfingers)

1 package unflavored gelatin

3 ounces unsweetened chocolate, finely chopped

¾ cup whole milk

½ cup (3.75 ounces) granulated sugar

1 teaspoon vanilla extract

1 cup heavy cream

½ recipe Vanilla Custard Sauce, chocolate variation (page 358), chilled, optional

¼ cup finely chopped pistachios

1. Set out a 1-quart-capacity (#16) charlotte mold or straight-sided soufflé dish and line it with plastic wrap. In a shallow bowl, combine the ⅓ cup of water with the Grand Marnier. Cut some of the ladyfingers so they fit the bottom of the mold and set out enough ladyfingers to line the inside of the mold.

2. Place ¼ cup cold water in a small saucepan and sprinkle the gelatin on top. Melt the chocolate in the top of a double boiler, stirring. In another small saucepan, combine the milk with the sugar and stir as you bring this to a simmer. Remove it from the heat, pour it over the chocolate, and whisk to combine. Gently heat the gelatin until liquefied, pour this into the hot chocolate mixture, and whisk together. Then add the vanilla. Set the top of the double boiler in a larger bowl filled with crushed ice and occasionally stir the mixture as it cools.

3. As the chocolate mixture is cooling, dip the flat side of the ladyfingers, cut to fit the bottom of the mold, in the Grand Marnier mixture, and line the bottom, setting the flat side facing up. Dip the remaining whole ladyfingers, flat side only, and set them upright, side by side, pressed against the sides of the mold, rounded side facing out so that you see this prettier side when you unmold the cake.

4. When the chocolate mixture thickens and feels like it is about to set, whip the heavy cream until it forms stiff peaks and fold it into the chocolate mixture. Spoon this into the cake-lined mold. Cover the top of the cream with more ladyfingers (do not dip them in Grand Marnier liquid) and, if necessary, cut off the tops of the ladyfingers that protrude above the rim of the mold. Cover the mold in plastic and chill for 24 hours.

5. To unmold the cake, unwrap the mold and cover the top with a plate. Invert the mold, lift it up, and peel off the plastic wrap. Spoon some of the chilled sauce around the bottom of the platter and scatter the pistachios over the sauce. Serve extra sauce on the side.

STORAGE: Keep in the refrigerator, wrapped airtight, and eat within 2 days.

Michele's Chocolate Zuccotto

This is my version of a fabulous Italian icebox cake that used to be a specialty of Florence but is now made and distributed throughout Italy. This particular cake got its name from the Italian word zucco, *which means "pumpkin," because it was prepared in pumpkinlike half-sphere molds that resembled the Duomo, the famous Florentine cathedral with its dome-shaped cupola. The cake is fashioned out of alcohol-soaked pieces of cake that envelop either a ricotta cheese or a whipped cream filling blended with nuts, chocolate, and candied fruit. I've changed things around quite a bit, making my zuccotto with slices of chocolate pound cake filled with both white and dark chocolate whipped ganaches blended with toasted almonds and grated chocolate. Be sure to soak the cake generously with alcohol or it will be hard to slice; however, even if your slices are not perfect, this is an amazingly delicious cake.*

Makes one 6-cup dome cake

Serves 6 to 8

Level of difficulty ★ ★

⅓ cup cognac or brandy

⅓ cup Kahlúa

Sixteen ⅜-inch-thick slices of Chocolate Chocolate Tea Cake (page 112) or a commercially prepared chocolate pound cake

One 2-ounce chunk of bittersweet chocolate

½ cup whole blanched almonds, toasted and finely chopped

½ recipe Whipped Ganache (page 321), made with 3 ounces white chocolate, whipped and chilled

½ recipe Whipped Ganache (page 321), made with 3 ounces bittersweet chocolate, whipped and chilled

---

1. Line a 6-cup-capacity round mixing bowl with plastic wrap and let the plastic drape over the sides of the bowl.
2. Combine the cognac and Kahlúa in a small mixing bowl. Cut 12 of the cake slices on the diagonal so each slice forms 2 triangles. With a pastry brush, moisten both sides of a cake triangle and set it in against the inside of the bowl in such a way that the narrow end points down to where the bowl tapers. Brush the next cake triangle and set it against the first one, facing the same way. Continue until the bowl is lined with cake. (Cut and halve more cake slices if you need to.) Make sure the entire inner surface of the bowl is covered with cake, and where there are gaps, stuff them with pieces of cake.
3. Grate the chunk of chocolate on the large holes of a grater (if your hands are very hot, hold the chocolate with disposable gloves so it doesn't melt all over your hands), or pulverize it in a food processor. Combine the grated chocolate with the chopped nuts.
4. Fold ½ of this mixture into the white chocolate whipped ganache and ½ into the dark chocolate whipped ganache. Spread the white chocolate mixture in the center of the mold and refrigerate it for 30 minutes. Spread the dark ganache mixture over the white ganache mixture. Slice more pieces of pound cake, moisten them with the remaining alcohol, and distribute them over the top of the filling. Make sure the entire surface is covered with cake. Pick up the sides of the plastic wrap and cover the top, then wrap the cake in more plastic so it is well sealed. Refrigerate for 24 hours.
5. Unwrap the cake, set a plate over the top, and turn the bowl upside down. Remove the bowl and plastic wrap. Serve in wedges; the first wedge is always the hardest to slice.

STORAGE: Keep in the refrigerator, wrapped airtight in plastic, for up to 2 days.

PART THREE

The Icing on the Cake

FROSTINGS, BUTTERCREAMS, ICINGS, FILLINGS, AND GLAZES

*T*HE ICING BETWEEN the layers and on the outside of the cake has as much personality and is as distinctive as the cake itself. For some of us, it is the icing that is the excuse for eating the cake, and for others the frosting is but a mere after-thought. In everyday language, "icing" and "frosting" are terms used interchangeably to describe buttercreams, confectioners' sugar glazes, and whipped cream toppings.

Although American layer cakes partner nicely with French buttercreams, in this book, for the most part, they are paired with confectioners' icings and frostings, which are uniquely American and absent from the French and professional pastry kitchen repertoire. Sponge and genoise cakes, which lie more in the classical pastry repertoire and are more European in character, are compatible with the European-style cooked sugar buttercreams, even though you can match them up with simpler confectioners' sugar frostings if you wish.

Almost all the recipes in this book pair cake with filling, but if you wish to deviate from my recommendations, keep in mind the following:

- Make sure the flavors and textures of cake and filling are compatible.
- If the cake itself, like a pound cake, requires no refrigeration, then match it with an icing that doesn't require refrigeration either.

- Reinforce the taste of the cake itself by pairing it with a similar-tasting frosting, or contrast the flavor of the cake with that of the frosting.
- Introduce different textural notes, such as filling a dense cake with an airy whipped cream filling, or adding nuts between the layers for crunch.
- Fill the inside of a cake with one type of icing and coat the outside with one that has a different texture or flavor.
- Be sure you check how much filling or frosting you need for the size cake you are icing so that you have enough.

Amounts Needed for Fillings and Frostings

THE CHART BELOW gives the amounts of filling and frosting required for different-size cakes. The amounts vary slightly, depending on the consistency of the filling and frosting, and on how thick a layer of frosting you like.

GLAZES AND POURABLE ICINGS

Top:
1 cup
  8.5 × 4.5 × 2.75-inch
  or 9 × 5 × 3-inch loaf cake
  12 standard-size (½-cup capacity) cupcakes

Top and sides:
1 to 1½ cups
  8-inch round, 2-layer cake
  8.5 × 4.5 × 2.75-inch
  or 9 × 5 × 3-inch loaf cake
1½ to 2 cups
  9- or 10-inch round, 2-layer cake
  9-inch tube cake
  9 × 13-inch sheet cake

BUTTERCREAMS AND THICK FROSTINGS

Top and sides:
1½ to 1¾ cups
  8-inch round, 2-layer cake
  8.5 × 4.5 × 2.75-inch
  or
  9 × 5 × 3-inch loaf cake

1¾ to 2¼ cups
  9-inch round, 2-layer cake
  12 standard-size (½-cup capacity) cupcakes

2½ to 3 cups
  10-inch round, 2-layer cake
  9 × 13-inch sheet cake

Top, sides, and middle:
2¾ to 3¼ cups
  8-inch round, 2-layer cake

3 to 3½ cups
  9-inch round, 2-layer cake

4 cups
    10-inch round, 2-layer cake
    8-inch round, 3-layer cake

Per layer:
    ½ to ¾ cup
        8-inch round cake

    ¾ to 1 cup
        9-inch round cake
        8-inch square cake

    1 to 1¼ cups
        10-inch round cake
        9 × 13-inch sheet cake

FLUFFY FROSTINGS SUCH AS BOILED ICING, ITALIAN MERINGUE, WHIPPED CREAM

Top and sides:
    2 to 2½ cups
        8-inch round, 2-layer cake

    2½ to 3 cups
        9-inch round, 2-layer cake

3 to 3½ cups
    10-inch round, 2-layer cake

3 to 4 cups
    9-inch round, 2-layer cake
    10-inch tube cake

Top, sides, and middle:
    3 to 3¾ cups
        8-inch round, 2-layer cake

    3¾ to 4¼ cups
        9-inch round, 2-layer cake

    4 to 4½ cups
        10-inch round, 2-layer cake

    5 cups
        10-inch tube cake

Per layer:
    ¾ to 1 cup
        8-inch round cake

    1 to 1½ cups
        9-inch round cake

    1½ to 1¾ cups
        10-inch round cake

Classic American Chocolate Frosting

I like the way this frosting sets up, with a whisper of a crunch, typical of American confectioners' sugar frostings. The amount of liquid you add depends on the weather and humidity, and on how soft you want the frosting to be. The color of this frosting is pale when freshly whipped but darkens upon standing.

Makes about 3 cups
Level of difficulty ★

3½ cups (1 pound) confectioners' sugar

Generous ¾ cup (2.5 ounces) unsweetened cocoa powder, sifted

1¼ sticks (5 ounces) unsalted butter, very soft

1 tablespoon vanilla extract

7 to 8 tablespoons milk or heavy cream

---

1. Sift the sugar and cocoa into a mixing bowl and blend with a whisk until well combined.
2. Add the butter, vanilla, and 7 tablespoons of the milk and, with an electric mixer on low speed, beat the frosting until the ingredients are combined. Increase the speed to medium and beat until light. Add more milk or cream if the frosting is too stiff, or more sifted confectioners' sugar if it is too loose.

MOCHA CHOCOLATE FROSTING

Omit the vanilla and substitute 2 teaspoons instant espresso coffee powder dissolved in 1 teaspoon hot water.

BRANDY CHOCOLATE FROSTING

Omit the vanilla and substitute brandy or cognac for ½ the milk.

ORANGE CHOCOLATE FROSTING

Omit the vanilla and substitute either 1 teaspoon freshly grated orange zest or 1 teaspoon orange extract or ¼ teaspoon orange oil. Also substitute ¼ cup thawed orange juice concentrate for ¼ cup of the milk.

Wicked Chocolate Frosting

This frosting is pure wickedness because of the abundance of chocolate. Substitute bittersweet chocolate for the unsweetened if you want a less intense chocolate taste.

Makes about 3 cups
Level of difficulty ★

---

1 pound confectioners' sugar

1 stick (4 ounces) unsalted butter, softened

5 ounces unsweetened chocolate, melted and cooled

2 teaspoons vanilla extract

About 6 tablespoons milk or cream

---

1. Sift the confectioners' sugar into a mixing bowl. Add the butter and combine with a wooden spoon. Add the chocolate and vanilla, and combine. Warm the milk in a microwave oven or on the stove and add it to the frosting.
2. With an electric mixer on low speed (use the paddle attachment if you have one), beat the frosting for 1 to 2 minutes, or until well blended and light. If the consistency is too loose, add more sugar; if too firm, add more milk.

Chocolate Malted Frosting

This frosting is terrific in devil's food cake layers. Malted milk powder is a combination of dry milk solids, barley, wheat flour, salt, and baking soda, and it is the baking soda that gives the icing a bit of a frothy lift.

Makes about 2½ cups
Level of difficulty ★

2 sticks (8 ounces) unsalted butter, softened

2½ cups (12 ounces) confectioners' sugar, sifted

⅓ cup (1 ounce) unsweetened cocoa powder, sifted

½ cup (2 ounces) or more malted milk powder

⅓ cup milk

1. With a wooden spoon or with an electric mixer on low speed, beat the butter for 1 minute to incorporate some air. Sift the sugar and cocoa powder over the butter, add the malted milk powder and milk, and beat until blended.
2. With an electric mixer on medium to high speed (preferably with the paddle attachment, if you have one), beat the frosting until light.
3. Add more malted milk to taste and adjust the consistency if necessary with more milk for a softer frosting or more confectioners' sugar for a firmer one.

Cream Cheese Chocolate Frosting

This is a rich, smooth frosting with a hint of tanginess and just the right note of sweetness. It is a dream frosting to use with white or golden layer cakes as well as with cupcakes.

Makes about 3½ cups
Level of difficulty ★

1 stick (4 ounces) unsalted butter, softened

8 ounces cream cheese, softened

5 ounces unsweetened chocolate, melted and cooled

About 3½ cups (1 pound) confectioners' sugar, sifted

1 to 2 tablespoons milk or heavy cream

1. With an electric mixer on low speed (or with the paddle attachment on a stationary mixer), beat the butter and cream cheese until blended and smooth. Add the chocolate and beat for a few seconds, or until combined.
2. In three additions, add the sugar by sifting it over the bowl and mixing it in by hand, or with a rubber spatula or wooden spoon. When all the sugar is in, beat the frosting with an electric mixer for about a minute, or until it is light and fluffy. Add the milk to make it smooth and spreadable.

VANILLA CREAM CHEESE FROSTING

Omit the chocolate and add 1 to 2 tablespoons more milk or cream to get the right consistency. Add 1 to 2 teaspoons of vanilla extract, to taste.

MINTED CREAM CHEESE FROSTING

Omit the chocolate and add 1 to 2 tablespoons more milk or cream to get the right consistency. Add ½ teaspoon peppermint oil or extract, plus a drop of green food coloring, if you wish.

Frostings, Buttercreams, Icings, Fillings, and Glazes 299

Mocha Frosting

I love the subtle coffee flavor in this frosting, which is great with any one of the standard American chocolate layer cakes.

Makes about 4 cups

Level of difficulty ★

1½ sticks (6 ounces) unsalted butter, softened

About 5 cups (1.5 pounds) confectioners' sugar, sifted

½ cup (1.5 ounces) unsweetened cocoa powder, sifted

2 tablespoons instant espresso coffee powder

About ¼ cup milk or heavy cream

1. With an electric mixer (or a stationary mixer fitted with the paddle attachment), beat the butter until light. Sift the sugar and cocoa powder into the butter. Dissolve the coffee in 2 tablespoons boiling or very hot tap water. With a rubber spatula or wooden spoon, gradually beat the ingredients until blended, then add the coffee and milk.
2. With an electric mixer on low speed, beat the frosting until light. Add more milk if the consistency is too firm or more sifted sugar, 1 tablespoon at a time, if the consistency is too loose.

Butterscotch Frosting

This frosting is much easier to work with if you spread it while it is still warm. Once the frosting is on the cake, don't move it around or it will lose its sheen.

Makes about 4 cups

Level of difficulty ★

1 cup packed (7.5 ounces) dark brown sugar

2 sticks (8 ounces) unsalted butter, cut into 1-inch chunks

¼ teaspoon salt

1 tablespoon vanilla extract

About 5 cups (1.5 pounds) confectioners' sugar

1. In a 2-quart saucepan over medium heat, bring the sugar, 1 stick of the butter, and ½ cup water to a simmer, stirring. Simmer over low heat for 5 minutes. Remove from the heat and cool for 10 minutes, then add the salt and vanilla.
2. While this is cooling, sift the confectioners' sugar into a large mixing bowl and add the second stick of butter. Add the warm sugar mixture and, with an electric mixer on low speed (preferably with the paddle attachment, if you have one), beat the frosting until well combined. Spread it while still warm.

Peanut Butter Chocolate Frosting

This frosting, which is not too sweet, is delicious with every type of American chocolate layer cake.

Makes about 2 cups

Level of difficulty ★

About 2 cups (9 ounces) confectioners' sugar, sifted

⅓ cup (1 ounce) unsweetened cocoa powder

½ cup (4 ounces) natural smooth peanut butter, preferably salted, at room temperature

About ¾ cup heavy cream, or more as needed

1 teaspoon vanilla extract or dark rum

1. Sift the confectioners' sugar with the cocoa powder into a mixing bowl and combine with a whisk.
2. With a rubber spatula, blend the peanut butter, heavy cream, and vanilla into the sugar and cocoa. Then, with an electric mixer on low speed (use the paddle attachment, if you have one), beat the frosting until well combined and light. If the consistency is too tight, it will tear at the cake. Spread some frosting on the cake first to see if it spreads smoothly and easily. If not, add more cream, 1 teaspoonful at a time.

Vanilla Frosting

This frosting is a nice change for those occasions when you want the contrast of a vanilla frosting with chocolate cake.

Makes about 2¼ cups

Level of difficulty ★

3½ cups (1 pound) confectioners' sugar

1 stick (4 ounces) unsalted butter, softened

1 tablespoon vanilla extract

3 tablespoons milk

1. Sift the sugar into a mixing bowl and, with a wooden spoon or rubber spatula, blend the butter, vanilla, and milk into the sugar. With an electric mixer on low speed (preferably with the paddle attachment, if you have one), beat the frosting until well combined and light.
2. If the consistency is too loose, add more sifted confectioners' sugar, 1 tablespoon at a time, or if too firm, add more milk.

ORANGE FROSTING

Use 2 teaspoons vanilla and add 1 teaspoon orange extract or ¼ teaspoon orange oil. You can also add ¼ teaspoon Fiori di Sicilia, which is an Italian baking seasoning consisting of vanillin and citrus oils. It is available through King Arthur's *Baker's Catalogue* (see page 390).

Classic French Buttercream

This luxurious buttercream is typical of those used in the professional French pastry kitchen. It is made by beating a hot sugar syrup into egg yolks and then adding lots of sweet butter and some flavorings. It is ideal to use for piping because it is soft enough to spread yet firm enough to hold its shape, even at room temperature. It is a bit cumbersome to make, but after you've practiced it a few times, you'll get the hang of it and understand how far superior it is to American confectioners' sugar frostings.

While you can make this with a handheld electric mixer, it is easier to do with a stationary mixer, as the mixer does the work of beating the yolks while you have both hands free to carefully pour the scalding sugar syrup into the eggs. For half batches, however, I use a handheld mixer because my stationary mixer bowl is too big.

Makes about 4 cups

Level of difficulty ★★★

1 cup (7.5 ounces) granulated sugar

2 teaspoons light corn syrup

6 large egg yolks

1 teaspoon vanilla extract, optional

4 sticks (1 pound) unsalted butter, softened

1. In a 1-quart saucepan, combine the sugar and corn syrup with ⅓ cup water and bring it to a simmer, stirring. Wash down the sides of the pan with a pastry brush dipped in cold water. Boil the sugar syrup without stirring until it reaches the soft ball stage, or 236° to 238°F on a candy thermometer.

2. When the syrup reaches 230°, start to beat the egg yolks with a stationary mixer fitted with the whip attachment on medium speed, and beat until light. Leave the machine running on the lowest speed.

3. When the syrup is at the right temperature, with the machine running on medium speed, pour it over the egg yolks, alongside an interior edge of the mixing bowl. Keep your eye on this point as you pour so the sugar syrup gets absorbed by the yolks. You can't pour the hot sugar in the center of the moving beaters because it will splatter against the sides of the mixing bowl and you'll waste about half the sugar. Continue to beat until the outside of the mixing bowl feels lukewarm.

4. At this stage, add the vanilla, if using, and beat in the butter, about 2 tablespoons at a time, adding another batch of butter to the eggs only after the first batch has been absorbed.

5. Use the buttercream right away or, if it is too soft, chill it in the refrigerator until it is of the right spreading consistency.

CHOCOLATE FRENCH BUTTERCREAM

Omit the vanilla. Fold into the finished buttercream 8 to 12 ounces melted and cooled semisweet or bittersweet chocolate.

PRALINE FRENCH BUTTERCREAM

Fold ⅓ cup praline paste (page 27) into the finished buttercream.

Quick Buttercreams

If you look at cookbooks from the 1960s and 1970s, you will find a number of recipes for "quick buttercreams" made by blending butter with confectioners' sugar, flavorings, and raw egg yolks, which give the buttercream a velvety unctuousness. Because of the risk of salmonella poisoning, however, we can no longer eat these quick buttercreams. It is thus useful to know how to make the old-fashioned buttercreams, which are safe to eat because the eggs are cooked by the scalding sugar syrup.

GIANDUJA FRENCH BUTTERCREAM

Make the chocolate buttercream with 6 ounces bittersweet chocolate and fold in ¼ to ⅓ cup (or to taste) praline paste (page 27).

COFFEE FRENCH BUTTERCREAM

Omit the vanilla. Fold into the finished buttercream 1 tablespoon instant espresso coffee powder dissolved in 1½ teaspoons hot water.

MOCHA FRENCH BUTTERCREAM

Make the coffee buttercream and fold into it 4 ounces melted and cooled semisweet or bittersweet chocolate.

ORANGE FRENCH BUTTERCREAM

Omit the vanilla and substitute 1 teaspoon orange extract or ¼ to ½ teaspoon orange oil. If you wish, add 2 teaspoons Grand Marnier or Cointreau as well.

PASTRY CREAM BUTTERCREAM

Mix, by weight, 2 parts of any of the classic French buttercreams above with 1 part of the Vanilla Pastry Cream, chocolate variation (page 322), or Italian Meringue Buttercream (page 308).

STORAGE: Store in the refrigerator, wrapped airtight, for up to 10 days, or in the freezer for up to 3 months. Let the buttercream come to room temperature and rewhip it for a few minutes with an electric mixer to get it to the right consistency before spreading.

About Boiled Sugar Syrups

Complicated, classically formed buttercreams and mousselike fillings are made with a boiled sugar syrup. To make a boiled sugar syrup, it is essential that you know how to properly execute the technique and what the texture and quality of the syrup should be, along with its correct temperature.

Sugar dissolves when you combine it with water. When you cook this solution, the water begins to evaporate and the sugar begins to concentrate, forming a syrup that changes in nature and thickness depending on the temperature. The more the water evaporates, the more concentrated and thicker the syrup becomes, and the harder the sugar is when it has cooled and set. The danger, when forming and boiling a sugar syrup, however, is the possibility of recrystallization when a single undissolved sugar crystal comes into contact with the rest of the syrup, transforming the smooth syrup into a lumpy, grainy mess.

There are precautions you can take, however. First, cook the syrup in a scrupulously clean pot. Add a pinch of cream of tartar or a drop of lemon juice to the sugar syrup before it comes to a boil. These acids cause a chemical reaction that helps prevent the sugar from crystallizing. Stir the sugar with a wooden spoon, or swirl the pot as the sugar dissolves in the water over heat to make sure no crystals are sneakily sticking to the bottom of the pot.

As you stir, make sure the sugar is entirely dissolved before you bring the syrup to a boil. You may throw undissolved sugar crystals against the sides of the pot while stirring, which could come into contact with the syrup and recrystallize the sugar. To prevent this from happening, wash down the insides of the pot several times during the boiling process with a pastry brush dipped in cold water.

There are two ways to determine the correct temperature of the sugar syrup: with a candy thermometer, or by feeling the texture and consistency of the sugar syrup. To do this with a candy thermometer, however, you need to be cooking enough sugar so that you have a deep enough mass in which the tip of the thermometer can be immersed. If you are boiling small quantities of sugar syrup, as we often do in this book, you need to learn to gauge how hot the syrup is by feeling its texture with your fingers. French pastry chefs feel the sugar by first dipping their fingertips in ice water, then pinching a drop of boiling sugar syrup and squeezing it between the fingers. Believe it or not, this really works and you don't feel the heat, provided you work fast enough. Even though I know how to do this, I am not recommending that you do it at home, because you could burn yourself. The other way to gauge by feel is to get a measuring cup of ice water ready along with a clean spoon. Dip the tip of the spoon in the sugar syrup, then immediately dip the spoon into the ice water and press the sugar (which cools instantly) from the spoon between your fingertips. This cooled piece of sugar will feel anywhere from an imperceptible thread to a crackling sharp shard, depending on how hot it was when you removed it from the pot.

The last tip you should know is that it takes a while for the sugar syrup to reach its first thread stage, but after that it passes quickly from one stage to another. This means you can walk away from the sugar syrup for a few moments at the beginning of cooking, but once it has reached the critical thread stage, keep a close eye on it.

Boiled Sugar Chart

Thread stage (230° to 234°F):

It is called the thread stage because, when you drop some of the sugar syrup into a bowl of ice water and press it between your fingers, which you then pull apart, the syrup forms a thin thread. Used for candies and syrups.

Soft ball stage (235° to 240°F):

This is the stage to know about for this book, because it is what I use almost exclusively to make buttercreams, fudge icings, and mousses. When you drop some of the sugar syrup into a bowl of ice water, it forms a mass you can squish between your fingertips into a soft ball shape.

Firm ball stage (245° to 250°F):

When you drop some of the sugar syrup into a bowl of ice water, it forms a firm mass you can still press between your fingertips, although the sugar is much firmer. Used for candies like soft caramels.

Hard ball stage (250° to 266°F):

When you drop some of the sugar syrup into a bowl of ice water and press it between your fingertips, it forms a hard ball. Used for hard candies.

Soft crack stage (280° to 290°F):

When you drop some of the sugar syrup into a bowl of ice water, it forms a crackling thread that has some flexibility and is pale yellow in color.

Hard crack stage (305° to 310°F):

When you drop some of the sugar syrup into a bowl of ice water, it forms a brittle thread that is golden in color. Used for coating candies.

Caramel (320° to 350°F):

The water has evaporated, the sugar ranges from a deep golden to dark brown, steam rises from the pot, and the sugar is hard like glass when it cools. Take care when you boil sugar to this stage because it burns easily.

Linda Dann's Swiss Meringue Buttercream

This is my favorite buttercream, and I thank Linda Dann for it. It is as light as an Italian meringue buttercream but so much easier to prepare that even a novice baker can make it. It has a delightful flavor and the perfect texture to use for piping.

Makes about 5 cups

Level of difficulty ★★

1 cup (7.5 ounces) granulated sugar

1 cup (7 to 8 large) egg whites, at room temperature

4 sticks (1 pound) unsalted butter, softened

6 ounces semisweet chocolate, melted and cooled

2 ounces unsweetened chocolate, melted and cooled

1. Combine the sugar and egg whites in a large bowl. Set the bowl over a saucepan of simmering water, and stir continuously with a whisk for several minutes, or until very hot to the touch (about 140°F on an instant-read thermometer).

2. Transfer the mixture to the bowl of a stationary mixer. With the whip attachment, beat the mixture on medium-low speed for about 1 minute, then increase the speed to high and whip for several minutes longer, or until cool and at least doubled in volume.

3. Turn the speed down to low and add tablespoon-size pieces of the softened butter while continuing to beat. When you begin to add the butter, the mixture deflates and at some point looks like cottage cheese. By the time all the butter is in, however, the buttercream is velvety smooth once again.

4. With a rubber spatula, fold in the two types of chocolate, then return the bowl to the mixer and beat for a few seconds longer, or until smooth and fluffy.

MOCHA SWISS MERINGUE BUTTERCREAM

Add to the chocolate buttercream 1 to 2 tablespoons instant espresso coffee powder dissolved in 2 teaspoons hot water.

STORAGE: Keep refrigerated for up to 3 days or in the freezer for up to 2 months. Let the buttercream come back to room temperature, then rewhip it for a few moments before using.

Italian Meringue Filling

An Italian meringue, known in America as "boiled icing," is made by beating a cooked sugar syrup into whipped egg whites. The function of the sugar syrup is to stabilize the meringue so it won't lose volume and shape over time, and it makes the meringue safe to eat because the heat of the sugar syrup cooks the egg whites. In European pastry kitchens, an Italian meringue is used primarily as one element in other preparations such as buttercreams and mousses, but occasionally you'll see it used as a filling or frosting, as Americans use boiled icing.

Makes about 5 cups
Level of difficulty ★★★

1⅓ cups (10 ounces) granulated sugar

1 tablespoon light corn syrup

5 large (5 ounces) egg whites, at room temperature

1. In a 2-quart saucepan, combine about ¾ of the sugar with the corn syrup and ½ cup water and bring to a simmer, stirring. Wash down the insides of the pan with a pastry brush dipped in cold water. Let the sugar syrup cook undisturbed until it reaches 238°F on a candy thermometer.
2. When the syrup reaches 220°, start to beat the egg whites with the remaining sugar in a stationary mixer fitted with the whip attachment, and beat until soft peaks form.
3. When the syrup is at the right temperature, start to rewhip the egg whites until peaked again and slowly, alongside one inside edge of the mixing bowl, drizzle the hot sugar syrup into the egg whites with the machine running. (Don't dump the hot sugar syrup into the middle of the egg whites with the machine running, or the syrup will splatter against the sides of the bowl.) Whip on medium speed until the mixture is tepid and the outside of the mixing bowl feels lukewarm.
4. Take care not to overbeat the meringue, or it will lose its billowy quality.

Italian Meringue Buttercream

This is a wonderful buttercream, especially valued for its pale ivory hue, perfect on wedding cakes. It is also prized because of its texture, which is lighter than that of a classic French buttercream. When you add the butter to the whipped egg whites, they will deflate and look curdled, but they will smooth out eventually when all the butter has been incorporated.

Makes about 4 cups
Level of difficulty ★ ★ ★

4 sticks less 2 tablespoons (15 ounces) unsalted butter, softened

Italian Meringue (page 308), freshly made and still in the mixer

Replace the whip attachment with the paddle attachment and beat the softened butter, 1 tablespoon at a time, into the meringue.

CHOCOLATE ITALIAN MERINGUE BUTTERCREAM

Add 8 ounces melted and cooled semisweet chocolate to the finished buttercream.

STORAGE: Store in the refrigerator, wrapped airtight in plastic, for up to 1 week or in the freezer for up to 1 month. Bring the buttercream to room temperature and rewhip it for a few minutes in an electric mixer to get it back to the right spreading consistency before using it.

Beginner's Chocolate Buttercream

This is the easiest and fastest buttercream to prepare because it entails zero cooking. You can double the recipe if need be.

Makes about 1½ cups
Level of difficulty ★

1 stick (4 ounces) unsalted butter, softened

½ cup confectioners' sugar, sifted

6 ounces semisweet or bittersweet chocolate, melted and cooled

2 teaspoons instant espresso coffee powder dissolved in 2 teaspoons water

With the electric mixer on low speed, cream the butter with the confectioners' sugar until fluffy, about 3 minutes. Fold in the chocolate and coffee, and beat until uniform in color.

Dione Lucas's Chocolate Buttercream

This recipe was adapted from one found in Dione Lucas's Cordon Bleu Cookbook, *and it is the only recipe I have seen for a buttercream made entirely with corn syrup rather than with a mixture of sugar and corn syrup. I am surmising that Dione Lucas was trying to duplicate at home a method used in French professional pastry kitchens whereby an already prepared sugar syrup, made with glucose, is heated up and poured into the yolks and blended with butter. She substituted for the prepared sugar syrup a corn syrup, which is more easily available to the home cook. Because this is far less sweet than buttercreams made with sugar, it works best when you add something else sweet, like melted semisweet chocolate or praline paste, to the mix.*

Makes about 2½ cups
Level of difficulty ★★★

---

4 large egg yolks

¾ cup light corn syrup

2½ sticks (10 ounces) unsalted butter, softened

6 ounces semisweet, milk, or white chocolate, melted and cooled

---

1. In a stationary mixer, whip the egg yolks until light. In a heavy 1-quart saucepan, bring the corn syrup to a simmer, stirring. Wash down the sides of the pan with a pastry brush dipped in cold water. Boil the syrup without stirring until it reaches the soft ball stage, or 236°F on a candy thermometer.
2. When the syrup reaches 230°, start beating the egg yolks again. With the machine running, when the syrup is at the right temperature, pour it into the egg yolks alongside one interior edge of the mixing bowl, and beat until the mixture is light, fluffy, lemon colored, and tepid.
3. Gradually beat in the butter, then the chocolate. Use the buttercream right away or, if too soft, chill in the refrigerator until it is of the right spreading consistency.

GIANDUJA

Add ⅓ cup praline paste (page 27) to the finished buttercream.

CHOCOLATE MOUSSELINE BUTTERCREAM

Fold into this recipe, ½ recipe for Vanilla Pastry Cream, chocolate variation (page 322).

COFFEE BUTTERCREAM

Make the syrup with ½ cup corn syrup and ¼ cup sugar. Omit the chocolate and fold in 2 teaspoons instant espresso coffee powder dissolved in 1 teaspoon very hot water.

STORAGE: Store in the refrigerator, wrapped airtight, for up to 10 days, or in the freezer for up to 3 months. Before spreading the buttercream on the cake, let it come to room temperature and rewhip it for a few minutes to get it back to the right consistency.

Custard Chocolate Buttercream

This buttercream, a lot easier to make than any of the cooked sugar syrup buttercreams, is unusual because it is fashioned out of a thickened custard sauce, melted chocolate, and softened butter. Its texture is a lot less dense than that of other buttercreams and will be appealing to those who think classic buttercreams taste too much of, well . . . butter! It is the perfect consistency to use as a filling for sponge, angel food, jelly roll, and meringue-style cakes, as well as rich enough to use as an icing for flourless nut tortes.

Makes about 2 cups
Level of difficulty ★★

---

1 cup milk

½ cup (3.75 ounces) granulated sugar

3 large egg yolks

1 tablespoon cornstarch

3 ounces semisweet chocolate, melted and cooled

2 sticks (8 ounces) unsalted butter, softened

---

1. In a small saucepan, combine the milk with ¼ cup of the sugar. Over low heat, bring the mixture to a simmer, stirring.
2. Meanwhile, in a mixing bowl, whisk the remaining ¼ cup sugar with the egg yolks and cornstarch. When the milk is at a simmer, drizzle it into the yolk mixture, whisking constantly.
3. When all the milk has been added to the yolks, return the mixture to the saucepan. Over low heat, whisking constantly, bring the mixture to a simmer and cook for about 1 minute, making sure to stir into the corners of the saucepan so that the custard does not scorch. When done, the custard will be very thick.
4. Remove the custard from the heat and, with an electric mixer on low speed, beat the custard until you can't see any more steam rising from its surface, and it feels warm to the touch. Beat in the chocolate, then the softened butter, 1 tablespoon at a time. Refrigerate the buttercream until it is firm enough to spread.

STORAGE: Store in the refrigerator, wrapped airtight, for up to 2 days.

Boiled Icing

Boiled icing is an American version of Italian meringue. There are two stages to making a proper boiled sugar icing: The first is to create a sugar syrup that is brought to the right temperature; the second is to whip egg whites until they are stiff but not overwhipped. You will be most successful if you have a stationary mixer so you can tend to the sugar syrup as the machine whips the egg whites.

Makes about 6 cups

Level of difficulty ★★★

---

1 generous cup (8 ounces) granulated sugar

2 tablespoons (1 ounce) light corn syrup

4 large egg whites

1 teaspoon vanilla or other flavored extract, optional

---

1. Set aside 2 tablespoons of the sugar. In a heavy 1-quart saucepan, over low heat, bring the remaining sugar, ½ cup water, and the corn syrup to a boil, stirring.
2. Dip a pastry brush in cold water and brush down the sides of the pan a few times to dissolve any sugar crystals. Let the syrup come to 200°F on a candy thermometer without stirring.
3. When the syrup is at that temperature, lower the heat and begin to whip the egg whites until they are semistiff. Gradually, with the machine running, add the reserved 2 tablespoons of sugar, and beat until the whites form soft peaks. Set the machine to its lowest speed and return to the sugar syrup.
4. Increase the heat under the syrup and let it reach 238° on a candy thermometer. Turn the electric mixer to medium speed to rewhip the whites. With the machine running, slowly pour the hot syrup into the egg whites alongside one interior point of the mixing bowl. (If you pour the syrup into the center of the bowl, where the syrup hits the beaters, it will splatter against the sides of the mixing bowl rather than be integrated into the egg whites.)
5. Once all the syrup is incorporated, continue to beat for 2 to 3 minutes, or until the icing is thick and glossy, forms stiff peaks, and is warm to the touch. With a rubber spatula, fold the vanilla, if using, into the icing and let it cool to room temperature. When you spread the icing on the cake, create characteristic swirls by making small circles with the back of a spoon, using a light touch.

CHOCOLATE BOILED ICING

Fold 2.5 ounces melted and cooled unsweetened chocolate into the finished icing.

ZEBRA BOILED ICING

Make the boiled icing and set half of it aside. To the other half add 1 ounce melted and cooled unsweetened chocolate. *Very minimally* blend the white and dark icings together; they will blend more into each other as you spread the icing on the cake.

COCONUT BOILED ICING

Fold ¾ cup grated coconut (fresh or packaged) into the icing and sprinkle more coconut on the top and sides of the cake after icing it.

OLD-FASHIONED MARSHMALLOW ICING

Sprinkle 2 teaspoons powdered unflavored gelatin over 2 tablespoons cold water set in a small skillet or saucepan. Over very low heat, stirring, melt the gelatin in the water until liquefied. Add the liquefied gelatin to the icing right after you add the hot syrup to the egg whites. Continue to whip, and use while warm.

Seven-Minute Icing

This is almost identical to a boiled icing but easier to make. The trick to the success of this recipe is to continue to beat the icing after it comes off the heat until it has cooled to room temperature. If you don't, the icing will collapse as it cools. Beat the icing with an electric mixer, because your arm will fall off if you beat it by hand!

Makes about 4 cups
Level of difficulty ★★

---

1 cup (7.5 ounces) granulated sugar

¼ teaspoon cream of tartar

2 large egg whites

½ teaspoon vanilla or other flavored extract

---

1. In a large mixing bowl, combine the sugar, ¼ cup water, the cream of tartar, and egg whites, and beat until blended with an electric handheld mixer on low speed.
2. Set the bowl with the egg whites over a saucepan of simmering water, making sure the bottom of the bowl does not come in direct contact with the water below. Beat the mixture with the electric mixer on medium speed for 7 minutes, until it is fluffy, glossy, and forms peaks.
3. Remove the bowl from the heat, add the vanilla, and continue to beat with the electric mixer until the icing is cool, thick, and glossy (it is easier to whip if you transfer the icing to a stationary mixer).
4. Spread the icing immediately, or it will develop a crust.

ORANGE SEVEN-MINUTE ICING

Proceed as above but substitute ¼ cup freshly squeezed orange juice for the water and ½ teaspoon freshly grated orange zest for the vanilla extract.

Chocolate Mousse Filling

I long for the days when chocolate mousse was easy and fast to make because it consisted simply of whipped egg whites or whipped cream blended into a mixture of egg yolk and melted chocolate. Now, of course, raw eggs are verboten *because people are terrified of salmonella poisoning. Today, to be on the safe side, I make chocolate mousse and mousse fillings the classic, professional French way—that is, with a base known as* pâte à bombe, *in which the eggs are cooked by the heat of a scalding sugar syrup. The pâte à bombe base is then blended into melted and cooled chocolate and folded into whipped cream. Unfortunately, this is not so easy to make and is a bit time-consuming as well. The key to success, however, is to have all three elements—pâte à bombe, melted chocolate, and whipped cream—at about the same temperature so that they form a smooth homogeneous mass when folded together. If the chocolate or pâte à bombe is too hot, the whipped cream deflates. Conversely, if the whipped cream is too cold, it causes the chocolate to seize into flecks, and the mousse will be grainy. (See Note.)*

Makes about 3½ cups

Level of difficulty ★ ★ ★

---

1 cup plus 2 tablespoons heavy cream

½ cup (3.75 ounces) granulated sugar

1 teaspoon light corn syrup

1 large egg

4 large egg yolks

10 ounces bittersweet or semisweet chocolate, melted and cooled

---

1. In a chilled bowl, with a chilled whisk or chilled beaters, begin to whip the cream, with the electric mixer on low, then on medium speed, until it is almost whipped and holds soft peaks. Set it aside.
2. In a heavy 1-quart saucepan, combine the sugar with the corn syrup and ¼ cup water and bring to a simmer, stirring. Wash down the sides of the pan with a pastry brush dipped in cold water. Boil the sugar syrup without stirring until it reaches the soft ball stage, or 236° to 238°F on a candy thermometer.
3. When the syrup reaches 230°, start to beat the egg and egg yolks with a stationary mixer fitted with the whip attachment, until light and lemon colored.
4. When the syrup is at the right temperature, with the machine running, pour the hot sugar syrup, alongside one inside edge of the mixing bowl, into the egg yolks, and whip until the mixture is light, fluffy, lemon colored, and tepid.
5. If the whipped cream has deflated somewhat, rewhip it until it holds soft peaks again, then fold ½ into the chocolate and the other ½ into the egg mixture. Fold the two mixtures together until homogeneously combined.

MILK CHOCOLATE MOUSSE

Substitute 6 ounces milk chocolate and 4 ounces semisweet chocolate for the bittersweet chocolate.

STORAGE: If made in advance, keep refrigerated in a covered bowl for up to 2 days.

NOTE: For a filling that has many of the qualities of chocolate mousse, although it is denser yet easier to make than this one, try the filling for the Coach House Chocolate Cake (page 268). It makes about 5 cups of mousse and can be made with white or milk chocolate in place of the bittersweet chocolate.

White Chocolate Mousse Filling

A white chocolate mousse is a bit harder to make than a dark chocolate one because white chocolate has a tendency to seize when it comes into contact with another ingredient. To compensate for this tendency, I blend the melted chocolate with melted butter and warm cream first, then add some liquefied gelatin to give the mousse more body. It is important to cool the mixture over ice before you fold in the whipped cream, or the whipped cream will deflate.

Makes about 6 cups
Level of difficulty ★★★

---

8 ounces white chocolate, finely chopped

1 stick (4 ounces) unsalted butter, cut into 1-inch chunks

3 cups heavy cream

1 envelope unflavored powdered gelatin

---

1. In a mixing bowl or the top of a double boiler set over simmering water, combine the white chocolate with the butter, and melt it, stirring. Remove from the heat and set aside. Bring 1 cup of the heavy cream to a simmer and whisk it into the butter and chocolate.

2. Set ¼ cup water in a small saucepan over low heat. Sprinkle the gelatin over the water and stir it until the gelatin is liquefied. Whisk this into the warm cream and white chocolate.

3. Set the bowl of white chocolate mixture in a larger bowl filled with crushed ice and, every now and then, stir the mixture with a rubber spatula until it is cool to the touch yet still fluid.

4. In a chilled bowl, with a chilled whisk or chilled beaters, begin to whip the remaining 2 cups cream with the mixer on low, then on medium speed, until the cream holds firm peaks.

5. In four additions, with a rubber spatula, fold the cooled white chocolate and butter into the whipped cream. Chill for 1 to 2 hours, or until of spreading consistency.

STORAGE: If made in advance, keep in the refrigerator, in a covered bowl, for up to 2 days.

Raspberry Mousse Filling

Raspberry is one of the few fruit flavors I love with dark chocolate. This raspberry mousse filling is a simple purée of raspberries thickened with gelatin and folded into whipped cream. It is the perfect filling for jelly roll–style cakes.

Makes about 4 cups

Level of difficulty ★★★

1 envelope unflavored powdered gelatin

1 package (12 ounces) individually quick frozen raspberries, thawed

¾ cup (5.5 ounces) granulated sugar

2 cups heavy cream

1. Set ¼ cup cold water in a small saucepan, sprinkle the gelatin on top, and let it soften.

2. In a blender or food processor, purée the raspberries with 2 to 3 tablespoons water, then pass the purée through a strainer and discard the seeds. Combine the raspberries and sugar in a medium saucepan and bring to a simmer over low heat, stirring. Also over low heat, stir the gelatin until it is liquefied.

3. When the raspberries are at a simmer, remove them from the heat, pour in the liquefied gelatin, and mix until blended. Transfer the mixture to a clean bowl. Set the bowl over crushed ice and stir every now and then with a rubber spatula until the mixture is at room temperature.

4. In a chilled bowl, with a chilled whisk or chilled beaters, begin to whip the cream with the electric mixer on low, then on medium speed until the cream is almost whipped and holding soft peaks. Set it aside in the refrigerator.

5. When the raspberry purée is cool, rewhip the cream until it forms stiff peaks. Begin by folding a quarter of the raspberry purée into the whipped cream, then keep on adding a little bit more of the purée as you fold it into the whipped cream. Refrigerate for at least 4 hours or, preferably, overnight.

PASSION FRUIT OR MANGO MOUSSE FILLING

Substitute 2 cups thawed frozen passion fruit purée or mango purée for the raspberries.

STORAGE: If made in advance, keep refrigerated in a covered bowl for up to 2 days.

Chocolate Sabayon Mousse

A sabayon is an alcohol-flavored egg yolk and sugar combination whipped over heat into a frothy mass and usually served as a dessert on its own or with fruit. Here, the sabayon is stabilized with gelatin, then blended with melted chocolate and whipped cream and turned into a mousse filling. It is especially lovely in sponge, biscuit, and jelly roll cakes. If you happen to make more than you need as a filling, serve the extra as a mousse, spooned into wineglasses, with butter cookies on the side.

Makes about 4 cups
Level of difficulty ★★

¼ cup brandy

1 envelope unflavored powdered gelatin

5 large egg yolks

½ cup (3.75 ounces) granulated sugar

½ cup brandy or dark rum

4 ounces semisweet chocolate, melted and cooled

2 cups heavy cream, chilled

1. Set the ¼ cup of brandy in a small saucepan. Sprinkle the gelatin over the brandy and set aside.
2. In a mixing bowl, with a whisk, blend the yolks with the sugar and the ½ cup of brandy. Place the bowl over a saucepan of barely simmering water (making sure the bottom of the bowl does not come in contact with the water below) and, preferably with a handheld electric mixer on medium speed, whip the mixture for about 5 minutes, or until it becomes thick and feels hot to the touch.
3. Remove the bowl from the heat and fold in the melted chocolate. Set the saucepan with the gelatin over very low heat and stir for a few seconds until the granules are dissolved and mixture is liquefied. With a rubber spatula, fold this into the egg yolk and chocolate base. Set the bowl over crushed ice and stir every now and then with a rubber spatula until the mixture is at room temperature.
4. Whip the cream until it forms softly firm peaks. Fold about ¼ of the whipped cream into the base and fold this lightened mixture back into the remaining whipped cream. Continue to fold until the mixture is homogeneous. Refrigerate for 15 minutes, or until firm enough to spread.

STORAGE: If made in advance, keep refrigerated in a covered bowl for up to 2 days.

Whipped Cream

There isn't another accompaniment that tastes quite as delicious with chocolate cake as does whipped cream. While plain whipped cream is superb, you should try some of the flavored variations as well. How much sugar to add to the whipped cream depends on your palate as well as the sweetness of the cake itself.

Makes about 4 cups

Level of difficulty ★

2 cups chilled heavy cream, preferably not ultrapasteurized

⅓ to ½ cup confectioners' sugar, sifted

1 to 2 teaspoons vanilla extract

1. In a chilled bowl, with a chilled whisk or chilled beaters, begin to whip the cream with the electric mixer on low, then on medium speed, until it begins to hold its shape and is ¾ whipped.
2. Sift the confectioners' sugar over the cream, add the vanilla, and beat for a few seconds longer, or until the cream forms soft billowy peaks. (If the mixture looks grainy, you have overwhipped it.)
3. Chill the whipped cream in the bowl until serving time. If it deflates, rewhip it for a few seconds in the machine, or by hand with a whisk.

COCOA WHIPPED CREAM

Omit the vanilla extract. Increase the confectioners' sugar to ¾ cup and sift 2 tablespoons unsweetened cocoa powder into the sugar before adding it to the whipped cream.

COFFEE WHIPPED CREAM

Eliminate the vanilla extract. Dissolve 2 teaspoons instant espresso coffee powder in 1 teaspoon hot water and cool. Increase the confectioners' sugar to ¾ cup and add the dissolved coffee at the point when you would add the vanilla.

MOCHA WHIPPED CREAM

Eliminate the vanilla extract. Dissolve 2 teaspoons instant espresso coffee powder in 1 teaspoon hot water and cool. Increase the confectioners' sugar to ¾ cup and sift 2 tablespoons unsweetened cocoa powder into the sugar before adding it to the whipped cream. Add the dissolved coffee at the point where you would add the vanilla.

CHOCOLATE MALTED WHIPPED CREAM

Omit the vanilla extract. Decrease the confectioners' sugar to ¼ cup. After the cream is ½ whipped, add 1 cup chocolate-flavored, sweetened malted milk powder and continue to whip until the cream is stiff.

SPICED WHIPPED CREAM

Stir ¼ to ½ teaspoon ground spice, such as allspice, cinnamon, cardamom, coriander, or ginger, into the confectioner's sugar before adding it to the whipped cream.

SPIRITED WHIPPED CREAM

After the cream is whipped, and just before serving, fold in 2 to 3 tablespoons dark rum, Grand Marnier, cognac, crème de cacao, Tia Maria, or any other alcohol you wish. Serve immediately, as the added liquid deflates the cream rather rapidly.

A Note on Whipping Cream

While making whipped cream is easy, there are a couple of precautions you should take so you don't overwhip the cream and turn it into butter. Remember that it is always better to underwhip heavy cream than to overwhip it. With a few swift strokes of a whisk, you can bring back a whipped cream that has deflated, but overbeaten whipped cream can't be saved. Properly whipped cream is soft and billowy, not stiff or grainy. One way of ensuring you don't overwhip the cream is to start off with a chilled bowl and chilled beaters (you can even set them in the freezer for a bit before you begin) and to stop whipping when the cream looks puffy but as if it still could stand more whipping.

Stabilized Whipped Cream

If you want to use whipped cream as a filling or frosting for your cakes, it will hold up better if you stabilize it first with gelatin. Because there is a residual graininess in a sta-bilized whipped cream, I like to camouflage this texture by sprinkling chopped nuts or shaved chocolate over the top and around the sides of the cake once it is frosted.

Makes about 4 cups

Level of difficulty ★

¼ cup cold water, milk, or coffee

2 teaspoons unflavored powdered gelatin

2 cups chilled heavy cream, preferably not ultrapasteurized

½ cup confectioners' sugar, sifted

1 teaspoon vanilla extract, optional

1. Set the water in a small skillet and sprinkle the gelatin over the top. Let the mixture stand until thickened, about 1 minute, then set the skillet over low heat and stir just long enough for the gelatin to liquefy. Remove from the heat and set aside.

2. In a chilled bowl with chilled beaters, begin to whip the cream with the electric mixer on low, then on medium speed, until the cream begins to form soft peaks. Sift the sugar over the cream and beat until it is ¾ whipped and holds soft peaks.

3. Remove 1 cup of the whipped cream to another bowl and quickly fold the liquefied gelatin into it, then fold this back into the remaining whipped cream. Fold in the vanilla extract, if using, and chill 10 minutes before spreading. Use right away.

Whipped Ganache

This works as both filling and frosting. It is different from an ordinary ganache in that you beat the chilled heavy cream and chocolate mixture as you would whipped cream. It is, however, far more intense in chocolate taste and holds its shape longer than does a cocoa-flavored whipped cream. The trick to this filling is to get it cold enough to whip yet not so cold that it seizes up. You should also take care to whip long enough to incorporate air, yet not so long that the mixture turns grainy.

Makes about 3 cups

Level of difficulty ★★

---

8 ounces bittersweet, milk, or white chocolate, finely chopped

2 cups heavy cream, preferably not ultrapasteurized

---

1. Set the chocolate in a medium bowl. In a saucepan, over medium heat, bring the cream barely to a simmer, and pour it over the chocolate. Let the mixture stand for 30 seconds, then whisk the ingredients together until homogenized. The best way to get this to the right temperature is to set the bowl in a larger bowl filled with crushed ice and whisk every now and then until the mixture is cold.

2. With an electric mixer on low speed, whip the mixture until it becomes a little lighter in texture, then increase the speed to medium and whip until the color turns light and the mixture holds soft peaks. If the ganache is not whipping properly, you may have to refrigerate it until it gets cold enough.

3. Refrigerate the whipped ganache for 15 minutes before spreading it on your cake.

STORAGE: It is best to make this on the day you use it as frosting or filling, or it will be too hard to spread.

Vanilla Pastry Cream

Pastry cream is a filling that is familiar to eclair-lovers, and it is terrific in chocolate cakes as well. It is made with egg yolks, so I recommend you eat anything made with it within 2 to 3 days. If you like a lighter version, fold 1 cup of whipped cream into the finished pastry cream.

Makes about 3 cups
Level of difficulty ★

---

2 cups milk

½ cup (3.75 ounces) granulated sugar

½ vanilla bean, split in half lengthwise

4 large egg yolks

6 tablespoons (1.5 ounces) cornstarch

½ stick (2 ounces) unsalted butter, cut into 4 chunks

---

1. Combine the milk with ¼ cup of the sugar in a 3-quart nonreactive saucepan. Scrape the vanilla seeds into the milk and add the emptied vanilla pod as well. Slowly bring the milk to a simmer over low heat, stirring.

2. Meanwhile, combine the remaining ¼ cup sugar with the egg yolks and beat with a whisk until thick, then fold in the cornstarch. Slowly pour the hot milk into the yolk mixture, whisking all the while. Strain the mixture back into the saucepan and bring it to a boil, stirring constantly so it doesn't stick to the bottom of the pan. When the mixture comes to a boil, it will thicken. After it comes to a boil, cook it for exactly 2 minutes over low heat, whisking continuously and reaching into the corners of the saucepan where the pastry cream tends to stick and burn.

3. Transfer the mixture to a clean bowl or to the bowl of a stationary mixer fitted with the paddle attachment. Beat for a few minutes, until no more steam rises from the surface of the pastry cream. Then beat in the butter, 1 tablespoon at a time, and refrigerate the cream with a piece of plastic wrap set directly on the surface so that it doesn't form a skin.

CHOCOLATE PASTRY CREAM

Omit the butter. Add 2 to 4 ounces of melted and cooled bittersweet or semisweet chocolate to the finished pastry cream.

COFFEE PASTRY CREAM

Omit the vanilla. Dissolve 1 tablespoon of instant espresso coffee powder in 1 tablespoon of very hot water and add this to the finished pastry cream.

MOCHA PASTRY CREAM

Add 2 ounces of melted and cooled bittersweet or semisweet chocolate to the coffee pastry cream.

PRALINE PASTRY CREAM

Omit the vanilla. Whisk some of the pastry cream into ⅓ to ½ cup praline paste (page 27), and fold this back into the remaining pastry cream.

GIANDUJA PASTRY CREAM

Add 2 ounces melted and cooled unsweetened chocolate to the praline pastry cream.

STORAGE: Do not make this more than 1 day ahead of using. Keep in the refrigerator, wrapped airtight.

Chocolate Pudding Filling

This is a soft filling, like a pastry cream, which is great in springy sponge and fragile meringue cakes. If you don't add the butter, the filling becomes reasonably low in cholesterol, which makes it a good partner for angel food cakes. Another reason I like it is that the filling is fast and easy to prepare, and, because it is free of eggs, it holds up better at room temperature than an egg-enriched pastry cream does.

Makes about 2½ cups

Level of difficulty ★ ★

¼ cup (1 ounce) cornstarch

1½ cups milk

¾ cup (5.5 ounces) granulated sugar

---

2 ounces semisweet chocolate, very finely chopped

---

2 ounces unsweetened chocolate, very finely chopped

---

2 sticks (8 ounces) unsalted butter, softened, optional

---

1. In a small mixing bowl, with a fork or a small whisk, combine the cornstarch with ½ cup of the milk.
2. In a small saucepan over low heat, bring the remaining 1 cup milk to a simmer with the sugar, stirring occasionally so the milk does not boil over. Remove the saucepan from the heat.
3. Whisk the cornstarch and milk again to make sure the cornstarch is dissolved, and add this to the hot milk and sugar mixture. Return the saucepan to the heat and bring to a simmer, whisking continuously. Simmer for 1 minute and remove from the heat. Transfer the pudding to a clean bowl, sprinkle both chocolates over the top, and whisk it into the pudding. With a rubber spatula, fold in the softened butter, if using, 1 tablespoon at a time. When all the butter is in, whisk the pudding to make sure it is well blended.

STORAGE: Keep in the refrigerator, wrapped airtight, for up to 2 days. If made in advance, return the filling to room temperature before spreading it on a cake.

Ganache

Ganache *is a French word that refers to a mixture of warm heavy cream blended with chocolate. This is an eternally popular icing because it has unbeatable texture and taste and is so easy to make. The icing tends to be on the thin side, so it may show the bumps and imperfections beneath it, but no one cares very much because it tastes so delicious. Depending on the proportion of heavy cream to chocolate, a ganache can be used as a thick chocolate candy center or as a light airy frosting.*

Makes about 2 cups

Level of difficulty ★

---

8 ounces bittersweet or semisweet chocolate, finely chopped

---

8 ounces heavy cream

---

1. Set the chopped chocolate in a mixing bowl.
2. In a small saucepan over low heat, bring the cream to just under a boil. Remove it from the heat and pour it over the chocolate. Let it stand for 30 seconds. With a rubber spatula, blend the ingredients together beginning from the center and mixing outward, so you don't form bubbles.
3. Let the ganache stand and come to room temperature before using, or cool it in the refrigerator, stirring occasionally, until spreadable.

MOCHA GANACHE

Add 1 tablespoon instant espresso coffee powder to the heavy cream before bringing it to a boil.

MILK CHOCOLATE GANACHE

Substitute 4 ounces milk chocolate for the bittersweet chocolate.

WHITE CHOCOLATE GANACHE

Substitute 10 ounces white chocolate for the bittersweet chocolate.

STORAGE: Keep leftovers for up to 5 days, covered airtight, in the refrigerator. Reheat in a microwave oven or in the top of a double boiler until spreadable but not hot.

Chocolate Water Icing

Linda Dann, of the Culinary Center of New York, shared this recipe, which I then discovered was from Albert Kumin, the legendary pastry chef. This glaze is firmer than a ganache because it is pure melted chocolate thinned slightly with water. It will taste only as good as the chocolate you put into it.

Makes about 1½ cups
Level of difficulty ★

1 pound semisweet or bittersweet chocolate, finely chopped

1 cup minus 1 tablespoon very hot tap water

1. Melt the chocolate in the top of a double boiler or a mixing bowl set over simmering water. Stir occasionally with a rubber spatula until the chocolate is completely melted. Remove it from the heat.
2. Add the hot water and immediately blend with a whisk, beating vigorously. Set the mixture back over the simmering water and finish blending with a wooden spoon until smooth. Use while tepid.

Glossy Chocolate Icing

The cornstarch in the confectioners' sugar gives this icing a sheen that holds even after refrigeration. Because the icing is quite fluid, you should use it to spread very thinly on single-layer cakes, or use it to ice the outside of a Bundt cake.

Makes about 2 cups
Level of difficulty ★

About 1¾ cups (8 ounces) confectioners' sugar

6 to 7 ounces unsweetened chocolate, finely chopped

½ stick (2 ounces) unsalted butter, cut into pieces

1. Sift the sugar into a heavy medium-size saucepan. Gradually whisk in ¾ cup water to make a paste. Bring the mixture to a simmer, remove it from the heat, and add the chocolate. Return the saucepan to the heat and bring the mixture to a boil, whisking; cook for exactly 6 minutes after it comes to a boil.
2. Remove from the heat, whisk in the butter, and transfer the icing to a clean bowl to cool for about 15 minutes, or until warm to the touch and spreadable. Stir the icing occasionally as it cools so that it does not develop a crust.

Midnight Icing

This icing is incredibly easy and quick to prepare and has a lovely smooth texture. Use all bittersweet or semisweet chocolate if you like your icings sweet.

Makes about 1 cup

Level of difficulty ★

1 cup (4.5 ounces) confectioners' sugar
1 tablespoon unsalted butter
2 ounces bittersweet chocolate, finely chopped
2 ounces unsweetened chocolate, finely chopped
1 teaspoon vanilla or other extract, such as orange

1. Sift the confectioners' sugar into a mixing bowl.
2. In a small saucepan, bring ¼ cup water and the butter to a simmer over low heat. Remove from the heat, add the chocolates and vanilla, and stir until smooth.
3. Gradually pour the hot chocolate mixture into the sugar, whisking all the while. If the icing is lumpy, pass it through a strainer. Spread the icing while it is still warm.

Sour Cream Chocolate Icing

This icing has a fabulous tangy taste and closely resembles a ganache in that it is composed of equal proportions of sour cream and chocolate. It is a dream icing to make because it is easy, tastes delicious, and has a fine velvety texture. Because of the sour cream, you must refrigerate all cakes frosted with this icing.

Makes about 1¾ cups

Level of difficulty ★

8 ounces bittersweet chocolate, finely chopped
1 cup (8 ounces) sour cream
1 teaspoon vanilla extract

1. Melt the chocolate in a microwave oven, or in a mixing bowl or the top of a double boiler set over barely simmering water. Transfer the melted chocolate to a clean bowl and cool for 10 minutes.
2. Beat in the sour cream, ¼ cup at a time, then add the vanilla. If the icing is too soft, refrigerate it for 15 minutes, or until firm enough to spread.

Real Fudge Icing

This fudge icing is a glorious American classic, but it is hard to get right. I tried this a dozen times before I figured out how to work with it. The icing, like fudge candy, is made by cooking sugar, milk, and chocolate to 236°F on a candy thermometer and beating it to achieve a fudgelike consistency. The problem is that you have a very small window of opportunity to work with the icing. Too warm, the icing doesn't hold its shape and runs off the cake, but too cool, it seizes up and you'll tear the cake as you spread the icing. Finally I figured out that I just had to divide the hot icing into 2 batches and beat and spread each batch separately. Now this recipe works like a charm, provided you follow the instructions exactly.

Makes about 3 cups
Level of difficulty ★ ★ ★

3 cups (22.5 ounces) granulated sugar

¾ cup milk

2 tablespoons light corn syrup

5 ounces unsweetened chocolate, finely chopped

2 tablespoons (1 ounce) unsalted butter

2 teaspoons vanilla extract

1. In a heavy 4-quart saucepan, combine the sugar with the milk, corn syrup, and chocolate. Over low heat, bring the mixture to a boil, stirring. Once the boil is reached, brush down the sides of the pan with a pastry brush dipped in cold water and don't stir the mixture anymore. Simmer the mixture until it reaches 236° to 238°F on a candy thermometer. (It takes about 10 minutes for the icing to reach the correct temperature.) *Do not let this get hotter than 240°* because the mixture continues to cook after you remove it from the heat, and it becomes unworkable if it gets any hotter.

2. Remove the saucepan from the heat and immediately stir in the butter. Transfer the icing, carefully (it is very hot), to 2 clean bowls, with about ⅓ in one bowl and ⅔ in the other. Cool the smaller batch for about 30 minutes, stirring it occasionally so it does not form a crust.

3. Add 1 teaspoon of vanilla to the smaller batch and begin to beat the mixture with an electric mixer on low speed for a couple of minutes, or until it just begins to lose its gloss and barely holds its shape (if it is too hot, the icing will fall back into the bowl in a puddle when you lift it up with the beaters). Pour the icing over one cake layer and quickly spread it to the edges with an offset spatula. Top the icing with the second cake layer.

4. Add the remaining vanilla to the larger batch of icing and beat the mixture until it is at the right temperature, as described above. At this point, pour the icing around the top edge of the cake so it drips down the sides, then pour it over the top layer. With an offset spatula, spread the icing over the top in one or two motions, then spread it around the sides. Use any remaining icing to patch up bare spots on the sides.

5. If the icing hardens too much, zap it in the microwave oven, at 100% power, at 15-second intervals until it is spreadable again.

REAL FUDGE GLAZE

Cut the recipe in half and use to glaze the top and sides only of a single- or 2-layer cake. After cooling for 45 minutes, beat the glaze for just 2 minutes. It will be quite warm, with a high shine, and pourable. Pour almost all the glaze over the top of the cake and it will slowly roll down the sides. Pour more icing (don't be stingy) right around the edges of the cake so it drips down and covers the sides. With a small offset spatula, spread the icing around the sides wherever there are bare spots, but don't continue working the top.

STORAGE: Cakes covered with this icing can be kept at room temperature for up to 3 days. If you wrap the cake airtight with foil, the icing will become softer over time. After several days, however, the sugar in the frosting reverts to a syrupy state and melts, at which point it's time to refrigerate the cake.

Fudge Caramel Icing

This delicious icing has wonderful undertones of caramel flavor running through the chocolate. A small amount of unsweetened chocolate puts into balance what might otherwise be too sweet an icing.

Makes about 3½ cups

Level of difficulty ★ ★ ★

---

3 cups (22.5 ounces) dark brown sugar

1½ cups heavy cream

---

1 tablespoon light corn syrup

---

2 ounces unsweetened chocolate, finely chopped

½ stick (2 ounces) unsalted butter

---

2 teaspoons vanilla extract

---

1. In a heavy 4-quart saucepan, combine the sugar with the cream and corn syrup and slowly bring the mixture to a simmer, stirring. Add the chocolate. With a pastry brush dipped in cold water, wash down any sugar crystals that form on the sides of the pan.

2. Cook the mixture without stirring until it reaches 236°F on a candy thermometer. Immediately remove the saucepan from the heat and add the butter. Transfer the mixture to a clean bowl and let it cool to 140°, stirring occasionally so a crust does not form. (This will take about an hour and a half). Add the vanilla and set aside about ¼ cup of the icing to use as a decorative element.

3. Beat the icing with an electric mixer (fitted with the paddle attachment, if you have one) on medium speed for about 5 minutes, or until it is at room temperature, begins to lose its shine, and thickens. Quickly spread the icing while still warm. After you have spread the icing on the top layer of the cake, drizzle the reserved amount in a crisscross or checkerboard pattern on top; it will be darker than the part you have beaten, and the patterns created by the different colors is quite lovely.

CARAMEL ICING

Omit the unsweetened chocolate and proceed with the recipe.

FUDGE CARAMEL GLAZE

Add the butter when you add the chocolate and cook to only 234°F. The icing will retain a fluidity and high gloss that is gorgeous.

Chocolate Satin Glaze

I love the brilliant shine of this glaze along with its rich taste, which hints at the flavor of caramel. It is sticky, so it clings readily to the sides of a cake. When you make the glaze, use a saucepan that is large enough so the cream does not boil over.

Makes about 1¼ cups

Level of difficulty ★

¾ cup (5.5 ounces) granulated sugar

¾ cup heavy cream

4 ounces unsweetened chocolate, finely chopped

1 teaspoon vanilla extract

1. In a 2-quart saucepan, combine the sugar with the cream and bring it to a boil, stirring over medium heat. (The mixture is at a boil when large bubbles burst furiously on the surface of the liquid.) Boil the mixture for exactly 2 minutes.
2. Add the chocolate and bring the mixture back to a boil, stirring continuously. Simmer over low heat for 2 minutes longer, stirring occasionally. Remove the saucepan from the heat, add the vanilla, and transfer the glaze to a clean bowl to cool. Stir it occasionally as it is cooling or it will develop a crust.
3. The glaze is ready to spread when it is slightly warm to the touch.

Jurgen's Chocolate Glaze

Jurgen David, an extraordinary young Austrian pastry chef and my instructor at the French Culinary Institute, used this glaze on one of his cakes, and I find it great. What is lovely is that you can halve or double the recipe and it always comes out well. This is a shiny glaze that dulls when refrigerated but comes back to life somehow at room temperature. To create the best finish possible, just like painting your house, you need to "double glaze" the cake. Pour a first coat of glaze over the cake, refrigerate the cake until the glaze hardens, then pour a second coat over the first one.

Makes about 1⅓ cups

Level of difficulty ★

½ pound bittersweet or semisweet chocolate, finely chopped

1 stick (4 ounces) unsalted butter, cut into 1-inch chunks

1 tablespoon light corn syrup

Combine the chocolate, butter, and corn syrup in a mixing bowl or the top of a doubler boiler set over simmering water. Stir occasionally until the ingredients are melted and smooth. Remove it from the heat and transfer it to a liquid measuring cup so you can easily pour it out. Use while still warm and fluid.

Maria's Best Chocolate Glaze

This is what I like best in my mother-in-law's repertoire of chocolate icings and glazes. It has a lovely sheen when just poured. Be sure to cook the glaze for as long as indicated, or it won't have the right consistency.

Makes about 1 cup

Level of difficulty ★

3 tablespoons granulated sugar

4 ounces bittersweet chocolate, finely chopped

2 tablespoons (1 ounce) cold butter, cut into ½-inch pieces

1. In a small saucepan, combine ¼ cup water and the sugar and bring to a simmer over low heat, stirring to dissolve the sugar. Add the chocolate, bring the liquid back to a simmer, and cook over low heat for exactly 5 minutes.
2. Immediately transfer the glaze to a clean bowl and add the butter. Whisk the butter with the chocolate until smooth. Cool thoroughly to room temperature before using, so it is fluid enough to pour yet cool enough to set immediately upon pouring.

MARIA'S MOCHA GLAZE

Substitute for the water an equal amount of double-strength freshly brewed coffee or 1 tablespoon instant espresso coffee powder dissolved in ¼ cup hot water.

White Chocolate Glaze

This glaze is thin and translucent. Because it allows the color and imperfections of the cake underneath to show through, it is best used to drizzle over tube cakes or single-layer cakes.

Makes about 2 cups

Level of difficulty ★

5 ounces white chocolate, finely chopped

¼ cup heavy cream

1 teaspoon corn syrup

1. Place the chocolate in a mixing bowl. Bring the cream and corn syrup to a simmer in a small saucepan over low heat. Pour it over the chocolate and stir, then return the mixture to the saucepan and heat gently until the chocolate is almost melted. Remove the saucepan from the heat and stir until the chocolate is thoroughly melted.
2. Transfer the mixture to a clean bowl and cool it thoroughly to room temperature before using.

Confectioners' Sugar Glaze

It is a bit difficult to come up with a recipe for a glaze you are constantly changing depending on how thick you want it or how much you'll need. What is fun, though, is to experiment with the myriad ways of flavoring the glaze, and I hope you'll try some of the more exotic suggestions.

Makes about 1 cup
Level of difficulty ★

About 1 cup (4.5 ounces) confectioners' sugar, sifted

About 4 teaspoons of liquid, such as lemon or orange juice; double-strength coffee or tea; brandy; rum; cognac; framboise or poire; 4 teaspoons water flavored to taste with drops of citrus oil; anise extract; rose or orange flower water

1. Sift the sugar for a second time into a mixing bowl. Make a well in the center and pour the liquid in the center. With a fork, a small whisk, or a spatula, work the liquid into the confectioners' sugar by gradually mixing the sugar into the center well.

2. Add only enough liquid to achieve the consistency you want. For some cakes you will need a fluid glaze that pours easily, so you will want to keep the glaze loose. For other cakes, you might need to sift in a bit more sugar to get it thick enough to use for piping designs.

PART FOUR

Decorative Techniques

DECORATING WHOLE CAKES

*F*ROM CAREME'S PASTILLAGE constructions of the nineteenth century to the exquisite gum paste flowers and buttercream roses that adorn today's wedding cakes, the work of pastry chefs has always had a decorative, architectural dimension which can sometimes overshadow the importance of flavor.

Sure, my 600 hours in pastry school introduced me to the art of decorating cakes with sugar ribbons and marzipan roses, but that doesn't mean I have mastered this unique and difficult decorative art. In fact, one of the most important lessons I learned was that the artistry, proficiency, and breadth of knowledge exhibited by the likes of a Dieter Schorner or Jacques Torres come from years of practice. They started their careers when they were sixteen years old while I began mine at age fifty, and that means I will never catch up or be as good as they are. But still, my cakes and desserts look glamorous and elegant because I make the best use of the skills I have.

When decorating whole cakes, I stick to techniques I do well, such as using a pure chocolate glaze on a cake and ornamenting it with a bouquet of gorgeous crystallized flowers in the center. I camouflage my imperfect icing technique by patting chopped nuts on the sides and am happy to finish frosted cakes with a simple bottom edging of buttercream rosettes. Remember that a cake decorated with confectioners' sugar dusted through a beautiful stencil is always more elegant than a cake garnished with sloppy-looking buttercream roses.

EQUIPMENT

The list below includes some special items needed specifically for decorating whole cakes, for making chocolate garnishes, or for creating plated desserts. For more detail on items listed but not discussed, see Baking Equipment: Miscellaneous Small Equipment (pages 44–49).

Bench Knife

Cardboard rounds and rectangles

(page 45)

Icing Comb

Nonstick Baking Mats

Paint Brush

Used for painting nuts with gold.

Paper and Plastic Cones

Paper and plastic cones are like pastry bags but are fashioned, in a pinch, out of parchment paper or plastic bags. This is what pastry chefs use for piping out small quantities of icing or for writing in chocolate. The great advantage of these cones is that they are disposable. You can buy parchment paper already cut into triangles for making paper cones, or you can cut a triangle out of a sheet of parchment you already have at home. (To make a paper cone, see page 349, Thin Icings and Paper Cone Designs.)

Pastry Bags, Tips, and Couplers

Serrated Knives

See: Knives (page 41)

Spatulas: Metal, Flat, and Offset

Squeeze Bottles (for plated desserts)

Turntable

If you enjoy cake decorating, you should invest in a heavy-duty turntable, the kind made of a lightweight stainless-steel round that swivels effortlessly on a heavy iron base. This may be more expensive than a cheap plastic one, but it will last you a lifetime. For simple decorative work on single tiers or lightweight cakes, you can get away with a lazy Susan or with holding the cake up to eye level in one hand and decorating it with the other hand.

INGREDIENTS

Below is a list of a few ingredients you should buy only if you are especially interested in cake decorating. Most are available through mail-order catalogues or can be purchased from stores that specialize in baking and cake decorating.

Food Coloring

I use food coloring to tint nonchocolate buttercreams. For frostings and buttercreams, use ordinary liquid food coloring.

Fresh Flowers

Be sure the flowers you crystallize are organic and edible. You can buy fresh edible flowers in gourmet produce stores or order them from the Herb Lady (page 389).

Crystallized Violets and Roses

You can crystallize fresh flowers on your own or buy candied violets and roses from cake-decorating supply houses, mail-order sources, and even from quality gourmet stores. The Herb Lady (page 389) makes and sells gorgeous crystallized flowers; her pansies are especially effective on chocolate cakes.

Gold and Silver Dust

You can use gold and silver dust to gild nuts.

Piping Gel

Piping gel is a clear gel used for writing on cakes. It is great to blend with melted chocolate because it prevents the chocolate from hardening as you pipe it out.

Meringue Powder

Meringue powder should be used instead of fresh egg whites in mixtures that are eaten raw; it is composed of dried egg whites that have been pasteurized so they are safe to eat. I use meringue powder for my crystallized flowers.

BEFORE YOU BEGIN

Planning a good design, knowing a few tricks, and mastering a couple of simple techniques will influence how beautiful your cake looks.

- Plan a design you know you can do successfully.
- Take a look at the suggestions I make and also look at photographs of cakes in other cookbooks.
- Read about the various decorative techniques before you begin.
- Make sure you have the ingredients at the ready, such as frosting, chopped nuts, or chocolate curls, as well as the necessary equipment like cardboard rounds, spatulas, and a turntable.

PLANNING THE DESIGN

Three basic elements come into play when designing a cake: the flavor and texture of the cake itself, the nature of the filling and frosting, and the decorative technique you are going to use. Most of the cakes in this book are planned with a particular design in mind, but should you wish to deviate from what is suggested, bear in mind the following:

- Single-layer cakes are best left plain, or finished with a thin icing or a light dusting of cocoa powder or confectioners' sugar.
- Double- and triple-layer cakes should be matched with a thick frosting or buttercream that camouflages the seams where layers and frosting meet.
- The cake layers should be level.
- The frosting will look better if you apply an undercoat of frosting, known as a "crumb coating," before you apply the topcoat.
- Measure and mark your cakes so that the decorations will be evenly spaced. Find the center of the cake and mark it with a pinprick hole made with a toothpick or metal cake tester. Then, if you want to mark portions with nuts or buttercream rosettes, divide the cake into whatever portions you want and mark these divisions with pinprick holes so you will know exactly where to place the decorations.
- It is easier for the novice cake decorator, with an unsure hand, to design a cake that does not require centered or evenly spaced decorative touches, like piping a trio of buttercream rosettes off-center.
- If you don't have a steady hand, don't pipe rosettes or shells around the top edge of the cake, but instead, pipe them around the bottom edge where they are less visible.
- When decorating with buttercreams, avoid piping out large rosettes on top, because then each person will get a slice of cake with too much frosting.

- If you don't know how to make the frosting look perfectly smooth, then make it look rustic by peaking it with a spatula or the back of a spoon.

- Nuts should be used as decoration only if they are also used in the cake or filling itself, and they must be the same as those already used.

- An ingredient not used in the cake or filling should be used as a decorative element only if it complements the taste of the cake.

- Novices with unsteady hands should think about adorning their cakes with commercially prepared garnishes, such as gold or silver beads, crystallized violets, candied ginger, gum paste flowers, or with shavings of colored chocolate. All these trimmings are available from mail-order catalogues, such as King Arthur's *Baker's Catalogue*, or from cake-decorating supply stores, such as the New York Cake and Baking Distributor (page 390).

HOW TO GLAZE, ICE, FILL, FROST, AND ASSEMBLE CAKES

BEFORE YOU APPLY any icing at all, make sure the cake itself is properly prepared, which means splitting it into layers or trimming the layers so they are level and straight, and brushing off the excess crumbs so they don't get embedded in the icing and make your cake look bumpy.

Cakes are easier to work on and slice through if you set them in the freezer for 5 minutes before you begin, and if you work on a turntable. You will also find it easier to trim and slice a cake with a professional-quality serrated knife.

Single-layer cakes, especially flourless tortes, are often smaller on top than on the bottom, which is fine if you are serving them to family or friends. But for a more finished, polished look, trim the sides with a serrated knife so they are straight.

The top of many a flourless cake can be cracked or sunken in the middle. Leave the cake as is if you are finishing it with a dusting of confectioners' sugar, but if you plan to glaze it, discard the pieces of the cracked top that fall away naturally and invert the cake onto a cardboard round so the flat bottom becomes the top. The new "top" still might sag a bit, but the overall look will be cleaner and the cake will be easier to ice.

It is all right if the top of a layer cake is domed, but you should always trim the interior layers so that when you stack them with filling the cake will be level.

CARDBOARD ROUNDS

Before I even trim the cake or slice it into layers, I set the cake on a rigid cardboard round so I don't risk the cake's breaking in half when I move it. After slicing a cake into two layers, I lift off the top layer with the help of another cardboard round or "cake lifter" (page 45) so it doesn't split apart.

If you are going to finish a cake with a thin glaze, set it on a cardboard round that is the same diameter or a tiny bit smaller than the cake so the icing doesn't pool on the cardboard.

When applying a thick frosting or buttercream, set the cake on a cardboard round that is ¼ inch larger than the diameter of the cake. This way the edge of the cardboard round guides the spatula when you apply the frosting and the sides will be straighter.

Cardboard rounds come in standard cake sizes. To allow for shrinkage of the cake, however, use a round that is one size smaller than the size of your cake pan. This means that for a cake baked in a 9-inch pan, you will need an 8-inch cardboard round.

SLICING THE CAKE INTO LAYERS

Set the cake on a cardboard round and then set it on a turntable or lazy Susan. If you are using a turntable, set a dampened piece of paper towel on the turntable, under the cardboard, so the cake doesn't slide around.

Set one hand, fingers spread open, on top of the cake. Hold the serrated knife with the other hand. Make a shallow cut all around the circumference of the cake to mark where you will split the cake into layers. Then, to slice the cake into even layers, keep the arm holding the knife immobile with the elbow at your waist and turn the turntable with your other hand. While you keep the knife still, keep on turning

the cake, until you have sliced through it. Resist the temptation to saw the cake with your knife.

To line up the cake layers after you frost them, you can first cut a V-shape vertical groove along the side of the cake. After you have frosted the first layer you can stack the second layer over the frosting in such a way that the cutout grooves line up.

APPLYING GLAZE OR THIN ICING

Brush off the cake crumbs. Use a cardboard round cut the same dimension or slightly smaller than the diameter of the cake. Anchor the cake to the cardboard with a dab of jam, corn syrup, or some of the glaze. Then set the cake, on the cardboard, on a wire rack set over a sheet of waxed paper to catch the drips of glaze.

There are two ways I like to spread thin glazes or icings. The first is to apply a thin coating of glaze around the sides of the cake, then pour the glaze over the top and let it drip down the sides. The excess glaze that pours down the sides now has something to adhere to and the sides will be smooth. Another method is to pour the glaze or icing over the top first, spread it across the cake from the center to the edge and over the sides. If necessary touch up the sides with more glaze or icing.

If you want the top of the cake as smooth as glass without showing the marks where the spatula touched the icing, pour the icing all over the top of the cake. Lift up the cake on the cardboard or cake rack on which it is set, and tilt the cake from side to side until the glaze spreads evenly and pours down the sides of the cake.

If you don't have cardboard rounds and must glaze the cake on a serving plate, this is how you do it so the glaze doesn't mess up the serving platter: Cut 4 strips of waxed paper, each about 3 inches wide.

Place them on the serving plate at right angles to each other in a square that is roughly the size of the circumference of the cake. Set the cake on top of the waxed paper strips so that part of the paper is underneath and part outside the cake. When the icing has set, slide the strips out from under the cake. If the bottom of the cake looks raggedy, pat chocolate shavings or ground nuts around the bottom or pipe a tiny border of frosting.

APPLYING THICK FROSTING OR BUTTERCREAM

Trim the cake, slice it into layers, and brush off the excess crumbs. With a dab of frosting, anchor the first cake layer to a cardboard round that is ¼ inch larger than the diameter of the cake. Set the cake on a flat surface, preferably a turntable or lazy Susan. Spread an even layer of frosting on the first layer. Lift the cake to eye level or bend down to judge if the frosting is level. If it is uneven, build up the side or area that needs more frosting so that it is level. Set the second cake layer on the frosting and spread the second layer with frosting, making sure it, too, is even and level. Repeat with a third or fourth layer, if necessary.

At this point, brush off the excess crumbs from the top and sides, then apply the thinnest layer imaginable of frosting or warm jam to "glue" down the excess crumbs. This is called a "crumb coating" and is the undercoat that ensures the topcoat of frosting will be smooth. Refrigerate the cake to set the crumb coating before you apply the topcoat of frosting.

There are a couple of ways you can then apply the topcoat of frosting. The first is to apply a massive amount of frosting to the top of the cake. With a straight or offset spatula spread the frosting across the top so that the excess drops over the sides, then spread the excess frosting around the sides of the cake. The second way is to reverse the order and spread the frosting around the sides of the cake first, then over the top.

If you are filling the cake with one type of icing and spreading the sides and top with another, there is a trick to making sure the inner filling doesn't "bleed" into the outer one. Pipe a ring of the outside frosting around the outside edge of each of the cake layers. Pipe the second frosting or filling inside the ring and stack the layers. Any frosting that pops out the sides will match the frosting on the outside of the cake.

LEVELING AND SMOOTHING THE TOP AND SIDES OF THE FROSTING

To make the top level, use a straight spatula or a ruler that is longer than the diameter of the cake and draw it straight across the top of the frosting in one sweeping level motion. Repeat if necessary to get a flat surface.

To make the frosting around the sides even, keep the spatula parallel and straight as you swivel the turntable. If you are working without a turntable, hold the cake up to eye level with one hand and keep on turning the cake as you spread the frosting with the other hand. Use the straight edges of the cardboard round to keep the frosting straight around the sides.

Sometimes you work the frosting in such a way that it is higher around the sides than the top of the cake. To make it level, pull the frosting from the edge toward the middle, using tiny swift strokes of the spatula. Work all around the outer edge of the cake until the height of the frosting on top and around the sides is the same.

It is often easier for the novice cake decorator to leave the frosting rough than to try to make it smooth. To give the frosting some life, however, make swirls across the cake by moving the convex side of a spoon or by dipping an icing spatula in half circles in the frosting, both across the top and around the sides of the cake. Another way is to make peaks and valleys in the frosting by pressing the top of a metal spatula into the frosting and pulling it up with the spatula.

To give the top and sides of a cake frosted with buttercream a very smooth finish, dip the icing spatula in a container of very hot or boiling water and wipe off the excess water on a towel. Pass the spatula around the sides or over the top of the cake and remove excess frosting from the spatula by scraping it against the inside of the bowl of frosting. Warm the spatula and scrape off the excess frosting each time you pass the spatula around the sides or top of the cake.

If you think the frosting or buttercream is getting too soft, refrigerate the cake and frosting for a few moments and then resume the frosting process.

PUTTING FINISHING TOUCHES ON THE SIDES AND BOTTOM

The sides and bottom of a glazed or frosted cake are hardest to make look neat and finished. This is easily rectified if you are working with a cake that contains some ingredient like nuts or coconut, because you can pat pieces of this ingredient around the sides of the cake and leave the top as is. The best way to do this is to set 1 to 2 cups of ground nuts (depending on how big the cake is) in a bowl or plate. (Nuts ground in a food processor should first be passed through a sieve to get rid of the powdery bits.) Hold the cake up to eye level with one hand and with the other hand pat the nuts against the sides. Do this over the bowl so the nuts that don't adhere to the sides fall back into the bowl and you can reuse them. Do this with icing that has been freshly applied and is moist, or the nuts won't adhere, and really press the nuts into the sides or they won't stick.

Another easy trick is to pat a ¼-inch border of chocolate shavings, curls, or ground nuts just around the bottom edge of the cake where it often looks most ragged.

The sides of cakes finished with thick frostings or buttercreams or whipped cream fillings look terrific if you ridge them with an icing comb. The easiest way to do this is to set the cake on a turntable, set the icing comb parallel to the sides of the cake and, lightly touching the icing, swivel the turntable, keeping the icing comb immobile. You can also striate and ridge the top with the icing comb.

DESIGNING THE DECORATIVE TOUCHES

W HETHER YOU HAVE frosted your cake with ganache or an American sugar icing, you will want to add some decorative touches to give the cake an elegant finished look. A decorative touch can be as simple as a dusting of confectioners' sugar or a cluster of gilded nuts or a bouquet of crystallized flowers. I have outlined below the bare beginnings of what is possible, and I hope these ideas will inspire you to come up with your own.

CONFECTIONERS' SUGAR AND COCOA POWDER DESIGNS

It is more dramatic to decorate dark cakes with a contrasting white confectioners' sugar and light cakes with dark cocoa powder. The best way to apply confectioners' sugar or cocoa powder to a cake is to shake it or force it with a spoon through a triple-meshed sieve.

A pretty effect is achieved by dusting the sugar or cocoa powder over a doily or stencil so the design gets transferred to the top of the cake when you lift up the stencil.

If you don't have a doily or stencil, set 1-inch paper strips perpendicular or crisscrossed across the top of cake at evenly spaced intervals. Dust the cake with sugar or cocoa powder, lift up the strips, and a pretty design will remain on your cake.

GLAZED AND ICED CAKE DESIGNS

Glazed cakes are effectively finished by placing a single element, such as a clump of crystallized flowers or a cluster of chocolate curls, either in the center of the cake or off to one side. They also look good with the sides and top ridged with an icing comb.

If the cake contains nuts, you can apply ground or chopped nuts to the sides, and then set whole or halved nuts around the top edge. For a supremely elegant look, you can first gild the nuts with gold dust (page 337) or dip part of each nut in melted chocolate (this is especially pretty with blanched almonds).

Glazed cakes also look elegant with the top drizzled with chocolate of a contrasting color. You can pipe or drizzle lines back and forth in a random pattern or create a grid effect by piping them in a crisscross pattern. You can do this with a paper cone or by waving a fork dipped in melted chocolate across the top of the cake so the chocolate falls in random drizzles and splashes. The effect is very Jackson Pollock–like!

BUTTERCREAM AND AMERICAN FROSTING DESIGNS

There are oodles of possibilities for designing a cake frosted with a thick icing. The ideas below are just the beginning.

Cakes filled and frosted with one type of icing

- Spread the top and sides with buttercream. Ridge the sides and the top with an icing comb dragged in a straight or wavy pattern.
- If the cake contains ground nuts, pat ground or finely chopped nuts around the sides of the cake and leave the top plain, or pipe a thin border of buttercream rosettes around the bottom edge only.
- Spread the top and sides with buttercream, then ridge the sides with an icing comb and scatter chocolate shavings or tempered chocolate across the top of the cake.
- Spread the top and sides with buttercream or frosting. Keep the sides plain or ridge them with an icing comb. Pipe out one small rosette per portion around the outside edge of the cake. If the cake itself contains nuts, top each of the rosettes with a whole or piece of the type of nut used in the cake.

Cakes filled and finished with two types of icing

- Spread the top and sides of the cake with one type of frosting. Keep the sides plain or ridge them with an icing comb. Pipe the second type of frosting in a border of rosettes or shells on the top or bottom edge of the cake.
- This trick works best with classic buttercreams. Spread the top and sides of the cake with one type of buttercream. Keep the sides plain or ridge them with an icing comb. Fill one side of a pastry bag with one type of buttercream and the other side of the bag with the second buttercream. Pipe a border of two-toned rosettes around the top or bottom edge of the cake. Or pipe a border of rosettes around the bottom edge of the cake and mark each serving by piping a rosette on the outside edge in the middle of the portion.

Cakes filled with buttercream or frosting and iced with ganache or glaze

- Spread the cake layers with buttercream or frosting, glaze the top with ganache, and finish according to any of the ideas for glazed cakes.

- Pat shaved chocolate around the sides of the cake, leaving the top plain.
- Write or pipe out delicate scrolls of melted chocolate in a contrasting hue.
- Glaze or ice the cake and garnish the top with store-bought marzipan fruit.

DESIGNS FOR WHIPPED CREAM OR OTHER FLUFFY FROSTINGS

Cakes frosted with whipped cream or fluffy mousse-like fillings need little else to make them look fabulous because the frosting itself is so luxurious.

- Drag an icing comb around the sides of the cake but leave the top plain.
- Drag an icing comb around the sides of the cake and pipe a border of shells around the bottom edge.
- Pat the sides of the cake with chocolate shavings or chopped nuts, if appropriate.
- Drag an icing comb around the sides of the cake, pipe huge rosettes around the top edge, and fill the center of the top with chocolate shavings or curls.
- Pat the sides of the cake with chocolate shavings, pipe rosettes around the top edge, and fill the center of the cake with chocolate curls, or shavings.

DECORATIVE PIPING

I am not the most adept with a pastry bag so I compensate by decorating my cakes with a minimum of fancy piping. However, even the simplest of piping needs to be executed with care, so you need to know at least the basics of working with a pastry bag or paper cone.

There are two large categories of piping work. The first is done with a pastry bag fitted with an assortment of tips and is best suited to thick frostings and buttercreams. The second is done with a paper cone filled with melted chocolate or fluid icings and is used for writing or for lacy delicate designs.

Thick Frostings and Buttercreams

American confectioners' sugar frostings and French buttercreams are thick enough to hold their shape when piped out of a pastry bag, which is why they are used for creating flowers, rosettes, shells, and borders. I am not going to get into buttercream piped flowers in this book because mastering that art deserves a book of its own. Here I just want to explain how to use the pastry bag effectively so that you are good enough to pipe out well-executed rosettes and other simple shapes.

Pastry Bags

I use a pastry bag fitted with a tip rather than a metal syringe type of decorating tube. A metal syringe tube does not hold enough frosting nor is it as effective or flexible as a pastry bag. The pastry bag of choice is a plastic-lined canvas bag or one made of nylon. I like to use a larger, 16- or 18-inch one because it holds a lot of frosting and I don't have to refill it as often as I do the smaller ones.

Pastry bags have a small hole cut out of the narrow end, which is where you fit the pastry tip. You will need to cut the end more to make it wider so a metal tip will fit into the opening. At home I have at least two of each size pastry bag, because some have larger openings for large tips, and others have smaller openings for small tips.

If you are doing complicated work and need to change tips during the piping process, use a coupler. Drop the coupler into the bag, slip the tip over the coupler, and anchor the tip to the coupler by screwing on the ring. This way, each time you need to change tips, you don't have to empty the bag of frosting; instead, you unscrew the ring and change the tip.

If you need to pipe out just a tiny amount of frosting, use a plastic zippered storage bag. Spoon some frosting in the bag, force it with your fingers down into one of the corners, and cut out an opening in the corner just as you would with a regular pastry bag. Or you can cut out a large enough opening in one of the corners to fit a tip or coupler and then fill the bag with frosting.

HOW TO FILL THE PASTRY BAG Before you begin, fold back the top quarter of the bag to form a cuff. Then, if you wish, set a tip or coupler in the bag, and place the empty bag in a tall container or jar so that the bag is upright and nothing oozes out the bottom. You will also have both hands free to hold and fill the bag. Use a wide rubber spatula to transfer the frosting to the bag. Be careful not to fill the bag more than halfway. Straighten out the cuff and press the frosting down into the bottom of the bag, into the tip. Twist the top of the bag closed. Over a bowl or a piece of waxed paper, press out some frosting to remove the air bubbles and make sure the frosting is flowing out properly. Before you tackle the cake, pipe out a few practice rosettes or other shapes onto a piece of waxed paper.

HOW TO CONTROL THE PASTRY BAG Beginners make the mistake of grabbing the top of the bag with one hand and the middle of the bag with the other. Holding it this way forces the frosting out from both the top and the bottom of the bag, which results in an awful mess. You need to twist the top of the bag closed and hold it closed between your thumb and index finger while the remaining three fingers squeeze out the frosting. The other hand is

HOW TO CONTROL THE PASTRY BAG

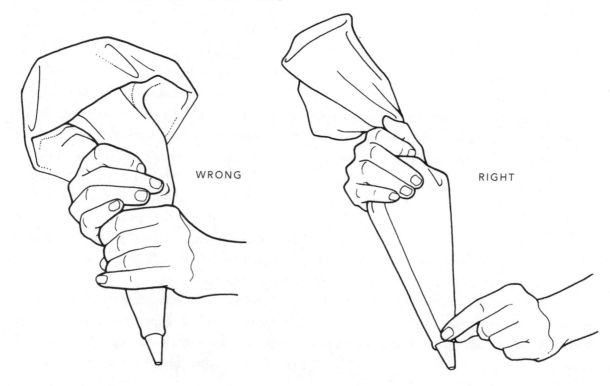

WRONG

RIGHT

placed toward the bottom of the bag and held lightly (no squeezing) to guide and control the tip.

PASTRY TIPS I find that star tips, closed and open, and round tips, each in a variety of widths, are enough for me to create great-looking borders and patterns. There are dozens of other tips from which to choose, most of which are designed for specific types of buttercream flowers.

If you want to experiment with different tips and create a wider variety of patterns, purchase a small set of pastry tips and buy some ready-made frosting with which to practice. Try piping out the different shapes and patterns on waxed paper so you can see what they look like before you apply them to a finished cake.

In deciding how large a tip to select, you must consider the nature of the frosting. If it is a light, airy whipped cream frosting, then use a wide tip; in fact, the larger the tip, the prettier the shape. Buttercream shapes, however, should be kept small or you'll end up with too much buttercream on each portion of cake.

The size of the cake can also determine the type of decorations you use, because a small cake looks out of balance with giant rosettes piped across the top, whereas tiny little stars will get lost on the surface of a multitiered cake.

The shapes, patterns, and borders described below are the easiest and most effective to make. Practice first so you know how the frosting is behaving and so you get into a rhythm. Before you begin, know your design exactly, and know where you'll place the decorations.

Plain or Round Tips. With a plain tip you can squeeze out dots, circles, lines, and ropes; you can use it for scroll work as well as for writing.

Dots: To make dots, hold the bag at a 90° angle, close to the surface of the cake. Squeeze out tiny mounds or dots, and when they are the right size, stop squeezing. With a sharp, clean movement, lift the pastry bag to stop the frosting from coming out.

Lines: Tips with small plain openings are great for writing as well as for piping out elegant thin lines of filigree or swags. The best way to pipe out lines is to hold the bag at a 90° angle to the cake, fairly high up, and let gravity do the work. Basically let the frosting drop from the pastry bag in a line, and when it is the length you want, stop squeezing; lay the line on the cake straight, in a squiggle, or in any pattern you like. If you try to pull on the line of frosting, as if the pastry bag were a pen, the line tends to break.

Star Tips. Star tips come open or closed. The closed one is good for beginners because you simply press out the frosting, but the open tip is more versatile and creates more graceful shapes.

Stars: To pipe out stars, hold the bag at a 90° angle and press the frosting out of the bag. The more frosting you press out, the larger the star will be. When you have the size you want, stop pressing on the bag and pull up quickly. At first you will be left with a tail in the center of the star, but the more adept you become, the smaller these tails will be. You can also knock them down by pressing them into the star.

Rosettes: To pipe out rosettes, use an open star tip, hold the bag at a 90° angle, and begin the rosette slightly off center. Make a spiral shape or circle ending in the center. Stop pressing the frosting, bury the tip in the frosting, and pull up. This motion creates softer, rounder shapes than the closed star tip.

Shells: To pipe out a shell, begin with an open or closed star tip, and hold the bag at a 45° angle to the cake. Press out some frosting to create a mound (the more you squeeze, the larger the size of the shell), then stop pressing as you pull away, straight or to one side. You should be left with a tapered tail of frosting that flows out of the mound.

Curved shells: To pipe out a curved shell, begin the shell as usual, but halfway through shaping it, curve it into a "C" form. To create an "S" out of shells, make one curved shell. Nestle the second shell in the first one by starting it in the tail end of the first shell so that the two shells together form an "S" shape.

Borders: Choose a tip you like. Set the dots or stars contiguous to one another all around the top or bottom edge of the cake. To create overlapping borders, which I think are the prettiest, form a shape you like, such as a dot, star, or shell. Stop squeezing to stop the flow of icing as you pull to one side and toward yourself, creating a small thin tail. Begin the second shape by overlapping it onto the tail of the first shape.

How to Clean Pastry Bags and Tips. Before you put them away, make sure your pastry bags and tips are clean. Press any leftover frosting from the bag into the garbage, turn the bag inside out, and scrub it with hot water and soap. Rinse it thoroughly, turn the bag right side out, and wash the outside. To dry the bag, hang it up or turn the top down to form a cuff and stand it upright on the cuff. With time though, even the best-kept bags begin to smell awful, so replace them.

Rinse the pastry tips in hot water, then soak them in a solution of hot water with a few drops of vinegar. Wash them again with hot water and soap, rinse thoroughly, and dry. For tips with tiny openings, use a tiny brush designed specifically to clean out the pastry tips.

THIN ICINGS AND PAPER CONE DESIGNS

A small quantity of icing or melted chocolate is easier to pipe out of a disposable paper cone than out of a pastry bag fitted with a tip.

How to Make a Paper Cone

Paper cones are fashioned out of triangles of parchment paper. The size of the cone depends on the size of the triangle. You can buy precut triangles measuring 15 × 15 × 21 inches in packages of 100. If you use these infrequently, however, fashion your own paper cone out of a sheet of parchment.

Cut 2 triangles out of a square of parchment (you can try this with waxed paper, but I find it tears too easily). Each triangle becomes a paper cone. The points of the triangle should be A, B, and C (see illustration). Find the midpoint of the longer side of the triangle, which is opposite point A (this midpoint is what eventually will be the point of your finished paper cone). From this midpoint, roll point B so it meets up exactly with point A. You now have shaped a cone on one side of the paper triangle. Wrap the other side of the paper around the first cone so that point C meets up with points A and B. Pull on the points of the paper so that the tip of the cone is sharp and closed. Tape the cone shut (professionals just hold it shut, but I find that if you are inexperienced, you let go of the tension and the paper cone opens up). Tuck the top ends of the paper inside the cone before you fill it.

How to Fill a Paper Cone

Fill a paper cone no more than halfway. Cut out a tiny hole at the tip; the smaller the opening, the more delicate the work will be. If you want to create more complicated piping with a disposable bag, you need to work with a large paper cone, cut out a larger hole, and drop a pastry tip in the cone before you fill it. Once the cone is halfway filled with frosting, fold down the top.

Start with a very small opening at the tip and make some test pipings on waxed paper to gauge if you need a larger opening. You can always cut out more of the tip if you want a thicker line of piping.

HOW TO MAKE A PAPER CONE

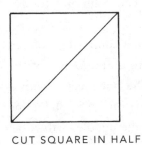

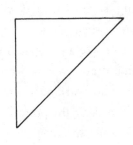

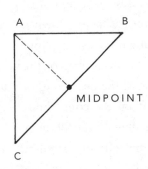

CUT SQUARE IN HALF

MIDPOINT

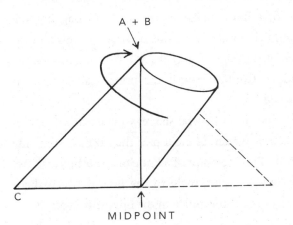

ROLL "B" UP SO IT MEETS WITH "A"

A + B

MIDPOINT

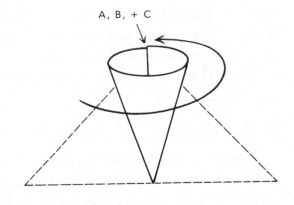

A, B, + C

WRAP "C" AROUND SO IT MEETS
WITH "A" AND "B"

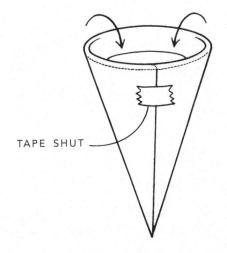

TAPE SHUT

TUCK THE TOP ENDS OF THE PAPER INSIDE BEFORE YOU FILL IT

How to Use a Paper Cone

The best way to control the flow of icing out of a paper cone is to imagine you are laying down a line of icing rather than pressing out frosting. Hold the paper cone at a 90° angle to the surface of the cake. Set the point of the cone at the beginning of where you want to go and lift up the cone about 1 inch above the cake. Gravity will make the filling or melted chocolate flow out of the cone in a straight line. You then lay the line, in the shape you want, on the surface of the cake. Always work so that the paper cone is held above the cake and slightly in front of the line of icing flowing out. Do not pull on the paper cone as if you were writing with a pen or the line of icing will break. Practice first on waxed paper before you tackle the cake.

Line Designs

Designs suitable for melted chocolate or thin icings are a series of tiny dots, scrolls, and, of course, writing. A classic design is a spiderweb, or feathery lines piped across the top of the cake. To do this, first glaze the cake with a chocolate glaze or icing. While the glaze is still tacky, pipe out a contrasting colored icing, such as melted white chocolate or a confectioners' sugar icing.

To make a spiderweb with a contrasting colored icing, draw a spiral beginning in the center of the cake and working toward the outer edge. With a toothpick or the point of a paring knife, pull a line across the spiral, starting in the middle of the cake and ending at the outer edge, as if you were marking a portion. Mark the cake with 6 or 8 lines. In between the first lines, make more lines by dragging the toothpick in the opposite direction, beginning at the outside edge of the cake and working toward the middle. Continue until the entire cake has been marked.

Rather than a spiral shape, you can draw parallel lines of icing across the top of the cake at 1-inch intervals. Pull the point of a knife or a toothpick across the lines at a 90° angle to the line. Between these lines, drag the toothpick in the opposite direction.

PRESENTATION AND THE PLATED DESSERT

A "PLATED DESSERT" IS the term used to describe the way two or three components, such as a slice of cake, a scoop of ice cream, and a round of custard, are presented on a dessert plate. The components aren't just posed on the plate, they are artfully arranged and complemented with additional elements like a zigzag or two of sauce, a spiral of crunchy caramel, or a chocolate butterfly perched on one of the components.

In restaurants, plated desserts have become so elaborate that they become miniature representations of objects, such as Jacques Torres's clever presentation of a cake inside a miniature chocolate stove, complete with chocolate saucepans, each of which contains a sauce. The idea of the plated dessert, novel and stunning at first, has, unfortunately, in many a fancy restaurant become a cliché with the architectural presentation overshadowing the taste of the dessert. Let me quickly reassure you that in this book, no such pastry feats will be required because the presentations are kept simple, are optional, and require no special skill or equipment except perhaps a couple of squeeze bottles.

While mostly a restaurant practice, the plated dessert offers advantages to the home cook as well because it allows bakers who don't have the skill or inclination to decorate a whole cake to come up with a pretty presentation for a slice. The plated dessert idea also allows for pairing additional flavors and textural notes with the cake, in the guise of a sauce, a berry garnish, or a crunchy caramel decoration.

I have divided suggestions for plated dessert presentations into two categories. The first category includes the more elaborate plated dessert ideas designed with a slice of unfrosted cake in mind because the cake itself is so simple. The second category includes the spare plated dessert ideas, designed to complement richly frosted cakes that need no further enriching sauce or garnish. For some cakes, I have also included, right after the recipe itself, a plated dessert idea for that specific cake, whereas for other cakes I refer you back to the more general suggestions outlined below.

Because the plated dessert presentation does involve last-minute work, don't attempt it for more than 6 or 8 servings at a time.

PLATED DESSERT SUGGESTIONS FOR UNFROSTED CAKES

The suggestions below are designed for plain, unfilled single-layer cakes, which benefit most from an enriching element such as whipped cream, a sauce, a moist berry garnish, or ice cream.

Make sure that the flavors of the decorative elements work well with the flavor of the cake itself. Never introduce an element for looks alone.

1. One or two thin sauces or melted ice creams:

   A. Pour or spoon a thin or medium-thick Vanilla Custard Sauce (page 358) or melted ice cream in a shallow bowl. Set a slice of cake in the middle of the sauce and garnish the sauce with Chocolate Shavings (page 380) or Curls (page 380).

   B. Pour or spoon Deadly Delicious Chocolate Sauce (page 362) or melted chocolate

ice cream in the center of a dessert plate. Set a slice of cake in the middle of the sauce and garnish the sauce with dots of a contrasting colored and flavored sauce, such as Raspberry Squeeze Sauce (page 368).

   C. Spoon one sauce on ½ the plate and a second sauce on the other ½. Center the slice of cake in the middle of the two sauces, which will run into each other in an impressionistic way.

2. Two or three heavier sauces:

   Make the sauces thick enough to hold their shape when squeezed on the plate. Make two or three sauces, one of which should be the Deadly Delicious Chocolate Sauce (page 362) or French Caramel Sauce (page 364), the other a contrasting creamy one, harmonious in flavor, such as a Flavored Custard Sauce, orange, mint, or spice variation (page 359).

   A. Center a slice of cake on a dinner-size plate. At random intervals, without touching each other, squeeze decorative dots, circles, or squiggles of sauce around the cake.

   B. Center a slice of cake on a dinner-size plate. Squeeze dots of sauce, of graduating sizes, in a crescent shape on one side of the cake. Spoon or squeeze a contrasting pool of sauce on the other side of the cake.

   C. Squeeze alternating bands of sauces, contiguous to one another, around the outside edge of a dinner-size plate. Set a slice of cake in the middle of the plate. At 1-inch intervals, drag the blunt end of a wooden skewer, pulling from the outer edge of the outside line of sauce through the other 2 or 3 bands of sauce toward the center of the plate. This creates a pretty spidery effect.

D. Squeeze or spoon a pool of chocolate sauce in the center or to one side of a dinner-size plate. Squeeze dots of another sauce, in a circle, on the chocolate sauce. Position the blunt end of a wooden skewer in the middle of one dot and drag it, moving it in a circle, through the center of the other dots so the skewer pulls the dots into heart shapes. Center the slice of cake in the sauce or set it to one side.

E. Pool a thick custard or Deadly Delicious Chocolate Sauce (page 362) in the middle of a dinner-size plate. Squeeze a thin spiral of an alternating sauce over the pool of the first sauce. Drag the blunt end of a wooden skewer, at ½-inch intervals, through the top sauce into the one below, always working in alternate directions, from the outside edge of the plate toward the center or from the center toward the outside. Center the cake in the middle of the sauce.

F. Squeeze a squiggle of plain melted chocolate or chocolate sauce down the center of the plate to divide it in half. Spoon or squeeze a second sauce to the left of the squiggle and a third sauce to the right. Center a slice of cake in the middle of the plate, over the squiggle.

G. Dot the plate with one or more sauces. To create starlike shapes, drag the blunt end of a wooden skewer, at 5 points, from the center of the dot working outward. For a "sunburst" effect, drag the skewer in a curved pattern. You can do this on dots of sauce on the plate or ones that have been squeezed on top of another sauce. Place a slice of cake in the center or to one side of the plate.

H. Make a variety of colorful sauces in contrasting flavors. Cut a plain chocolate pound cake, brownie, or batter cake into an oversized slice, then cut that slice into 3 smaller squares or other shapes. Dot the plate with two or three 2-inch-wide pools of sauce (the same or different types) and center a small piece of cake in the middle of each sauce.

3. Trios of Color:

Make 3 sauces of different colors and place them in squeeze bottles. A contrasting colorful trio that tastes delicious together is Sour Cream Sauce (page 370), Raspberry Squeeze Sauce (page 368), and Deadly Delicious Chocolate Sauce (page 362).

For all the following patterns, set the slice of cake in the middle of a 10-inch plate.

A. Squeeze the 3 sauces in alternating colored dots around the outside edge of the plate. Run the blunt end of a wooden skewer around the plate, through the center of each dot, so they run into each other forming heart shapes.

B. Randomly squeeze the 3 sauces into different-size dots or circles.

C. In a pattern, or randomly, squeeze large dots of 3 sauces around the plate. Squeeze smaller dots of another color sauce in the center of the larger ones to create multicolored bull's-eye patterns.

4. Fruit Sauces and Fruit:

Cheesecakes, coconut cakes, or white chocolate cakes work best with the following ideas.

A. Choose 2 or 3 different-colored, fruit-flavored sauces (or 2 fruit and 1 sour cream sauce) and create some of the same effects described in Trios of Color.

B. Set a slice of cake to one side or in the middle of a large plate. Spoon or squeeze a pool of fruit sauce next to or underneath the cake. Center a clump of a tiny dice of fresh fruit in the center of the sauce, and set a mint leaf in the middle of the fruit.

PLATED DESSERT SUGGESTIONS FOR FROSTED CAKES

What makes these plated dessert presentations different from those for unfrosted cakes is that they are meant as pure decoration, not as a way to add more flavor or texture.

To help you speed up the service of the dessert, you can decorate the plates in advance and keep them lined up on a counter. When you are ready to serve dessert, cut the cake and center a slice in the middle of each of the decorated plates.

1. Decorating with melted chocolate and chocolate shavings:

   Use melted chocolate in a paper cone to pipe out decorations. The opening at the bottom of the cone should be as small as possible so the designs will be thin and elegant. Use an oversized dinner plate.

   A. Pipe out squiggles, dots of the same or different sizes, or write out names or sayings around the outside edge of a plate.

   B. Pipe the outline of a tree with branches or outlines of balloons or butterflies. With a squeeze bottle, fill in the spaces with 1 or 2 fruit sauces of different colors.

C. Strew chocolate shavings (using whatever type of chocolate you prefer) around a slice of cake.

2. Decorating the plate with powdered cocoa or confectioners' sugar:

   Spoon confectioners' sugar into a sieve and, with a spoon, tap the sieve so the sugar is dusted evenly over the surface of the plate. This is so that the cocoa powder you dust over the sugar will have something to cling to and won't move.

   A. Lay strips of paper in a pattern (diagonals, crisscross, or some other way) over the plate. Dust the plate evenly with cocoa powder by tapping it with a spoon through a fine-meshed sieve. Carefully remove the strips of paper.

   B. Lay a stencil over the confectioners' sugar and dust cocoa powder over the stencil. Carefully lift up the stencil and the design will have been transferred to the plate.

   C. Lay a fork and spoon, upside down, in a crisscross pattern on the plate. Dust cocoa powder over the plate, then carefully remove them. The outline of the fork and spoon will be transferred to the plate.

3. Decorating with fruit:

   A Cut colorful fruit that matches the flavor of the cake into uniform dice no larger than ½ inch. Center the slice of cake on the plate and strew the dice of fruit around the slice. Some fruits are best left whole or sliced. Good fruits to use as decorative elements include rounds of kiwi; a dice of mango or passion fruit; whole raspberries or blueberries; whole, sliced, or cubed strawberries; slices of star fruit; or pomegranate seeds. You can complement the dice of fruit with tiny dots of fruit sauce as well. Avoid fruits like apples that discolor and are too hard to complement the texture of the cake.

B. Make a strawberry flower, which is a technique that works especially well with individually portioned chocolate cakes. Remove the stems and cut the strawberries (preferably of about the same size) into ¼-inch slices. Make a circle of the slices of strawberry in the middle of the plate, leaving a hollow space in the circle where the cake will go. Place the strawberries so the points face toward the outside of the plate. Pose the slice of cake over the strawberries with the strawberry points peaking out from underneath. Pipe some whipped cream in the center of the cake, and set the tip or point of a whole strawberry in the middle of the whipped cream.

4. Decorating with caramel, nut brittle, or crystallized flowers:

A Strew broken-up Shards of Caramel (page 374) or nut brittle on the plate, around the slice of cake.

B. Crystallize mint, roses, or other organic leaves or flower petals. Strew the whole leaves or petals on the plate around the slice of cake, or break up the flowers first and scatter the pieces around the cake.

SAUCES

Vanilla Custard Sauce (Crème Anglaise)

A crème anglaise *is a French custard sauce, usually spooned over cakes, fruit, or other desserts. In France, the sauce is made with milk, but I prefer it with cream so that it is thicker and richer. You can create a thinner sauce, as I explain below. Be sure you make the sauce in a nonreactive saucepan, or it might turn a gray or greenish hue. There are myriad ways of flavoring this sauce, which will you will see as you read on. Because of the yolks, the sauce is highly perishable and should be eaten within 2 days.*

Makes about 2¼ cups

Level of difficulty ★ ★ ★

6 egg yolks
2 cups heavy cream
½ cup (3.75 ounces) granulated sugar
One 2-inch length vanilla bean, split in two (see Note), *or* 2 teaspoons vanilla extract

1. Before you begin, set a clean stainless-steel or other nonreactive bowl, with a strainer over it, into a larger bowl filled with crushed ice. Place the egg yolks in a second stainless-steel bowl.
2. Combine the cream and sugar in a nonreactive 9-inch skillet or shallow saucepan. With the tip of a paring knife, scrape the vanilla seeds out of the pod into the cream. Add the vanilla pod to the cream, then set the saucepan over low heat and bring the cream to just under a boil, stirring occasionally with a heatproof rubber spatula or spoon.
3. When the cream is hot, stir the yolks with a rubber spatula to mix them, then add the hot cream, by tablespoonfuls, stirring continuously so the yolks don't scramble. When ½ the cream has been incorporated, stir the warmed egg yolks back into the saucepan and return it to low heat.
4. Cook the sauce, stirring continuously, for about 2 minutes, or until the mixture thickens and steam begins to lift from the surface of the sauce (the temperature will register about 150°F on an instant-read thermometer).
5. Immediately pour the sauce through the strainer into the clean bowl set over ice and cool for 5 minutes. Set a piece of plastic wrap directly on the surface of the sauce so it does not develop a skin, and refrigerate until ready to use. If you are using vanilla extract, stir it into the sauce right before refrigerating it.

MEDIUM-THICK SAUCE

Substitute light cream for the heavy cream.

THIN SAUCE

Substitute milk for the heavy cream.

THICK SAUCE FOR PLATED DESSERTS

Reduce the amount of cream to 1 cup. This sauce is thick enough to hold its shape on a plate when drizzled out of a squeeze bottle.

STORAGE: Keep in the refrigerator in a covered glass jar for up to 2 days.

NOTE: You can rinse the vanilla pod after cooking, air-dry it, and stick it in a jar of granulated or superfine sugar to make vanilla sugar.

Flavored Custard Sauces

What I love about flavored custard sauces is that they give me a way of pairing chocolate cake with unexpected spices and seasonings without imposing those exotic combinations on anyone who doesn't choose to accompany their piece of cake with the sauce.

You can flavor custard sauces in a variety of ways, and the suggestions below are only the tip of the iceberg. There are two methods of imparting flavor to these sauces: by adding flavorings to the finished sauce or by infusing the cream first with seasonings and then making the sauce with the infused cream. When you add flavorings to the finished sauce, begin with the smallest amount and add more as you go, because you can't take out what you have already incorporated.

1 recipe Vanilla Custard Sauce (page 358)

TO FLAVOR THE FINISHED SAUCE

CHOCOLATE: Simmer the heavy cream with 3 tablespoons of cocoa powder and use ¾ cup (5.5 ounces) sugar instead of ½ cup.

COFFEE: Add to the finished sauce: ¾ to 1 teaspoon instant espresso coffee powder dissolved in 1 teaspoon hot water.

CUMIN: Add ½ to ¾ teaspoon ground cumin to the finished sauce. You can add a drop of rose water or orange flower water to the sauce as well. This is delicious with warm flourless chocolate cakes.

FLORAL: Add to the finished sauce: ¼ to ½ teaspoon rose water, orange flower water, or Fiori di Sicilia. It is available through King Arthur's *Baker's Catalogue* (page 390).

ORANGE: Add ½ to 1 teaspoon orange extract to the finished sauce.

PEPPERED: Simmer the cream with 2 teaspoons cracked black peppercorns in addition to the vanilla bean. This is delicious with plain chocolate pound cakes.

PRALINE: Whisk 3 tablespoons praline paste (page 27) into the finished sauce.

SAFFRON: Simmer the cream with 1 teaspoon saffron threads instead of the vanilla bean. This is delicious with coconut cakes.

SPICE: Add to the finished sauce: ¾ to 1 teaspoon ground cardamom or cinnamon, or ¼ teaspoon ground nutmeg or allspice.

SPIRITED: Add to the finished sauce: 2½ to 3 tablespoons alcoholic flavoring of choice, such as brandy, cognac, or dark rum. If you want a sweet alcoholic flavoring like amaretto or Grand Marnier, add 2 tablespoons of the liqueur along with 1 tablespoon of brandy or cognac to cut the sweetness.

continued on next page

Flavored Custard Sauces

continued from previous page

TO FLAVOR THE SAUCE BY INFUSION

Combine the cream with any one of the following ingredients and bring it to a simmer, remove the saucepan from the heat, and transfer the cream to a clean bowl. Refrigerate, covered, for 24 hours before making the custard sauce with the infused cream.

CINNAMON: Simmer the cream with 2 to 3 cinnamon sticks. Remove the sticks before finishing the custard sauce.

GINGER: Simmer the cream with 1 tablespoon finely minced fresh ginger. Strain out the ginger before finishing the custard sauce.

MINT: Simmer the cream with 1 cup chopped fresh mint leaves and stems. Strain out the leaves and stems before finishing the custard sauce.

MIXED SPICE: Simmer the cream with ¼ cup pickling or mulling spice. Strain out the spice before finishing the custard sauce.

SZECHUAN PEPPER: Simmer the cream with 1 tablespoon cracked Szechuan peppercorns. Strain out the peppercorns before finishing the custard sauce.

TEA: Simmer the cream with ¼ cup loose tea leaves. Strain out the tea leaves before finishing the custard sauce.

Stabilized Custard Sauce

This is a little easier to make than the classic Vanilla Custard Sauce (page 358) because it is stabilized with cornstarch. For ways to flavor this sauce, see all the variations for the Vanilla Custard Sauce.

Makes about 2 cups

Level of difficulty ★★

---

4 large egg yolks

2 cups milk

2 teaspoons cornstarch

⅓ cup (2.5 ounces) granulated sugar

2 teaspoons vanilla extract or alcoholic flavoring of choice

---

1. Before you begin, set a clean stainless-steel or other nonreactive bowl into a larger one filled with crushed ice and set a strainer over the mixing bowl. Place the egg yolks in a second stainless-steel bowl of 1-quart capacity.
2. Pour the milk into a heavy, nonreactive 1-quart saucepan and slowly bring it to a simmer over low heat.
3. Meanwhile, with a rubber spatula, break up the yolks and blend them with the cornstarch and sugar. When the milk is hot, drizzle it by tablespoonfuls into the yolks, stirring the yolks continuously with the spatula so they don't scramble. When ½ the milk is in, pour the rest into the yolks in a steady stream, continuing to stir.
4. Return the mixture to the saucepan and cook over low heat, stirring continuously for about 2 minutes, or until the mixture thickens, steam just begins to lift from the sauce, and the temperature registers 150°F on an instant-read thermometer.
5. Immediately pour the sauce through the strainer into the clean bowl set over ice and cool it for 5 minutes. Stir in vanilla. Set a piece of plastic wrap flush on the surface of the sauce so it does not develop a skin. Refrigerate until ready to use.

STORAGE: Keep in a covered glass jar in the refrigerator, for up to 2 days.

**Deadly Delicious Chocolate Sauce

There is hardly a cake that does not benefit from a spoonful or two of this delicious sauce. It's the sauce I used to make at Restaurant Luna for our ice cream sundaes, and it's the one of choice to use in squeeze bottles for plated desserts.

Makes about 1½ cups

Level of difficulty ★

½ cup milk

½ cup heavy cream

3 tablespoons sugar

5 ounces bittersweet chocolate, finely chopped

1 tablespoon unsalted butter, optional

1. In a small saucepan, combine the milk, cream, and sugar and slowly bring the mixture to a boil, stirring occasionally.
2. Remove the saucepan from the heat, add the chocolate, and stir until the chocolate is almost melted. Return the saucepan to the heat and bring the sauce to a simmer, stirring occasionally. Remove the pan from the heat and strain the sauce into a clean bowl. Cool for 20 minutes. If you like a shiny sauce, whisk in the butter.
3. Serve the sauce warm or at room temperature.

STORAGE: Keep in a covered glass jar in the refrigerator for up to 5 days, but bring it back to room temperature, or warm it in a double boiler or microwave oven, before serving.

Orange Juice Custard Sauce

This is marvelous with any of the plainer chocolate pound cakes.

Makes about 1½ cups

Level of difficulty ★ ★ ★

1 cup orange juice

1 teaspoon freshly grated orange zest

¾ cup (5.5 ounces) granulated sugar

2 large eggs

1. Before you begin, set a strainer over a stainless-steel mixing bowl. In a heavy, nonreactive 1-quart saucepan, combine the orange juice with the orange zest and ½ cup of the sugar and bring to a simmer, stirring, over low heat.
2. When the juice is hot, remove it from the heat. Whisk the eggs with the remaining ¼ cup sugar. Slowly drizzle the hot juice into the eggs, stirring continuously with a whisk so the eggs don't scramble.
3. Return the mixture to the saucepan and cook over low heat, stirring continuously with a heat-resistant rubber spatula or wooden spoon, until the mixture thickens and steam begins to lift from the surface of the sauce. (The temperature will register about 150°F on an instant-read thermometer.)
4. Immediately pour the sauce through the strainer into the clean bowl and cool for 5 minutes. Set a piece of plastic wrap flush on the surface of the sauce so it does not develop a skin, and refrigerate until ready to use.

STORAGE: Keep in the refrigerator in a covered glass jar up to 2 days.

**Bourbon Sauce

This voluptuous, delicate sauce is absolutely addictive. It is similar to a custard sauce but thicker.

Makes about 1¼ cups
Level of difficulty ★ ★ ★

---

4 egg yolks

---

1 cup heavy cream

½ cup (3.75 ounces) granulated sugar

---

2 tablespoons bourbon or whiskey

---

1. Before you begin, set a clean stainless-steel or other nonreactive bowl, with a strainer set over it, into a larger bowl filled with crushed ice. Place the egg yolks in a second stainless-steel bowl of about 1-quart capacity.

2. Combine the cream and 6 tablespoons of the sugar in a heavy, nonreactive 1-quart saucepan. Over low heat, bring the mixture to a simmer, stirring. When the cream is hot, remove it from the heat. Whisk the yolks with the remaining 2 tablespoons sugar and the bourbon. Drizzle the hot cream, by tablespoonfuls, into the yolks, stirring continuously with a whisk so the yolks don't scramble. When ½ the cream has been incorporated, pour the remaining cream into the yolks a little bit faster, still stirring continuously.

3. Return the mixture to the saucepan and cook it over low heat, stirring continuously with a wooden spoon or heat-resistant rubber spatula, for about 2 minutes, or until the mixture thickens and steam begins to lift from the surface of the sauce. (The temperature will register about 150°F on an instant-read thermometer.)

4. Immediately pour the sauce through the strainer into the clean bowl set over ice and cool for 5 minutes, stirring occasionally. Set a piece of plastic wrap flush on the surface of the sauce so it does not develop a skin, and refrigerate until ready to use.

STORAGE: Because of the eggs, keep this in the refrigerator in a covered glass jar for no longer than 2 days.

French Caramel Sauce

Makes about 1½ cups

Level of difficulty ★ ★ ★

1 cup (7.5 ounces) granulated sugar

1 teaspoon fresh lemon juice

¾ cup heavy cream

¼ cup milk

1. In a heavy 3-quart saucepan, combine the sugar, ¼ cup water, and the lemon juice and bring to a boil, stirring. Wash down the insides of the saucepan with a pastry brush dipped in water to dissolve any sugar crystals.
2. Cook the syrup over low heat, without stirring, to the caramel stage, about 320°F on a candy thermometer, or until it looks golden brown and smells of caramel.
3. Remove the saucepan from the heat and let the caramel cool for a couple of minutes while you bring the cream to a simmer in another saucepan.
4. Slowly, averting your face, add the hot cream to the caramel. The sauce will bubble up furiously. Return the saucepan to low heat and stir until it is smooth. Remove the sauce from the heat, transfer it to a clean stainless-steel bowl, and add the milk. If you are not going to use this right away, cool it down to room temperature before storing it in the refrigerator.

STORAGE: Keep refrigerated in a covered glass jar for up to 1 week. If you want to serve this warm, reheat the sauce in a double boiler or in a microwave oven.

Butterscotch Sauce

This is close to, although not as refined in taste as, the French Caramel Sauce (page 364), but it is faster and easier to prepare.

Makes about 1½ cups

Level of difficulty ★

1 stick (4 ounces) unsalted butter, cut into 1-inch pieces

1 cup heavy cream

1¼ cups packed (9.5 ounces) dark brown sugar

In a 2-quart saucepan, cook the butter over low heat, stirring, until it begins to turn brown and emits a lovely nutty aroma. Add the cream and sugar and bring to a simmer, stirring. After the sauce comes to a simmer, cook it over low heat, stirring occasionally, for 5 to 6 minutes, or until it is syrupy and thick. Remove the sauce from the heat and skim off the foam that forms on top. Cool to room temperature.

STORAGE: Keep refrigerated in a covered glass jar for up to 1 week. Before using, reheat in a double boiler or in a microwave oven until fluid and warm.

Grand Marnier Sauce

I particularly like this glorious sauce as a change from the Orange Juice Custard Sauce (page 362) I usually serve with chocolate cake. It has a translucent quality and tastes delicious served either cold or at room temperature.

Makes 2 cups

Level of difficulty ★

---

1 teaspoon freshly grated orange zest

---

1 cup orange juice, preferably freshly squeezed

½ cup (3.75 ounces) granulated sugar

¼ cup Grand Marnier, Cointreau, or Triple Sec

---

1 tablespoon cornstarch

---

1. In a nonreactive saucepan, combine the orange zest, juice, sugar, and ½ cup water and bring it to a boil over medium heat, stirring. Reduce the heat, add the Grand Marnier, and bring the sauce back to a boil.
2. Combine the cornstarch and 1 tablespoon water with a fork and drizzle it into the sauce. Whisking occasionally, bring the sauce up to a boil again and simmer for 30 seconds, or until lightly thickened. Remove it from the heat, cool to room temperature, and refrigerate.

STORAGE: Keep refrigerated in a covered glass jar for up to 1 week.

Fresh Mango Sauce

This delicious sauce is easy to make and looks quite spectacular on the plate. It is especially pleasing with white chocolate cakes, which need some tartness to balance their sweetness.

Makes about 2 cups

Level of difficulty ★

---

2 medium (about 14 ounces each) mangos, peeled and diced (1½ cups diced)

---

1 tablespoon fresh lemon juice

---

3 tablespoons light corn syrup

In a blender, purée the mangos with the lemon juice, ½ cup water, and the corn syrup. If the sauce is too thick, slowly add more water until you like the consistency or add more corn syrup if you want a sweeter sauce.

STORAGE: Keep refrigerated in a covered glass jar for up to 3 days.

Canned Mango Sauce

Makes about 1 cup

Level of difficulty ★

1 cup sweetened mango pulp
(Indian brand Alphonso)

1 tablespoon lemon juice or
vodka

Blend the mango pulp with the lemon juice or vodka and add enough warm water to achieve the consistency you like (1 tablespoon or so).

STORAGE: Keep refrigerated in a covered glass jar for up to 3 days.

Passion Fruit Sauce

I adore the flavor of passion fruit and have always been frustrated that professional pastry chefs had frozen passion fruit purée available to them whereas ordinary home cooks did not. Lo and behold, I have discovered a similar frozen purée in my local Hispanic market. This product is a bit thinner than the professional product I was used to, so I thicken it with egg yolks.

Makes about 1⅔ cups

Level of difficulty ★

3 large egg yolks

1½ cups thawed frozen passion
fruit purée

¼ cup granulated sugar

1. Before you begin, set a clean stainless-steel or other nonreactive bowl in a larger one filled with crushed ice. Set a strainer over the empty bowl. Place the egg yolks in a second stainless-steel bowl of about 1-quart capacity.
2. Pour the passion fruit purée, ¼ cup water, and the sugar into a heavy, nonreactive 1-quart saucepan. Set the saucepan over medium heat and stir occasionally as the liquid comes to a simmer.
3. Meanwhile, stir the yolks with a rubber spatula. When the passion fruit liquid is hot, drizzle it, by tablespoonfuls, into the yolks as you continue to stir so the yolks don't scramble. When ½ the liquid is in, pour in the rest more rapidly, stirring.
4. Return the mixture to the saucepan and cook over low heat, stirring continuously, for about 2 minutes, or until the mixture thickens, steam just begins to lift from the surface of the sauce, and the temperature registers about 150°F on an instant-read thermometer.
5. Immediately pour the sauce through the strainer into the clean bowl set over ice and cool for 5 minutes. Set a piece of plastic wrap flush on the surface of the sauce so it does not develop a skin. Refrigerate until ready to use.

STORAGE: Keep refrigerated in a covered glass jar for no longer than 2 days.

Pink Pear Sauce

This sauce is from my book Cooking the Nouvelle Cuisine in America *(New York: Workman Publishing, 1978). You must use Comice pears, available only in fall and early winter, because they are the juiciest and most aromatic.*

Makes about 2 cups

Level of difficulty ★

1 cup red wine, such as a Beaujolais

⅓ cup (2.5 ounces) granulated sugar

3 medium (1½ pounds) Comice pears

¼ stick (1 ounce) unsalted butter

1. In a nonreactive saucepan, combine the wine, ½ cup water, and the sugar and bring to a boil, stirring. While this is coming to a boil, peel, core, and cut the pears into eighths.
2. When the liquid is at a boil, add the pears, reduce the heat, and simmer, partially covered, for 7 to 10 minutes, or until the pears are tender but not falling apart.
3. With a slotted spoon, remove the pears from the syrup and transfer them to the bowl of a food processor or blender. Over medium heat, boil the wine poaching liquid down until only ⅓ to ¼ cup remains (it will look dark and glossy at this point), 3 to 5 minutes, and remove it from the heat.
4. Meanwhile, purée the pears with the butter until smooth, and transfer the purée to a clean bowl. Stir the reduced wine syrup into the purée and serve warm.

STORAGE: Keep in the refrigerator, covered, for up to 1 week. Before using, reheat in a double boiler until hot.

Raspberry Squeeze Sauce

Modern pastry chefs would be lost without their squeeze bottles filled with colorful sauces, which they use to decorate their plates as an artist uses her paints. Professionals have available to them an extraordinary array of wonderfully and sometimes exotically flavored frozen fruit purées from which they fashion not only sorbets but sauces as well. I have discovered, however, that the ordinary home baker is not without resources. Under your nose, in your supermarket, you have the vehicle from which to produce a raspberry sauce with a texture and weight that's perfect for decorating the plate. Don't add anything to the purée or you won't achieve the perfect texture for a squeeze sauce.

Makes about 1 cup
Level of difficulty ★

1 package (10 ounces) frozen raspberries in syrup, thawed

Purée the raspberries with their syrup in a blender. Strain the sauce through a sieve and transfer to a squeeze bottle.

STORAGE: Keep in the refrigerator in a covered glass jar for no longer than 1 week. After that, the purée will start to ferment.

Apricot Squeeze Sauce

It doesn't matter that the flavor of the canned apricots is not as fine as that of dried apricots, because this sauce is meant to be used as a decorative element only in plated dessert presentations.

Makes about 1 cup
Level of difficulty ★

1 pound canned apricots, packed in syrup

Purée the apricots with some of their syrup until you achieve a consistency that allows the sauce to hold its shape when squeezed on a plate. Thin with water if necessary, and pass it through a strainer.

STORAGE: Keep in the refrigerator in a covered glass jar for up to 1 week.

Fruit Plate Sauce

This sauce is too thick to squeeze out of a bottle. Instead, spoon it either beside the slice of cake or underneath it.

Makes about 1 cup

Level of difficulty ★

---
1 package (10 ounces) individually quick frozen fruit such as strawberries, blueberries, or raspberries

---
½ cup Simple Syrup (page 370)

Purée the fruit with the syrup in a blender.

STORAGE: Keep refrigerated in a covered glass jar for up to 1 week.

Ivory Chocolate Sauce

This plated dessert sauce, made with white chocolate and a sugar syrup, is unusual and lovely to look at but should be used sparingly because it is quite sweet.

Makes about 1¼ cups

Level of difficulty ★

---
4 ounces white chocolate, very finely chopped

⅓ cup (2.5 ounces) granulated sugar

---
1 tablespoon light corn syrup

Set the chocolate in a mixing bowl. In a small saucepan, combine the sugar, corn syrup, and ¼ cup water and bring slowly to a boil, stirring occasionally. Remove the saucepan from the heat and pour it over the white chocolate. Whisk the sugar syrup into the chocolate and mix until smooth. Serve at room temperature.

STORAGE: Keep in the refrigerator, in a covered glass jar, for 1 week, but bring back to room temperature before using.

Sour Cream Sauce

There isn't much to this sauce because there isn't much you want to do with it other than use it for decorative purposes in plated dessert presentations. It is a great, handy garnish to use in conjunction with other sauces because it has a pure white color and enough heft so it doesn't run into other sauces.

Makes about ½ cup

Level of difficulty ★

½ cup sour cream

About 2 tablespoons heavy cream

Whisk the ingredients together until smooth and well blended. Add a bit of water if the sauce is too thick to use in a squeeze bottle.

Simple Syrup

This is an essential ingredient to have on hand. It is used as a soaking syrup for sponge cakes to make them moist, as well as with frozen fruit to make plated dessert sauces.

Makes 1 cup

1 cup (7.5 ounces) granulated sugar

In a small saucepan, bring the sugar and 1 cup water to a boil, stirring. The moment the syrup comes to a boil, remove it from the heat and cool it to room temperature.

VANILLA SYRUP

Simmer the sugar and water with the seeds of 2 vanilla pods.

CITRUS SYRUP

Simmer the sugar and water with 4 pieces of citrus peel such as orange, tangerine, or lemon, each about ½ × 2 inches.

SPIRITED SYRUP

To ¼ cup of simple syrup, add 1 to 2 tablespoons of alcohol such as dark rum, whiskey, brandy, cognac, framboise, or another of your choice.

STORAGE: This keeps indefinitely in a covered glass jar in the refrigerator.

GARNISHES

*T*HESE ACCOMPANIMENTS BRING a lovely last touch to a plated dessert or add a new flavor note to a slice of cake.

Fig Compote

This is best served with plain, unfrosted chocolate cakes.

Makes about 2 cups

Level of difficulty ★

2 cups packed (12 ounces) dry California figs, quartered

1 cup ruby port wine

2 tablespoons honey

2 × ½-inch strip of fresh lemon peel

2 × ½-inch strip of fresh orange peel

1. Combine the ingredients in a nonreactive 2-quart saucepan and bring to a simmer, stirring, over low heat.
2. Cover and simmer gently for about 30 minutes, or until the figs have absorbed all the liquid and are tender. Discard the lemon and orange peels; cool, then refrigerate until ready to serve.

STORAGE: Keeps up to 3 days in the refrigerator.

Very Berry Compote

When I was the pastry chef at Restaurant Luna in Mount Kisco, I used to serve this with cheesecake, although it also works well with white chocolate cakes. It is so delicious that you can, in fact, serve it as a dessert on its own, with lightly sweetened whipped cream, in chilled wineglasses.

Makes about 1 quart

Level of difficulty ★

One 12-ounce package individually quick frozen blueberries or raspberries, thawed

2 tablespoons cornstarch

Scant ¼ cup granulated sugar

3 cups fresh berries, such as blackberries, blueberries, raspberries, or sliced strawberries

1. In a food processor, purée the thawed frozen berries with ½ cup water. Transfer the purée to a sieve set over a bowl. With a spoon, push the purée through the sieve and discard the seeds.
2. In a nonreactive saucepan, dissolve the cornstarch in 2 tablespoons water. Add the fruit purée and sugar and, over low heat, bring the mixture to a boil, stirring occasionally. Boil, stirring continuously so the bottom doesn't scorch, for 30 seconds to make sure the cornstarch swells up.
3. Add the fresh berries, bring the mixture back to a simmer, and remove from the heat. Transfer the compote to a clean bowl and let it cool to room temperature before refrigerating.

STORAGE: Keep in the refrigerator, covered, for up to 1 week.

Sugared Chestnuts

One of my favorite taste treats are marrons glacés, *a confection consisting of fresh whole chestnuts enveloped in crystallized sugar. It is a candy widely available in Europe in the fall and winter. In this country,* marrons glacés *turn up, on occasion, in the finer gourmet stores around Christmastime. I use* marrons glacés *only as the occasional garnish for a plated dessert or as part of a cake filling, and when I can't find the real McCoy, I make this recipe. Take care to use roasted whole chestnuts, not the canned unsweetened variety, which are too watery.*

Makes 2 cups
Level of difficulty ★★

1 cup (7.5 ounces) granulated sugar

2 teaspoons light corn syrup

1 jar (14 to 15 ounces) roasted whole chestnuts, coarsely chopped

1. Set out a nonstick baking mat, or oil a marble counter or the back of a heavy-duty baking sheet with a flavorless vegetable oil.
2. Combine the sugar with the corn syrup and 1 cup water in a heavy-duty saucepan. Bring the ingredients to a boil, stirring occasionally, and boil hard until the sugar looks bubbly all over.
3. Dip a pastry brush in cold water and brush down the sides of the pan to dissolve any sugar crystals. Without stirring, let the syrup cook until it begins to smell of caramel and turn a pale golden yellow. At this stage add the chestnuts and immediately remove the saucepan from the heat. Swirl the ingredients around to coat the chestnuts with the caramel and quickly pour the mixture onto the baking sheet or oiled marble to cool.
4. When cool, break up the chestnuts and caramel bits with your fingers.

STORAGE: Keeps covered at room temperature for up to 1 week.

Shards of Caramel

These are simply broken-up pieces of hard caramel that look fabulous stuck on an individual slice of cake or strewn around the plate.

Level of difficulty ★★

½ cup (3.75 ounces) granulated sugar

1. Set out a nonstick baking mat or, if you don't have one, lightly coat a jelly roll pan or marble surface with about a teaspoon of a flavorless vegetable oil.

2. In a heavy 1-quart saucepan, bring the sugar and ¼ cup water to a boil, stirring. Brush down the sides of the pan a couple of times with a pastry brush dipped in cold water to prevent the sugar from crystallizing. Stop stirring. Let the mixture cook until it turns golden amber, smells of caramel, and is about 320°F on a candy thermometer.

3. Remove the pan from the heat and immediately pour the mixture onto the baking mat. Pick up the mat by the corners and let the caramel spread out as thinly as possible. Or on a jelly roll pan or marble, spread the caramel as thin as possible with a heat-resistant rubber spatula or wooden spoon. Work fast because the mixture sets quickly.

4. An alternate method is to pour the mixture into long thin strands or shapes that you can then use, as is, for decoration.

5. When the caramel has set and is completely cold, break up the pieces into long slender shards or into interesting shapes. Be careful how you handle these pieces because they are as sharp as glass.

COLORED SHARDS OF CARAMEL

When the caramel turns golden, add a drop of red or yellow food coloring, then swirl it around in the pan before pouring the caramel onto the surface to cool.

BUBBLE SHARDS OF CARAMEL

Pour the caramel onto a sheet of natural parchment. Pick up the parchment by its corners and shake it as the caramel drips down. Or rub a nonstick baking mat with denatured alcohol before pouring on the caramel. Pick up the mat by its corners and shake it as the caramel drips down. Tiny air bubbles will form under the caramel, giving it a bubbly, glassy look.

STORAGE: Keep at room temperature, in an airtight container, for up to 1 week.

Nut Brittle Powder

This pulverized caramelized almond powder, sometimes known as praline powder or krokant, adds sweetness, nut flavor, and crunch to plated desserts as well as to buttercreams, frostings, and even cakes.

Makes about 1 cup

Level of difficulty ★★

¾ cup (5.5 ounces) granulated sugar

½ cup toasted sliced almonds, or chopped toasted and skinned hazelnuts

1. Set out a nonstick baking mat or, if you don't have one, lightly coat a jelly roll pan or marble surface with about a teaspoon of a flavorless vegetable oil.
2. In a heavy 1-quart saucepan, bring the sugar and 2 tablespoons water to a boil, stirring. Brush down the sides of the pan a couple of times with a pastry brush dipped in cold water to prevent the sugar from crystallizing. Stop stirring. Let the mixture cook until it turns golden amber, smells of caramel, and registers about 320°F on a candy thermometer.
3. Remove the pan from the heat, add the nuts all at once, swirl them around in the pan until well coated, and immediately pour them onto the mat. Pick up the mat by the corners and let the mixture spread out as thinly as possible, or spread it with a buttered metal spatula. When the mixture has set for 5 minutes, loosen it from the mat and let it harden completely.
4. Break the nut brittle into chunks, wrap them in towels, and crush them coarsely with a hammer. Transfer the pieces to the bowl of a food processor fitted with a steel blade and pulse until the mixture is chopped or powdery, as you wish.

STORAGE: Keep in a cool dry place, in an airtight container, for up to 4 weeks.

Meringue Mushrooms

This meringue batter is piped out and assembled to simulate adorable little mushrooms, which are used to adorn a a bûche de noël, *a cake served in France on Christmas Eve.*

Makes 16 to 18 "mushrooms"

Level of difficulty ★★

¾ cup confectioners' sugar, sifted

1½ teaspoons flour

2 large egg whites, at room temperature

⅛ teaspoon salt

⅛ teaspoon cream of tartar

⅓ cup (2.5 ounces) superfine sugar

Unsweetened cocoa powder, for dusting

About ¼ cup buttercream, used to frost the outside of the Double Chocolate Christmas Log (page 199)

1. Preheat the oven to 250°F. Line a 12 × 16 × 1-inch baking pan with parchment or a nonstick baking mat. If you don't have parchment, then butter and flour the pan, and line it with waxed paper. Set out a 14-inch pastry bag fitted with a ⅜-inch-wide plain tip.

2. Sift the confectioners' sugar with the flour twice and set it aside.

3. With a handheld electric mixer on low speed, beat the egg whites until frothy. Add the salt and cream of tartar and beat on medium speed until the whites are semistiff. Add the superfine sugar, 1 tablespoon at a time, and whip on high speed until the egg whites are stiff and glossy.

4. Shake the confectioners' sugar and flour through a strainer over the egg whites, in several additions. With a rubber spatula, fold the ingredients together. Transfer the mixture to the prepared pastry bag.

5. Pipe out the mushroom "stems" with about ½ the batter by holding the bag vertically and perpendicular to the prepared baking pan and piping out a cone shape about ½ inch wide at the base and ¾ inch high. (You can also make some a bit smaller if you wish.) Stop piping and pull the pastry bag straight up to form a pointed tip on top of the cone.

6. With the other ½ of the batter, pipe out the mushroom "caps." To do so, press out some dome shapes that are about 1 inch in diameter and ¾ inch thick, as well as some that are smaller. When you are finished piping each dome, release the pressure on the bag and pull the bag away sideways rather than straight up to avoid little points on the caps. If, however, you do shape the points, dip your fingertip in water and gently knock them down into the piped-out meringue.

7. Through a strainer, sift some cocoa powder over the caps and bake for about 40 minutes, or until the meringues are dry and firm to the touch. Cool them on a wire rack.

TO ASSEMBLE

1. Line a small cookie sheet with waxed paper.

2. With the tip of a paring knife, make a small hole on the flat underside of each of the mushroom caps. Stick the point of the stem into some buttercream and push it into the hole you created beneath the mushroom cap. Set some caps straight on top of the stems and others slightly askew to make the mushrooms look a little more realistic.

3. Line up the assembled mushrooms on the lined cookie sheet.

STORAGE: Don't make these more than 24 hours in advance. Keep them in a dry cool place, loosely covered with foil, rather than in the refrigerator, where the moisture will make them soggy.

MUSHROOM CAPS AND STEMS

MUSHROOM STEM

MUSHROOM CAP

CAN KNOCK DOWN TIP OF CAP

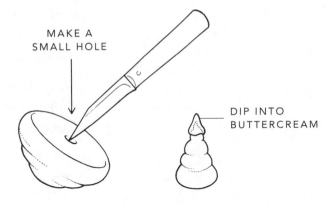

MAKE A
SMALL HOLE

DIP INTO
BUTTERCREAM

ASSEMBLING DRIED PIECES

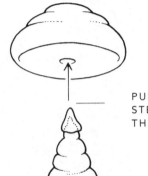

PUSH THE
STEM INTO
THE HOLE

SET SOME CAPS
STRAIGHT AND
SOME ASKEW

Sugared Flowers

Candied flowers are gorgeous on all cakes but are especially dazzling on chocolate cakes. It takes a little bit of planning and time to do this, but the effort is well worth it. You must use organically grown flowers, which are used as a food source, and never ornamental flowers, which have been sprayed with toxic poisons. (You can buy organically grown flowers, as well as flowers already candied, from The Herb Lady—see Source List, page 389, for address.) Be sure to make these on a dry day.

Level of difficulty ★★

Edible, organic flowers (see Note)

¼ cup egg whites, reconstituted from dried egg whites, or meringue powder

1 cup (7.5 ounces) superfine sugar

1. With small scissors, cut off the green stems as close as possible to the base of the flowers.
2. Cover an icing grid or wire rack with parchment or waxed paper.
3. Dip a paintbrush or your fingers in the egg white mixture. Carefully coat each surface of each of the flower petals. (If you are using your fingers, massage the egg whites into the petals without saturating them.) Gather some sugar in one hand, or in a strainer, and sprinkle the sugar lavishly over one side of the flower. Shake off the excess sugar. Turn the flower over, coat the other side with sugar, and shake off the excess.
4. Set the flowers, face up, on the paper-covered grid and dry them in a cool place for 24 to 36 hours.

STORAGE: Store in a covered metal box, like a cookie box. If dried correctly, they will keep for several months.

NOTE: There are dozens of edible flowers and leaves, but the ones below are the prettiest:

Apple blossoms

Nasturtiums

Pansies

Roses

Violets

Mint leaves

QUICK AND EASY CHOCOLATE DECORATIONS

*F*OR PRETTY but optional decorative touches, try your hand at these easy-to-prepare chocolate decorations.

Chocolate Curls

The only trick to making chocolate curls is to have the chocolate at room temperature. If the chocolate is too cold, it will crack into shards. It is easiest to do this with white chocolate.

Makes about 2 cups

Level of difficulty ★

One 8-ounce block bittersweet, milk, or white chocolate, at room temperature

If your hands are very hot, wear white cotton or latex disposable gloves. Set out a bowl or piece of waxed paper to catch the curls. Hold the block of chocolate in one hand over the bowl or paper and, with a swivel-type vegetable peeler, peel the length of one side of the block of chocolate. The peeled chocolate will fall into "curls." Continue "peeling" the chocolate, turning the block so you work each side, until you have enough curls.

Chocolate Shavings

Shavings are different from curls because for shavings you grate cold chocolate into pieces that look like wood shavings.

Makes about 1 cup

Level of difficulty ★

One 4-ounce block bittersweet, milk, or white chocolate, chilled

Grate the chocolate directly over the cake you want to decorate, over a sheet of waxed paper, or over a bowl. Rub the side of the chocolate against the medium holes of a box grater, or shave each side with a swivel-type vegetable peeler.

Chocolate Writing

There are two ways to "write" on cakes or on plates for pretty plated dessert presentations. You can pipe out either pure melted and cooled chocolate or a mixture of melted chocolate and piping gel. Writing with the piping gel is easier because it does not harden in the paper cone as melted chocolate can, but it does not dry as firm as plain chocolate does. You can buy piping gel from any store or a mail-order source that specializes in baking or cake-decorating supplies.

Makes

Level of difficulty ★

MELTED-CHOCOLATE METHOD

1 ounce bittersweet, semisweet, milk, or white chocolate, finely chopped

Paper cone (page 349)

GEL METHOD

1 part clear piping gel

1 part bittersweet or semisweet chocolate, melted and cooled

Paper cone (page 349)

FOR THE MELTED CHOCOLATE METHOD

1. In a microwave oven or in the top of a double boiler, partially melt the chocolate and then remove it from the heat. Stir until the unmelted chocolate has disappeared into the melted chocolate, and set it aside until cool to the touch but still fluid. Transfer it to the paper cone.

FOR THE GEL METHOD

2. Combine the piping gel and chocolate in a mixing bowl and, with a rubber spatula, blend them until homogeneously combined. Line a strainer with a double thickness of cotton cheesecloth. With the rubber spatula, press the chocolate piping gel through the cheesecloth. This is done to make sure you have a smooth gel. Transfer the gel to the paper cone.

APPENDIX A

Michele's Favorite Recipes

PLAIN AND EASY BATTER CAKES

Gisèle's Raspberry Chocolate Cake, page 76

Reine de Saba, page 83

CHEESECAKES

Berry White Chocolate Cheesecake, page 99

BUTTER CAKES: POUND AND LAYER

Chocolate Chocolate Tea Cake, page 112

Chocolate *Pain de Gênes*, page 115

Potato Chocolate Chip Cake, page 124

Tea-Infused White Chocolate Cake, page 131

Aztec Devil's Food Cake, page 143

Chocolate Blitz Torte, page 160

Hawaiian Coconut Cake with White Chocolate Ganache, page 166

FOAM CAKES

Chocolate Praline Cake, page 192

FLOURLESS CAKES

Macaroon Cake, page 246

The Michele: A Pecan Extravaganza, page 248

SPECIAL CAKES

The Alessia: A Marzipan-Lover's Dream Cake, page 263

Chocolate Linzer Torte, page 278

The Gianduja, page 270

Michele's Marjolaine Cake, page 272

INDIVIDUAL CAKES

Chocolate Volcanoes, page 282

SAUCES

Deadly Delicious Chocolate Sauce, page 362

Bourbon Sauce, page 363

Glossary of Terms and Phrases

BEAT: To mix ingredients rapidly and in a circular motion to create a smooth and light mixture.

BEAT THE BUTTER UNTIL LIGHT: To whip enough air into the butter so that it becomes light in color and fluffy in texture.

BLANCH: To remove the outer skin of nuts or fruit by boiling or roasting the ingredient.

BLEND: To combine two or more ingredients so they are smoothly and evenly mixed.

BOIL: To heat a liquid to a point where large bubbles break the surface.

BUTTER, MELTED AND COOLED: Melted butter that is about as warm as body temperature.

BUTTER, SOFTENED: Butter that is at room temperature and soft enough so you can poke your finger in it easily, yet not so soft that it melts.

CAKE TESTER: See Baking Equipment: Miscellaneous Small Equipment (pages 45–49).

CARAMELIZE: To cook sugar to the point at which it liquefies, turns amber, smells of caramel, and registers anywhere from 320° to 350°F on a candy thermometer.

CHOP COARSELY: To cut an ingredient into uneven pieces that are about ¼ inch in size.

CHOP FINELY: To cut an ingredient into uneven pieces that are about ⅛ inch in size. A finely chopped ingredient is larger than one that is minced.

CREAM THE BUTTER: To combine and beat the butter with sugar until it has an ivory hue and a texture somewhere between mayonnaise and whipped cream.

CRUMB COATING: A very thin, transparent coating of icing applied to the cake to anchor the crumbs. This is an undercoating that makes the top coat of frosting adhere better.

DIVIDE THE BATTER: To transfer the batter from mixing bowl to cake pans so that each pan receives an equal share of batter.

DRY INGREDIENTS: Usually refers to flour, cornstarch, cocoa powder, or other ingredients that are not in liquid form.

DUST: To coat a food or work surface with a light sprinkling of a dry ingredient such as flour, confectioners' sugar, or nuts.

FOAMY: To beat air into eggs to the point at which the surface shows air bubbles that look like foam. The word can be used interchangeably with "frothy."

FOLD: See Baking Information and Techniques: Folding (page 50).

FROSTING: An American confectioners' sugar icing.

FROTHY: See Foamy.

GANACHE: A French word that describes a mixture of melted chocolate and heavy cream.

GARNISH: Anything edible used to decorate, finish, or accompany a cake. Also, the act of decorating or finishing the cake.

GENEROUS: Refers to a volume measurement that is mounded slightly over the top of the measuring tool.

GLAZE: A thin icing usually poured over cakes.

GRATE: To rub an ingredient, like a lemon, against a rough surface so its skin comes off in small shreds or flakes.

GREASE AND FLOUR THE PANS: See Preparing Pans (page 52).

GRIND THE NUTS: To process whole nuts in the food processor so they are pulverized into fine particles almost as tiny as flour.

HOMOGENIZED: When two disparate ingredients are mixed so they become thoroughly and completely blended.

ICE BATH: A bowl filled with crushed ice into which you set another, smaller bowl. This is done when you want to quickly chill a mixture.

ICING: A word used interchangeably with "frosting." An icing has a texture between a frosting and a glaze. Also, the act of applying a frosting to a cake.

INVERT: To turn a cake upside down so that the bottom is facing up.

MERINGUE: Egg whites and sugar beaten until glossy and stiff. There are several types of meringues. A French meringue is made simply by whipping sugar into egg whites. A Swiss meringue is made by heating the egg whites and sugar before you whip them. An Italian meringue is made by

whipping a 236°F sugar syrup into beaten egg whites.

MINCE: To chop food into tiny pieces.

PINCH: A minute amount of a dry powdery ingredient equal to what you can pinch between your thumb and index finger.

PIPE OUT: To press out batter or frosting from a pastry bag.

PIPING CHOCOLATE: Refers to a mix, created out of melted chocolate mixed with piping gel (see page 381), used to write on cakes.

PITH: The white bitter layer of citrus fruit skin that lies directly beneath the colored layer of skin.

PRALINE PASTE: A ready-to-eat paste made of toasted hazelnuts and caramelized sugar.

RIBBON, TO: To beat eggs with sugar long enough for them to thicken and lighten in color.

ROASTED NUTS: To bake nuts until they smell toasted and darken in color.

SCANT: Refers to a volume measurement that is just shy of being full.

SEMISTIFF EGG WHITES: See Soft Peaks.

SEPARATE EGGS: To crack open an egg and set aside the yolk in one bowl and the white in another. See Ingredients: Eggs (page 9).

SHEET CAKE: A thin cake that is baked in a shallow rectangular pan such as a jelly roll or 9 × 13 × 2-inch pan.

SIFT: To strain dry ingredients such as flour, cornstarch, or confectioners' sugar to remove lumps.

SIMMER: To cook food in liquid at a temperature that is below boiling, and when small bubbles begin to break the surface.

SKINNED HAZELNUTS: Hazelnuts with their outer skin rubbed off. Also known as "blanched."

SOFT PEAKS: The point at which whipped egg whites or heavy cream stand up in soft peaks that droop slightly. Also known as "semistiff" egg whites.

STIFF PEAKS: The point at which whipped egg whites or heavy cream stand up in firm peaks with pointy tops.

SUPREMES, ORANGE: Refers to orange sections with all the skin and membrane removed.

TAP OUT EXCESS: Before baking, when you butter and flour baking pans, "tap out excess" flour which, if you don't, turns "clumpy" after baking. To remove the excess flour, after you have greased and dusted the pans with flour, invert them and give the pans a couple of sharp raps against the side of a sink or garbage pail.

TEMPERING: Warming eggs with some hot liquid to get them ready to be heated up to a higher temperature.

TOP IS SPRINGY: When you lightly press the top of a cake to determine if the cake is done and the surface springs back.

TORTE: In German, this word means simply "cake," but it also has come to describe a flat or flourless cake.

ULTRAPASTEURIZED CREAM: Refers to cream that has been heated to a very high temperature so that its shelf life has been extended. Does not whip as well as heavy cream that has not been ultra-pasteurized.

UNMOLD THE CAKE: To turn the cake out of its pan.

WATER BATH: A larger vessel into which you set a smaller vessel and then fill the larger one with water. This can be done in the oven or on top of the stove, and is a technique reserved for ingredients or preparations that require gentle, indirect heat so that they don't curdle or separate.

WHIP: To incorporate air into heavy cream or egg whites in order to increase their volume.

ZEST: The colored outer peel of a citrus fruit.

Source List

Below are the sources for equipment and ingredients of which I have firsthand knowledge. There are dozens more such sources throughout the country, but I didn't feel right listing them because I have no experience with their service or reliability.

Bridge Kitchenware
214 East 52nd Street
New York, New York 10022
(212) 688-4220

> A great store for professional-quality equipment, including odd-sized pans, knives, turntables, etc.

Broadway Panhandler
477 Broome Street
New York, New York 10013
(212) 966-3434

> A great store for cooking equipment in general, and for a terrific selection of baking equipment such as nonstick baking mats, and decorating equipment including tips, colors, etc.

Dean & DeLuca
560 Broadway
New York, New York 10012
(800) 999-0306

> A good source for professional-style equipment and some cake-decorating items. Very expensive, however. Mail-order catalogue information: (800) 221-7714.

The Herb Lady
52792 42nd Avenue
Lawrence, Michigan 49064
(616) 674-3879

> One of the best sources for organic flowers with which to decorate your cakes. She also sells crystallized flowers such as pansies and roses. Excellent service.

King Arthur Flour Co.
P.O. Box 876
Norwich, Vermont 05055-0876
(800) 827-6836

Mail-order source, *The Baker's Catalogue*. Has a good selection of baking equipment such as nonstick baking mats and is the best mail-order source for ingredients such as cake flour, praline and almond paste, roasted skinned hazelnuts, and Boyajian citrus oils. This is my favorite source for baking ingredients. The service is fast, professional, and courteous, and I cannot recommend the company highly enough.

Martha By Mail
P.O. Box 60060
Tampa, Florida 33660-0060
(800) 950-7130

Great mail-order source for pretty cake stands and for the best grater in the world. The grater is long and thin, comes from Japan, and cannot be beat for zesting citrus fruits. However, be sure that once you get on their mailing list, you ask that they not rent out your name, or you will be inundated, as I was, with more unwanted catalogues than you can imagine.

New York Cake and Baking Distributor
56 West 22nd Street
New York, New York 10010
(800) 942-2539

A store and mail-order source that offers a lot of cake-decorating equipment, and other baking supplies such as gum paste flowers with which to decorate cakes.

Penzeys Spices
P.O. Box 933
Muskego, Wisconsin 53150
(262) 679-7207

The best source for spices and extracts. A wonderful selection of vanilla beans.

J. B. Prince Co.
36 East 31st Street; 11th floor
New York, New York 10016
(212) 683-3553

Great professional equipment, including the best-quality squeeze bottles, which must, however, be bought by the case (24/case).

Sweet Celebrations
P.O. Box 39426
Edina, Minnesota 55439-0426
(800) 328-6722

A good mail-order source for some equipment, and especially strong on cake-decorating items, including gold leaf. Includes a good selection of useful paper goods such as doilies, corrugated cardboard rounds, parchment circles, and cake boxes.

Albert Uster Imports, Inc.
9211 Gaither Road
Gaithersburg, Maryland 20877
(800) 231-8154

Mail-order catalogue of specialty ingredients like prepared dessert sauces you can use for plated desserts. They also have ready-to-eat decorative elements you can use to beautify your cakes.

Williams-Sonoma
Mail-Order Department
10000 Covington Cross
Las Vegas, Nevada 89114
(800) 541-2233

Stores nationwide and mail-order catalogue. An expensive collection of cooking and baking equipment. Useful because they are a national source.

Wilton Industries
2240 West 75th Street
Woodridge, Illinois 60517
www.wilton.com
(630) 963-7100

The end-all of cake-decorating supplies.

Zabar's
2245 Broadway
New York, New York 10024
(212) 787-2000

Has a lot of good-quality baking equipment at excellent prices. Also sells hard-to-find ingredients like almond paste, canned poppy-seed mix, and chestnut purée.

Selected Bibliography

In theory, I should list all 700 titles in my cookbook collection, because I am inspired by everything I read. However, space does not permit such a luxury, so instead I have compiled a bibliography of the books that helped me the most with this particular book.

Amendola, Joseph. *The Baker's Manual,* 4th ed. New York: Van Nostrand Reinhold, 1993.

Amendola, Joseph, and Donald E. Lundbeg. *Understanding Baking,* 2nd ed. New York: Van Nostrand Reinhold, 1992.

American Egg Board. *Eggcyclopedia.* Park Ridge, Illinois, 1989. Pamphlet.

Anderson, Jean. *American Century Cookbook: The Most Popular Recipes of the 20th Century.* New York: Clarkson Potter Publishers, 1997.

Bailey, Janet. *Keeping Food Fresh.* New York: Perennial Library, Harper & Row Publishers, 1989.

Bennion, E. G., and G. S. T. Bamford. *The Technology of Cake Making,* 6th ed. London: Chapman and Hall, 1997.

Bilheux, Roland, and Alain Escoffier. *French Professional Pastry Series,* vols. 1–4, trans. Rhona Poritzky-Lauvand and James Peterson. New York: Van Nostrand Reinhold, 1988.

Coe, Sophie D., and Michael D. Coe. *True History of Chocolate.* London: Thames and Hudson, 1996.

Corriher, Shirley O. *Cookwise.* New York: William Morrow and Company, 1997.

Giraud, Daniel. *Le Patissier Chocolatier.* Ed. Luxe, #171. Aix-en-Provence: Maraval à Saint-Pons, 1986.

Gisslen, Wayne. *Professional Baking,* 2nd ed. New York: John Wiley & Sons, 1994.

Gonzalez, Elaine. *Chocolate Artistry: Techniques for Molding, Decorating and Designing with Chocolate.* Chicago: Contemporary Books, 1983.

Healy, Bruce, and Paul Bugat. *Mastering the Art of French Pastry.* Woodbury, N.Y.: Barron's Educational Series, 1984.

Hermé, Pierre. *Larousse des Desserts.* Paris: Larousse, 1997.

Kander, Mrs. Simon. *The Settlement Cook Book.* Milwaukee, Wis.: The Settlement Cook Book Co., 1949.

Kochbuch der Deutschen Koschschule im Prag. Prague: 1917.

Larousse Gastronomique: Avec le Concours du Comite Gastronomique preside par Joel Robuchon. Larousse-Bordas, 1996.

Lenotre, Gaston. *Lenotre's Desserts and Pastries.* Woodbury, N.Y.: Barron's Educational Series, 1977.

Linxe, Robert. *La Maison du Chocolat.* Paris: Robert Laffont, 1992.

Lucas, Dione. *The Cordon Bleu Cook Book.* Boston: Little Brown and Company, 1947.

Malgieri, Nick. *Perfect Pastry.* New York: Macmillan Publishing, 1989.

———. *Chocolate: From Simple Cookies to Extravagant Showstoppers.* New York: HarperCollins Publishers, 1998.

Mariani, John F. *The Dictionary of American Food and Drink.* New York: Hearst Books, 1994.

McGee, Harold. *On Food and Cooking: The Science and Love of the Kitchen.* New York: Charles Scribner's Sons, 1984.

Medrich, Alice. *Chocolat: Extraordinary Chocolate Desserts.* New York: Warner Books, 1990.

Moritz, Mrs. C. F., and Miss Adele Kahn. *The Twentieth Century Cook Book,* 5th ed. New York: G. W. Dillingham Co., 1898.

The New Settlement Cook Book, revised. New York: Simon and Schuster, 1954.

Peck, Paula. *The Art of Fine Baking.* New York: Simon and Schuster, 1961.

Purdy, Susan G. *A Piece of Cake.* New York: Macmillan Publishing Company, 1989.

Reich, Lily Joss. *The Viennese Pastry Cookbook.* New York: The Macmillan Company, 1970.

Rombauer, Irma S. *The Joy of Cooking.* Indianapolis: Bobbs-Merrill Company, 1943.

———. *The Joy of Cooking.* Indianapolis: Bobbs-Merrill Company, 1946.

Rombauer, Irma S., and Marion Rombauer Becker. *The Joy of Cooking.* Indianapolis: Bobbs-Merrill Company, 1975.

Roux, Michel, and Albert Roux. *The Roux Brothers on Patisserie.* London: Little, Brown and Company, 1986. 1993 reprint ed.

Sultan, William J. *Professional Baking,* 5th ed. New York: Van Nostrand Reinhold, 1990.

Thuries, Yves. *The Classic and Contemporary Recipes of Yves Thuries: French Pastry,* trans. Rhona Poritzky-Lauvand. New York: Van Nostrand Reinhold, 1996.

Urvater, Michele, and David Liederman. *Cooking the Nouvelle Cuisine in America.* New York: Workman Publishing, 1979.

Woman's Day Collector's Cookbook. New York: Simon and Schuster, 1970.

INDEX

Note: When a cake recipe has more than one page reference, the page number(s) in **boldface** refer to the recipe itself; page numbers which follow refer to other recipes in which the cake recipe is used.

A

Alessia's Banana Chocolate Cream Cake, 214–15
The Alessia: A Marzipan-Lover's Dream Cake, 263
all-purpose flour, 15, 16, 51
Almond(s). *See also* Nut(s)
  The Alessia: A Marzipan-Lover's Dream Cake, 263
  Biscuit, Chocolate, **212**, 213
  buying, 25–26
  Cake, Chocolate, Our Family's Favorite, **252–53**, 263
  Cake, White Chocolate, 86–87
  Cardamom Carrot Cocoa Cake, 88–89
  Chocolate Blitz Torte, 160–61
  Chocolate Cake with Ganache, 110
  Chocolate *Pain de Gênes*, **115**, 286
  Glorious Amaretto Cake, 213
  Macaroon Cake, 246–47
  Michele's Marjolaine Cake, 272–73
  Mohr im Hemd, 284–85
  Nut Brittle Powder, 375
  Nut Meringue Cake, **259**, 260

  paste, about, 26
  Potato Chocolate Chip Cake, 124–25
  Prune and Ginger Chocolate Cake, 93
  Rehrucken (Chocolate Saddle of Venison), 243
  Reine de Saba, 83
Amaretto Cake, Glorious, 213
American Icebox Cake, 286
Angel Food Cake(s), **227**, 229
  about, 178–79
  checklist for, 182–83
  Chocolate Pudding-Filled, 229
  Cocoa Puff, **226–27**, 228, 286
  cooling, 55
  Filled, 228
  fillings and icings for, 183
  oven heat for, 181
  pans for, 38, 39
  preparing batter for, 179–81
  preparing pans for, 54
  tips for, 231
Ann Rothschild's Cake, 233
"Antique" Chocolate Pound Cake, 105
Apple Pecan Chocolate Cake, 234–35

appliances, major, 35–37
Apricot(s), 24
  Squeeze Sauce, 368
  Upside-Down Cake, Chocolate, 134
Austrian Dobos Torte, 216–17
Autumn Chestnut Cake, 236–37
Aztec Devil's Food Cake, 143

B

baking chocolate, defined, 30, 32
baking equipment, 35–49
  baking pans, 38–40
  food processors, 37
  kitchen scales, 40–41
  knives, 41
  measuring tools, 41–42
  miscellaneous, 44–49
  mixers, 36–37
  mixing bowls, 42
  ovens, 35–36
  saucepans, 41–43
  thermometers, 43–44
baking information. *See* baking equipment; ingredients; techniques

baking pans
  dusting with flour, 53
  filling with batter, 53–54
  greasing, 52–53
  lining with paper, 53
  substituting, in recipes, 39–40
  types and sizes, 38–40
  volume capacity of, 39–40
baking parchment, 44
baking powder, 17
baking soda, 16–17
Banana
  Chocolate Cream Cake, Alessia's, 214–15
  Tea Cake, Chocolate, 111
batter cakes, 61–93
  about, 61–62
  Boozy Mud, 71
  Brownie Torte, 70
  Brownies
    Best, 69
    Classic, 68
    Coconut, 68
    Espresso, 68
    Jammy, 68
  Cardamom Carrot Cocoa, 88–89
  Cherry Milk-Chocolate, 72–73
  Chocolate
    Beet, 90
    Date and Walnut, 92
    Fissure Spiced, 77
    Fruit, Christmas, 74
    Mayonnaise, Pecan, 65
    Not-So Wacky, 64
    One-Bowl, with Tutti-Frutti Filling, 78
    Orange-Blossom, 79
    Peanut, 80–81
    Prune and Ginger, 93
    Pudding, 66
    Pudding, King Arthur, 67
    Quintessential French, 82
    Raspberry, Gisèle's, 76
    Rum Chestnut, 84–85
    Wacky, 63
    Zucchini Quick Bread, 91
  Ginger Honey, with Chocolate, 75
  Reine de Saba, 83
  White Chocolate Almond, 86–87
Bean Torte, Chocolate, 239
Beet Cake, Chocolate, 90

Beginner's Chocolate Buttercream, 309
bench knife, 44
Berry. *See also specific berry*
  Compote, Very, 372
  White Chocolate Cheesecake, 99
Best Brownies, 69
biscuit cakes, 207–25
  about, 178–79, 207
  Amaretto, Glorious, 213
  Austrian Dobos Torte, 216–17
  Banana Chocolate Cream, Alessia's, 214–15
  Blonde Biscuit, 209
  checklist for, 182–83
  Chocolate Almond Biscuit, **212**, 213
  Chocolate Biscuit, **208–9**, 288–89
  Chocolate Nut Biscuit, 210–11
  Chocolate Swiss Roll, Dione Lucas's, 224–25
  Dark Chocolate Swiss Roll, 222–23
  fillings and icings for, 183
  The Lorenzini, 218–19
  making into roll cakes, 181–82
  preparing batter for, 179–81
  Rigo Jansci, 220–21
bittersweet chocolate, about, 31, 32
Black Forest Cake, Dieter Schorner's, 196–97
Blackout Cake, Boston, 158
bleached flour, 14, 15
Blonde Biscuit, 209
Blueberries
  Berry White Chocolate Cheesecake, 99
  Fruit Plate Sauce, 369
  Very Berry Compote, 372
Boiled Icing, 312
  amounts needed for cakes, 297
  Chocolate, 312
  Coconut, 313
  Marshmallow, Old-Fashioned, 313
  Zebra, 312
boiled sugar syrups, about, 304–6
Boozy Mud Cake, 71
Boston Blackout Cake, 158
Bourbon
  Boozy Mud Cake, 71
  Chocolate Cake, Pecan, 119

Christmas Chocolate Fruit Cake, 74
  Fudge Cake, Pecan, 119
  Sauce, 363
bowls, mixing, 42
Brandy
  Chocolate Frosting, 298
  Chocolate Sabayon Mousse, 317
  Christmas Chocolate Fruit Cake, 74
  Spirited Custard Sauce, 359
  Spirited Syrup, 370
bread flour, 15, 51
brown sugar, 20, 21, 52
Brownie Torte, 70
Brownies, Best, 69
Brownies, Classic, 68
Brownies, Coconut, 68
Brownies, Espresso, 68
Brownies, Jammy, 68
Bubble Shards of Caramel, 374
Bundt pans, 38, 39
butter, in baked goods, 12–13
butter cakes, 100–135. *See also* layer
    butter cakes; Pound Cake; Tea
    Cake
  checklist for, 103
  Chocolate
    Almond, with Ganache, 110
    Bundt, Orange and, 122–23
    Cake Pudding, 135
    Cherry and Hazelnut, 114
    Coffee Cake, Streusel-Woven, 130
    Deep-Dish, with Sour Cream Icing, **113**, 281
    Hazelnut, **116**, 135
    Pecan Bourbon, 119
    Upside-Down, Apricot, 134
  Cocoa, Raspberry-Scented, 126–27
  Cocoa Coconut, Glazed, 120–21
  Fudge, Pecan Bourbon, 119
  Fudge, Tunnel of, 132
  Midnight, 118
  oven heat for, 103
  Potato Chocolate Chip, 124–25
  preparing batter for, 101–3
  Walnut-Chocolate Filled Kugelhopf, 133
  White Chocolate, Tea-Infused, 131
Butter Sponge Cake Layers
    (Genoise). *See* Sponge Cake(s)

Buttercream
  amounts needed for cakes, 296–97
  applying to cake, 341
  Chocolate, Beginner's, 309
  Chocolate, Custard, 311
  Chocolate, Dione Lucas's, 310
  Chocolate Mousseline, 310
  Coffee, 310
  finishing touches for, 342, 344–45
  French
    Chocolate, 302
    Classic, 302
    Coffee, 303
    Gianduja, 303
    Mocha, 303
    Orange, 303
    Pastry Cream, 303
    Praline, 302
  Gianduja, 310
  Italian Meringue, 309
    Chocolate, 309
  matching with cakes, 295–96
  piping from pastry bag, 345–48
  quick, about, 303
  Swiss Meringue
    Linda Dann's, 307
    Mocha, 307
buttermilk, in recipes, 18
Buttermilk Chocolate Cake Layers,
  148, 287
Butterscotch Frosting, 300
Butterscotch Sauce, 364

C

cake breaker, 44
cake dome, 44–45
cake flour, 14, 15, 16, 51
cake lifter, 45
cake testers, 45
candy thermometer, 43–44
Canned Mango Sauce, 366
Caramel
  Glaze, Fudge, 329
  Icing, 329
  Icing, Fudge, 329
  plated dessert ideas for, 355
  preparing, temperature for, 306
  Sauce, French, 364
  Shards of; variations, 374
Cardamom Carrot Cocoa Cake, 88–89

cardboard boxes, 45
cardboard rounds and triangles, 45
Carrot Cocoa Cake, Cardamom,
  88–89
charlotte mold, 45, 290
charlotte russe, about, 290
Checkerboard Cake, 159
cheese. *See* Cream Cheese; Mascar-
  pone; Ricotta
Cheesecake
  about, 94–95
  Berry White Chocolate, 99
  Chocolate, 96
  slicing, 95
  White and Black Chocolate, 98
  White Chocolate, 97
Cherry(ies)
  Dieter Schorner's Black Forest
    Cake, 196–97
  and Hazelnut Chocolate Cake, 114
  Milk-Chocolate Cake, 72–73
Chestnut(s), 26
  Cake, Autumn, 236–37
  Chocolate Cake, Rum, 84–85
  Chocolate Meringue Cake, 264–65
  Sugared, 373
Chewy Chocolate Pound Cake, 105
Chiffon Cake(s)
  about, 178–79
  checklist for, 182–83
  Chocolate, 230–31
  cooling, 55
  preparing batter for, 179–81
  preparing pans for, 54
Chile Chocolate Peanut Torte, 238
Chipped Chocolate Pound Cake,
  105
chocolate, 28–34
  buttons or *pistoles*, 32
  chopping, 33
  history of, 28
  melting, 33–34
  plated dessert ideas for, 354
  production of, 29–30
  "seized," tip for, 34
  storing, 32
  types of, 30–33
Christmas Chocolate Fruit Cake, 74
Christmas Log, Double Chocolate,
  199
Cinnamon Custard Sauce, 360

Cinnamon-Chocolate-Walnut Cake,
  163
citrus oils, 22
Citrus Syrup, 370
Classic American Chocolate Frost-
  ing, 298
Classic Brownie, The, 68
Classic Devil's Food Cake Layers,
  139–40, 279
Classic French Buttercream, 302
Coach House Chocolate Cake,
  268–69
coating chocolate, defined, 32
cocoa powder
  decorating with, 343
  plated dessert ideas for, 354
  types of, 32–33
  volume and weight equivalences,
    51
Cocoa Puff, **226–27**, 228, 286
Cocoa Whipped Cream, 318
Coconut
  Boiled Icing, 313
  Brownies, 68
  Cake, Glazed Cocoa, 120–21
  Cake, Hawaiian, with White
    Chocolate Ganache, 166–67
  Chocolate Pound Cake, 105
  cream, how to make, 27
  fresh, opening, 26
  Linda's "Comfort Food" Chocolate
    Cake, 168–69
  Macaroon Cake, 246–47
  Michele's German Chocolate Cake,
    170–71
  milk, how to make, 27
  milk, unsweetened, 19
  packaged, 26
Coffee. *See also* Mocha
  Buttercream, 310
  Custard Sauce, 359
  Espresso Brownies, 68
  extract, 22
  French Buttercream, 303
  The Java, 242
  Pastry Cream, 322
  Whipped Cream, 318
Coffee Cake, Streusel-Woven
  Chocolate, 130
Colored Shards of Caramel, 374
Compote, Fig, 372

Compote, Very Berry, 372
confectionary chocolate, about, 31, 32
Confectioners' Sugar
  about, 20
  decorating with, 343
  Glaze, 332
  measuring, 21
  plated dessert ideas for, 354
  volume and weight equivalences, 52
convection ovens, 36
cooling cakes, 55
copper saucepan, 43
corn syrup, 21–22
cornstarch, 16, 51
couplers, 48
covering chocolate, defined, 32
"Crazy Quilt" Chocolate Pound Cake, 105
cream. *See also* Pastry Cream; Sour Cream; Whipped Cream
  types of, 18
Cream Cheese, 13. *See also* Cheesecake
  Frosting, Chocolate, 299
  Frosting, Minted, 299
  Frosting, Vanilla, 299
cream of tartar, 28
creaming method, 101–3
crystallized flowers, 336, 355
Cumin Custard Sauce, 359
Cupcakes, 279
  Fudge Nut, 280
  Michele's Fantasy, 281
Curls, Chocolate, 380
currants, in baked goods, 24
Custard Chocolate Buttercream, 311
Custard Devil's Food Cake Layers, **141–42**, 143, 144
Custard Sauce
  Flavored, 359–60
  Orange Juice, 362
  Stabilized, 361
  Vanilla (Crème Anglaise), 358
cutting boards, 45–46

D

Dacquoise, 260
dark chocolate, types of, 30–31
Dark Chocolate Swiss Roll, 222–23

Date and Walnut Chocolate Cake, 92
dates, buying, 24
Deadly Delicious Chocolate Sauce, 362
decorating combs, 46
decorations, quick and easy, 380–81
decorative techniques, 335–55
  decorative piping, 345–48
  designs created with
    American frosting, 344–45
    buttercream, 344–45
    cocoa powder, 343
    confectioners' sugar, 343
    fluffy frosting, 345
    glazed and iced cakes, 344
    paper cones, 348–50
    thin icings, 348–50
    whipped cream, 345
  equipment for, 46–49, 336
  ingredients for, 336–37
  preparing cake for
    applying buttercream, 341
    applying glaze, 340–41
    applying thick frosting, 341
    applying thin icing, 340–41
    cardboard rounds for, 340
    frosted sides and bottom, 342
    frosted top and sides, 341–42
    slicing into layers, 340
  preparing design for, 337–38
Deep-Dish Chocolate Cake with Sour Cream Icing, **113**, 281
Dependable Chocolate Pound Cake, **104–6**, 135, 286
Devil's Food Cake
  Aztec, 143
  Classic, Layers, **139–40**, 279
  Custard, Layers, **141–42**, 143, 144
  Linda's Quintessential, **146–47**, 279
  Mocha, 144
  Sweet, Layers, 145
Dieter Schorner's
  Black Forest Cake, 196–97
  Chocolate Gateau, 198
Dione Lucas's
  Chocolate Buttercream, 310
  Chocolate Swiss Roll, 224–25
  Roulade Leontine, 257–58
Dobos Torte, Austrian, 216–17
doilies, 46
doneness, testing for, 54–55

double boiler, 43
Double Chocolate Christmas Log, 199
dry measuring cups, 41–42
Dutch-processed cocoa powder, 32

E

egg(s), 9–12
  in angel food cakes, 179, 180
  beating, 11, 178–79
  buying and storing, 10
  in chiffon cakes, 179
  separating, 10–11
  in sponge cakes, 178–79, 180
  whipping, 11–12, 180
  whites, dried, 10
enriched flour, 14, 15
equipment, baking. *See* baking equipment
equipment, decorating, 46–49, 336
Espresso Brownies, 68
extracts, 22–23

F

fats, in baked goods, 12–13
Fig Compote, 372
figs, buying, 24
Filled Angel Food Cake, 228
Filling
  amounts needed for cakes, 296–97
  Chocolate Pudding, 323
  finishing touches for, 342, 345
  Italian Meringue, 308
  matching with cakes, 295–96
  Mousse
    Chocolate, 314–15
    Chocolate Sabayon, 317
    Mango, 316
    Milk Chocolate, 314
    Passion Fruit, 316
    Raspberry, 316
    White Chocolate, 315
  Pastry Cream
    Chocolate, 322
    Coffee, 322
    Gianduja, 322
    Mocha, 322
    Praline, 322
    Vanilla, 322

Whipped Cream, 318–19
  Chocolate Malted, 318
  Cocoa, 318
  Coffee, 318
  Mocha, 318
  Spiced, 319
  Spirited, 319
  Stabilized, 320
  Whipped Ganache, 321
Fissure Spiced Chocolate Cake, 77
flat spatulas, 48
Flavored Custard Sauces, 359–60
flavorings, 22–23
Floral Custard Sauce, 359
flour
  almond, 25–26
  chestnut, 26
  measuring, 15–16
  sifting, 16
  storing, 15
  types of, 14–15
  volume and weight equivalences,
    51
flourless cakes, 232–61. *See also* Torte
    (flourless)
  about, 232
  Ann Rothschild's, 233
  Chestnut, Autumn, 236–37
  Chocolate
    Almond, Our Family's Favorite,
      252–53, 263
    Apple Pecan, 234–35
    Souffléed, 254
  Dacquoise, 260
  Dione Lucas's Roulade Leontine,
    257–58
  The Java, 242
  Macaroon, 246–47
  The Michele: A Pecan Extrava-
    ganza, 248–49
  Nut Meringue, **259**, 260
  Rehrucken (Chocolate Saddle of
    Venison), 243
  White Chocolate, with Lemon, 256
flowers, crystallized, 336, 355
flowers, fresh, 336
Flowers, Sugared, 378
foam cakes, 178–79. *See also* Angel
    Food Cake(s); biscuit cakes;
    Chiffon Cake(s); Sponge
    Cake(s)

folding, 50–51
food coloring, 336
food processors, 37
freezing cakes, 56, 95
French buttercream. *See* Buttercream
French Caramel Sauce, 364
French Chocolate Cake, Quintessen-
    tial, 82
Fresh Mango Sauce, 365
Frosting. *See also* Buttercream; Fill-
    ing; Glaze; Icing
  amounts needed for cakes, 296–97
  applying to cake, 341
  Butterscotch, 300
  Chocolate
    Brandy, 298
    Classic American, 298
    Malted, 299
    Mocha, 298
    Orange, 298
    Peanut Butter, 301
    Wicked, 298
  Cream Cheese
    Chocolate, 299
    Minted, 299
    Vanilla, 299
  finishing touches for, 342, 344–45
  leveling and smoothing, 341–42
  matching with cakes, 295–96
  Mocha, 300
  Orange, 301
  piping from pastry bag, 345–48
  Vanilla, 301
Fruit. *See also specific fruit*
  Cake, Christmas Chocolate, 74
  canned, buying, 24
  Chewy Chocolate Pound Cake, 105
  "Crazy Quilt" Chocolate Pound
    Cake, 105
  dried, selecting, 23–24
  frozen, buying, 24
  jarred, buying, 24
  One-Bowl Chocolate Cake with
    Tutti-Frutti Filling, 78
  Plate Sauce, 369
  plated dessert ideas for, 354–55
  purées, making, 24
Fudge
  Cake, 164–65
  Cake, Tunnel of, 132
  Caramel Glaze, 329

Caramel Icing, 329
Glaze, Real, 328
Icing, Real, 327–28
Nut Cupcakes, 280

G

Ganache, 324
  how to make, 34
  Milk Chocolate, 324
  Mocha, 324
  Whipped, 321
  White Chocolate, 324
garnishes, 372–78
  Fig Compote, 372
  Meringue Mushrooms, 376–77
  Nut Brittle Powder, 375
  Shards of Caramel, 374
  Sugared Chestnuts, 373
  Sugared Flowers, 378
  Very Berry Compote, 372
gelatin, 28
German Chocolate, 31
  Cake, Michele's, 170–71
Gianduja, The, 270–71
Gianduja Buttercream, 310
Gianduja French Buttercream, 303
Gianduja Pastry Cream, 322
Ginger
  crystallized, 22
  Custard Sauce, 360
  Honey Cake with Chocolate, 75
  and Prune Chocolate Cake, 93
Gisèle's Raspberry Chocolate Cake,
    76
glass pans, 38
Glaze
  amounts needed for cakes, 296
  applying to cake, 340–41
  Chocolate, Jurgen's, 330
  Chocolate, Maria's Best, 331
  Chocolate Satin, 330
  Confectioners' Sugar, 332
  finishing touches for, 342, 344–45
  Fudge, Real, 328
  Fudge Caramel, 329
  matching with cakes, 295–96
  Mocha, Maria's, 331
  White Chocolate, 331
Glazed Chocolate Pound Cake, 105
Glazed Cocoa Coconut Cake, 120–21

Glorious Amaretto Cake, 213
Glossy Chocolate Icing, 325
gold and silver dust, 337
Grand Marnier
  Chocolate Cake, 200
  Sauce, 365
  Spirited Custard Sauce, 359
  Spirited Whipped Cream, 319
granulated sugar, 19, 21, 52
graters, 46

H

half-sheet pans, 38–39, 54
handheld electric mixers, 37
Hawaiian Coconut Cake with White
  Chocolate Ganache, 166–67
Hazelnut(s), 27. *See also* Nut(s); Pra-
  line
  Chocolate Cake, **116**, 135
  Chocolate Cake, Cherry and, 114
  Chocolate Linzer Torte, 278
  Chocolate Praline Cake, 192–93
  Dacquoise, 260
  The Gianduja, 270–71
  Kata Torte, 261
  Michele's Marjolaine Cake,
    272–73
  Mohr im Hemd, 284–85
  Nut Brittle Powder, 375
  Nut Meringue Cake, **259**, 260
  Nutty Chocolate Pound Cake, 105
  Torte, Chocolate, Karen's, 244–45
herbs, 22
high-altitude baking, 57
Honey, 21–22
  Cake, Ginger, with Chocolate, 75
  Orange-Blossom Chocolate Cake,
    79
Hubert, Eric, 285
hydrogenated vegetable shortening,
  13

I

ice chipper, 46
icebox cakes. *See* refrigerated cakes
Icing. *See also* Buttercream; Filling;
    Frosting; Glaze
  amounts needed for cakes, 296
  applying to cake, 340–41

Boiled, 312
  Chocolate, 312
  Coconut, 313
  Marshmallow, Old-Fashioned,
    313
  Zebra, 312
Caramel, 329
Chocolate, Glossy, 325
Chocolate, Sour Cream, 326
Chocolate Water, 325
finishing touches for, 342, 344–45
Fudge, Real, 327–28
Fudge Caramel, 329
Ganache, 324
  Milk Chocolate, 324
  Mocha, 324
  White Chocolate, 324
matching with cakes, 295–96
Midnight, 326
piping from paper cone, 348–50
Seven-Minute, 313
  Orange, 313
icing combs, 46
imitation chocolate, defined, 32
individual cakes
  Chocolate Volcanoes, 282
  Cupcakes, 279
  Fudge Nut Cupcakes, 280
  Michele's Fantasy Cupcakes, 281
  Mohr im Hemd, 284–85
ingredients, 9–34
  chocolate, 28–34
  cream of tartar, 28
  for decorating, 336–37
  eggs, 9–12
  extracts and flavorings, 22–23
  fats, 12–13
  flours, 14–16
  fruits, 23–24
  gelatin, 28
  leaveners, 16–17
  liquid sweeteners, 21–22
  liquids, 17–19
  nuts and seeds, 24–28
  starches, 16
  sugars, 19–21
instant-read thermometer, 44
Italian Chocolate Icebox Cake, 287
Italian Meringue
  amounts needed for cakes, 297
  Buttercream, 309

Buttercream, Chocolate, 309
  Filling, 308
Ivory Chocolate Sauce, 369

J

Jammy Brownies, 68
The Java, 242
jelly roll pans, 38–39, 54
jelly rolls. *See* rolled cakes
Jurgen's Chocolate Glaze, 330

K

Kahlúa Chocolate Cake, 202–3
Karen's Chocolate Hazelnut Torte,
    244–45
Kata Torte, 261
King Arthur Chocolate Pudding
    Cake, 67
kitchen scales, 40–41
kitchen shears, 46
knives, 41
Kugelhopf
  pans, 38, 39
  Walnut-Chocolate Filled, 133

L

ladyfingers
  Blonde Biscuit, 209
  Chocolate Biscuit, **208–9**, 288–89
  piped from biscuit batter, 207
layer butter cakes, 136–77. *See also*
    Devil's Food Cake
  Boston Blackout, 158
  Checkerboard, 159
  checklist for, 103
  Chocolate
    Blitz Torte, 160–61
    Buttermilk, **148**, 287
    Chip, 162
    -Cinnamon-Walnut, 163
    German, Michele's, 170–71
    Light, **149**, 279
    Linda's "Comfort Food,"
      168–69
    Minted, 172
    Silky, **150**, 158
    Sour Cream, **153**, 158, 279
    Yeasted, 176–77

Coconut, Hawaiian, with White
    Chocolate Ganache, 166–67
frosting combinations for, 137–38
Fudge, 164–65
Golden, One, Two, Three, Four,
    155, 159
matching layer to frosting, 136–38
oven heat for, 103
preparing batter for, 101–3
Red Velvet, 173
Sacher Torte, 174–75
Sin City Cake, 152
  Layers, **151**, 152
White, 157
White Chocolate, 154
Yellow, **156**, 279
leaveners, 16–17
lemon zester, 46
Light Chocolate Cake Layers, **149**, 279
Light Chocolate Pound Cake, **107**,
    135, 286
Linda Dann's
  "Comfort Food" Chocolate Cake,
    168–69
  Quintessential Devil's Food Cake,
    146–47, 279
  Swiss Meringue Buttercream, 307
Linzer Torte, Chocolate, 278
liquid measuring cups, 42
liquid sweeteners, 21–22
liquids, in cake batters, 17–19
loaf pans, 38, 39
Lorenzini, Francis, 219
Lorenzini, The, 218–19

M

Macadamia nuts, 27
  Coconut Brownies, 68
  Hawaiian Coconut Cake with White
    Chocolate Ganache, 166–67
Macaroon Cake, 246–47
Malted Frosting, Chocolate, 299
Malted Whipped Cream, Chocolate,
    318
Mango Mousse Filling, 316
Mango Sauce, Canned, 366
Mango Sauce, Fresh, 365
Marbled Chocolate Pound Cake,
    108, 286
margarine, in cakes, 12–13

Maria's Best Chocolate Glaze, 331
Maria's Mocha Glaze, 331
Marshmallow Icing, Old-Fashioned,
    313
Marzipan-Lover's Dream Cake: The
    Alessia, 263
Mascarpone
  Chocolate Tiramisu, 283
mats, baking, 47
Mayonnaise
  Cake, Pecan Chocolate, 65
  in Wacky Chocolate Cake, 63
measuring chart, 42
measuring ingredients, 51–52
measuring tools, 41–42
Meringue. *See also* Italian Meringue;
    Swiss Meringue
  Mushrooms, 376–77
  powder, about, 337
  whipping egg whites for, 12, 180
meringue-type cakes
  Chestnut Chocolate, 264–65
  Dacquoise, 260
  Kata Torte, 261
  Macaroon, 246–47
  Michele's Marjolaine, 272–73
  The Michele: A Pecan Extrava-
    ganza, 248–49
  Nut Meringue, **259**, 260
  Opera, 274–75
Michele's
  Chocolate Zuccotto, 292
  Fantasy Cupcakes, 281
  German Chocolate Cake, 170–71
  Marjolaine Cake, 272–73
  Marvelous Mistake, 204–5
The Michele: A Pecan Extravaganza,
    248–49
microwave ovens, 36
Midnight Cake, 118
Midnight Icing, 326
milk, in baked goods, 18
Milk Chocolate, 31, 32
  Ganache, 324
  Mousse Filling, 314
milk products, in baked goods, 18–19
Mincemeat Torte, Chocolate, 266–67
mint, storing, 22
Mint Custard Sauce, 360
Minted Chocolate Cake, 172
Minted Cream Cheese Frosting, 299

Mixed Spice Custard Sauce, 360
mixers, 36–37
mixing bowls, 42
Mocha
  Chocolate Frosting, 298
  Devil's Food Cake, 144
  French Buttercream, 303
  Frosting, 300
  Ganache, 324
  Glaze, Maria's, 331
  Nut Sponge Cake, 188
  Pastry Cream, 322
  Sponge Cake, **188**, 201
  Swiss Meringue Buttercream, 307
  Tea Cake, **117**, 286
  Whipped Cream, 318
Mohn Torte (Poppy Seed Cake),
    250–51
Mohr im Hemd, 284–85
molasses, in recipes, 21–22
Mousse. *See* Filling
Mud Cake, Boozy, 71
muffin pans, 39
Mushrooms, Meringue, 376–77

N

natural flavorings, 22
nonalkalized cocoa powder, 32
nonstick baking mats, 47
Not-So-Wacky Chocolate Cake, 64
Nut(s). *See also specific nuts*
  Biscuit, Chocolate, 210–11
  Brittle Powder, 375
  Butter Sponge Cake, 186
  Chocolate Pumpernickel Torte,
    240–41
  chopping, 25
  "Crazy Quilt" Chocolate Pound
    Cake, 105
  Filled Angel Food Cake, 228
  measuring, 25
  Meringue Cake, **259**, 260
  Nutty Chocolate Pound Cake, 105
  plated dessert ideas for, 355
  Sponge Cake
    Chocolate, 188
    Layers, Chocolate, **189**, 200
    Mocha, 188
  toasting, 25
  volume and weight equivalences, 52

O

offset spatula, 48
oil, vegetable, 13
Old-Fashioned Marshmallow Icing, 313
One, Two, Three, Four Golden Cake Layers, **155**, 159
One-Bowl Chocolate Cake with Tutti-Frutti Filling, 78
Opera Cake, 274–75
Orange
  -Blossom Chocolate Cake, 79
  Butter Sponge Cake Layers, 185
  and Chocolate Bundt Cake, 122–23
  Chocolate Frosting, 298
  Custard Sauce, 359
  flower water, 22
  French Buttercream, 303
  Frosting, 301
  juice concentrate, in cakes, 19
  Juice Custard Sauce, 362
  Seven-Minute Icing, 313
Our Family's Favorite Chocolate Almond Cake, **252–53**, 263
ovens
  preparing, 52
  thermometers for, 44
  types of, 35–36

P

pans. *See* baking pans
paper cones, 348–50
Passion Fruit Mousse Filling, 316
Passion Fruit Sauce, 366
pastry bags, 47, 345–47, 348
pastry brushes, 47
pastry combs, 46
Pastry Cream
  Buttercream, 303
  Chocolate, 322
  Coffee, 322
  Gianduja, 322
  Mocha, 322
  Praline, 322
  Vanilla, 322
pastry flour, 15, 51
pastry tips, 47–48, 347–48
pastry tubes, 47–48

Peanut Butter Chocolate Frosting, 301
Peanut Chocolate Cake, 80–81
Peanut Torte, Chile Chocolate, 238
Pear Sauce, Pink, 367
Pecan(s), 27. *See also* Nut(s)
  Best Brownies, 69
  Bourbon Chocolate Cake, 119
  Bourbon Fudge Cake, 119
  Brownie Torte, 70
  Cardamom Carrot Cocoa Cake, 88–89
  Chocolate Apricot Upside-Down Cake, 134
  Chocolate Cake, Apple, 234–35
  Chocolate Mayonnaise Cake, 65
  Chocolate Zucchini Quick Bread, 91
  Christmas Chocolate Fruit Cake, 74
  Extravaganza: The Michele, 248–49
  Fudge Nut Cupcakes, 280
  King Arthur Chocolate Pudding Cake, 67
  Michele's German Chocolate Cake, 170–71
  Nutty Chocolate Pound Cake, 105
  Red Velvet Cake, 173
Peppercorns
  Aztec Devil's Food Cake, 143
  Chocolate Pumpernickel Torte, 240–41
  Peppered Custard Sauce, 359
  Szechuan Pepper Custard Sauce, 360
Pink Pear Sauce, 367
piping, decorative, 345–48
piping gel, 337
pistachios, in recipes, 27
plated dessert presentations, 351–55
  for frosted cakes, 354–55
  for unfrosted cakes, 352–54
Poppy Seed(s), 27
  Cake (Mohn Torte), 250–51
  Chocolate Pound Cake, 105
  White Chocolate Flourless Cake with Lemon, 256
Potato Chocolate Chip Cake, 124–25
potato starch, about, 16
Pound Cake, Chocolate
  Dependable, **104–6**, 135, 286
  variations, 105

  Light, **107**, 135, 286
  Marbled, **108**, 286
  Pain de Gênes, **115**, 286
  Spicy, with Brandy Glaze, 128–29
  Super Rich, **109**, 135
Powder, Nut Brittle, 375
powdered sugar, about, 20
Praline
  Cake, Chocolate, 192–93
  Custard Sauce, 359
  French Buttercream, 302
  Gianduja, The, 270–71
  Gianduja Buttercream, 310
  Gianduja French Buttercream, 303
  Gianduja Pastry Cream, 322
  Michele's Marjolaine Cake, 272–73
  Opera Cake, 274–75
  paste, about, 27
  Pastry Cream, 322
Prinzregenten Torte, 276–77
Prune and Ginger Chocolate Cake, 93
Pudding
  Cake, Chocolate, 66
  Cake, Chocolate, King Arthur, 67
  Chocolate, -Filled Angel Food Cake, 229
  Chocolate Cake, 135
  Filling, Chocolate, 323
Pumpernickel Torte, Chocolate, 240–41

Q

Quintessential French Chocolate Cake, 82

R

raisins, in baked goods, 24
Raspberry(ies)
  Berry White Chocolate Cheesecake, 99
  Butter Sponge Cake Layers, **186**, 206
  Cake, 206
  Chocolate Cake, Gisèle's, 76
  Filled Angel Food Cake, 228
  Fruit Plate Sauce, 369

Mousse Filling, 316
-Scented Cocoa Cake, 126–27
Squeeze Sauce, 368
Very Berry Compote, 372
Real Fudge Glaze, 328
Real Fudge Icing, 327–28
recipes, tips for, 58
Red Velvet Cake, 173
refrigerated cakes
  American Icebox, 286
  Chocolate Tiramisu, 283
  Chocolate Velvet, 288–89
  Italian Chocolate Icebox, 287
  Michele's Chocolate Zuccotto, 292
  Rob Russe, 291
refrigerating cakes, 55–56, 95
Rehrucken (Chocolate Saddle of
  Venison), 243
Reine de Saba, 83
Ricotta
  Berry White Chocolate Cheesecake,
  99
  Italian Chocolate Icebox Cake, 287
Rigo Jansci, 220–21
Rob Russe, 291
rolled cakes
  Blonde Biscuit, 209
  Chocolate Biscuit, **208–9**, 288–89
  Chocolate Sponge Sheet Cake,
  190–91, 199
  cooling, 55
  Dark Chocolate Swiss Roll, 222–23
  Dione Lucas's Chocolate Swiss
  Roll, 224–25
  Dione Lucas's Roulade Leontine,
  257–58
  Double Chocolate Christmas Log,
  199
  preparing, 181–82
rose water, about, 22
round cake pans, 39
rubber spatula, 48–49
Rum
  Cake, Chocolate, Wilkinson's, 201
  Chestnut Chocolate Cake, 84–85
  Chocolate Sabayon Mousse, 317
  Christmas Chocolate Fruit Cake,
  74
  Spirited Custard Sauce, 359
  Spirited Syrup, 370
  Spirited Whipped Cream, 319

S

Sabayon Mousse, Chocolate, 317
Sacher Torte, 174–75
Saffron Custard Sauce, 359
salt, in recipes, 22
Sauce, 358–70
  Apricot Squeeze, 368
  Bourbon, 363
  Butterscotch, 364
  Caramel, French, 364
  Chocolate, Deadly Delicious, 362
  Chocolate, Ivory, 369
  Custard
    Flavored, 359–60
    Orange Juice, 362
    Stabilized, 361
    Vanilla (Crème Anglaise), 358
  Fruit Plate, 369
  Grand Marnier, 365
  Mango, Canned, 366
  Mango, Fresh, 365
  Passion Fruit, 366
  Pear, Pink, 367
  plated dessert ideas for, 352–54
  Raspberry Squeeze, 368
  Sour Cream, 370
saucepans, 42–43
scales, kitchen, 40–41
Schorner, Dieter, 197
semisweet chocolate, about, 31, 32
Seven-Minute Icing, 313
  Orange, 313
Shards of Caramel; variations, 374
Shavings, Chocolate, 380
shortened cakes. *See* butter cakes
shortening, vegetable, 13
sifters, 48
Silky Chocolate Cake Layers, **150**, 158
Silpat, 47
Simple Syrup, 370
  Citrus, 370
  Spirited, 370
  Vanilla, 370
Sin City Cake, 152
Sin City Cake Layers, **151**, 152
soft ball stage, 306
Souffléed Chocolate Cake, 254
Sour Cream, 18
  Chocolate Cake Layers, **153**, 158,
  279

Chocolate Icing, 326
Sauce, 370
spatulas, 48–49
special cakes
  The Alessia: A Marzipan-Lover's
  Dream, 263
  Chocolate, Coach House, 268–69
  Chocolate Linzer Torte, 278
  Chocolate Mincemeat Torte,
  266–67
  The Gianduja, 270–71
  Marjolaine, Michele's, 272–73
  Meringue, Chestnut Chocolate,
  264–65
  Opera, 274–75
  Prinzregenten Torte, 276–77
Spices, 23. *See also specific spices*
  Fissure Spiced Chocolate Cake,
  77
  Mixed Spice Custard Sauce, 360
  Spice Custard Sauce, 359
  Spiced Whipped Cream, 319
  Spicy Chocolate Pound Cake,
  105
  Spicy Chocolate Pound Cake with
  Brandy Glaze, 128–29
Spirited Custard Sauce, 359
Spirited Syrup, 370
Spirited Whipped Cream, 319
spirits, in baked goods, 23
Sponge Cake(s), 178–206. *See also*
  biscuit cakes
  about, 178–79
  Black Forest, Dieter Schorner's,
  196–97
  Butter (Genoise), **184–86**, 206
  Nut, 186
  Orange, 185
  Raspberry, **186**, 206
  checklist for, 182–83
  Chocolate
    Double, Christmas Log, 199
    Gateau, Dieter Schorner's, 198
    Grand Marnier, 200
    Kahlúa, 202–3
    Nut, Layers, **189**, 200
    Praline, 192–93
    Rum, Wilkinson's, 201
    Sheet, **190–91**, 199
    with White Chocolate Mousse,
    194–95

Chocolate Butter (Chocolate Genoise), **187–88**, 196–97, 198, 201
  Chocolate Nut, 188
  Mocha, **188**, 201
  Mocha Nut, 188
  fillings and icings for, 183
  frosting, tips for, 181
  making into rolled cakes, 181–82
  matching with frosting, 295
  Michele's Marvelous Mistake, 204–5
  oven heat for, 181
  preparing batter for, 179–81
  preparing pans for, 54
  Raspberry, 206
spoons, measuring, 42
spoons, stirring, 49
springform pans, 38, 39
square pans, 38, 39
squeeze bottles, 49
Squeeze Sauce, Apricot, 368
Squeeze Sauce, Raspberry, 368
Stabilized Custard Sauce, 361
Stabilized Whipped Cream, 320
starches, types of, 16
stationary mixers, 36–37
storing cakes, 55–56, 95
strainers, 48
Streusel-Woven Chocolate Coffee Cake, 130
sugar
  measuring, 20–21
  sifting, 21
  types of, 19–20
  volume and weight equivalences, 52
sugar syrups, boiled, about, 304–6
Sugared Chestnuts, 373
Sugared Flowers, 378
summer chocolate, defined, 32
summer coating, defined, 31
Super Rich Chocolate Pound Cake, **109**, 135
superfine sugar, about, 20, 21, 52
sweet chocolate, about, 31
Sweet Devil's Food Cake Layers, 145
sweetened condensed milk, 18
Swiss Meringue
  Buttercream, Linda Dann's, 307
  Buttercream, Mocha, 307

Swiss Roll
  Chocolate, Dione Lucas's, 224–25
  Dark Chocolate, 222–23
swivel-action vegetable peeler, 49
Syrup, boiled sugar, about, 304–6
Syrup, Simple, 370
  Citrus, 370
  Spirited, 370
  Vanilla, 370
Szechuan Pepper Custard Sauce, 360

T

Tea Cake
  Chocolate Banana, 111
  Chocolate Chocolate, **112**, 135, 286, 292
  Mocha, **117**, 286
Tea Custard Sauce, 360
Tea-Infused White Chocolate Cake, 131
techniques, 50–58
  cooling cakes, 55
  folding, 50–51
  high-altitude baking, 57
  measuring, 51–52
  preparing the oven, 52
  preparing the pans, 52–54
  storing cakes, 55–56, 95
  testing for doneness, 54–55
  tips for successful baking, 57–58
  transporting cakes, 45, 56–57
  unmolding cakes, 55, 182
testing for doneness, 54–55
thermometers, 43–44
thread stage, 306
Tiramisu, Chocolate, 283
Torte (flourless)
  Chile Chocolate Peanut, 238
  Chocolate Bean, 239
  Chocolate Hazelnut, Karen's, 244–45
  Chocolate Pumpernickel, 240–41
  Kata, 261
  Mohn (Poppy Seed Cake), 250–51
  Walnut Chocolate, 255
Torte (with flour)
  Brownie, 70
  Chocolate Blitz, 160–61
  Chocolate Mincemeat, 266–67
  Dobos, Austrian, 216–17

  Linzer, Chocolate, 278
  Prinzregenten, 276–77
  Sacher, 174–75
transporting cakes, 45, 56–57
tube pans, 38, 39
Tunnel of Fudge Cake, 132

U

unbleached flour, 14, 15
unmolding cakes, 55, 182
unsweetened chocolate, about, 30, 32
unsweetened cocoa powder, in recipes, 32
unsweetened coconut milk, 19
Upside-Down Cake, Chocolate Apricot, 134

V

Vanilla
  Cream Cheese Frosting, 299
  Custard Sauce (Crème Anglaise), 358
  extract and beans, 23
  Frosting, 301
  Pastry Cream, 322
  sugar, 20
  Syrup, 370
vegetable oil, 13
vegetable shortening, 13
Very Berry Compote, 372
volume and weight equivalences, 51–52

W

Wacky Chocolate Cake, 63
Wacky Chocolate Cake, Not-So-, 64
Walnut(s), 27. *See also* Nut(s)
  Best Brownies, 69
  Brownie Torte, 70
  Cake, Cinnamon-Chocolate-, 163
  Chocolate Bean Torte, 239
  -Chocolate Filled Kugelhopf, 133
  Chocolate Torte, 255
  Chocolate Zucchini Quick Bread, 91
  Christmas Chocolate Fruit Cake, 74
  and Date Chocolate Cake, 92

King Arthur Chocolate Pudding
 Cake, 67
Nutty Chocolate Pound Cake, 105
Tunnel of Fudge Cake, 132
Whipped Cream, 318–19
 amounts needed for cakes, 297
 buying cream for, 18
 Chocolate Malted, 318
 Cocoa, 318
 Coffee, 318
 Mocha, 318
 Spiced, 319
 Spirited, 319
 Stabilized, 320
 tips for making, 319
Whipped Ganache, 321
whisks, 49
White and Black Chocolate Cheese-
 cake, 98
White Cake Layers, 157

White Chocolate, 31, 32
 Almond Cake, 86–87
 Cake, Tea-Infused, 131
 Cake Layers, 154
 Cheesecake, 97
 Cheesecake, Berry, 99
 Flourless Cake with Lemon, 256
 Ganache, 324
 Glaze, 331
 Hawaiian Coconut Cake with White
  Chocolate Ganache, 166–67
 Ivory Chocolate Sauce, 369
 Macaroon Cake, 246–47
 Mousse Filling, 315
 White and Black Chocolate
  Cheesecake, 98
Wicked Chocolate Frosting, 298
Wilkinson's Chocolate Rum Cake,
 201
wire racks, 49

wire whips, 49
wooden skewers, 45
Writing, Chocolate, 381

Y

yeast, 17
Yeasted Chocolate Cake, 176–77
Yellow Cake
 Layers, **156**, 279
 One, Two, Three, Four Golden
  Cake Layers, **155**, 159
yogurt, in recipes, 19

Z

Zebra Boiled Icing, 312
zest, grating and mincing, 23
zester, lemon, 46
Zucchini Quick Bread, Chocolate, 91